Industry, State, and Society in Stalin's Russia

Industry, State, and Society in Stalin's Russia, 1926–1934

DAVID R. SHEARER

CORNELL UNIVERSITY PRESS

ITHACA AND LONDON

First published 1996 by Cornell University Press.

Printed in the United States of America

Library of Congress Cataloging-in-Publication Data
Shearer, David, 1952–
    Industry, state, and society in Stalin's Russia, 1926–1934 / David
R. Shearer.
        p.   cm.
    Includes bibliographical references (p.   ) and index.
    ISBN 0-8014-3207-3 (alk. paper)
    1. Industry and state—Soviet Union.   2. Soviet Union—Economic
policy—1917–1928.   3. Soviet Union—Economic policy—1928–1932.
HD3616.S472S5   1996
338.947′009′0042—dc20   96-8178

This book is printed on Lyons Falls Turin Book,
a paper that is totally chlorine-free and acid-free.

FOR MOSHE LEWIN

Contents

Acknowledgments   ix

Abbreviations   xiii

Introduction: Stalinism and the Industrial State   1

I.   THE STATE(S) OF THE ECONOMY IN THE LATE 1920S

1.   Unruly Bureaucracies, Fragmented Markets   25

2.   Wheeling and Dealing in Soviet Industry   53

3.   Rabkrin and the Militarized Campaign Economy   76

II. THE STRUGGLE FOR A NEW STATE, 1928–1930

4.   What Kind of State?   111

5.   The Politics of Modernization   134

III. WORKING IN THE MADHOUSE, 1930–1934

6.   Daily Work in the *Apparat*   167

7.   Purge and Patronage   187

8.   The Pathologies of Modernization   204

Conclusion: Socialism, Dictatorship, and Despotism
in Stalin's Russia   232

Glossary   243
Bibliography   247
Index   259

Acknowledgments

This book would not have been written without support from many people and institutions. Generous grants from the International Research and Exchanges Board (IREX) and the Social Sciences Research Council (SSRC) made research travel possible. Fellowship years at the Hoover Institution on War, Revolution, and Peace and at Harvard's Russian Research Center allowed me to mine those institutions' rich resources. They provided very different but equally collegial and stimulating work environments. I am indebted to them for their support. I am also grateful to the University of Delaware for providing crucial leave time and for funding research trips to Russia and to professional conferences.

I have presented portions of my ideas in various forums and have benefited from the comments and suggestions of my colleagues, especially the organizers of and participants in the annual European Seminar on Russian and Soviet History and the Michigan State University conference on labor and working-class history, held in November 1990. Portions of Chapter 2 have appeared in slightly altered form in *Cahiers du monde russe* 36 (January–June 1995): 139–59, copyright © Ecole des Hautes Etudes en Sciences Sociales. Parts of Chapter 8 are included in the essay "Factories within Factories: Changes in the Structure of Work and Management in Soviet Machine-Building Factories, 1926–1934," in *Social Dimensions of Soviet Industrialization*, edited by William G. Rosenberg and Lewis H. Siegelbaum (Bloomington: Indiana University Press, 1993). I am grateful for permission to use this material here. I am also grateful to the Hoover Institution and the director and staff of the Gosudarstvennyi Arkhiv

Rossiiskoi Federatsii (GARF) for permission to reproduce photographs from their collections.

Competent and helpful staff at several libraries made my research tasks easier than I had anticipated. I appreciate the assistance given me by the staff of the Alexander Baykov Library at the Center for Russian and East European Studies of the University of Birmingham, England; the Bibliothèque de Documentation Internationale Contemporaine, Paris; the library of the Deutsches Museum, Munich; the library of the International Labor Office, Geneva; the archive and library of the Hoover Institution; and Widener Library, Harvard University.

I conducted the main body of research for this book in archives of the Soviet Union and Russia. I owe thanks to many people and organizations there for making my various research trips productive. I am deeply indebted to the staffs at what for many years were TsGAOR and TsGANKh, the Soviet state and economic archives (now GARF and RGAE), and to the staff of RTsKhIDNI, the former central archive of the Communist Party of the Soviet Union. Throughout the early 1990s, when I conducted most of the research for this book, the staffs of those institutions worked under enormous pressures. Political, economic, and administrative upheavals associated with the collapse of the Soviet Union were followed by the invasion of scholars into newly opened archives. Facing constant uncertainty and difficult working conditions, the many men and women with whom I consulted went about their business with courage, patience, good humor, and generous spirit. Their expertise and help were invaluable to me and the many other historians who sought their assistance.

I am also grateful to the staff of the Russian (formerly Lenin) State Library in Moscow and to the staff at INION, the library of the former Soviet and now Russian Academy of Social Sciences. The reproduction staff at INION, especially, was gracious in providing many hundreds of pages of microfilm. They should take pride in proving that the abacus is still faster than the electronic calculator. I thank the Center for Humanities and Social Sciences at Moscow State University, especially Aleksei Surin and Aleksei Barabashev, for providing financial support and an academic home, replete with generous portions of tea, on several of my visits. I am also grateful to the Institute of History of the Soviet and Russian Academy of Sciences and to Viktor P. Danilov in particular for his sponsorship and the time we spent discussing Russian and Soviet history.

I owe the greatest intellectual debt to Moshe Lewin, who has always set the highest standard of excellence. His sense of historical process—especially its incongruities, ironies, and ambiguities—has shaped the way I think about Soviet history. His exhortations to push beyond ideological and historiographic stereotypes are an inspiration and a challenge. I am also indebted to many others for constructive criticisms and encouragement. First, I thank my colleagues in the history department at the University of Delaware. It is a pleasure to work among such a group of genial and active scholars. I also thank John Barber, Mary Fissell, John Hatch, Roger Horowitz, Val Kivelson, Henrika Kuklick, James Millar, Jack Pressman, Alfred Rieber, David Sedik, Merritt Roe Smith, and Elizabeth Wood. Sheila Fitzpatrick, Diane Koenker, Daniel Orlovsky, John Shearer, Lewis Siegelbaum, Ron Suny, and Reginald Zelnik have read parts of this book in its various incarnations as chapters, conference papers, and article drafts. I am grateful for their numerous comments and suggestions. I thank Andrea Graziosi, Jim Heinzen, and Oleg Khlevniuk especially for their careful reading of various chapters and for our many discussions. I have also benefited from the constructive criticisms provided by anonymous readers for Cornell University Press. I have followed many of their suggestions and the book is much better for them. In addition, I am grateful for the support and active interest of John G. Ackerman, director of Cornell University Press, and for the work of his staff. Barbara Salazar's patient editing saved me from many errors and turned a raw manuscript into a book.

Finally, I thank Sarah Tracy, who has read and discussed with me the numerous drafts of my chapters. Her astute criticisms as a historian and a first-rate stylist have helped me immeasurably. Her support has sustained me. I am grateful for her companionship over the years.

D. R. S.

Abbreviations

d., dd.	*delo, dela* (file, files)
f.	*fond* (collection)
GARF (formerly TsGAOR)	Gosudarstvennyi arkhiv Rossiiskoi Federatsii (State Archive of the Russian Federation)
GEU	General'noe ekonomicheskoe upravlenie (General Economic Administration)
IuMT	Iuzhnyi mashinostroitel'nyi trest (Iuzhmashtrest; Southern Machine Building Trust)
l., ll.	*list, listy* (folio, folios)
LMT	Leningradskii mashinostroitel'nyi trest (Lenmashtrest; Leningrad Machine Building Trust)
MMT	Moskovskii mashinostroitel'nyi trest (Mosmashtrest; Moscow Machine Building Trust)
NKPS	Narodnyi komissariat putei soobshcheniia (Narkomput'; People's Commissariat of Means of Communication [Transportation])
NOT	nauchnaia organizatsiia truda (scientific organization of work)
OGPU	Ob"edinennoe gosudarstvennoe politicheskoe upravlenie (Unified State Political Administration [political police])
op.	*opis'* (inventory)
ORNOT	Obshchestvo rabotnikov nauchnoi organizatsii truda (Society for the Scientific Organization of Work)

PEU   Planovo-ekonomicheskoe upravlenie (Planning-Eco-
                    nomic Administration [of Vesenkha])
RGAE (formerly   Rossiiskii gosudarstvennyi arkhiv ekonomiki (Russian
  TsGANKh)   State Archive of the Economy)
RKI   Narodnyi komissariat raboche-krest'ianskoi inspektsii
                    (Rabkrin; People's Commissariat of Workers' and
                    Peasants' Inspection)
RTsKhIDNI   Rossiiskii tsentr khraneniia i izucheniia dokumentov
                    noveishei istorii (Russian Center for the Preservation
                    and Study of Documents of Contemporary History)
SSI   Soiuzstankoinstrument   (Vsesoiuznoe   stankostroi-
                    tel'noe i instrumental'noe ob"edinenie; All-Union
                    Engineering and Machine Tool Association)
STO   Sovet truda i oborony (Council on Labor and Defense)
TPG   *Torgovo-promyshlennaia gazeta* (Trade and industrial
                    journal; Vesenkha newspaper)
TsIK   Tsentral'nyi ispolnitel'nyi komitet (Central Executive
                    Committee [of the USSR Soviets])
TsK   Tsentral'nyi komitet (Central Committe [of the Com-
                    munist Party])
TsKK   Tsentral'naia kontrol'naia komissiia (Central Control
                    Commission)
VAI   Vsesoiuznaia assotsiatsiia inzhenerov (All-Union Asso-
                    ciation of Engineers)
VDW   Verein Deutscher Werkzeugmaschine (German Ma-
                    chine Tool Society; by extension, a lathe it produced)
VMS   Vsesoiuznyi metallurgicheskii sindikat (All-Union
                    Metal Syndicate)
VMTS   Vsesoiuznyi mashinotekhnicheskii sindikat (All-Union
                    Engineering Syndicate)
VSNKh   Vysshii sovet narodnogo khoziaistva (Vesenkha; Su-
                    preme Council of the People's Economy)
VSS   Vsesoiuznyi sovet sindikatov (All-Union Council of
                    Syndicates)
VTS   Vsesoiuznyi tekstil'nyi sindikat (All-Union Textile Syn-
                    dicate)

Industry, State,
and Society
in Stalin's Russia

Introduction: Stalinism and the Industrial State

In his book *The Twenty Years' Crisis*, E. H. Carr wrote that World War I, Europe's Great War, marked an irrevocable break with the continent's past. The magnitude of the war's slaughter—several million died in the four years from 1914 through 1918—and the chaos that followed the fighting led many Europeans to reject the predominantly liberal economic and political values of the nineteenth century. In the 1920s and increasingly during the troubled years of the Great Depression, European nations turned to authoritarian solutions in efforts to resolve their societies' many problems. As Carr wrote, these decades of unprecedented economic and social instability polarized European societies and gave rise to mass political movements of both the extreme left and extreme right.[1]

In southern and central Europe, the rejection of liberalism and parliamentary politics culminated in the two great dictatorships of Benito Mussolini's Fascist Italy and Adolf Hitler's National Socialist Germany. Throughout much of the rest of the continent—in Spain, Poland, Romania, Hungary, and elsewhere—fragile monarchies and republics fell victim to military juntas and despots. In Russia, the Great War ended in socialist revolution and the overthrow of the country's ruling autocracy. The social-democratic impulses of the 1917 revolution quickly turned to dictatorship in the 1920s and 1930s under Joseph Stalin, general secretary of the ruling Communist Party of the Soviet Union.

Stalin's name is linked most recognizably to the system of political despotism and terror that the Soviet dictator created during his lifetime. As a

[1] E. H. Carr, *The Twenty Years' Crisis, 1919–1939: An Introduction to the Study of International Relations* (New York, 1946).

historical phenomenon, however, Stalinism is also associated with an industrial revolution that in a decade transformed the USSR from an agrarian peasant society into a military-industrial superstate.[2] The scale of change in the Soviet Union during the late 1920s and 1930s was breathtaking, as was the reckless audacity of the Communist Party and government officials who led the country's industrial drive. They and the millions of people who built and worked in Soviet factories and on Soviet farms perceived themselves, and rightly, as Russia's modernizers. Stalin's industrial builders saw themselves engaged in a world-historical struggle to conquer Russia's vast empty spaces and to create, almost from whole cloth, a new civilization. What they built was supposedly a socialist state, the first in the history of the world.

Certainly Stalin's Great Leap Forward, as the Soviet industrialization drive was called, radically altered the industrial economy. These years also witnessed a chaotic and violent restructuring of social and economic relations and a reorganization of power and hierarchy. What emerged in the 1930s, however, was and continues to be a subject of passionate disagreement. Many observers regard terror and authoritarianism as the defining essence of Stalinism; indeed, the lens through which all of Soviet history must be viewed. Others have justified the Stalinist version of state dictatorship as the only viable defense of socialism against the reconstruction of European capitalism and then fascism after World War I. Conversely, Stalinism has been condemned as the ultimate betrayal of socialism, the means by which Stalin and his political entourage amassed personal power through the willful and cynical destruction of Soviet society. Some scholars have emphasized continuity in Russian history and argued that Stalin's dictatorship was predominantly a revived Russian state, the revenge of history, as it were, on the Communist revolution. Still others, in an attempt to eschew ideology, have insisted that the Soviet industrialization drive was essentially an extreme form of modernization, a repudiation of Russia's past and a continuation of trends that began in Europe with the Industrial Revolution of the eighteenth and nineteenth centuries.[3]

In fact, while the appeal to socialist construction provided a central justification for Stalin's industrialization drive, Stalinism as an industrial and state system was not socialist. Neither was it simply a betrayal of socialism. Stalinism was certainly more than just a revived Russian state, and it was more than just another chapter in the supposedly ongoing march of progress and the Industrial Revolution. Stalinism represented a unique

[2]See Moshe Lewin, *Russia/USSR/Russia: The Drive and Drift of a Super-State* (New York, 1995).

[3]For a summary of these arguments, see Giuseppi Boffa, *The Stalin Phenomenon*, trans. Nicholas Fersen (Ithaca, 1992).

kind of modern industrial state despotism, a complex, often contradictory, and constantly evolving system of political economy, state bureaucratic relationships, and social forms of organization. The Stalinist state certainly had roots in a Russian past, a peasant past in particular, that fundamentaly shaped the new state and regime. Yet that state was also, and mainly, a product of the twentieth-century European experience. The massive industrialization drive started by Stalin in the late 1920s and the creation of a powerful Soviet state that accompanied the Soviet industrial revolution did not take place in historical isolation; it was part of the crisis and reconstruction that engulfed all of Europe after World War I. How Stalin's industrial revolution came about, what was unique about it, and what derived from common European trends is the subject of this book. In the chapters that follow, I reexamine some of the central issues of Stalinism through a close study of the Soviet state and industrial economy during the late 1920s and early 1930s, and through an examination of the struggles during that period to shape a new Soviet state and society.

The Historical Context: Revolution and Reconstruction

As World War I drew to a close, social and political upheavals swept Europe. In almost every country, conflict arose between democratic and socialist "forces of movement" and the conservative "forces of order."[4] Autocratic forms of government collapsed in all of the defeated empire-nations: Austria-Hungary, Germany, and Russia. Throughout the territories of these former empires, a wave of radical unrest threatened to turn the political overthrow of the old order into full-scale social revolution. Postwar revolutionary movement challenged the property and power relations on which European capitalism and conservative bourgeois dominance had been founded.

The first and most serious revolutionary outbreak occurred immediately after the armistice ended the military conflict in 1918. During this time, Europe's conservative elites defended their interests either through outright repression and civil war or by making compromises with newly formed democratic governments, as in Germany. In the end, however, the revolutionary wave was contained. By 1921, political conservativism had recovered the upper hand, and by the end of 1923, the last real revolutionary threat dissipated in the aborted German "October," a failed attempt by the German Communist Party to incite popular rebellion against the fledgling Weimar Republic. During the middle part of the decade, conservative elites fashioned new arrangements—through international financial agreements, corporate consolidation, increased political authoritarianism,

[4]These are the terms of Charles Maier, *Recasting Bourgeois Europe: Stabilization in France, Germany, and Italy in the Decade after World War I* (Princeton, 1975), p. 4.

and industrial rationalization—that secured the defense of bourgeois Europe against the immediate postwar challenges. Whether in Raymond Poincaré's France, Gustav Stresemann's Germany, or Mussolini's Italy, government support for private interests led to a new stage of state-sponsored capitalism that was aggressively nationalist, antiparliamentary, and antisocialist.[5]

If in Western Europe the postwar crisis resulted in the recostruction of conservative bourgeois power, in Russia the collapse of the old order precipitated a full-scale popular revolution. Complete political breakdown occurred in February 1917, with the abdication of Tsar Nicholas II after several years of debilitating war with Germany. For nine months a fragile coalition government attempted to rule Russia. The Provisional Government, composed of representatives of Russia's propertied and conservative classes, sought legitimacy and stability by committing itself to constitutional government, to the defense of property rights, and above all to defense of the Russian nation through continuation of the war against Germany. The Provisional Government, too, was swept away by the force of revolutionary upheaval. Throughout 1917, spontaneous peasant rebellions in the countryside dispossessed landowners and redistributed land. In the cities, armed soldiers and workers' councils, the soviets, checked what little authority the Provisional Government possessed and effectively controlled political power. After a series of political crises in July and August 1917, the popular revolutionary movement culminated in October in the seizure of power by Vladimir Lenin and armed detachments loyal to the Bolshevik faction of the Russian Social Democratic Party. To save the revolution from what they feared would be a reactionary counterrevolution, Lenin's Bolsheviks arrested the remaining few members of the Provisional Government, banned other political parties, and declared the founding of Europe's first socialist republic.

Soviet Russia in the 1920s: One Step Forward, Two Steps Back

Lenin and his Bolsheviks attempted to resolve the crisis of power in Russia by establishing a dictatorship that would rule in the name of the country's urban and rural laboring population rather than in the interests of its propertied classes. Within the first few weeks of taking power, the Bolshevik government issued orders legalizing all land seizures. The new government also ended the unpopular war with Germany, albeit by signing a treaty that dismembered much of the old Russian empire and left German armies still poised on Russia's borders. Measures such as these found popular support. From the beginning, however, the Bolshevik gov-

---

[5] I take the chronology and outlines of European middle-class reconstruction from Maier, *Recasting Bourgeois Europe*.

ernment was plagued by a host of crises that fundamentally shaped the institutional formation of the government and the political consciousness of its leaders. The first of these crises came in the form of a direct military challenge to Bolshevik rule. From the summer of 1918 through the spring of 1921, Russia and the territories of the old empire suffered a series of savage national and civil wars. At times the Bolsheviks were hard-pressed to defend themselves against the opposition White armies that encircled the central core of Bolshevik-held Russia. After establishing a secure military hold on Russia, however, the revolutionary government used the fighting to expand Bolshevik power to many areas of the old empire that had gained independence after the fall of the autocracy. The fighting was especially brutal in Ukraine, Georgia, Central Asia, and the Northern Caucasus. There Bolshevik armies met fierce resistance from nationalist, religious, and even local Communist and Peasant Party forces.

By 1921 the Bolsheviks had overcome the last of the organized military opposition to their rule. Yet organized military opposition was only one of the Bolsheviks' problems, and, as it turned out, not the most serious. The brutality of Bolshevik dictatorship during the revolutionary war period was unprecedented. Policies of economic nationalization, the widespread use of political and organized military terror, food requisitioning, and forced military and labor conscription combined to keep the Bolsheviks in power, but the harshness of their rule triggered massive uprisings in the countryside and increasingly among what were supposed to be the regime's staunchest social allies: Russia's urban workers. Lenin's government brutally suppressed these uprisings. At the same time, it acted to mitigate the harsh economic and political conditions that had come to be known as "war communism." Beginning in the spring of 1921, Lenin and the Bolshevik leaders introduced a series of measures designed to bring social peace and foster economic recovery. New laws ended food requisitioning and introduced taxes in kind. Soon agricultural taxes were monetarized as the government allowed free trade and permitted a limited range of free market activities. Reforms in the early 1920s also ended inflation and helped stabilize the Soviet currency. Lenin defended this series of reforms, called the New Economic Policy (NEP), as a necessary step backward from war communism into a quasi-capitalist economic and social order. The country, he declared, was too weak and underdeveloped to move rapidly into full-scale socialism. To many Communists, however, the NEP compromised socialist principles and threatened to hold the Bolshevik government hostage to hostile social classes and dangerous economic trends.

To some degree, both sides were correct in the debate over NEP. By the spring of 1921, Lenin realized that, as a result of the harsh policies of war communism, the regime faced a far more serious threat from its own supporters than it had from opposition military forces. Lenin and other Bolshevik leaders hoped that NEP reforms would relieve the worst shortages of food and commodities, and would restart the engine of economic recovery. NEP reforms produced the desired effect, and quickly. Those policies brought a measure of stability, recovery, and social peace to Russia and the newly constituted Union of Soviet Socialist Republics, the USSR, officially founded in 1922. Yet the years of NEP also seemed to bear out the truth of the left opposition's warnings. Throughout the 1920s, the Bolshevik government faced a series of economic crises that disrupted efforts to plan the economy and move ahead with industrial development. For the most part, these crises were caused by tensions between the regime and the country's large number of smallholding peasant agricultural producers. Many peasants mistrusted the Bolshevik regime as a government of the industrial cities, a government that had let the peasants keep their land but had starved and persecuted them throughout the revolutionary war years. Agricultural policies during the 1920s, which alternately punished and rewarded private farming and trade, reflected the Bolsheviks' ambivalence toward the peasantry as a potentially hostile social class. Thus, because of political and social tensions, and especially for economic reasons, large numbers of peasants refused to trade with the state. Many peasant farmers preferred to trade through the more profitable private and semiprivate grain and produce markets. Many others withdrew altogether from the national markets and produced for their own consumption and seasonal needs within relatively self-contained regional markets.[6]

Even as government policies alienated the peasant producers, they hurt the urban workers. Disparities between agricultural and industrial prices exacerbated food shortages in the cities and contributed to rising unemployment because of forced cuts in state subsidies to industries. The fiscal restrictions of NEP also required the government to reduce spending on education and medicine, child care, unemployment insurance, and other social programs to which the Bolsheviks were committed. Russia's cities, which had suffered from the neglect and fighting of the revolutionary war years, experienced a revival during the NEP. On the surface, however, the revival was associated with capitalist restoration, not with socialist construction. Urban streets seemed populated with increasing numbers of unemployed workers, prostitutes, orphans, criminal gangs, well-fed bureaucrats, and ostentatiously dressed traders and entrepreneurs.[7] The last, the

[6]On rural conditions, see Viktor Danilov, *Rural Russia under the New Regime*, trans. Orlando Figes (Bloomington, 1988); Lewin, *Russia/USSR/Russia*, pp. 23–41; Teodor Shanin, *The Awkward Class: Political Sociology of Peasantry in a Developing Society* (London, 1972).

[7]Alan Ball, *And Now My Heart Is Hardened: Abandoned Children in Soviet Russia, 1918–1930* (Berkeley, 1994); idem, *Russia's Last Capitalists: The Nepmen, 1921–1929* (Berkeley, 1987).

infamous Nepmen, were not numerous, but they were prominent fixtures of the cities by the mid-1920s. Many workers and soldiers who had fought for the Revolution now watched from unemployment lines as merchants and government officials passed to and fro in motor cars. Hotels, bars, and night clubs catered to foreign dignitaries and to the new Soviet political and business elite.[8]

As the country drifted further into NEP, policy and ideological differences sharpened among leaders of the Communist Party. The failure of the German revolution in October 1923 and Lenin's death in 1924 exacerbated a deepening sense of isolation and crisis. A struggle among contenders for Lenin's role split the Communist Party into bitter factions. The power struggle distracted Party leaders from the urgent tasks of economic and social governance and focused attention and energies instead on issues of personal antagonism, Party procedures, and the true legacy of Leninism. By the mid-1920s the Party also faced a serious crisis of identity. Bolshevik leaders worried that the rising number of administrative employees (slushashchie) joining the Party would soon overwhelm and obscure the Party's proletarian and socialist origins. Even before Lenin died, there was already widespread concern that the Party had been transformed from a revolutionary political movement into a bureaucratized governmental apparatus. The Party crisis that arose in the mid-1920s only confirmed to many people that the Bolshevik leaders had lost their way and that the socialist revolution was foundering on the rocks of NEP.

As if these problems were not enough, two crises in 1927 and 1928 threatened the very existence of the regime. A serious downturn in grain sales to the state jeopardized the government's projected export plans, and worse, created the need for food rationing again for the first time since the early years of the Revolution.[9] The unexpected shortfall in agricultural revenue left such a scarcity of capital for industrial construction that economists in the Commissariat of Finance feared the imminent collapse of the state's ruble currency. The financial crisis was so severe that foreign governments were discussing the possibility that the Soviet economy would disintegrate and the country would be plunged into yet a new period of revolutionary upheaval.[10] A war scare in 1927 heightened the sense of vulnerability felt by Bolshevik leaders, and all this occurred at a

[8]On industrial workers and unemployment, see especially John Hatch, "Bringing Economics Back In: Industrial Arbitration and Collective Bargaining during NEP," paper presented at the conference "The Making of the Soviet Working Class," Michigan State University, 9–11 November 1990; William Chase, Workers, Society, and the Soviet State: Labor and Life in Moscow, 1918–1929 (Urbana, 1987).

[9]The supply of goods to markets was in a disastrous state, having fallen nearly 16 percent in the single month of December 1927. In some provincial cities supplies were so low that the needs of the population could be met for only a few days at a time. See Michal Reiman, The Birth of Stalinism: The USSR on the Eve of the Second Revolution (Bloomington, 1987), p. 44.

[10]Ibid., p. 48.

time when European capitalism seemed not only to have stabilized and recovered from the war, but to have surged to new strength through its alliance with powerful state and international forces.

The Return to Revolution, Stalin's Version

It was in this context of domestic crisis and gathering international danger that Stalin, general secretary of the Communist Party since Lenin's death, launched the Great Leap Forward. The Great Leap Forward was supposed to return the Party to the path of revolution and to accelerate the country into a period of true socialist construction. In fact, with the advent of the first five-year plan in 1928, the regime plunged the country into a bacchanalian frenzy of forced industrial construction and economic modernization.[11] Rapid industrialization was accompanied by a frontal assault on the economic structures and social relations of NEP. The regime moved swiftly to abolish private farming and trade, to collectivize the country's agricultural lands under state control, and to extend centralized planning to every sector of the economy. Famine-producing policies of agricultural extraction recalled the worst years of the revolutionary war era, and a series of ruthless social wars decimated the peasantry, the professions, and other social elements supposedly hostile to Communist power.

Even as Stalin destroyed the economic and social foundations of NEP, he laid the foundation for a new industrial state and society. At the center of the Soviet industrial revolution was the rapid expansion and modernization of the country's heavy industry: iron, steel, and engineering production. These were the Soviet Union's capital producer and advanced technology industries; these were the industries that would make the tanks and locomotives that would secure the military and economic might of the new Soviet state. Heavy industry received a large infusion of investment funding, labor resources, and supplies, even as other industrial and economic branches suffered crippling shortages. Construction of the country's new hydroelectric dams, steel factories, and automobile plants received great publicity and the personal attention of Stalin and the Politbiuro, the inner ruling council of the Communist Party.

Before the industrialization drive, Soviet manufacturing capacity had been limited, and the country relied heavily on foreign imports. With some notable exceptions, most factories were relatively small and served regional markets. Even in the large state-run factories, work was unsystematic and based largely on artisanal forms of labor and production organization. By the early 1930s, however, scores of new industrial

[11]Naum Jasny was the first to describe Soviet industrial policies during the first five-year plan as "bacchanalian." See his *Soviet Industrialization, 1928–1952* (Chicago, 1961), p. 7.

branches had been created, and hundreds of new factories had been raised on the urban and rural landscapes. State policies gave priority to the development of large-scale factory complexes engaged in mass production, which were built to employ the most up-to-date engineering techniques, managerial practices, and work methods. Some of the Soviet Union's factories were the largest of their kind in the world.[12] Each employed thousands of workers and was equipped with the latest in modern machinery. Existing factories were reconstructed and expanded, often changed beyond recognition. Old workshops were razed or stripped and then abandoned as production lines started up in new, often half-completed structures.

All of the country's resources were mobilized for industrial modernization, which was achieved against all odds and at a staggering cost in human lives, brutal social conflict, and squandered economic resources. Millions of Soviet citizens and hundreds of thousands of non-Soviet citizens gave their labor, even their lives, to the industrialization effort. Many pledged themselves voluntarily, enthusiastically, because they believed they were building socialism. At the same time, millions were worked to death as industrial slaves in penal colonies, on farms, and on the state's new construction projects. Still, the goal was achieved. By the end of the 1930s, Soviet leaders could boast that the USSR was one of the world's major industrial producer countries, competitive with such industrial giants as the United States, Germany, and Great Britain.

The Historiographic Context: The State and Political Economy

The story of the Soviet industrial revolution is an oft-told one. It is a story so well known that we think of the events it describes as part of an inexorable historical process. The years 1928 through 1932 are often described as a period of "socialist transformation" from something we think we know as NEP to something we call a "planned" or a "command administrative economy."[13] The destruction of private trade after 1928, the centralization of economic and industrial administration, and the creation of a massive state bureaucratic dictatorship have generally been treated as an inevitable consequence of the policy of rapid industrialization. E. H. Carr argued that the necessity of defending socialism in one country predisposed Soviet leaders to replace NEP with a policy of aggressive industrialization.[14] Carr also argued, as have other scholars, that the growth of a

---

[12] The steel works built in the early 1930s at Kuznetskstroi and Magnitogorsk, for example, rivaled the mills of the Ruhr Valley and of Gary, Indiana.

[13] For this characterization, see R. W. Davies, *The Soviet Economy in Turmoil, 1929–1930* (Cambridge, Mass., 1989), pp. xiv–xviii, 465–69.

[14] E. H. Carr, *Socialism in One Country, 1924–1926*, vol. 2 (New York, 1959), p. 49.

strong state was inevitable, given the scale of the Party's industrialization plans and the weakness of the Soviet society and economy. Moshe Lewin, Carr's successor as historian of the Soviet state, emphasizes the "enfeebled" social basis, the "homogenized, illiterate and semiliterate" social structure of the 1920s. The devastation of revolution and war from 1918 through 1921, Lewin argues, destroyed the urban and rural basis of the new regime, depriving the Bolsheviks of the most "experienced" and "sophisticated" layers of social support. The "archaization" of society that resulted from the revolutionary wars provided a "breeding ground" for the authoritarianism and the statization characteristic of the Soviet economy and society. In Lewin's account, the "two retreating curves" of urban and rural devolution "simplified" the social structure and opened up a space for Stalinism and the expansion of state power.[15]

R. W. Davies has detailed many of the links between industrialization and the growth of a powerful state apparatus. According to Davies, the combination of several trends—the decision to force the pace of industrialization, the elimination of private trade and markets, and the introduction of planning—required an unavoidable "shift from NEP to the centrally planned economy." Economic planning and market economics were incompatible, so the story goes, and once Stalinist leaders began to dismantle the mixed-market system of the NEP, planning led inevitably to a centrally administered economy. The year 1928, the year the first five-year plan was launched, is the crucial date in this narrative. This was the year NEP died and Stalinism as an economic system was born. According to most accounts, especially those by economic historians, once the Stalinist regime embarked on rapid industrialization and "socialization" of property relations, the mechanisms of a centralized state dictatorship followed inevitably.[16]

It would be difficult to challenge the economic logic of this argument. It is very likely true that the market and commercial mechanisms of NEP would have been inadequate to finance the pace and scale of industrial development that Stalinist leaders eventually achieved. Massive state intervention *was* inevitable, given the kind of industrialization frenzy into which Stalin drove the country. Yet what may seem inevitable in hindsight

[15]Moshe Lewin, *The Making of the Soviet System: Essays in the Social History of Interwar Russia* (New York, 1985), pp. 311–12. Lewin is careful to distinguish himself from Carr, who, he argues, treats the state as an autonomous agent, making and unmaking society without being affected by it. In constructing his vision of the state, Lewin is concerned with how the state of society conditioned and constrained the state of the state (p. 288).

[16]Davies, *Soviet Economy in Turmoil*, p. xviii. Davies describes the elimination of private trade and commerce as part of the process of "socialist transformation" (pp. 465, 469). Lewin, in contrast, distinguishes between socialization and statization of property relations, and argues that what occurred under Stalin was statization, not socialization. It is on the basis of that distinction that Lewin asserts that the Stalin revolution was not socialist. See Lewin, *Making of the Soviet System*, p. 308.

was not seen as inevitable by those caught up in the events of the late 1920s. Stalin and those around him had not yet created the Stalinist state as we have come to understand it. Ideas about the NEP were not yet schematized and fixed in hindsight from the perspective of a bureau-cratized economy and a bureaucratic dictatorship.

Indeed, questions about the role of the state in organizing the economy were far from settled in 1928 and 1929. Ideas about how to combine plan-ning, industrialization, commerce, trade, and administration were still quite flexible, even as the first five-year plan was launched. For many officials, economic planning was not incompatible with an economy driven by commercial trade. Administration did not mean centralization, nor was NEP incompatible with rapid industrialization. There was cer-tainly nothing in the logic of industrialization, even rapid industrializa-tion, that entailed construction of a massive state dictatorship over society and the economy. It is only in hindsight that we have come to use the terms "planned industrialization" and "command administrative econ-omy" interchangeably to describe the Stalinist system of industrial admin-istration. We distinguish this system from the mixed-market economic system of NEP. Yet conflict and debate within the Soviet political economy in the late 1920s did not cut neatly along lines of state vs. private or ad-ministered vs. market. Participants in the organizational struggles of the late 1920s were careful to distinguish a "planned" from an "administered" and a "command" economy. To the many officials working in the Party and government bureaucracies that managed the economy, these descrip-tive terms were not interchangeable. Officials proposed and debated nu-merous economic and organizational models. Competing agencies enacted contradictory policies in attempts to create the necessary economic condi-tions for industrialization. Even many of those who called for drastic al-terations in the economy and institutional structures of the state did not envision the kind of alterations Stalin came to implement. That the Stalin-ist industrial state became what it was—a highly centralized, dictatorial command economy—can be attributed not to inexorable social or eco-nomic forces but to a fierce organizational and political struggle for con-trol of the emerging Soviet state.

Organizational conflicts in the last years of the 1920s consumed much of the political passion, time, and energy of Party and state officials. These organizational politics were one of the defining moments of the early Sta-linist state. Yet historians have largely ignored this struggle for the state, because much of that struggle occurred between 1928 and 1930, after the start of the first five-year plan.[17] In discussing the end of NEP and the transition from the 1920s to the 1930s, most political-economic histories

---

[17]One of the exceptions to this rule is Sheila Fitzpatrick, "Sergo Ordzhonikidze and the Takeover of VSNKh," *Soviet Studies* 36 (April 1985): 153–72.

focus primary attention on the great industrialization debates of the mid-1920s.[18] Those debates concluded in 1927 and 1928 with the defeat of Party moderates, with Stalin's decision to engage in rapid industrialization, and with the consequent shift in resources from agriculture and trade to industrial construction.[19] The industrialization debates were a crucial turning point in Soviet history. They deserve much of the attention given to them. Yet those debates decided questions of investment priorities; they did not address the question how a state system, let alone a socialist state, should be organized for rapid industrialization.

In the chapters that follow, I reconstruct the politics of industrial state-building, not from hindsight but as the struggle for the state unfolded from the mid-1920s through the early 1930s. The point I wish to make, however, is not just that we need to resettle the boundaries of NEP. I do not argue simply that on the basis of new evidence we should shift the end of NEP from 1928 to 1930 or 1931 to include all of the problems and politics of policy implementation. We need to re-conceptualize the nature of NEP and the transformation of the Soviet political economy during the first five-year plan period.

As the following chapters will show, the construction of a powerful, centralized state apparatus in the late 1920s and early 1930s was not the inevitable consequence of rapid industrialization. Nor was the amassing of central state power a necessary condition for economic planning. For Stalin's state-builders, the drive to create an administrative dictatorship did not spring from the decision to industrialize the country rapidly. Consolidation of a powerful state, free from social and economic constraints, had always been a central goal of the Stalinists. Industrialization gave renewed impetus to their efforts. In fact, the ways in which Stalinist leaders went about building a state industrial dictatorship undermined the foundations of the Soviet planned economy. As E. H. Carr and R. W. Davies have shown, those foundations were laid in the mid-1920s.[20] The experiments in commercial and economic planning that were started in those years gathered momentum in the latter part of the decade. These

---

[18]Alec Nove, for example, takes a whole chapter to review the industrialization debates, but then passes over state reforms after the beginning of the five-year plan. See Alec Nove, *An Economic History of the USSR* (London, 1969). Davies, *Soviet Economy in Turmoil*, recounts, at times in detail, many of the financial and organizational reforms of 1929 and 1930. See esp. pp. 162–73. As two reviewers have noted, however, Davies does not analyze topics of economic history in the context of "the relationship of state and society and the positions and actions of social classes and groups": Lewis H. Siegelbaum and Ronald Grigor Suny, "Making the Command Economy: Western Historians on Soviet Industrialization," *International Labor and Working-Class History* 43 (Spring, 1993): 69.

[19]See the classic work by Alexander Erlich, *The Soviet Industrialization Debates, 1924–1928* (Cambridge, Mass., 1960).

[20]E. H. Carr and R. W. Davies, *Foundations of a Planned Economy, 1926–1929*, 2 vols. (London, 1969).

experiments were cut short by the Stalinist reorganization of the industrial economy in 1930. What emerged after that date can be called a command economy of sorts, but not a planned one. Whether the brief period of planning that characterized the last years of the 1920s was a continuation of NEP or something different was hotly debated by contemporaries. To many observers, however, it was clear that the evolution of the Soviet state and economy in the late 1920s was different not only from that of the early NEP but from what they saw developing in the early 1930s.

Much of the struggle over state formation during the first five-year plan period revolved around arcane issues of finance, commerce, and bureaucratic organization of the Soviet industrial economy. Conflicts over such issues were not the most publicly dramatic of the era. Yet, as contemporaries involved in those conflicts understood, the issues they debated were fundamentally important to the reconstruction of state power and to the relationship of the Soviet state to its citizens. This book, then, is not a history of the Soviet political economy or of the Soviet industrialization drive; it is a political, economic, and social history of the Stalinist industrial state during its formative period.

The Social Basis of Stalin's Revolution

Histories of the interwar period have proliferated in recent decades. Much has been written especially about the social bases of support for Stalin and industrialization. Apart from the political-economic foundation of the Stalinist state, the social basis of support for the Stalinist regime is one of the most well-developed aspects of the Stalin historiography. Reacting against an older tradition of elite political history, scholars have added a social dimension to what is still a preoccupation with the politics of Stalinism. Much of the new scholarship revolves around issues of working-class formation and the influence of class struggle on conflicts in Soviet political culture during the 1920s and 1930s.[21] There are sound historical reasons for such an approach. The Bolshevik regime during the 1920s

[21]See Vladimir Andrle, *Workers in Stalin's Russia: Industrialization and Social Change in a Planned Economy* (Brighton, 1988); Chase, *Workers, Society, and the Soviet State;* Donald Filtzer, *Soviet Workers and Stalinist Industrialization: The Formation of Modern Soviet Production Relations, 1928–1941* (Armonk, N.Y., 1986); John Hatch, "The 'Lenin Levy' and the Social Origins of Stalinism: Workers and the Communist Party in Moscow, 1921–1928," *Slavic Review* 48, no. 4 (1989): 558–77; Hiroaki Kuromiya, *Stalin's Industrial Revolution: Politics and Workers, 1928–1931* (Cambridge, 1988); Gert Meyer, *Sozialstruktur sowjetischer Industriearbeiter am Ende der Zwanziger Jahre: Ergebnisse der Gewerkschaftsumfrage unter Metall-, Textil-, und Bergarbeitern, 1929* (Marburg, 1981); Lynn Viola, *Best Sons of the Fatherland* (New York, 1987); Chris Ward, *Russia's Cotton Workers and the New Economic Policy: Shop Floor Culture and State Policy, 1921–1929* (Cambridge, 1990). For a summary of this historiographic trend, see Lewis H. Siegelbaum, *Stakhanovism and the Politics of Productivity in the USSR, 1935–1941* (New York, 1988), pp. 16–65.

proclaimed itself the vanguard of a proletarian, socialist dictatorship. The Party looked to the working class as the source of its legitimacy and power. Yet political leaders also feared a growing alienation from the working masses as the Party, over the course of the 1920s, became more a governing bureaucratic organization than a mass revolutionary movement. To remedy this situation, Party leaders in the mid- and late 1920s sought ways—recruitment drives, worker promotion campaigns, Party membership reviews—to renew and solidify its links to the working classes. Only by reinvigorating the Party's proletarian character, officials believed, could the Party realize the goals of working-class hegemony in the processes of social, economic, and state formation.

The proletarian posture that the Party adopted in the 1920s redounded to the benefit of the Stalinist faction within the Party's leadership. Indeed, Stalin allied himself aggressively with the Party's proletarian goals. As a result, according to social historians, the Stalinist faction was able to draw on significant working-class support for the brutal assault, launched in 1928, on Party moderates, the state's bureaucratic apparatus, and the conciliatory economic and social policies of the 1920s.[22] It is an increasingly accepted view that this alliance between Stalinist political leaders and key segments of the working classes proved crucial to the Stalinists' success in their bid for power in the Party and governmental bureaucracies. According to the new historiography, the key to the so-called Stalin revolution lies not in Stalin's skill at factional politics, the traditional consensus of political historians, but in the class alignment of social and political forces during the 1920s.[23]

As the number of social-political histories of the working class has grown, studies of other groups have been fitted integrally into the class-conflict interpretation of the Stalinist revolution. Studies of the professional strata of Soviet industrial managers and engineers emphasize the inherent conflict between these groups and Party politicians.[24] Specialists were subjected to political pressure because, in the received interpretation,

[22]For the most explicit statements of this view see Chase, *Workers, Society, and the Soviet State*, Hatch, "'Lenin Levy'"; Hiroaki Kuromiya, "*Edinonachalie* and the Soviet Industrial Manager, 1928–1937," *Soviet Studies* 36, no. 2 (1984): 185–204, and "The Crisis of Proletarian Identity in the Soviet Factory, 1928–1929," *Slavic Review* 44, no. 2 (1985): 280–97; Lynn Viola, *Best Sons*.

[23]Chris Ward has objected that to organize working class history around such issues as Stalinism and the Revolution is to distort social history into political history. See his "Languages of Trade or Languages of Class? Work Culture in Russian Cotton Mills in the 1920s," in *Making Workers Soviet: Power, Class, and Identity*, ed. Lewis H. Siegelbaum and Ronald Grigor Suny (Ithaca, 1994), pp. 194–219, esp. 195, n. 2.

[24]See Jeremy Azrael, *Managerial Power and Soviet Politics* (Cambridge, Mass., 1966); David Granick, *Red Executive: A Study of the Organization Man in Russian Industry* (New York, 1960); Kendall Bailes, *Technology and Society under Lenin and Stalin: Origins of the Soviet Technical Intelligentsia* (Princeton, 1978); Fitzpatrick, "Sergo Ordzhonikidze"; Nicholas Lampert, *The Technical Intelligentsia and the Soviet State* (New York, 1979).

their professional expertise and authority posed a challenge to the Party's control over the country's economic administration. Moreover, many specialists in key decision-making positions were trained before the Revolution. They were not of working-class backgrounds and were not Communist Party members. These so-called bourgeois specialists were, in fact, bourgeois, drawn from the ranks of Russia's prerevolutionary professional middle classes. Although most professionals worked loyally for the regime, Bolshevik Party leaders were deeply suspicious of them, and for good reason. According to most accounts, the great majority of specialists in the bureaucracies opposed Stalinist industrialization policies as reckless adventurism, dangerous to the fragile economic and social recovery under way during NEP.[25]

There is no doubt that Communist Party officials were suspicious of the loyalty of the country's technical and administrative intelligentsia, and feared being held hostage to their technical expertise. As a result, the Stalinist regime attacked the privilege and authority of specialists, especially those identified as bourgeois specialists, who Party officials believed were sabotaging the country's industrialization plans. Thousands of specialists were persecuted, arrested, and made the scapegoats for the catastrophic failure of the very policies many specialists had opposed. In the infamous Shakhty trials of mining engineers in 1928, and again in the trial of industrial "wreckers" in 1930, some of the country's top engineers and managers were tried on fabricated charges of sabotage and political conspiracy. Many were convicted and some shot for supposedly plotting with foreign governments to wreck the state's industrialization plans and bring about the collapse of the Soviet regime.

At the factory level, much of the social conflict of the late 1920s erupted in harassment and physical violence against managers and engineers—the infamous *spetseedstvo*, or specialist-baiting campaigns, of 1928 and 1929. According to most histories, this conflict cut along class lines. Militant workers formed shock brigades and engaged in socialist competitions that directly challenged the authority of managers on the shop floor. Encouraged by Party activists and official propaganda, these groups sought to wrest control of production from the established managerial hierarchy and to fulfill the revolutionary goal of worker self-management. The official press trumpeted the success of shock groups in reducing waste, increasing productivity, and raising working-class political consciousness. Determined to turn industrialization into class war, so the story goes, Stalinist political leaders greeted the new labor methods as historically unprecedented, uniquely socialist forms of rationalization and work organization.

[25] See Lampert, *Technical Intelligentsia*, esp. chap. 3.

The message from the wreckers' trials and the antispecialist campaign of the late 1920s seems clear. Regardless of guilt or innocence, class—or rather the perception of class—mattered. Anyone could fall under suspicion, but most people who did run afoul of the regime in those years had social, professional, or occupational backgrounds that identified them as bourgeois. Through intimidation and arrest, and by fueling the class hostility of workers, the Stalinist regime accomplished two related goals: it successfully subjugated professional autonomy to political ends and it laid the foundation for a new specifically Soviet technical intelligentsia.[26]

Certainly the harsh economic and political policies associated with the first five-year plan created a volatile and chaotic situation that verged on social warfare. In those years it was better to be known as a "red" than a "bourgeois" manager or engineer.[27] Yet, as important as the perception of class was, a class analysis leaves much unexplained about the dynamics of social identity and conflict during the Soviet industrial revolution. The rhetoric of building socialism, used to legitimate class war, masked a more complex fracturing and restructuring of social relations and hierarchies of authority. At the factory level, industrial reconstruction and rationalization did not foster class solidarity, but exacerbated social divisions within the working class, giving rise to a variety of conflicting economic and political responses by workers to state-initiated policies. At the same time, the workers' conflicting responses to rationalization and industrial reconstruction overlapped and played into bitter struggles between different managerial strata, occupational groups, and industrial bureaucracies. As has traditionally been argued, many managers and specialists opposed Stalinist industrial policies on the grounds of economic irrationality. Yet other groups—within the industrial administrative apparatus, the trade union organizations, and the professional engineering and managerial strata—enthusiastically supported the regime's goals and plans. They did so precisely because of the technocratic and pro-managerial implications of those plans, or because those plans evoked a vision of modern industrialism that mesmerized Party members and professionals alike.[28] These

---

[26]See Loren Graham, *The Ghost of the Executed Engineer: Technology and the Fall of the Soviet Union* (Cambridge, Mass., 1993). Graham notes especially that the engineer Petr Palchinskii was so well respected that the Bolshevik authorities executed him secretly rather than risk putting him on public trial.

[27]"Red" identified one's political sympathies and did not automatically imply anything about one's social background. In practice, however, "red" was often used synonymously with "proletarian." For more on the social construction of identity during this period, see Sheila Fitzpatrick, "The Problem of Class Identity in NEP Society," in Fitzpatrick et al., *Russia in the Era of NEP* (Bloomington, 1991), pp. 12–33; and her "Ascribing Class: The Construction of Social Identity in Soviet Russia," *Journal of Modern History* 65, no. 4 (1993): 745–70.

[28]"Technocracy" implies (1) the ability of technically trained specialists to exercise autonomous authority within an expanding sphere of professional and administrative competence, and (2) the attempted implementation of singularly technological or bureaucratic solutions to resolve social, economic, and political problems. Thus Stalinist industrialization policies,

groups also perceived and justified their interests in the language of so-cialist construction. Moreover, they played a significant role in designing the policies and administrative institutions of the Stalinist industrializa-tion drive.

Stalinist policies, then, despite the class rhetoric in which they were presented, drew support across a wide spectrum of social and occupa-tional groups; not just within the working class, but also within the largely middle-level professional strata of specialists, administrators, and planners who worked in the state's industrial administrative apparatus. Stalinist policies drew support not because of their appeal to a particular class-based social or political ideology, but because of the many social and ideological cross-currents that those policies encompassed. As a criterion of historical analysis, class alone does not explain why such a diverse crosssection of Soviet society supported Stalin and industrialization, or why certain groups supported the regime and its goals and others did not. Nor does class explain why certain individuals and occupational groups were able to exert such a formative influence on policies and insti-tutions and others could not. Class does not explain how Stalinist indus-trial strategies and state institutions came into being, or why a particular administrative culture or a certain set of bureaucratic relations came to dominate the state's industrial system. Class, in other words, is too broad a category to be useful in efforts to understand the process of state con-struction under Stalin. As we shall see, other conflicts—occupational, gen-erational, regional, and bureaucratic—shaped Soviet industrial policies and relations as much as the conflicts that we have traditionally empha-sized between Stalinists and non-Stalinists, Party officials and specialists, Communists and non-communists, workers and managers.[29]

Beyond Class

Over the last twenty years, two historians, Sheila Fitzpatrick and Moshe Lewin, have attempted to analyze the social foundations of Stalin-ism in ways that go beyond the categories of class conflict. Both describe the making of a new Soviet elite in the 1930s as part of a plebeian up-heaval rather than as the culmination of a class revolution.[30] Rapid eco-

though economically irrational, were often technocratic and drew support from segments of the managerial and technical strata.

[29]For a discussion of the importance of occupational categories and their difference from class forms of social identification, see Thomas Childers, "The Social Language of Politics: The Sociology of Political Discourse in the Weimar Republic," *American Historical Review* 95, no. 2 (1990): 331–58.

[30]See esp. Sheila Fitzpatrick, "Stalin and the Making of a New Elite, 1928–1939," *Slavic Review* 38, no. 2 (1979): 377–402; idem, "'Middle-Class Values' and Soviet Life in the 1930s," in *Soviet Society and Culture: Essays in Honor of Vera S. Dunham*, ed. Terry Thompson and

nomic expansion, coupled with the destruction of the old intelligentsia, according to both Fitzpatrick and Lewin, created a vortex of social mobility that made factory directors, Party heads, and even commissars out of barely literate peasant-workers. This process created an instant ruling elite that supported Stalin and, according to Fitzpatrick, quickly assimilated middle-class rather than proletarian or socialist values.[31] Elite or not, according to Lewin, the Soviet ruling "class" that emerged in the 1930s could barely read the signs in canteens that admonished comrades not to spit on the floor. What occurred in the 1930s, writes Lewin, was a crude process of social destruction and creation that had "little to do with the working class" and less to do with the creation of socialism or any kind of intelligentsia. Indeed, Russia's "rural nexus" and the "acceleration of backwardness" caused by years of war and social destruction so shaped the formation of state institutions and policies that Stalin's rule is best described as a peasant or serf despotism, albeit one that accomplished an industrial revolution.[32]

Fitzpatrick and Lewin focus on the broad sweep of time and take in the mostly glacial, sometimes cataclysmic movement of large social formations. Scholars of a younger generation, inspired largely by newly accessible archival material, have veered sharply away from social history and returned to the realm of biography, both individual and collective, to explain the political culture of Stalinism. Some have pioneered new studies of Stalin and his entourage, or *druzhina*.[33] These scholars argue that we do not need to resort to broad social explanations of class conflict or complex reconstructions of the "rural nexus" to understand the mentality, policies, and institutions of the Stalinist state in the 1930s. In their view, the shared experiences of the revolutionary war fundamentally shaped not only the psychology of Stalin and the Stalinists but also specific policies. The tactics of mass organization, dictatorship, and political violence adopted in 1920

Richard Sheldon (Boulder, 1988), pp. 20–38; idem, *Education and Social Mobility in the Soviet Union, 1921–1934* (Cambridge, 1979); Lewin, *Making of the Soviet System*.

[31]Fitzpatrick, "'Middle-Class Values.'"

[32]Lewin, *Making of the Soviet System*, pp. 37, 266–68. In, *Magnetic Mountain: Stalinism as a Civilization* (Berkeley, 1995), Stephen Kotkin argues that Stalinist rule enjoyed widespread legitimacy not just because the regime created its own elite or because it destroyed the old intelligentsia, but because millions of Soviet people believed that the Communist Party under Stalin was in fact building socialism.

[33]See esp. Oleg Khlevniuk, *Stalin i Ordzhonikidze: Konflikty v Politbiuro v 30-gody* (Moscow, 1993), published in English as *In Stalin's Shadow: The Career of Sergo Ordzhonikidze*, trans. David J. Nordlander (Armonk, N.Y., 1995); Andrea Graziosi is currently writing a biography of Georgii Piatakov, one of the most important Bolshevik administrative figures. Parts of this work have appeared as "'Building the First System of State Industry in History': Piatakov's VSNKh and the Crisis of NEP, 1923–1926," *Cahiers du monde russe et soviétique* 32 (1991): 539–81, and "At the Roots of Soviet Industrial Relations and Practices: Piatakov's Donbass in 1921," *Cahiers du monde russe* 36 (1995): 95–138. *Druzhina*, which denoted the personal bodyguard of the medieval tsars, is Graziosi's term.

Instilling values: a factory shame board in the early 1930s exhorts workers to shave, and punishes Comrade "Shirker" for disorderly conduct by stripping him of shock work privileges for three months. GARF.

and 1921 prefigured the same brutal tactics of state-building used in the early 1930s.[34]

These historians certainly do not deny the impact of society on the state, but each has moved from an early interest in the social-political history of labor to a new focus on the Stalinist elite.[35] The collective efforts of this group to gather material on the workings of the Politbiuro during the 1920s and 1930s is indicative of this new focus.[36] Their study, which is fundamentally important to any understanding of Soviet history, also reflects the view of this group of scholars about Stalinism and the process of Soviet state formation. That process was centered in the Politbiuro, from which all significant initiatives flowed, and without whose support no initiatives became significant. In the collective view of this group, "the leaders of the Politbiuro could assert, with full justification, 'Gosudarstvo—eto my' [We are the state]—an ironic echo of Louis XIV's "L'état, c'est moi."[37]

In fact, the biographical and social approaches complement each other. Both are needed to understand Stalinism. Though there was no precedent for what a socialist society should look like, the architects of Stalin's industrial state had specific ideas about what they were doing, and those ideas had to have the support of the Politbiuro. It is important, therefore, to know who those officials were, their backgrounds, and what kind of state it was they thought they were building. At the same time, as Lewin and others have pointed out, social relations and the political and bureaucratic culture that came to characterize the Soviet industrial system during the 1930s reflected very little of the schemes of those who were supposedly in charge of that system.[38] Indeed, the new state that took shape in the chaos of the industrialization drive was unruly and unstable, the more so as its creators tried to plan and gain control over it. This contradiction—between the centralization of power and the loss of control, and between rational planning and wholly unplanned consequences—is one of the central problems of Stalinism that needs explaining. It is difficult to

[34]This is the central argument of Graziosi, "At the Roots of Soviet Industrial Relations," which denies any fundamental historical significance to NEP.

[35]See O. V. Khlevniuk, Udarniki pervoi piatiletki (Moscow, 1989); V. A. Kozlov and O. V. Khlevniuk, Nachinaetsia s cheloveka: chelovecheskii faktor v sotsialisticheskom stroitel'stve (Moscow, 1988); Andrea Graziosi, "'Visitors from Other Times': Foreign Workers in the Prewar Piatiletki," in Cahiers du monde russe et soviétique 29 (April–June 1988): 161–80.

[36]See the collection of archive documents Stalinskoe politbiuro v 30-e gody, ed. Oleg Khlevniuk, Aleksandr Kvashonkin, L. P. Kosheleva, and L. A. Rogovaia (Moscow, 1995). This collective is planning a second and third series of documents. See also Kosheleva et al., eds., Pis'ma I. V. Stalina V. M. Molotovu, 1925–1936 gg: Sbornik dokumentov (Moscow, 1995).

[37]Khlevniuk et al., Stalinskoe politbiuro, p. 7.

[38]In addition to Lewin's works, cited above, see J. Arch Getty, The Origins of the Great Purges: The Soviet Communist Party Reconsidered (New York, 1985), and G. T. Rittersporn, Stalinist Simplifications and Soviet Complications: Social Tensions and Political Conflicts in the USSR, 1933–1953 (New York, 1991). Getty and Rittersporn take this argument much further than Lewin.

find a single appropriate label for the Soviet industrial state that evolved in the 1930s. It was neither socialist nor planned nor quite the administrative command dictatorship that Stalinist leaders had hoped to create. Yet discernible patterns, both formal and especially informal, of administration, social relations, and production organization can be described and analyzed. Explaining how the Soviet industrial system actually worked, as opposed to how it was supposed to work, is one of the central tasks of this book.

In 1928 and 1929, the Communist Party and Soviet government, led by Stalin, supposedly stood for rapid industrialization, modernization, and above all a socialist Russia. So did millions of Soviet citizens, including key groups in the state's industrial administrative apparatus. Yet the support of these groups for Stalin and the goals of the regime did not imply support of Stalinism as it came to be practiced or as we have since come to understand it. Different groups had radically different ideas about the meaning of modernization, industrialization, and socialism, and many could find support for their ideas in the often vague and contradictory policies of the regime. Let us see how these individuals and groups interpreted and attempted to act on the goals of the regime as they understood them. Their actions and influence shaped the emerging Soviet industrial state, at times successfully, at times unsuccessfully and with harsh consequences.

PART I

The State(s) of the Economy in the Late 1920s

1

Unruly Bureaucracies, Fragmented Markets

The various parts of the administrative apparatus are
engaged in economic war with each other.
                    —V. N. Mantsev, August 1929

On 17 October 1927, Valerian Kuibyshev, the head of the Soviet Union's Supreme Economic Council, or Vesenkha, delivered a report to the Central Executive Committee of the government, TsIK, on the preparedness of the economy for the tasks of rapid industrialization. As chairman of Vesenkha, Kuibyshev routinely reported on the state of the economy to the government and to executive bodies of the Communist Party. This report, however, was a crucial one. Over the previous year, Vesenkha and the state's planning agency, Gosplan, had presented several competing versions of a five-year industrialization plan, and those reports had aroused heated political debate and factional infighting within the government and the Party.[1] The 15th Party Congress was approaching in December 1927, and factional groups opposed to Party policies were preparing platforms for the anticipated debates. Kuibyshev's speech to the Executive Committee in late October 1927 would be one of the last opportunities before the congress convened for Vesenkha to defend its proposals in a highly publicized forum.

Economic disagreements among Party and government leaders at this time centered on questions about the pace of industrialization. Kuibyshev was among the inner circle of Party leaders around Joseph Stalin, the Party's general secretary, who by 1927 were beginning to push the government and Party toward increasingly ambitious industrialization plans. As a result, Kuibyshev's report to the TsIK was optimistic about the ability of the country's economy to achieve industrialization rapidly. Kuibyshev

[1]For a discussion of the industrialization debates during 1927, see Carr and Davies, *Foundations of a Planned Economy*, 2:837–98.

noted the continuing unemployment, high industrial costs and prices, and shortages of materials and resources. Still, he argued, much progress had been made to stabilize and rationalize the industrial economy. Accounting methods, while still not widespread, were being implemented, and Vesenkha was moving "vigorously" to strengthen factory administration, as the government instructed. Vesenkha was proceeding apace with the reorganization and rationalization of production, Kuibyshev announced, and the system of sales and distribution of supplies was working tolerably well through syndicated trade cartels for the various branches of industry. Vesenkha was also moving forward with plans for construction and reconstruction of industry, in accordance with recently revised proposals for a five-year plan. Kuibyshev acknowledged that problems existed, but, he declared, the system was operating as it should. All was in order, according to Kuibyshev, and the industrial apparatus was ready to achieve the goals set before it by the Party and the government.[2]

In fact, all was not in order. Kuibyshev's sanguine assessments contrasted sharply with the critical evaluations offered by officials in the Soviet government's inspectorate and control agency, the Narodnyi Komissariat Raboche-Krest'ianskoi Inspektsii, or Rabkrin. Rabkrin's numerous investigations of Vesenkha in the last years of the decade revealed serious organizational problems, which hampered the council's administration of industry and the economy. Moreover, if Rabkrin's reports were to be believed, the situation was getting worse, not better. According to Rabkrin's officials, weak central leadership had led to pervasive mismanagement and chaotic planning. On numerous occasions in the late 1920s, Rabkrin reports accused Vesenkha officials of criminal negligence and outright fraud.

These accusations were bad enough, but there was more. Vesenkha, declared many Rabkrin investigations, allowed the private sectors of the economy to overwhelm and drive policy in the state-owned sectors. Economic decisions were subject to the whims of the market and its control by alien social classes, the peasantry and the hated Nepmen, the private traders and entrepreneurs. Even within the state sectors, claimed Rabkrin, the absence of effective administrative controls allowed regional centers to distort national policies. Vesenkha's policies, Rabkrin officials declared, resulted in loose financial control, an orgy of spending, and a system of interregional rivalry that threatened central state control of the economy.[3]

---

[2]V. Kuibyshev, *Itogi i perspektivy khoziaistvennogo stroitel'stva SSSR: Doklad na 2–i sessii TsIK SSSR 17/X/27 g.* (Moscow, 1927), pp. 33–42, 44–61. This was, in fact, Vesenkha's third draft of a five-year plan, far more ambitious than its previous one, and much more so than proposals put forward by Gosplan. See Carr and Davies, *Foundations of a Planned Economy*, p. 868. See also the massive report on rationalization issued by Kuibyshev in 1928, *Ratsionalizatsiia promyshlennosti SSSR* (Moscow, 1928), esp. pp. 4–23.

[3]Rabkrin summarized its criticisms of Vesenkha in a report edited by A. P. Rozengol'ts,

The contrast in tone and substance of Vesenkha's and Rabkrin's assessments of the industrial economy was so striking that it is hard to believe they referred to the same industrial system. Where the one struck a positive note, the other delivered scathing criticism. Where the one depicted ordered progress, the other described chaos. In fact, the truth lay somewhere between the contrasting descriptions. The Soviet industrial economy on the eve of the first five-year plan was not so well ordered as Kuibyshev claimed, but it was not quite so chaotic as Rabkrin officials charged. Not quite, but Soviet industry on the eve of the great industrialization drive corresponded more to Rabkrin's descriptions than to Kuibyshev's. Despite Kuibyshev's optimistic pronouncements, Vesenkha exercised little authority over its fragmented and unruly economic empire. As the 1920s drew to a close, the agency was unprepared for the tasks of industrialization that lay ahead.

Soviet Russia's NEP Economy: An Overview

The state's industrial economy was only one part, although a significant part, of a complex economic system that had evolved over the course of the 1920s. It was not just one economy, but a mixture of several economies. A basic division existed between state-owned and private sectors, a division that was established officially in 1921 with the beginning of the New Economic Policy, or NEP. The existence of any private sector was against the Bolsheviks' socialist ideals, but the Party and the government accepted the necessity of a mixed economy for political as well as economic reasons. Private control of the agrarian economy, especially, was the compromise that the Bolsheviks accepted to keep social peace with a peasant class that was wary of the government's socialist goals, if not openly hostile to them. The government and Party also tolerated private ownership and market forces in retail trade, small business, and many consumer industries. The government and Party encouraged market forces in these sectors, primarily in the early 1920s, as a temporary measure to stimulate economic and social recovery after the war with Germany and the revolutionary wars that had swept the Russian empire from 1914 to 1921. In 1922 and 1923, at the height of NEP, Nepmen accounted for as much as 80 percent of retail trade in the country. Party and governmental authorities began to curtail private trade activities after mid-decade, but as late as 1927 close to 40 percent of trade still passed through private hands.[4]

To ensure basic control over the economy, the government maintained

---

Promyshlennost': Sbornik statei po materialam TsKK VKP(b)-NK RKI (Moscow, 1930). More is said about Rabkrin's criticisms of Vesenkha in Chapter 3.

[4]Ball, *Russia's Last Capitalists*, p. 104.

ownership of most of the capital or heavy industries, such as mining, metallurgy, machine building, and petrochemicals. State control also extended to the country's major banking and financial institutions. State-owned industry employed the vast majority of workers and was administered through the system of state bureaucracies under Vesenkha. Prices, wages, contracts, and working conditions in these sectors were established not by market forces but by the government in accordance with the goals determined by its planning agencies and by the Communist Party.[5]

By controlling the activities in these dominant sectors, the government controlled what was called the "commanding heights" of the economy. The military metaphor was deliberate, for the Bolsheviks felt themselves besieged by the hostile forces that controlled the private, market-driven sectors of the economy. It was the prospect of being overwhelmed by capitalist economic and social forces that many officials feared when they accused Vesenkha of not doing enough to bolster and extend the influence of the socialized sectors of the economy.

State and private sectors interacted through cooperatives and semistate and semiprivate commercial associations, which the government alternately encouraged and repressed through its economic and price policies. This interaction between state and private sectors was an integral and officially accepted part of the NEP economy, notwithstanding fears about the influence of the market over the state-owned sector. Though often exaggerated, such fears had a basis in reality. Hidden market forces operated within state industry, but those forces did not infiltrate state sectors from the private sectors of the economy, as many people believed. Market and other competitive forces arose out of economic and administrative relations within the state sector.

Vesenkha's Bureaucratic Economy

The Supreme Economic Council, or Vesenkha, administered the country's industrial economy. Vesenkha's headquarters on Ploshchad' Nogina (Nogin Square), were less than a three-minute direct drive from the main gates of the Kremlin fortress on Red Square, the seat of the government and Communist Party headquarters. Vesenkha's offices and those of its subdepartments covered nearly a whole city block and were housed in one of the city's modern glass, iron, and masonry structures. Its closeness to the Kremlin, the center of political power, bespoke Vesenkha's importance in the hierarchy of governmental agencies. The functional rationality of its architecture symbolized the agency's mission to administer a

[5]For how the NEP economic system worked, see Carr, *Socialism in One Country*, and Carr and Davies, *Foundations of a Planned Economy*.

planned socialist economy. Vesenkha was one of the largest and most powerful of the country's governing bureaucracies.

Vesenkha exercised nominal administrative control over the industrial system through a vast and multilayered hierarchy of bureaucracies. At the top was the presidium, composed of the top two dozen or so administrative and planning leaders in Vesenkha. Directly beneath the presidium in the hierarchy, with offices in the same building, were the chief planning and economic administrations. In the early 1920s, authority was divided at this level between the ten directorates (*direktoraty*) of the Central Administration of State Industry (TsUGProm) and the subdepartments of the General Economic Administration (GEU). Until 1927 the Industrial Planning Commission, Promplan, was one of the most important departments in Vesenkha, but operated as a subdepartment of the GEU. Reforms in 1927 simplified somewhat Vesenkha's complex administrative structure. Officials disbanded TsUGProm and the GEU and combined their subdepartments into eight new chief industrial administrations called *glavnye upravlenie*, or *glavki* (see Figure 1). The eight glavki supervised administration of the major industrial branches of the economy and were directly subordinate to Vesenkha's presidium. Promplan, which had been a subdepartment of the GEU, was transformed into an independent economic and planning administration for the whole of the economy, the Planovo-Ekonomicheskoe Upravlenie, or PEU, and it too was placed under direct authority of the presidium. The PEU was charged to coordinate the activities of the chief industrial administrations, the glavki, although the hierarchy of authority between these two agencies was never clearly defined. Glavmetall (Glavnoe Upravlenie Metallicheskoi Promyshlennosti), for example, was the chief administration for all the metal and machine fabricating industries under government ownership. In 1927 Glavmetall employed slightly more than 300 people in its central offices. It had six major departments, each with several subdepartments. Departments were well equipped with telephones and typewriters, and several had telegraphic cable machines to communicate with regional administrative offices.[6]

In 1927 Glavmetall administered seventy-six regionally organized production trusts, including nineteen of all-union designation. An all-union designation meant that a trust was administered under direct supervision of Vesenkha SSSR. Eleven trusts were administered under republic control, and forty-six trusts fell within the jurisdiction of local or city economic councils. All-union trusts maintained bureau staffs in Moscow but had their main offices in regional industrial centers. Trusts provided the most immediate supervisory functions over the various metal fabricating works in their areas. In all, Glavmetall administered, through its trusts,

---

[6]"Polozhenie o glavmetalle i ego otdelakh," in RGAE, f. 4086, op. 1, d. 641, ll. 3–4.

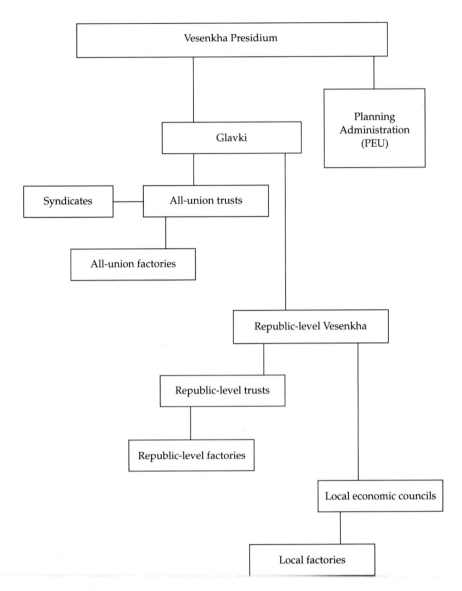

Figure 1. The Vesenkha system, 1926–1929

364 factories with 335,000 workers. These factories accounted for over 90 percent of all metal fabricating production in the country and the same proportion of the country's metalworkers. The remaining production fell under the supervision of cooperative organizations, private companies, or foreign concessions.[7] Vesenkha's administration amounted to a near monopoly in the metal fabricating and metallurgical industries, a reflection of the "commanding heights" strategy of the New Economic Policy.

Trusts varied in size and status. Those all-union trusts under Vesenkha's direct supervision usually encompassed the most significant and largest factories in their geographic regions. In 1927 Gomzy, the State Association of Metal Factories, was the largest of these trusts. Its authority encompassed the machine building works in the central industrial region, particularly in Moscow, and stretched west to include the giant metallurgical and machine building complexes at Briansk, on the upper reaches of the Dnieper River. Because Gomzy administered the central region, it was one of the few major trusts to have its central offices in Moscow. Other trusts of all-union significance included Uralmet, with headquarters in Sverdlovsk; Iugostal', the powerful southern metal trust, with offices in Khar'kov; and the Kramatorsk machine building complex in southern Russia. Factories in these trusts were generally the most favored in receipt of supplies and personnel. Because of the privileges that accompanied the all-union designation, factories fought to attain and to keep their status within all-union trusts.

Not all factories of significance fell under the administration of all-union trusts. Some operated under the supervision of republic or even city economic administrations. The Moscow Machine Building Trust, Mosmashtrest (MMT), for example, was administered under the Moscow City Economic Council. The factories in its jurisdiction were therefore only of "local" (*mestnoe*) significance. The largest of the MMT factories, the Krasnyi Proletarii works (formerly the Bromley factory), squatted in the near southeastern suburbs of the capital. It employed nine hundred workers, technical personnel, and administrators at the height of its operating capacity before 1930. The Krasnyi Proletarii was small by comparison to a giant manufacturing works such as the Kolomenskii factory, administered by Gomzy and situated farther outside Moscow. The Kolomenskii employed nearly two thousand workers by the end of the 1920s. Yet despite its local significance and modest size, the Krasnyi Proletarii was the most important, technologically sophisticated machine tool factory in the USSR. It produced some of the country's most advanced industrial lathes, planers, and cutting machines and a good many of the precision industrial instruments used in other machine manufacturing works.

[7]*Metallopromyshlennost' za 10 let* (Moscow, 1927), pp. 35, 46, 72. *Kontsentratsia fabrichno-zavodskoi i trestirovannoi tsenzovoi promyshlennosti* (Moscow, 1929), p. 48, gives somewhat higher figures.

Trusts under republic or city supervision usually lacked the prestige and power of all-union trusts, but this was not uniformly the case. By the end of the decade, Mosmashtrest, with the Krasnyi Proletarii as its flagship factory, achieved the status of fourth largest machine building trust in the country in combined production output. Similarly, the Leningrad machine building trust, Lenmashtrest (LMT), reported to the city economic council, not directly to Vesenkha SSSR. Nonetheless, the LMT administered the massive Putilov works, which sprawled throughout the southeastern sections of the city and were among the largest manufacturing complexes in all of Europe. With the Putilov works as its banner factory, Lenmashtrest was one of the most influential trusts in the Vesenkha system.

Officially, economic administration was organized within Vesenkha by industrial branch. Branch or horizontal organization meant that Glavmetall, for example, administered affairs in all the metal fabricating industries, including ferrous and nonferrous metallurgy and machine building. Glavelektro ran the electrical generating facilities in the country, Glavtekstil controlled all textile manufacture, and so on.[8] After June 1928, Glavmetall split into three separate administrations. Each new glavk was concerned with a different aspect of metal manufacture, but the branch principle remained the primary organizing principle. Thus Glavchermet took over control of all ferrous metal manufacture, Glavtsvetmet handled nonferrous metallurgy, and Glavmashinstroi administered all machine building production. Other industrial branches were organized similarly under their chief administrations.

Vesenkha's officials attempted to administer their vast bureaucratic economy in accordance with the latest methods of scientific management. In the early 1920s, Vesenkha began a study of these techniques in advanced capitalist countries with the intention of adapting them to Soviet factory conditions. Vesenkha sponsored numerous conferences and meetings at which Soviet specialists examined in detail the organization of such works as Ford's River Rouge automobile plant in Michigan. They also examined factories reorganized under functional departments of administration developed by Frederick Taylor, the premier American expert on scientific management. Vesenkha officials traveled to the United States to study the organization of production and management in these and other plants. Soviet experts also toured British firms, especially the fa-

[8]Horizontal organization differed from vertical integration, the principle on which most German firms were organized, in that vertically organized cartels sought control over a manufacturing process from raw materials to finished product. Thus a vertically integrated steel cartel might own coal mines and iron ore foundries as well as rolling and blooming mills for steel products.

mous Vickers engineering works, and the large German manufacturing firms of the Ruhr and northern Germany—Krupp, MAN, Siemens.

Debates continued throughout the 1920s over whether to reorganize Soviet factory administration within functional departments or to retain traditional shop forms of management. Desiring greater specialization and control, those who favored functionalism argued that traditional managerial methods, such as contracting between shop heads and factory management, left too much discretion to lower administrative personnel and workers as to how and when to work. Under the old ways, shop administrators and foremen determined wages and allocation of work assignments. New technologies, especially mass-production systems, required standardized work procedures and precise coordination of the various aspects of manufacture and assembly. Vesenkha's specialists believed that cost-effective operation of modern production technologies demanded systematic managerial intervention in the production process.[9]

On the basis of their experience in reorganizing production and management at several machine building factories near Khar'kov, Ukrainian experts especially lobbied vigorously for functionalist types of administration. In the Ukrainian factories, the traditional rights of shop administrators and production foremen were abolished, and a separate department of specialists was established for each aspect of production organization and economic management. Analogous departments were established and linked at the factory, trust, and republic administrative levels. Each department had complete authority over its area of expertise, whether over supplies and inventory, quality control of materials, production planning, labor organization and wage determination, or financial accounting. Each department gave orders directly to its counterpart at the next lowest administrative level, until orders reached shop administrators and foremen. Shop administrators were to ensure the proper execution of work orders they received from central factory departments.[10]

Advocates of functionalism acknowledged the potential confusion inherent in this type of managerial structure. When instructions arrived in the shop from different departments of the central administration, foremen and workers found themselves subordinate to a number of overseers instead of just one. Functional management was designed to specialize

[9]For an articulate statement of the connection between mass production and managerial control, see V. L. Leder, ed., *Sovremennoe sostoianie rabot po ratsionalizatsii v promyshlennosti SSSR* (Moscow, 1926). See also L. Ia. Shukgalter, ed., *Rabota nepreryvnym potokom: Sbornik statei* (Moscow, 1930).

[10]*Doklady VSNKh USSR po voprosam organizatsii i ratsionalizatsii proizvodstva na promyshlennykh predpriiatiikh za 1925–1926 god,"* in RGAE, f. 3429, op. 3, d. 469, ll. 25–113. For a discussion of the reorganization at the Khar'kov locomotive plant, see ll. 25–87. See also ll. 88–113 on managerial restructuring.

and thereby enhance control over work activities. To that extent it potentially sacrificed unity of command for a high degree of specialization. But functionalists naively argued that proper coordination would be preserved by the centralization of planning within a socialist economy.[11]

Whether the Ukrainian influence proved decisive is not clear, but in the early spring of 1927, Vesenkha ordered its trusts to begin production surveys of factories for transfer to functional forms of management.[12] In addition, Vesenkha ordered the introduction of a range of other reforms. Like functional management, these measures were designed to reduce costs by bringing production processes under systematic managerial control. Authorities renewed an ongoing campaign to bring financial discipline to state enterprises through the introduction of modern accounting methods. Vesenkha's Bureau of Standardization and Rationalization encouraged state trusts and enterprises to establish universal operating standards for equipment, to systematize work routines, and to reduce the number and standardize the types of machines and other equipment manufactured by individual plants. Vesenkha also urged trusts to modernize factory dispatching and routing systems. Through the use of standardized forms and specifications, Vesenkha hoped that managers could increase the rate of flow of materials through the factory. Such methods were also supposed to eliminate redundancy, confusion, and loss as pieces moved through the manufacturing and assembly stages of production.

Industrial Administration and Administrative Entrepreneurs

Vesenkha's organization charts looked tidy, with rows of administrative boxes and lines of authority that ran true and straight. Russia's industrial economy, by contrast, was anything but tidy. The factory system that the Soviets inherited had developed historically in a piecemeal fashion. As a result, individual factories encompassed a range of production processes and types. The Putilov works in Leningrad, for example, combined so many diverse manufacturing processes that no one knew exactly how many products it manufactured. The number reached certainly into the hundreds. The factory manufactured just about anything that was metal, from hatpins to steam boilers and locomotives. The Putilov works, like many factories, was its own production kingdom. The works contained its

---

[11]For a concise and illuminating description of functionalism in the Soviet managerial context, see S. A. Billon, "Soviet Management Structure: Stability and Change," in *Evolution of International Management Structures*, ed. Harold F. Williamson (Newark, Del., 1979), pp. 114–43. See also the interesting comment by Vsevelod Holubnychy that follows, pp. 144–58. The other essays in this book describe the systematic managerial movement in an international context, as does Judith Merkle, *Management and Ideology: The Legacy of the International Scientific Management Movement* (Berkeley, 1980).

[12]*Industrializatsiia SSSR: Dokumenty i materialy, 1926–1928* (Moscow, 1969), pp. 498–99.

own foundry and metal fabricating complex, and, like many machine manufactories, it built its own machine tools. Clearly the branch organization of industrial administration was ill suited to a production complex such as the Putilov works.

In the Ural region, factory complexes were often integrated vertically; that is, they combined metallurgical and machine building works with mining and forestry operations and even railroad lines. This kind of arrangement was called a combine, or *kombinat*. Often these complexes were not concentrated in one location, but were scattered over a wide geographical area. Thus Vesenkha officials had to decide whether to administer the various parts of a *kombinat* under a single glavk—mining, metallurgy, or machine building—or under three separate glavki. As often as not, Vesenkha chose the latter alternative. Indeed, different parts of a single factory were often administered by different glavki. This was the case at the Kramatorsk works, whose administration was divided between Vesenkha's metallurgical and machine building administrations. More often, the opposite situation obtained. Foundry work at the Krasnyi Profintern works in Briansk was administered not through the metallurgical administration but through Glavmashinstroi, Vesenkha's chief administration for machine building. Similarly, forging and foundry work at the Krasnyi Proletarii plant in Moscow was administered under the machine building branch of Vesenkha, not under the metallurgical branch. Conversely, machine shops at the Taganrog metallurgical works in southern Russia fell under the jurisdiction of the metallurgical and not the machine building branch of Vesenkha's administration.[13]

The absence of clear jurisdictional lines of authority led trusts and glavki into constant bureaucratic squabbles. Officials at Gomzy, for example, successfully incorporated the Krasnyi Putilovets, the prize factory of Lenmashtrest, into its organizational structure in 1927. On the other hand, the trust tried unsuccessfully for several years to wrest control of the Krasnyi Proletarii factory in Moscow away from Mosmashtrest and the Moscow city economic administration. On the verge of success in late 1929, Gomzy itself was abolished and absorbed into a newly created association of machine manufacturing plants, Mashinoob"edinenie. Not long after, the Krasnyi Proletarii was incorporated into the all-union machine tool trust, Stankotrest, but only after an intense campaign by the Moscow economic council to retain the factory.

Similarly, Donugol', one of the country's large coal cartels, fought re-

---

[13]For a summary of these problems and an excellent organizational history of industrial administration in the metal industries during the interwar period, see V. A. Shakhovoi, "Organizatsionnye formy upravleniia metallopromyshlennost'iu, 1917–1932" (candidate diss., Moscow State University, 1971). See also V. Z. Drobizhev, *Glavnyi shtab sotsialisticheskoi promyshlennosti: Ocherki istorii VSNKha, 1917–1932* (Moscow, 1966), esp. pp. 165–70.

peatedly to keep control of several machine repair and small machine tool manufactories in southern Russia that the Kramatorsk metallurgical and machine manufacturing *kombinat* argued rightfully belonged under its jurisdiction. Still other trusts joined the fray. *Torgovo-promyshlennaia gazeta* (*TPG*), Vesenkha's official newspaper, reported in November 1928 that the fight over these machine shops had developed into a four-way battle. The squabble involved not only the coal cartel and the metallurgical *kombinat*, but also Iugostal' and the Ukrainian machine building trust, Ukrmashtrest. Vesenkha established a special commission to look into the matter, and in early January 1929 *TPG* reported that Vesenkha had decided the issue in favor of the *kombinat*. Donugol' officials were planning to fight back.[14]

Such bureaucratic infighting occurred regularly. For several weeks in October 1928, *TPG* relayed the ongoing battle by Glavmashinstroi to upgrade the status of the southern machine building trust, Iushmashtrest, from a republic-level to an all-union trust. Glavmashinstroi argued that the trust's factories were large enough and important enough to warrant the change, which would bring the trust and its factories under Glavmashinstroi's jurisdiction. The Ukrainian economic council, which administered the trust, charged that this was not just an economic matter; it was one more example of the center's encroachment on republic rights. It was a direct attack against Ukraine. Glavmashinstroi won its case, but not before the matter was referred to the Council of People's Commissars, Sovnarkom, the highest governmental body.[15]

Such disputes seemed to belong more to the world of competitive corporate capitalism than to the realm of cooperative state socialism. In fact, in the mid-1920s state trusts and factories operated in a set of administrative and financial conditions that fostered aggressive corporate behavior. Two major factors were driving trust officials to expand their corporate control: the economics of scarcity and a bureaucratic system that was notorious for its inefficiency and inability to enforce regulations and contracts. Trusts could rarely depend on the timely receipt of materials and equipment for their factories. Such delays disrupted production schedules, caused idleness, and adversely affected the trusts' yearly account balances. As a result, trust officials sought to maintain a diverse range of production within individual factories and to the extent possible within the trust as a whole. In other words, Vesenkha's erratic administrative system fostered the socialist equivalent of a drive toward vertical integration. Trusts sought to maintain or gain as much control as possible over production processes, from raw materials to making machine tools to making the metal to make the machines.

[14]*TPG*, 5 November 1928, p. 2; 5 January 1929, p. 1.
[15]*TPG*, 16 October 1928, p. 3.

The pressures to integrate vertically contradicted the branch, or horizontal, organization of trusts and factories under the chief administrations. Thus metallurgical trusts sought to retain or to acquire machine making shops, and machine building trusts and factories sought to keep or to gain control over foundry works. The case of Donugol' exemplified trust considerations. The trust was loath to part with the machine shops under its control, even though, administratively, those shops did not fit within the jurisdiction of a coal-producing trust. When a *TPG* reporter asked how, given Vesenkha's policy of branch specialization, he could justify keeping the machine building complexes in question, the head of Donugol' replied that the reason was "obvious." Without its machine shops, Donugol' would be forced to contract with a separate machine building trust for the manufacture of equipment it currently controlled within its own organization. *TPG* reported this response sympathetically, noting also the machine plants' traditionally close commercial and professional ties to the coal pits of the Don region. A change in administration, the newspaper noted, would disrupt those ties and the expertise built up in those plants over decades.[16]

The trusts' commercial relation to the state also forced them into aggressive entrepreneurial behavior. Large industrial trusts in Vesenkha received the overwhelming majority of their contracts from state-owned capital goods consumers. The Commissariat of Transportation (NKPS), for example, which controlled all rail shipping in the country, was one of the largest state consumers. Contracts with state agencies, such as with the NKPS, were generally large and for long terms. These contracts provided security for a factory, but work on state orders often ran far over schedule. Such work tied up labor and factory resources for months and even years without showing a profit or a finished product. Large amounts of unproductive or "dead" capital adversely affected yearly account balances, which central Vesenkha officials watched closely.

To redress the deficits in yearly account balances, factories and trusts sought contracts for single or small-batch orders—specialized orders for only a few pieces. Because these orders could be completed quickly, they improved a factory's or trust's rate of capital turnover; that is, the amount of time it took between payment for raw materials and receipt of payment for a finished product. Trusts and factories negotiated for these orders themselves, outside the general distribution of contracts through the Vesenkha hierarchy. Production for these kinds of orders was referred to as on-the-side production, or *proizvodstvo na storone*. Factories and trusts made on-the-side contracts with other state industrial enterprises or with trade and production organizations outside the state system. On-the-side

---

[16]*TPG*, 5 November 1928, p. 3.

production was legal under NEP so long as state-contracted supplies were not used and so long as it did not interfere with the fulfillment of state orders.

On-the-side contracts usually accounted for a small percentage of the production profile of a factory or a trust. They made up about 13 percent of Iugostal''s production program in 1928, for example.[17] Yet on-the-side contracts often made the difference between solvency and insolvency. Sometimes whole shops were devoted to the manufacture of items not listed on the factory's official production profile. For example, despite orders from Vesenkha that the Krasnyi Profintern factory at Briansk was to specialize solely in the production of locomotives and railroad cars, the factory continued to produce dozens of items. Steel plows, for example, were sold outside the system of state orders received from NKPS through the trust directorate Gomzy. The factory had produced steel plows since well before the Revolution, and they sold well within an established regional agricultural market. In the latter part of the 1920s, the factory expanded production of plows, even though it experienced increasing difficulties keeping within cost limits and production schedules in its locomotive production.[18]

For several years Gomzy pressured factory management to cease or curtail its production of plows because the factory was not meeting its obligations in locomotive and railroad car manufacture. In 1928 the factory and trust finally reached a compromise: the trust allowed the factory to use its market connections to expand plow sales in return for a share of the profits. From that date, Gomzy officials defended plow production at the Krasnyi Profintern even against pressure from the NKPS.[19] Thus trusts were not, in principle, averse to factory ties with traditional economic markets so as long as they themselves received a portion of the profits.

Producing for a side market improved a trust's account balance. The necessity of doing so, however, combined with the problems caused by the state's inefficient supply and distribution system, set trusts against Vesenkha's rationalization policies. Vesenkha's drive for production efficiency and administrative simplicity created demand for greater specialization of factory production, but the commercial and accounting conditions under which trusts operated encouraged them to produce a diversity of products. Strict specialization threatened to deny trusts the production flexibility they needed to take advantage of rapidly chang-

[17]For an example of Iugostal' customer lists, see RGAE, f. 4086, op. 3, d. 24, ll. 13–15.

[18]"Protokol zasedanii proizvodstvennogo pluzhnogo tsekha, 27.2.1926," in GARF, f. 7952, op. 6, d. 32, ll. 154–64. See esp. the resolution of the session, ll. 162–64.

[19]See the comments by the factory director, K. P. Portenko, defending this practice: "Stenogramma doklada direktora zavoda K.P. Portenko na obshchezavodskoi konferentsii rabochikh i sluzhashchikh, 18–19.4.1928," ibid., ll. 211, 230. See also the critical comments of an NKPS inspector, ll. 236–45.

ing market opportunities and to stay ahead of Vesenkha's accounting game.

Certainly, market considerations played a negligible role in some types of production. A practically unlimited market existed for such equipment as agricultural and transportation machines. In these areas, trusts went far toward instituting continuous-flow mass-production techniques.[20] Yet, as the Krasnyi Profintern case shows, even factories engaged in mass production for large and secure state markets did a brisk on-the-side business. Trusts whose factories turned out tractors, automobiles, and locomotives might also produce tools for local blacksmiths and agricultural cooperatives or special equipment for other trusts on the side.[21]

It is difficult to assess the scope and effect of this entrepreneurial aspect of the state's economy, but the practice of on-the-side contracting seems to have been widespread. On-the-side contracting very likely provided many scarce products not covered by Vesenkha's cumbersome system of contract distribution. Yet newspaper reports complained about the unabashedly commercial activities of state production trusts.[22] Even the Party's Central Committee heard complaints that such activities disrupted the state's attempt to plan commercial costs. Because on-the-side contracting was not subject to direct price controls by state agencies, the practice created inflationary pressures and added yet another price tier to the several already used within the state's industrial system. Moreover, the trusts' entrepreneurial activities reinforced traditional trading and commercial networks, despite Vesenkha's attempts to create a nationally administered state market.[23]

Still, no serious action was taken against the trusts. Regional officials fought successfully against what they perceived as Vesenkha's excessive meddling. Throughout the decade, trusts maintained production flexibility and a diverse product range in their factories. They produced for the state, but also traded for profit across a range of local and national markets. Trust officials did not defy central authorities simply out of will-

[20]Shukgalter, *Rabota nepreryunym potokom*, p. 12.

[21]The memoir by the young engineer A. I. Gorbunkov in GARF, f. 7952, op. 3, d. 94, gives a good description of the entrepreneurial activities of the trust officials of Mosmashtrest (ll. 84–117).

[22]For complaints about the entrepreneurial activities of Mosmashtrest and other trusts, see the article by an engineer who signed himself Neverov (Unbeliever) in *TPG*, 29 July 1928, p. 2. After complaining about lack of specialization at the Krasnyi Proletarii, he went on to list a number of factories that continued to purchase contracts and patents outside their officially designated areas of specialization.

[23]See N. M. Shvernik's brief report of semilegal trading by southern metal factories in the Central Committee's plenum meetings of 10–17 November 1929 in RTsKhIDNI, f. 17, op. 2, d. 441, l. 46. Shvernik described factory and trust entrepreneurial activities by using an old expression, "They work and work to trade and trade"; Vesenkha's vice chairman, I. V. Kosior, added, "They trade, rejoice, count their money, and shed tears [Torgovali, veselilis', podshchitali, proslezilis']."

fulness, but were reacting to administrative and commercial pressures placed on them within the state's economic system. Nonetheless, their commercial activities gave rise to market forces that disrupted efforts by central authorities to plan and control state industry.

Accounting Reforms, Budgetary Politics, and the Russian Accordion Game

If central authorities failed to impose market discipline on state-owned sectors of the economy, they found it no less difficult to implement accounting and commercial reforms. Vesenkha's financial officers depended on accurate accounting reports from trusts and their factories, since these were the crucial documents used to construct yearly control figures for the economy. The yearly control figures were the financial and commercial indices of economic performance on which Vesenkha constructed its annual budgets. Without systematic accounting procedures, Vesenkha's financial planners could not know to what extent their control and budgetary calculations had a basis in economic reality; industrial managers could not direct the economy with any degree of precision.

Despite the importance of proper accounting, methods of financial reporting and control remained at a primitive level in Soviet industry throughout the 1920s. As late as 1928, a Rabkrin survey committee reported that "not one factory" had implemented full financial accounting procedures. The RKI report noted that none of Vesenkha's trusts, with the exception of Iugostal' and Gomzy, had taken even the "first steps" toward fulfillment of Vesenkha's and the government's orders to introduce accounting and administrative reforms in their factories.[24] Such a state of affairs was bad enough. Yet according to I. Matrozov, a Vesenkha economist, even when trusts, let alone factories, submitted accounting records, they were not used in the construction of control figures; control and budgetary figures were a "myth" and bore little relation to actual production capabilities.[25] Another official, V. Ol'khov, complained to a Rabkrin commission that systematic calculation of production costs was a "dream." What typically happened, Ol'khov said, was that different governmental commissions arrived at completely different cost figures, using "God only knows what divining methods." How higher officials chose one set over another Ol'khov professed not to understand. Neither did he understand how Vesenkha developed its industrial politics. "It is certainly not on the basis of accurate cost accounting calculations."[26]

---

[24]GARF, f. 374, op. 1, d. 596, l. 255.
[25]TPG, 4 October 1928, p. 3.
[26]GARF, f. 374, op. 1, d. 616, l. 239. In December 1926 Sergo Ordzhonikidze, the head of Rabkrin, also recounted the problem caused by varying assessments of profitability, in this

Ol'khov might have been enlightened about the budgetary process had he listened to Stepan Birman's address to the June 1928 Iugostal' production conference. Birman, the head of the Southern Metallurgical Trust, was the kind of industrial autocrat Soviet leaders both feared and needed. A refugee Hungarian Communist, Birman was both competent and outspoken. He was pugnacious, even fractious, in his dealings with higher officials, but he successfully defended "southern" interests within Vesenkha. Birman's enormous energy, his managerial abilities, and even his sometimes high-handed methods made Iugostal' one of the most influential and successful trusts. At the same time, his maverick managerial style made Birman many enemies and embroiled him in scandal and political intrigue.[27]

Birman gave delegates to the June 1928 Iugostal' conference a typical demonstration of his acerbic wit. He unsettled his listeners by explaining that in Vesenkha's supposedly planned economy there existed no plan and no planning. The budgetary process, which included financial and production planning, did not proceed in the orderly fashion everyone assumed. A trust's yearly budget allocations could, and usually did, change quarterly and often monthly. These changes resulted from mistaken assessments of financial constraints, Birman noted, but more often than not from the tug-of-war of personal, factional, and especially regional lobbying within Vesenkha. Constructing industry's budget was, in other words, a political rather than an economic process.[28]

Birman likened the budgetary and planning process to playing the Russian accordion, *igra garmoshki*, in his words. A trust's allocations "swelled" and "deflated," according to Birman, like an accordion bellows, depending on who was "playing the tune" in Vesenkha. To illustrate his analogy, Birman gave a month-by-month description of the changes in Iugostal''s 1926–27 budgetary allocation. From October 1926, the beginning of the fiscal operating year, until April 1927, the trust had no official financial or production plan. Even after April 1927 its construction and operating budget was subject to change without warning. Typically, the final version of a trust's plan was not established until after the fact, that is, after the end of the operating year.[29] The "fits and starts" so characteristic of Soviet industrial production, Birman argued, resulted more from Vesenkha's erratic budgetary and planning process than from the trusts' poor manage-

---

case in the textile industries. His speech is printed in G. K. Ordzhonikidze, *Stat'i i rechi*, vol. 2, *1926–1937* (Moscow, 1957), p. 10.

[27]See Fitzpatrick, "Sergo Ordzhonikidze."

[28]*Vseukrainskaia proizvodstvennaia konferentsiia rabochikh metallistov zavodov Iugostali, 28 iunia–5 iulia 1928 goda: Stenograficheskii otchet* (Khar'kov, 1928), p. 16.

[29]Ibid., pp. 16, 17, 159, 160. Ordzhonikidze reports a similar complaint by an unnamed industrial official in his *Stat'i i rechi*, 2:14.

ment. Justifying his own "sometimes reckless" style of leadership, Birman argued that, within Vesenkha's chaotic administrative culture, a trust manager had to get whatever financial allocations he could when he could, and spend them immediately.[30] One never knew when money might be snatched away in the great Russian accordion game.

The Tail That Wags the Dog: Trust-Glavki Relations

To maintain economic discipline throughout its industrial empire, Vesenkha relied on its administrative hierarchy as well as on commercial and financial mechanisms. As chief administrations, glavki were supposed to regulate the activities of trusts and ensure a smooth and orderly budgetary process. Glavki stood at the pinnacle of Vesenkha's bureaucratic economy. In practice, however, it was the trusts that administered the glavki. Glavki, the all-powerful arbiters of industry in the early 1920s, had shrunk in size and significance by the middle of the decade. Most had small clerical and technical staffs in relation to the large number of trusts and enterprises they oversaw. Even Glavmetall and its successor, Glavmashinstroi, still among the largest and most active of the glavki in the late 1920s, operated with "probably one of the worst" staff shortages of any of the chief administrations.[31]

Because of poor staffing, glavki relied on economic data supplied by their respective trusts. Kh. Rapoport, a member of Vesenkha's Planning Administration, the PEU, summarized the consequences of such a situation. Because glavki had no independent source of information, Rapoport wrote in 1929, they became "ideological dependents" of the trusts.[32] B. Klimov-Verkhovskii, a Vesenkha administrator, confirmed that glavki had no independent means to assess industrial needs or capabilities. They operated "merely" as "registrars" of the trusts.[33] Neither, according to Rapoport, did glavki have any authority over credit allocations. This function belonged to the state's commercial trade syndicates. Separation of financial politics from the glavki, in Rapoport's view, was what "killed" the chief administrations.[34] Stripped of their commercial power and dependent on trusts for information, glavki could not formulate policy and "lead" their trusts. The chief administrations acted more in the role of advocate for the policies of their various trusts inside Vesenkha's presidium and the PEU, Vesenkha's primary policy-making body.[35] In effect,

[30]*Vseukrainskaia proizvodstvennaia konferentsiia*, p. 159.

[31]Assessment by B. N. Dobrovol'skii, member of Glavmashinstroi's presidium, 28 January 1930: RGAE, f. 5716, op. 2, d. 2, l. 16.

[32]Kh. Rapoport to Ordzhonikidze, 22 July 1929, in GARF, f. 374, op. 1, d. 616, l. 253.

[33]*TPG*, 15 December 1929, p. 2.

[34]Rapoport to Ordzhonikidze, 22 July 1929.

[35]Dobrovol'skii, in RGAE, f. 5716, op. 2, d. 2, l. 16. Rapoport gave the same assessment in

glavki became lobbying agents for their respective trusts rather than authoritative planning and administrative centers.

The authority of Vesenkha's chief administrations was so weak that powerful trusts controlled contract procedures in the state sector. Rather than distribute production contracts rationally and systematically, glavki found themselves in the position of beggars, pleading with their trusts to take orders. Vesenkha could not enforce contract discipline even in such vitally important areas as agricultural machinery. In February 1929, for example, on the basis of projected agricultural needs for the fall harvest, the Council on Labor and Defense, STO, ordered Vesenkha to increase the production of spare parts for agricultural machinery by an unspecified amount. In the administrative hierarchy of Vesenkha, this task fell logically to Glavmashinstroi, the chief administration for machine building. This was a crucial harvest year, and spare parts for agricultural equipment were desperately needed. Consequently, to ensure the quality of work and materials, especially of steel, the government instructed the glavk to place its orders with Soviet armament factories.[36]

Despite the national importance and urgency of this type of production, the state's armaments trust refused the contract, as did fourteen other trusts and enterprises. The weapons trust, like the other enterprises, calculated that the price offered by the government was too little to cover production and distribution costs. Other trusts claimed that their factories were already overcontracted. Finally, in the summer of 1929, Glavmashinstroi was able to place part of the order with the Krasnyi Putilovets works in Leningrad and part with the Urals machine building factory in Zlatoust. Still, the chief administration was able to contract only half of the order; the rest went unfilled.[37]

Vesenkha not only was unable to enforce contract discipline but could not even communicate effectively with its enterprises and trusts. Instructions, regulations, and orders poured out of the Supreme Economic Council at the rate of six to seven a day.[38] Yet the trusts deliberately ignored many of them. Worse yet, as a Rabkrin survey showed, many trust officials were entirely unaware of even major decisions, such as the June 1927 regulations governing relations between trusts and factories.[39] Some man-

his letter to Ordzhonikidze of 22 July, and a representative at Vesenkha's fourth plenum meeting in November 1928 commented that "glavki had lost the confidence of economic managers": *TPG*, 30 November 1928, p. 4.

[36]RGAE, f. 5735, op. 2, d. 2, ll. 26–27.

[37]Ibid., l. 27.

[38]Kosior at fourth Vesenkha plenum, *TPG*, 1 December 1928, p. 3.

[39]GARF, f. 374, op. 1, d. 596, l. 254. Rabkrin's survey was conducted in 1928. A survey of Moscow and Leningrad trusts conducted by the Central Committee in early 1930 found that still nothing had been done to implement the government's decrees on industrial relations. See RTsKhIDNI, f. 17, op. 74, d. 30, l. 99.

agers, when informed of the content of certain instructions or orders, expressed skepticism about their validity. Others did not understand the intent of regulations or did not have the time and personnel to enact them. One official reported to the Seventh Trade Union Congress in December 1928 that of seventy-six orders issued by Sovnarkom to the Russian Federation Vesenkha in 1927, only 36 percent had been fulfilled. One trust official reportedly admitted to Ordzhonikidze that he and his colleagues had established a permanent group of five to six people specifically to rebuff the "countless" demands Vesenkha made on them.[40]

Rabkrin's findings highlighted one of the major problems with Vesenkha's administrative structure. The logistics of communication within such a scattered and complex bureaucratic system was staggering. The country's paper manufacturers could not keep up with Vesenkha's demands, and paper shortages continued in Vesenkha throughout the decade. Telegrams and telephone usually sufficed to link the major industrial centers with Moscow, but communications with many trusts and enterprises were problematic. Vesenkha had to rely on publication of decrees and orders in *Torgovo-promyshlennaia gazeta*. As a result, many smaller works simply fell through the administrative cracks. In discussing the five-year plans drawn up in 1927 and 1928, for example, B. Klimov-Verkhovskii claimed that "numerous" works, even within Glavmashinstroi, had been overlooked and were not included in the plan.[41]

Vesenkha was supposed to act as a central planning and control organ. Its task was to meld interests and mold the disparate elements of the old Russia into a nationally unified and integrated industrial economy. Instead of reshaping the old economy, Vesenkha became shaped by it.

Trusts and Regional Organization of the Industrial Economy

If the glavki represented the interests of their respective industries in the planning councils of Vesenkha, they and Vesenkha became the battle ground for regional rivalries and infighting. Arkady Rozengol'ts, deputy head of Rabkrin, confirmed to the 11th Ukrainian Communist Party Congress in 1930 that much of the factional politics in the state's planning and administrative organs cut along regional lines. Regional interests even cut across bureaucratic lines outside of Vesenkha. Local Party and trade union organs lobbied on behalf of "their" trusts, hoping to persuade influential people in central organs to intervene in Vesenkha's budgetary process. Selection of factory construction sites, for example, depended at times on the influence wielded by regional Party organizations.[42] Trust directors

---

[40] Ordzhonikidze, *Stat'i i rechi*, 2:141, 14.

[41] *TPG*, 15 December 1929, p. 2.

[42] A. P. Rozengol'ts, *Za sotsializm protiv biurokratizma: Doklad o rabote TsKK-NKRKI SSSR na XI s''ezde KP(b)U* (Moscow, 1930), p. 27.

were frequently gone from their home offices. They traveled constantly to Moscow, making the rounds of committees, commissions, and other state trusts to lobby for their regional interests.

Rabkrin surveys in late 1926 and 1927 revealed an extensive network of lobbying and trade offices in the capital. Lenmashtrest, for example, kept a staff of forty-five people in Moscow.[43] Iugostal' and other major industrial concerns also maintained large permanent offices in the city. Even regional Soviet organs kept offices in Moscow. All-union enterprises were supposed to have small liaison bureaus in key economic centers, but Rabkrin's investigations found that these offices were being used for much more than liaison: they were functioning as large-scale trade and influence-peddling operations. In late 1926 Rabkrin counted over 700 such offices in Moscow alone, employing over 5,000 people—slightly less than 4 percent of all officials working in the capital at the time.[44] Rabkrin directed that as many as 400 of these offices be closed, but an agency report in 1928 estimated that these representatives of regional interests accounted for nearly 6 percent of the capital's bureaucratic strata.[45]

With Birman as its head, Iugostal' was one of the most powerful of the regional trusts, not only because of its size and economic importance but because of the personal connections and influence of its managing director. Iugostal', and Birman in particular, found a strong advocate in I. V. Kosior, member of Vesenkha's presidium and Birman's predecessor as head of Iugostal'. V. I. Mezhlauk, the head of Glavmetall, had also been head of Iugostal' early in the 1920s, and had also come to Vesenkha from the southern metal industries. Kosior and Mezhlauk drew heavily on the southern region for personnel, and as a result, many of Glavmetall's important functionaries came from the South. Their common background led to a discernible policy bias in favor of metallurgy over machine building and in favor of the southern areas of industrial development. This bias was so strong that references were often made in Vesenkha and other governmental bodies to the "southern" or "Ukrainian" bloc.

Gomzy, the central region's machine manufacturing trust organization, also provided a conduit to high-level influence in Vesenkha. A. F. Tolokontsev made his way up the administrative ladder at Gomzy, from factory director at the Kolomensk locomotive works to head of the trust. From there he was appointed to the sensitive position of head of the country's defense industries. In 1928 Tolokontsev became the first director of Vesenkha's machine building administration, Glavmashinstroi. He also took a seat on Vesenkha's presidium. Like Tolokontsev, K. P. (sometimes listed as F. I. or K. I.) Portenko also worked in Gomzy as director of the Krasnyi Profintern factory. When Tolokontsev became head of Glav-

[43]GARF, f. 374, op. 19, d. 33.
[44]See Ordzhonikidze, Stat'i i rechi, 2:19, 24.
[45]GARF, f. 374, op. 19, d. 2, l. 33.

mashinstroi in 1928, he brought Portenko to Moscow. Tolokontsev appointed Portenko his deputy head when the new machine building cartel, Mashinoob"edinenie, replaced Glavmashinstroi in early 1930. As a result, Portenko also gained a seat on Vesenkha's presidium.

Tolokontsev and Portenko, like others before them, brought their own men to staff key offices in the chief administration. This practice created a coterie of *tsentristy*, or "centrists," in Glavmashinstroi and later in Mashinoob"edinenie. Though not as influential as Mezhlauk, Kosior, and the "Ukrainians," Portenko, Tolokontsev, and others in Glavmashinstroi showed themselves to be effective advocates for the interests of the machine manufacturing branches in general and for the central industrial region in particular. Through Glavmashinstroi, they provided a balance in Vesenkha to the interests of the powerfully entrenched southern bloc.

To counter the influence of both the central and southern groups, industrial trusts in Leningrad and other northern areas of the country banded together in two associations, the Northwestern Industrial Bureau, the Severo-zapadnoe Prombiuro, and the Northwestern Economic Council, the Severo-zapadnyi Ekonomicheskii Sovet. Formed in the early 1920s, these organizations were patterned after the prerevolutionary association of northern machine manufacturers. In the mid-1920s, M. S. Mikhailov, the head of Lenmashtrest, played a prominent role in this group, which also maintained close ties to the Russian republican leadership in Vesenkha under S. S. Lobov. The two associations promoted plans for northern economic integration and were among the strongest supporters of regional trust control over industry.[46]

The Urals was the most underrepresented of the major industrial regions. The influence of the southern or Ukrainian bloc overshadowed that of Uralmet, the Urals metallurgical trust, but at least Uralmet gave the Urals metal interests a voice in Vesenkha. According to a prominent engineer, N. Vol'pert, machine building in the Urals remained "completely" underdeveloped because of the lack of a strong trust organization to represent those interests. Only the establishment of Uralmashtrest in 1928 helped to redress this balance. Until then, according to Vol'pert, prerevolutionary manufacturing centers such as Nadeshdinsk, Tagilsk, and Aleksandrovsk remained underused and technically backward. Because they lacked regional political clout, these centers had missed out on the money and credit made available for the reconstruction boom of the mid-1920s. As a result, the Urals machine manufacturing industries had fallen to the status of "colonial subsidiaries" of the more powerful central and northern machine building and metallurgical regions.[47]

[46]See, e.g., *TPG*, 3 December 1926, p. 3.
[47]*TPG*, 13 November 1929, p. 1.

The Great German Gold Rush

Able and willing to take advantage of the state's budgetary largess, powerful trusts maintained a great deal of autonomy. One of the biggest scandals of the decade, and one that clearly demonstrated lack of central Vesenkha control, involved what came to be called the great German gold rush. It began in 1925 when the Weimar government granted the Soviet government 400 million Reichsmarks—about 300 million gold rubles—in credits for industrial reconstruction.[48] The German offer was motivated by a desire to open markets for its own overcapitalized machine building industry. Yet in this case, what was good for the entrepreneurs of capitalist Germany, by then Soviet Russia's biggest trading partner, was also good for the entrepreneurs of socialist industry. German credit terms made the lure of German machines irresistible to Soviet trust heads eager to reequip their factories and stay ahead in the economic accounting game.

Formally, the process by which trusts acquired foreign machinery involved complicated bureaucratic procedures with numerous levels of review and control. The foreign trade section of Vesenkha, along with the Commissariat of Trade and the foreign trade department of Gosbank, approved jointly any purchase of equipment abroad that required payment in gold rubles or foreign currency. In cases involving large-scale reconstruction or the construction of new facilities, plans were supposed to be drawn up by Vesenkha's central engineering and construction design agencies, Gipromez and Orgametall. These agencies were to consult with trust and factory personnel, but the final drafts, approved by the appropriate glavk, were submitted to Vesenkha's industrial and economic administration, the PEU, and to the presidium of Vesenkha. Vesenkha based its recommendations for approval or amendment on the yearly control figures and the overall industrial needs of the economy. Sovnarkom also reviewed these matters for approval, especially if they involved large-scale purchases of foreign equipment.

In practice, the situation allowed a great deal of political and entrepreneurial maneuvering by the trusts. Influential trust heads such as Birman, Mikhailov, and Portenko took the initiative in drawing up reconstruction plans, which regional Party and trade union officials actively supported. Throughout the decade, their recommendations met little resistance in discussions at the all-union Vesenkha level. Approval was facilitated by close personal ties with leaders in Vesenkha and the Party.[49] Between 1925 and

[48]L. M. Kheifets, "Problema zameshcheniia importa oborudovaniia," *Metall*, 1928, no. 12, p. 56.

[49]A Rabkrin survey in 1929 confirmed that, rather than submit its requests to Gipromez, the southern trust did all its own design work for reconstruction. See GARF, f. 374, op. 15, d. 1056, l. 229b.

1929, for example, Iugostal' engaged in a massive reconstruction campaign that required the expenditure of millions of gold rubles for German machinery and expertise. As a result of Birman's shrewdness, Iugostal' received the largest single share of the German credit bonanza—45 million gold rubles, he reported in June 1928.[50]

Iugostal''s extravagant outlays for foreign equipment, coupled with the large amounts it received from the state budget for reconstruction, drew the attention of Rabkrin and investigators of the political police, the OGPU. After numerous surveys in 1928 and 1929, the inspectorate and police agencies made public charges against the trust, and against Birman in particular. According to a 1929 Rabkrin survey presented to the Politbiuro, much of the equipment was inappropriate for the trust's factories. According to Rabkrin, orders had been placed hastily with no regard for proper specifications or preliminary surveys of production needs. Iugostal' had placed 50 million rubles' worth of equipment orders and 38.6 million rubles' worth had arrived by 1 October 1928, yet less than one-quarter of the equipment had been installed and was operational. The rest still sat, either defective or otherwise unused, in Iugostal''s warehouses. In the Rykov metal complex alone a "colossal" 94 percent of foreign equipment remained unused.[51] In the Petrovsk factory, only 2 of 8 million rubles' worth of new German machinery was in use. According to a *TPG* article in late 1929, 112 heavy hauling cranes, "with their motors intact," sat in the factory's warehouse.[52]

Rabkrin officials estimated that the cost of the trust's buying spree amounted to 50 percent more than the trust could expect to earn with the equipment it had purchased. Iugostal''s behavior, declared Rabkrin's report, represented the worst of a widespread practice of abusing foreign credits and the availability of foreign equipment. More to the point, the scandal showed everything that was bad about Vesenkha's lack of control over the trusts.[53] Three members of Iugostal''s ruling board were arrested for wrecking in late 1928, in part because of the machine-buying scandal, and Birman's own position became precarious for a time.

Predictably, the revelations of Iugostal''s actions drew sharp protests from other trusts. Officials of the Ural Metal Trust, for example, complained bitterly at a 1928 Vesenkha presidium meeting about regional favoritism and the aggressive tactics of what they called the southern and central regional cliques. Ural Party and trade union leaders joined in this criticism and demanded a greater share of the industrial pie. They went

[50]*Vseukrainskaia proizvodstvennaia konferentsiia*, 14.
[51]GARF, f. 374, op. 15, d. 484, l. 163b; d. 1056, l. 233.
[52]*TPG*, 25 October 1929, p. 3.
[53]Ibid.

further and accused Iugostal', and Birman in particular, of engaging in an indiscriminate "orgy of machine buying" far beyond what economic rationality could justify. Ural officials charged that the Iugostal' trust leader was engaged in no less than an economic war against the Urals. One Ural official was diplomatic enough to say that in the Urals "we do not have as big an appetite as those in the south."[54]

Charges of malfeasance were repeated by others including Kuibyshev, who usually remained neutral in such confrontations. Vesenkha's chairman admonished Iugostal' officials publicly for buying equipment indiscriminately, without a specific plan for its use. It was irresponsible, he argued, for the trust to lay out money and to buy whatever was available, "regardless of whether it will be set up or put in storage." Kuibyshev's admonition should have carried considerable moral force, but it did not. A member of the audience brusquely interrupted to declare that in view of Vesenkha's weak leadership, Iugostal''s indiscriminate buying was "a good principle."[55]

This exchange unleashed a flood of criticism, directed not against the trusts but against Vesenkha's leader. Speaker after speaker criticized the lack of systematic order in budgeting and in the allocation of reconstruction funding and methods used to define reconstruction priorities. In defending Iugostal''s policies, a Ukrainian summarized the problem succinctly. He applauded the trusts for taking initiative because, he said, "no one knows who is to have the final say over building. The trust leadership? The republic economic council? The central Vesenkha council? You can't tell me because no one knows." Another delegate noted that many localities started construction projects in order to present central authorities with a fait accompli, so that Vesenkha would be forced to fund their projects.[56] Many trusts and factories juggled their accounts in order to gain initial funding for these projects. They used short-term commercial credit to finance construction—a practice that was illegal but commonplace—in the hope that Vesenkha or Gosbank would grant long-term construction credits to finish the job. Once the credits were in hand, local officials would repay their commercial creditors and hope that central officials did not audit their accounts too carefully.[57]

Kuibyshev admitted that Vesenkha had little control over the trusts, which another delegate called "wild" and "uncontrollable." Using his oft-repeated line, Kuibyshev pleaded that he had always been guided by the

[54]GARF, f. 5451, op. 12, d. 69, ll. 118, 121. The political consequences of the Iugostal' scandal are explored further in Chapter 3.

[55]Ibid., l. 18.

[56]Ibid., ll. 75–76, 81.

[57]Juggling commercial credit to pay for construction projects was only one of the many ways enterprises manipulated their accounts, as we shall see.

principle that the less interference from the center in trust affairs, the bet-ter.[58] To most delegates, this must have seemed an excuse for poor leadership.

True to character, Birman defended his actions with no apologies. At the June 1928 Iugostal' meeting, Birman admitted, in understated tones, that the trust's reconstruction and reequipment policies were "not based entirely on the principles of economic accountability." Yet Iugostal''s outspoken chief told a sympathetic audience that hoarding and overpurchasing were the only recourse left to industrial heads to protect their factories against Vesenkha's "capricious" industrial policies. Moreover, Birman said, it was not just Iugostal' that acted in this way. "All of us," he declared, "not just Iugostal' but also those in the higher organs . . . had to make a choice. Either we ordered the equipment and used the credit, not knowing if we would actually be able to use the machinery when it arrived; or we could have refrained, waiting to make proper calculations, not knowing how long the offer of credit would last. We all decided on the first variant, both Iugostal' and Vesenkha officials." To blame Iugostal' alone was wrong, Birman concluded.[59]

Conclusions

The attack on Iugostal' and the bitter feuding that broke out at the 1928 Vesenkha meeting revealed the weakness of central authority and the extent to which regional interests distorted national economic and industrial policy. The strength of regional interests and the competition among regions thwarted Vesenkha's attempts to create a national system of industrial planning and administration. The trust administrative system that existed throughout the 1920s grew out of Russia's regional historical development. That system was neither planned nor created, but because it was so deeply embedded in the trade and commercial structures of Russia's prerevolutionary economy, the trust system proved a particularly stable and enduring form of industrial organization. Regional trade ties shaped trusts' interests and led trust officials into constant conflict with central authorities.

Industrial trusts operated within a network of regional markets and commercial interests that often included close ties to Party, trade union, and local governmental institutions. These groups often supported one another in confrontations with authorities in other regions and in the center. Patterns of patronage and professional mobility from the trusts to central Vesenkha bureaucracies reinforced regional influences and factionalism at the higher levels of the industrial apparatus. In dealing with

[58]GARF, f. 5451, op. 12, d. 69, ll. 121, 147.
[59]Vseukrainskaia proizvodstvennaia konferentsiia, pp. 26, 14.

obstinate trust officials such as Stepan Birman, central authorities were also confronting Russia's past.

Vesenkha's authorities attempted to reduce trust and regional influence in the economy through financial and accounting reforms and by formally separating trusts from decisions about capital investments, commercial credits, and production design. Despite these measures, trusts continued to exercise a considerable amount of informal control in almost all of these areas, especially in production organization, planning, and technological reconstruction in their factories. Trusts successfully resisted many of Vesenkha's rationalization policies or, as in the case of financial and accounting reform, turned them to their own advantage. But these practices by no means indicated an inherent conservatism or resistance to change. The most successful and powerful trust officials were aggressively entrepreneurial and fashioned creative solutions to respond to the changing commercial and administrative conditions of state industry in NEP Russia. It was the smaller trusts in the less developed and less influential regions that relied on Vesenkha to defend their interests against the more powerful regions. The most powerful trusts even came to wield a decisive influence over foreign trade policies and the allocation of state investment funds.

As influential as trusts were, however, they did not dominate policy formulation at the highest levels of Vesenkha. Trusts were strong enough to resist the pressure of central authorities and to disrupt the industrial system, but not to provide a constructive basis for its further development. The behavior of trust officials exaggerated regional divisions in the economy and industrial administration, but the persistence of regional influences served more to weaken Vesenkha's authority than to strengthen the trusts' control over the economy.

Kuibyshev was not the kind of strong leader who could rein in the trusts and stop the centrifugal forces pulling the industrial economy apart. Indeed, Vesenkha's unsuccessful attempts to reform the industrial administrative system contributed to its chaotic character. Central authorities could strip trusts of much of their formal administrative powers, but their inability to formalize central administrative control only exacerbated the disruptive influence of regional, commercial, and personal politics. These were the very problems reforms were designed to resolve. By the beginning of the first five-year plan in 1928, the power of the trusts over production strategies, patterns of technological reconstruction, and market relations threatened the state's control of its own industrial sectors, supposedly the most centrally controlled of all economic sectors. As the decade drew to a close and the tasks of rapid industrialization loomed ahead, it was apparent that Vesenkha commanded very little of the commanding heights of the industrial economy. As Vesenkha's influence waned, authority shifted to the state's trade syndicates, once the small sales offices of the production trusts. By the end of the 1920s, the growing commercial power of the syndicates threatened the production and entrepreneurial autonomy of the trusts and challenged the planning and administrative authority of Vesenkha.

2

Wheeling and Dealing in Soviet Industry

> We should remember, the first chapter of volume one of
> *Kapital* begins with the words "market" and "trade."
> —M. A. Granovskii, 7 October 1928

Vesenkha's fourth plenum session met in November 1928 in an atmosphere of tension and uncertainty. The regime's first five-year plan had begun, and the economy was undergoing the shock of rapid industrialization. A grain procurement crisis threatened the regime's economic plans and raised the specter of social warfare in the countryside. Inflation, mild until 1928, showed signs of spiraling out of control as the government's presses printed ever more rubles to fund industrial expansion. In the factories, an unruly and volatile labor force threatened to turn hostility against management into class war. Rumors of war and economic sabotage ran rampant, and the ever-present possibility loomed that Party leaders would set industrial targets ever higher. Yet the most divisive issue to arise at Vesenkha's plenum meeting had little to do with the major debates we have come to associate with this period: shifting investment priorities, industrial tempos, the organization of agriculture, economic financing, progress on major construction projects. Delegates were concerned almost exclusively with the growing commercial influence of the state's industrial trade syndicates.

The rise of the syndicates to their preeminent position during the last years of the 1920s was rapid and unexpected. By the end of the decade, the growth of the syndicates and their increasing power challenged Vesenkha itself as the center of industrial planning and administration.[1] Increasing syndicate control sharply curtailed the production planning and entrepreneurial discretion of trusts, on the one side, and on the other side

---

[1] In this assessment, I agree with Iu. Avdakov, *Gosudarstvennaia promyshlennost', SSSR v perekhodnom periode* (Moscow, 1977), p. 196.

usurped the regulatory functions of Vesenkha's chief industrial administrations, the glavki. By 1929, at the height of the movement, syndicate
spokesmen did not hide their intention to concentrate all production and
planning activities of state industry within their operations.[2]

The rise of the syndicate movement is one of the most remarkable yet
virtually unknown stories of the Soviet economic experiments of the
1920s. The *sindikaty* were established in the early 1920s as sales and supply offices of the state's major production cartels, the trusts. As the economy recovered and trade expanded, these offices outgrew their obscure
origins and became distinct trade organizations for the various industrial
branches of the economy. By the end of the decade, the syndicates controlled nearly 90 percent of all exchanges of goods within the state sector.
In some branches, such as oil, metallurgy, mining, and salt production,
syndicate control reached nearly 100 percent. In the industrial branches
under their influence, syndicates not only controlled sales but regulated
all commercial and financial relations among the various manufacturing
trusts. Control over state credit allocations, especially, allowed the syndicates to exert increasing influence over production organization and planning decisions. Because of their financial leverage, for example, syndicates
regulated the volume of output of factories and the range of products
manufactured. To ensure proper use of investment funds, syndicates also
became involved in quality control inspection and in the planning of new
production types and technologies.[3]

The little that has been written about the syndicate movement supports
the view that it was part of the "general process of the erosion of market
relations" in the late 1920s. According to this view, Stalinist leaders used
the syndicates' monopolistic practices as a weapon against the country's
market-oriented economy.[4] Yet, in 1930, at the height of their influence, the
syndicates were abruptly eliminated. Stalinist officials initiated sweeping
organizational reforms in that year to create the administrative structure
of an industrial state. Why, then, eliminate the syndicates? Was it because,
having destroyed the market policies of the 1920s, the Stalinists found the
syndicates no longer necessary? Were the syndicates part of the Stalinist
attack against NEP, or were they, as their opponents feared, the institutional gates through which NEP market forces would enter and overwhelm the state's economy?

Iosef Kosior, the keynote speaker at Vesenkha's fourth plenum in late
November 1928, articulated the fears of many in the economic bureau-

---

[2]For discussion of syndicate plans to develop planning mechanisms, see S. E. Veitsman,
"Puti razvitiia mashino-tekhnicheskogo sindikata," *Metall*, 1928, no. 1, pp. 67–68.

[3]V. Ia. Kantorovich, *Sindikatskaia sistema* (Moscow, 1929), p. 73. On the expanding role of the
syndicates see ibid., pp. 9–13. See also Avdakov, *Gosudarstvennaia promyshlennost'*, pp. 193–97.

[4]Carr and Davies, *Foundations of a Planned Economy*, 2:641.

cracies. Kosior began his comments with conciliatory words but ended with a stinging attack on the syndicates. He accused syndicate officials of "starting a war to strengthen their power over the economy: to eliminate the glavki, dismantle the trusts, and subordinate all economic managerial functions under their own control." The growing influence of the syndicates was bad enough, but the real danger lay in the purpose to which syndicate leaders wished to apply their newfound organizational power. According to Kosior, the syndicates' ultimate goal was "to allow the petty-bourgeois spontaneity of the market to rule the state."[5]

Kosior's criticisms, though overdrawn, had some legitimacy. Syndicate officials saw their movement as a link connecting the commercially based NEP economy to the planned economy of the industrialization drive. Syndicate officials were committed to fulfilling the tasks of planned industrialization, but they believed the best way to do that was within NEP's commercial and financial framework. The syndicates pursued monopolistic market practices against Vesenkha's trusts, but not with the goal of subjugating consumers to producers or of supplanting market relations with administrative mechanisms. On the contrary, syndicate leaders conceived of their tasks in entrepreneurial and commercial terms. They saw themselves as capital agents of the state, but not as state monopolies engaged in a war against the market. In fact, syndicates fought aggressively to subordinate producers to the commercial discipline of market and consumer demand. As we have seen, the glavki embodied the bureaucratic culture of industrial administration and the trusts reflected the producer-driven economy of Vesenkha. The syndicates represented the growing influence of a commercial trade culture within state industry.

Here lay both the promise and the problem of the syndicates. On the one hand, the syndicate movement seemed to offer a viable alternative to Vesenkha's ill-fated administrative attempts to organize the industrial system. The commercial power that syndicates came to wield over the production trusts promised to break the hold of regionalism in the economy and to bring financial and contractual discipline to the state's economy. Syndicate leaders claimed that their movement was the only hope of integrating the state's producers into a truly national system of trade and commercial relations.

On the other hand, permitting the syndicates to usurp the authority and functions of the glavki and trusts represented more than just the replacement of one pair of regulatory organizations with another. Allowing the syndicates to run industry represented a radical experiment in commercial forms of state socialism. Advocates of the syndicate system hailed it as a model for the future organization of Soviet industry. Critics saw the syn-

[5]TPG, 2 December 1928.

dicates as the Trojan horses of NEP capitalism sneaking into the state industrial sector.

The VMTS: Building a Commercial Trade Network

By 1930, when the syndicates were eliminated, they had come to provide vital commercial ties among state-owned industrial manufacturers
and between state industry and the increasingly complex networks of industrial consumers outside the state system. The phenomenal growth of
the syndicate movement in the late 1920s testified to the syndicates' success in integrating planning with commercial mechanisms in the economy.
In pursuing this goal, however, the syndicates met resistance from Vesenkha's major production trusts; and nowhere more strongly than from the
metal and machine building trusts. Although the metallurgical syndicate
controlled nearly 100 percent of trade in that branch, strong trust leaders
made their presence felt in the monthly meetings of the syndicate's institutional shareholders, or *paishchiki*. A similar situation obtained in the engineering and machine building branches, although there the syndicate's
market control was not so strong as in other branches.

In June 1926 the Vsesoiuznyi Mashinotekhnicheskii Sindikat, the VMTS,
was established to service the machine manufacturing and engineering
branches of the Soviet economy. Like syndicates in other industrial
branches, the VMTS operated warehouses and sold goods on order from
its controlling parent organizations, the industrial production trusts. The
VMTS traded in everything metal, from plows to sophisticated machine
tools. While bartering among its parent organizations, the VMTS also sold
state-manufactured products on the broader private and semiprivate markets of NEP Russia. Most of these products passed through semiprivate
trading cooperatives and into the agricultural and small-scale metal industries of rural Russia.

The VMTS began with a small head office in Moscow of about forty
people and four regional offices in Leningrad, Khar'kov, Kiev, and
Sverdlovsk. Its initial operating capital base amounted to 8 million rubles,
which it received from Glavmashinstroi and from its parent trust organizations. The latter constituted the shareholders, the *paishchiki*, of the
VMTS, and in 1926 only eight trusts or industrial combines (*kombinaty*)
purchased shares. The 8 million rubles was barely enough to cover the
syndicate's yearly operating and trading costs.

These were modest beginnings and the syndicate had difficulties establishing itself and gaining ground in the machine manufacturing market.
For those goods that were syndicated, mostly mass-produced or standardized types of production, the VMTS maintained nearly complete control. By 1929, however, the VMTS still controlled only 35 to 40 percent of

goods turnover covered under state contracts with machine building trusts. In fact, syndicate-controlled exchange and distribution actually declined from 1927 through 1928. Machine building was the only industrial branch of the economy in which syndicate control showed a decline during that year. Only the perfume syndicate gave as poor a showing as the VMTS.[6]

The syndicate's failure to gain a controlling share of the machine building market testified to the strength of the industry's trust system. Purchasing shares in the syndicate was optional, and at first only a few large production trusts did so. Most of the syndicate's initial shareholders came from the ranks of the less powerful regional trusts, the Southern Machine Building Trust, for example, and a few metal and machine building *kombinaty* in the Ural region. Even shareholding trusts continued to maintain their own sales offices and resisted what they considered the syndicate's encroachment on their commercial prerogatives.

Moreover, syndication of goods proceeded on an adhoc basis at the discretion of the producers, not according to any market stimulus or on any regular contractual basis. Thus during the first years of its existence, the syndicate had no choice in what it sold. VMTS took sales instructions from its producer parents and tried to sell whatever it was given. Most of these consignments consisted of equipment that the trusts had difficulty selling through their own commercial organizations. The trusts preferred to use their own sales offices to move the majority of profitable goods, shunting the less profitable items over to the VMTS. The trusts used the syndicate, in the words of one frustrated VMTS official, as the "dumping ground for the industry's garbage."[7]

In addition to capital shortages, the syndicate experienced credit problems. When the syndicate was founded, it inherited a vast system of warehouses and unused stock from its predecessor, Metallosklad. Forced by Glavmashinstroi to take over these operations, VMTS had to "purchase" the stocks in the warehouses, which went into VMTS accounts as a debt. As a result, until April 1928, when the VMTS finally rid itself of these warehouses, Gosbank severely restricted VMTS's ability to issue commercial credit to purchasers.[8] The bank also refused entirely to issue the syndicate long-term developmental credits. Capital poor and with no credit possibilities, VMTS could hardly move goods, let alone increase its rate of

[6]S. E. Veitsman, "Puti razvitiia mashino-tekhnicheskogo sindikata," *Metall*, 1928, no. 1, pp. 56–68. See also N. D. Koniukov, "Vsesoiuznyi mashinotekhnicheskii sindikat v 1928–1929," *Metall*, 1929, no. 4, pp. 100–110.

[7]"Istoriia VMTS i perepiski s kontorami," in RGAE, f. 5715, op. 7, d. 187, ll. 182–83b. See also "Stenogramma s"ezda unolnomochennykh trestov-paishchikov VMTS, 27.10.1928," ibid., d. 26, l. 4b.

[8]The syndicate's warehouses, in the words of one official, "hung like a dead weight on the syndicate's neck": RGAE, f. 5715, op. 7, d. 26, l. 8. See also ibid., d. 187, l. 182.

goods turnover and achieve commercial profitability. For the first several years of its existence, the syndicate survived on cash infusions from a special Glavmashinstroi fund.

VMTS officials were not deterred, however. Through commercial, financial, and administrative means, the syndicate waged a concerted campaign to improve its situation and bring the state's producers to heel. In 1928 the syndicate's fortunes began to change. The VMTS emerged from its burdensome debt, improved its capital standing, and, with greater cash reserves and new credit allocations, began to fight the powerful trusts on an equal footing.

Much of the credit for this turnaround belonged to the competent and vigorous leadership of the syndicate, especially to its chief, N. D. Koniukov. Koniukov, an economically trained manager who had worked in Soviet industry since the early 1920s, was appointed head of the VMTS in early 1927. Determined to establish the VMTS as the commercial engine of industry, he reorganized its operations and recruited talented and trained engineers, financial accountants, and office administrators. Most of them came from the glavki and other Vesenkha bureaucracies, especially its planning administration, the PEU. Among the new functionaries was the prerevolution-trained economist and engineer N. Orentlikher, former head of Vesenkha's industrial rationalization bureau. Orentlikher became head of the syndicate's newly established experimental machine tool and engineering directorate.

This directorate was one of six originally established to cover the areas of machine manufacturing equipment that the syndicate planned to monopolize. A trained engineer headed each directorate, but the staff included economists and accountants as well. Together these groups were charged to study equipment needs and production capabilities; to consult with producers and buyers; to find markets; but also to alter and adapt production designs to fit specific market niches. These directorates became the nucleus of a new production design and market research organization within the syndicate. By the end of the decade, the VMTS became a major design center for new production systems. The work of the directorates, greatly expanded in personnel and funding, rivaled that of Orgametall, Vesenkha's independent rationalization and production design consultation organization.

Koniukov inaugurated what can only be described as an aggressive marketing policy. He expanded the syndicate's regional office network and relied increasingly on those offices to pursue contracts and customers. He urged his regional office heads to change "from being merely selling agents . . . to acting as engineering consultants to industry. Don't wait for customers to come to you," Koniukov told them: "Go to your customers. Establish a longstanding relationship; consult with them on their particular forms of production; find out what kind of capital constraints they have, what kind of equipment they need, what kind they can purchase from us." Koniukov encouraged his offices to establish ties with customers "so that they will be serviced by us as authoritative consultants in areas where their need matches our expertise."[9]

Through local consulting work and surveys the VMTS began to piece together a systematic picture of the Soviet machine manufacturing market, and in 1928 it published a catalog of machine products available from state industrial enterprises. VMTS distributed the catalogs to its regional offices for use in consulting work and made them available on the general market. This was the first such catalog issued in the country, and the VMTS published it with great fanfare. According to one newspaper article, these catalogs would stimulate "every kind" of contact between producers and consumers. Their distribution would help create a truly national market and would, it was hoped, reduce the number of imports as consumers discovered that domestic factories could fulfill their equipment needs.[10]

As it moved to a more active marketing strategy, the VMTS came into competition with the commercial apparatus of the production trusts. Trusts and syndicate did not compete over prices because most prices in the state sector were strictly regulated, but rates of capital turnover and transaction fees affected the difference between fixed prices and trading or production costs and made competition inevitable. Trusts, for example, contracted with VMTS, but continued to sell the same goods through their own offices in order to avoid what trusts considered high sales commissions—3 to 5 percent—charged by the syndicate. Koniukov countered by exhorting local offices to move goods out of warehouses quickly and get them to customers before the trusts established their own contracts. Getting to industrial consumers first gained a greater market share for the syndicate and increased its rate of capital turnover.[11]

Trusts and the syndicate also competed in the sale of equipment outside the state sector. Both the syndicate and the state's production trusts sold machinery and equipment to a variety of corporate customers, directly to industrial factories, but also to agents acting as buyers for republic and local industrial trusts. Through its regional offices, the syndicate also sold to private and semiprivate cooperative organizations acting on behalf of farms, small workshops, or other local networks of industrial consumers. At this level of local trading, the boundary between state and broad private markets became blurred and competition with other trading organizations was fierce. The syndicate's main rivals in local trading markets

[9]"Stenogramma s"ezda unolnomochennykh trestov-paishchikov VMTS," l. 6b.
[10]See, e.g., "Sovetskii mashinotekhnicheskii katalog," *TPG*, 11 January 1928, p. 3.
[11]RGAE, f. 5715, op. 7, d. 26, ll. 29–32.

were not the state's industrial producers but the regional branches of Sov-torg, the federation of trading cooperatives.

Memoranda from the syndicate's main office to its local bureaus reveals a free-for-all trading atmosphere at the end of NEP. Koniukov warned local offices constantly to be on guard against local Sovtorg activities. Re-gional syndicate offices kept a close watch on which types of machinery Sovtorg and other cooperative organizations were selling, and whether they were trying to undersell the syndicate or capture its customers. Ko-niukov worried especially that Sovtorg and other organizations were un-derselling equipment already syndicated through VMTS. Until Glav-mashinstroi regulated contract practices in late 1929, it was common practice for producers to contract with VMTS at set prices and then sell the same type of equipment more cheaply through Sovtorg or through the producers' own sales offices. They more than compensated for the lower price in quicker rates of capital turnover and by avoiding the syndicate's sales commissions. Koniukov often reprimanded producers for such be-havior; not only was it illegal, but it was "inappropriate for the establish-ment of normal, friendly commercial relations."[12]

The Politics of Credit and Trade

The syndicate fought producers' competitive practices by filing nu-merous complaints with state regulatory agencies such as Glav-mashinstroi and Narkomtorg, the state regulatory agency for trade. More important, VMTS countered competitive tactics with its own commercial strategy. The range of commercial options open to the VMTS was limited by state regulatory practices, since the state determined both wholesale and retail prices. Regulations allowed latitude in lowering but not in rais-ing prices for industrial consumer goods. Thus producers and marketers could not accumulate capital primarily through price increases. Increasing rates of goods turnover—that is, selling more products faster, even at lower prices than competitors—provided one of the main means to in-crease profitability and accumulate capital.

Koniukov made certain the syndicate excelled at this practice. Mem-oranda and reports from the central office constantly compared turnover rates and encouraged slacking bureaus to improve the time between con-tract closures, receipt of goods, delivery, and payment. Just as important, the syndicate's chief accountant often reminded local bureaus to speed accounting work so that transactions could be registered as quickly as possible in the active balance columns of the syndicate's books.[13]

Increasing its rates of turnover helped VMTS to gain and keep pro-

[12]Ibid., d. 187, ll. 26–30; d. 26, ll. 31–32.
[13]See ibid., d. 187, ll. 16–26.

ducers' business and to compete successfully with other sellers. Still, credit restrictions limited the syndicate's ability to expand its activities significantly. In the spring of 1928, however, Koniukov, with the help of A. I. Tolokontsev, the new head of Glavmashinstroi, persuaded Gosbank to lift restrictions on the syndicate's ability to extend commercial credit. VMTS was also permitted, in April 1928, to apply for long-term credits to fund production design and development projects. The central directorates of VMTS, such as Orentlikher's machine tool bureau, used these long-term credits to establish new production lines and adapt old ones to supply specific machine tools and instruments needed by industrial consumers. These credits and the work of the directorates allowed the VMTS to link market needs with producer capabilities. Availability of long-term credits also permitted the syndicate for the first time to become more than a commercial agent. The syndicate was now in a position to influence directly the design and organization of production in its shareholders' factories.

The VMTS used its newfound commercial credit power to begin moving goods on a large scale. By the end of the 1927–28 operating year, VMTS had quadrupled its rate of goods turnover from the previous year, but it did so almost entirely through the use of promissory notes and commercial credit rather than by cash transactions. The syndicate was supposed to pay at least 20 percent of any transaction in cash, but in 1927–28, only 15 percent of syndicate contracts were paid in cash. The syndicate's goal, of course, was to accumulate enough operating capital so that it did have to rely so heavily on credit. In the meantime, credit became the principal mechanism of trade. In reporting the figure of 15 percent to shareholders in October 1928, Koniukov noted optimistically that this was at least better than the 13 percent cash payment of the previous year.[14]

The VMTS, like other syndicates, operated within an intricate and extensive web of credit relations. In fact, the syndicate's accounting books reveal that at any one time its cash reserves amounted to a small fraction of the total of promissory notes due.[15] In other words, the syndicate, like all other state institutions, lived on credit. It purchased equipment on credit or promissory notes from producers, and it extended credit to buyers. VMTS also advanced credit to producers to work up new production lines and designs, and it covered shortfalls in cash flows with further extensions of credit from producers, or with temporary cash loans from Gosbank or Glavmashinstroi. The VMTS carried the huge amounts of credit that accumulated in one year over to the next year's balance sheets. As a result, keeping track of the various kinds of credit, whether short-

[14]Ibid., d. 26, ll. 9–10.
[15]Ibid., d. 90, l. 105b. See also d. 26, l. 6.

term promissory notes, loans, or bills of exchange, became extremely complicated and took up far more accounting time and a comparable amount of space in the account books than did the tracking of goods.[16] At times it seemed that the circulation of credit and the circulation of goods had little to do with each other, and nothing to do with real money. VMTS officials made concerted efforts to increase cash levels, but throughout its existence the VMTS, like other syndicates, relied on credit and used it liberally to facilitate commercial transactions.

Tensions between Trusts and Syndicate

Whether by cash or credit, the syndicate moved goods. Its aggressiveness transformed VMTS into an increasingly powerful commercial organization. By the end of 1928, VMTS syndicated nearly 100 percent of machine tools and instruments in the state industrial sector. It controlled the marketing of nearly 50 percent of all other mass- or serially produced machinery. In fact, the syndicate was rapidly gaining monopoly control in key areas of the machine manufacturing market. VMTS used its monopoly powers, too, but not to subjugate markets to state producers. By the spring of 1928, VMTS was commercially strong enough to refuse what it regarded as unwanted or unneeded goods, and it used its new power to enforce market discipline on the industrial trusts.

The syndicate tried to force trusts to produce for the market by making them sign "preliminary" (predvaritel'nye) contracts with the syndicate before the start of each year. These contracts would establish legally binding delivery dates and prices and specify sanctions for noncompliance. Moreover, production programs established in the contracts were to be based on syndicate surveys of consumer needs and specific orders received by the syndicate from its network of customers. The trusts resisted adoption of these contracts because they feared, correctly, that their implementation would allow the syndicate, and thus the market, to control the trusts' production decisions.[17] By enforcing contractual discipline on producers, VMTS hoped to end cycles of glut and scarcity and to smooth out the resulting wild price fluctuations in the private markets. It also hoped to regulate the selling wars among trusts, Sovtorg offices, and syndicates in both the state and nonstate markets. These selling wars did little to benefit consumers and they played havoc with the syndicate's ability to anticipate demand and plan production accordingly.

[16]Extensive monthly and quarterly accounts exist for VMTS for 1928 and 1929, showing the movement of credit, goods, and money. See ibid., d. 90. For a complete accounting record of 1928–29 see ibid., d. 212; for 1927–28, d. 26, ll. 61–63.

[17]Koniukov urged trusts to adopt this contracting system at the October 1928 shareholders meeting: ibid., d. 26, l. 7.

The trusts relied on the specialized skills of the syndicate to sell their products faster and, in most cases, more cheaply than they could themselves. At the same time, industrial producers were becoming concerned about the increasing commercial power of the syndicate to dictate relations with its shareholders. Conflicts between trusts and syndicate surfaced at the October 1928 shareholders' meeting. There the syndicate confronted the trusts with the necessity of doubling capital shareholdings and adopting the new contract system. Anticipating resistance, Koniukov gave trust representatives an elementary lesson in market economics. The trusts, he said, should bring their products more into line with market demands. "The market does not exist for you," explained Koniukov, "you exist to supply market needs." He suggested strongly but diplomatically that the trusts accept binding contracts as the basis for a new relationship between trusts and syndicate: between industry and the market.[18]

Trust representatives refused to submit to the new contracts, and without apparent irony charged the syndicate with monopolistic practices. V. Fedorov, of Iuzhmashtrest (IuMT), the Southern Machine Building Trust, voiced the concerns of many trust representatives when he charged that the syndicate wanted to use the contracts to dictate to industry what to produce. This was a thinly veiled attempt, he said, to establish the "whimsical" and "capricious" dictatorship of the market over industry, with the syndicate acting as the market's agent. Mikhailov, of Lenmashtrest, the powerful Leningrad Machine Building Trust, favored full syndication of only mass-produced goods—items that, once produced, needed no more attention from producers. Special orders requiring complex technical work, tailored design, and almost daily contact with the customer could not be syndicated. Despite clear regulations from Glavmashinstroi, Mikhailov noted, the syndicate was attempting to usurp the producers' design and development functions as well as their commercial activities.[19]

Representatives of smaller trusts endorsed syndicate work. They welcomed, for example, the syndicate's help in working up new production designs. In this matter, the syndicate provided a valuable service that the smaller trusts, with limited staff and facilities, could not perform. Further, S. Ivanov of the Urals Izhorsk instrument *kombinat* lauded the VMTS's marketing expertise. Before the syndicate took over their sales, Ivanov noted, "we couldn't move anything." VMTS did a "colossal job" in selling the *kombinat*'s instruments and in advising Izhorsk how to retool to produce instruments that would sell. The production and accounting indices of the trust were now in good shape, thanks to the syndicate.[20]

Such glowing testimonials did little to blunt criticism from the larger

[18]Ibid., ll. 6b, 8b–9.
[19]Ibid., ll. 12, 18–19.
[20]Ibid., l. 23.

trusts. The most severe charge turned on the issue of commissions. Mikhail Sukhanov, of the Moscow Machine Building Trust, MMT, expressed indignation at the arbitrary and "outrageous" commissions charged by VMTS on syndicated sales, which could go over 5 percent. Fedorov, of IuMT, claimed that their own sales offices operated at less than 1 percent of the cost of a contract. Savitskii, another trust representative, accused VMTS of outright robbery and noted that such fees made it difficult for trusts to stay within their already tight production costs.[21]

One official, Zubzhitskii, added that the syndicate took not only a hefty commission but the cream of producers' goods. "They say they want to regulate production programs, interfere in production programs, but then say that anything left in factory warehouses—that is, anything that won't sell—'must be supported by the trusts' working capital." In plain language, Zubzhitskii argued, this meant that the syndicate dictated to the trusts what to produce, took the best products, added a commission, and then left the trusts with junk. Mikhailov, of Lenmashtrest, added that VMTS engaged in unfair pricing practices. The syndicate, he said, habitually negotiated widely varying prices with different producers for similar equipment. Zubzhitskii concluded that, instead of taking such high commissions from producers and forcing manufacturers' output prices down, the syndicate should "lean" (lech') on the consumer. Consumers, he argued, should bear the burden of capital accumulation.[22]

VMTS officials reacted angrily. S. E. Veitsman, a member of VMTS's governing board, scolded trust representatives for resisting the numerous orders and regulations on syndication. Trust officials, Veitsman sarcastically noted, wanted to run their trusts like medieval principalities. "The prince wakes," Veitsman mimicked, "and says 'my left leg wants such-and-such, and so I'll do such-and-such.' You, Comrade Mikhailov, and you representatives from MMT, and the armature trust, all of you want to relate to us as princes to vassals." Veitsman dismissed complaints about the syndicate's commission policies. He argued that the trusts' claim to such low marketing costs was a fiction. The trusts, he charged, routinely transferred what should be considered trading costs into other accounting categories in order to make their books look good. Besides, the syndicate incurred higher trading costs because it marketed goods nationwide. And as for the charge that the syndicate sold the best and left the trusts with poor-quality equipment, now the trusts were having to swallow their own bad medicine.[23]

I. Golovko, from the Urals office of VMTS, challenged Fedorov's complaints that the syndicate was throwing the trusts to the whims of the

[21]Ibid., ll. 24, 14b.
[22]Ibid., ll. 19, 22.
[23]Ibid., ll. 15–15b.

market. He reminded Fedorov that in the state sector especially the market was inseparable from the machinery requirements of producers themselves. Those requirements were defined by tasks set forth in yearly control figures of the five-year plan. Using Smithian phrases of market rationality, Golovko argued that the market was not capricious. "In fact," he argued, "the market organizes the tasks of industry in accordance with regular changes in the demands of technology and the rational organization of production." Producers, on the other hand, displayed extreme inertia, accustomed as they were to a monopoly position. Here was the "real truth" behind the trusts' complaints about the capricious market. Complacency and fear lay behind their resistance to new production changes and to the syndicate's influence over producers.[24]

Koniukov pressed the syndicate's position in his closing statement even as he tried to bring peace to the two sides. He admitted irregularities in syndicate price negotiations and promised to correct those practices. He could not resist pointing out, however, that such irregularities would be smoothed over with the adoption of regular contracting procedures. Koniukov also defended the syndicate's commission policies. He argued that, as the syndicate took over the trusts' commercial and supply functions, it protected producers but exposed itself to the brunt of state wholesale price reductions and the government's commercial tax policies. To press his point, Koniukov recalled that in 1927–28 Vesenkha reduced industrial retail prices by 4 percent. As a result, the syndicate suffered a loss for the year. The syndicate, Koniukov reasoned, had to maintain a wide margin of profitability, and it responded to state regulatory policies in the only way it could, by raising the fees it charged manufacturers.[25]

The October meeting with shareholder trusts was stormy, but Koniukov reported to the syndicate's managerial board two weeks later that VMTS got most of what it wanted. It failed to win approval of new contract procedures, but Koniukov expressed confidence that the contracts would be adopted soon, either voluntarily or under pressure from Glavmashinstroi. More important, eight new trusts purchased shares in VMTS at the meeting, and the original shareholders agreed to double their share capital in the syndicate. The syndicate was in good shape. It would begin the 1929 calendar year with twenty major shareholders and a capital base of well over 20 million rubles.[26]

Koniukov had urged trust representatives not to think of themselves as orderlies, (prikazchiky) to the VMTS masters (khoziaeva). To his colleagues, however, Koniukov declared triumphantly that the syndicate was now the undisputed master (khoziain) of industry. He congratulated his staff on the

[24]Ibid., l. 24.
[25]Ibid., ll. 28–39.
[26]Ibid., l. 23.

year just past, and he noted that control figures and five-year plan estimates would create a strain in the current year. Koniukov looked forward
confidently, however, to an annual commercial plan of 260 million rubles,
nearly double that of the previous year. Several more trusts had asked to
join, and plans were afoot to expand regional sales offices, enlarge the
syndicate's directorates, and become even more deeply involved in both
market and production planning.

Koniukov gained one other victory at the syndicate's meeting.
A. Tolokontsev, head of Glavmashinstroi, attended the VMTS session to
discuss relations between the syndicate and the chief administration. The
discussion was congenial, and Tolokontsev agreed to most of the syndicate's suggestions on how to discipline the trusts. He gave his specific
support to the idea of binding contracts and promised to use what administrative measures he could to force trusts to agree to them. More important, he conceded that the government's arbitrary price reductions on raw
materials played havoc with the commercial activities of state industry,
with adverse affects on industry's profitability and the process of capital
formation. Tolokontsev acknowledged that at the very least, the syndicate
should be brought into pricing discussions at the glavk level to represent
industry's commercial interests and to be forewarned of any price
changes.[27]

This concession cost Tolokontsev little. Decisions about major price
movements were political matters and made at the highest levels of the
government and Party, within Sovnarkom, the STO, and the Politbiuro.
Allowing syndicate representatives a voice in discussions at the Vesenkha
level probably would not have a significant effect on these decisions.
Tolokontsev's gesture was not meaningless, however. Vesenkha made
many decisions about small price increments, transaction fees, commissions, and exceptions to the government's general pricing policies. Multi-
plied by tens of millions of rubles, these small decisions had a significant
impact on the economy. To permit syndicate representation in these decisions was not only to recognize the growing influence of the syndicates
but also to acknowledge the legitimate role of commercial interests in state
industry.

Vesenkha's Fourth Plenum Meeting, November 1928

It was precisely the issue of commercial and syndicate influence that
was at the heart of the rancorous debate at Vesenkha's November 1928
plenum session. To resolve these issues, Iosef Kosior, former head of

---

[27]RGAE, f. 5715, op. 7, d. 26, l. 7. It is interesting to note that the syndicate, despite its
commitment to commercial mechanisms, was willing to use Glavmashinstroi's muscle to further its ends.

Iugostal' and an outspoken defender of trust interests, presented an over-all framework for the regulation of relations among glavki, trusts, and syndicates. While conciliatory to the syndicates, he made it clear that they were to be subordinate to the trusts. And in case anyone misunderstood the import of his comments, Kosior made it known that this was not just a matter of organizational hegemony but involved fundamental principles of political economy.

The syndicates' main function, Kosior said, should be "sales, that is, to organize the market." He conceded that some influence should go the other way and that the syndicates might also exercise some influence over financing and supply. Kosior also admitted that syndicates might play a larger role in industries where glavki were weak or small or where pro-duction was designated for a broader consumer market. They should not, however, play a dominant role in branches with strong trusts and strong chief administrations. In the next sentence Kosior returned to his funda-mental point. He reiterated that syndicates "should be organizations of the trust" [at this point a delegate interrupted with a corroborating "Yes!"] because production, in this phase of our socialist economy, should have the greatest influence in our industrial system, not the market." With these comments, Kosior allied himself unmistakably on the side of the state's manufacturing interests.[28]

When Stepan Birman, the fiery head of Iugostal', spoke, he unburdened himself, in typical style, of numerous complaints. First, he upbraided the miners' trade union leader, I. I. Shvarts, who had disparaged industrial leaders in his comments at the plenum. Birman minced no words, calling Shvarts a "milksop" (shliapa). Next he flailed away at Vesenkha's leaders, then against Vesenkha's industrial bank, and then against Rabkrin, the state inspectorate. When he finally got to the subject of syndicates, Birman referred to them as a movement of "little Alexanders and their little Ma-cedonias." This, he said, is how he would characterize the syndicates' at-tempts "to lord it over the trusts." Birman referred to the "constant, exas-perating, and fierce" (ozhestochennuiu) struggles against the "imperialist tendencies" of the metallurgical syndicate during the formulation of the 1928–29 financial and production plans. He chided Kuibyshev for not "stepping in" to put the syndicates in their place, and he declared that all the "lack of clarity and friction" could be avoided if Vesenkha would fi-nally realize that the syndicates "are the sales apparatus of the trusts." Vesenkha's leaders acted as if the situation were reversed, as if the trusts "were the production departments of the all-powerful syndicates."[29]

Birman's comments reveal the rancor and disagreement that divided

[28]TPG, 30 November 1928.
[29]TPG, 1 December 1928. "They are *our* organizations," Birman said, "but now they dream about ruling the trusts, how they will 'take us in hand'" (italics mine).

Vesenkha over the issue of how to organize the industrial economy. The united front of the trusts against the syndicates also reveals the extent to which the big trusts dominated Vesenkha politics. Representatives of Vesenkha's smaller trusts, who generally supported the syndicate movement, did not speak at the plenum. If they appeared, their comments were not reported. All of the trust officials whose comments were reproduced in the newspapers were representatives of Vesenkha's major all-union production cartels.

Syndicate officials gave as good as they got. Gavrilov of the chemical syndicate told the gathering that Kosior undervalued the syndicate movement because he failed to comprehend the evolution of the Soviet political economy over the last years. "To limit them [the syndicates] merely as sales or even trade organizations," he said, "contradicts an understanding of present economic conditions." Gavrilov pointed out that ownership of industry by the state and the advent of planning did not mean that the market disappeared. The state-owned industrial market was "much harsher" than the wider market in its demands on manufacturers. Moreover, the distinction that trusts drew between consumers and producers was artificial, since state producers were also consumers of all manner of supplies and raw materials, as well as finished machine products. Emphasis on policies that favored only producers would hurt state enterprises in their capacity as consumers. The syndicates, he concluded, were the only institutions capable, through commercial activities, to regulate relations between producers and their markets. "Yes, and I am talking about markets inside the state sector."[30]

V. N. Mantsev, member of Vesenkha's presidium and head of the All-Union Council of Syndicates, the Vsesoiuznyi Sovet Sindikatov (VSS), refuted the charge that the syndicates represented the influence of petty-bourgeois market spontaneity. This "simplistic prattle" ignored the pressing need to organize production within the socialized, or state, economic sectors. Koniukov put the syndicate case succinctly and bluntly: the syndicates needed influence over production "not just to rule over the trusts but to ensure that there will be fewer mistakes, less junk produced, and fewer warehouses full of unneeded and worthless products." Kilevitz, of the textile syndicate, said he understood that the current campaign to reduce production costs was important as part of the process of capital formation, but he failed to understand why more weight was not given to capital formation through syndicated commercial activities?[31]

The atmosphere of the discussion period was so hostile that Kosior was much harsher toward the syndicates in his closing remarks than in his opening comments. Speakers exchanged barbs and open insults as they

[30]Ibid.
[31]Ibid.

debated the past and future role of the syndicates. One delegate remarked that all the fighting reminded him of squabbles among capitalist conglomerates over market shares.[32] Delegates angrily denied the validity of the analogy, yet there was some truth to it. Despite the vehemence of their disagreements, all the disputants shared the assumption that commercial relations should be an important, if not the most important, organizing and regulating principle of industry. More to the point, the trusts, though state producers, were certainly no strangers to entrepreneurial commercial activity. Shareholders' meetings of the syndicate organizations made that clear. Much of the anger trust officials projected was not over matters of principle but over loss of control over commercial activity to the syndicates. The dispute between trusts and syndicates came down to a disagreement over who should be the state's institutional entrepreneurs, which institutions should be at the center of the production and commercial trading nexus of the industrial economy.

Yet if disagreement between trusts and syndicates was a matter of degree, the distinction was important. Trusts may have engaged in entrepreneurial activities in order to improve their profitability and their account balances, but they nonetheless lived off the state's budget. V. I. Mezhlauk, deputy chair of Vesenkha and head of the metal industries until 1928, vigorously defended state subsidies of industry, even at the height of the cost-accounting NEP era. Mezhlauk's attitude reflected the producer-driven mentality of Vesenkha's chief administrations and its trusts. Syndicates, in contrast, could draw on emergency Vesenkha funds to cover temporary shortfalls, but they lived off the capital turnover they generated through their commercial activities. This is how they measured their profitability and how they made money for the state. The commercial basis of their work promoted a mentality that their counterparts in the trusts did not share. Trust officials conceived of their tasks in terms of a producer-driven bureaucratic economy; syndicate officials thought of theirs in commercial and entrepreneurial terms.

Syndicate officials were so confident of their movement that in 1929 they proclaimed it their goal to commercialize the whole of the state's economy by the end of the first five-year plan.[33] In mid-January they also planned how best to promote syndicate interests and to advertise the syndicates' importance as "the center of the industrial system." V. N. Mantsev, the head of the All-Union Council of Syndicates (VSS) urged his fellow presidium members to engage in more public activities that would draw attention to the syndicates. He encouraged his colleagues to give more interviews, for example, and to organize debates, especially in forums such as the well-known managerial society Club Dzerzhinskii. In the

[32]*TPG*, 1 December 1928.
[33]Kantorovich, *Sindikatskaia sistema*, p. 10.

same vein, Mantsev announced that he had contacted the editors of the *Torgovo-promyshlennaia gazeta*, which would regularly send a reporter to cover meetings of the VSS presidium. Mantsev also reported that he had given 10,000 rubles to the journal *Puti industrializatsii* to do the same.[34] The second year of the five-year plan promised to be an even better year for the syndicates than the first.

Financial Politics and the Credit Debacle of 1930

Despite severe strains in the economy, 1929 proceeded well for the syndicates commercially. By the end of the year, however, they faced yet another crisis. This time the threat came not from the trusts but from Rabkrin and Gosbank. Rabkrin's organizational plans to centralize administrative control of the economy threatened the end of the syndicate movement, as did plans jointly developed by Rabkrin and Gosbank to centralize all financial and credit transactions. At a meeting of the All-Union Council of Syndicates on 11 March 1929, A. Fushman, of Rabkrin, and G. Piatakov, the head of Gosbank, presented the particulars of a proposal to reform commercial credit and financial transactions. They explained that the extension of commercial or short-term credit had gotten out of hand: syndicate credit policies had failed to discipline industrial trusts financially. Syndicate advances and credit extensions had not led to any significant stimulus in production and had not spurred factories to mobilize capital or reduce costs more effectively. Issues of printed money were as high as ever. According to Fushman, for every ruble that industry gained by turnover of goods it received three in printed issues. Plans for rapid industrial construction were already straining the budget, causing inflation, and driving the purchasing power of the ruble down. Syndicate credit policies, argued Fushman, were exacerbating the problem.[35]

Piatakov expanded on Fushman's arguments. Gosbank, he said, had to act to regulate credit in order to slow inflation. According to a new plan the two of them had worked out, Gosbank would centralize all credit operations in its branches and would set strict limits on commercial credit allocations. This measure, Fushman reasoned, would wean industry off credit and stabilize the purchasing power of the ruble. After 15 January 1930, syndicates could no longer issue commercial credits under their own authority. They had to apply to Gosbank for each transaction.[36]

Syndicate representatives were appalled. M. Sokolovskii, of VSS, argued

[34] RGAE, f. 3915, op. 1, d. 241, l. 63.

[35] "Stenogrammy zasedanii prezidiuma VSS o ratsionalizatsii finansovogo khoziaistva promyshlennosti i otnoshenii promyshlennosti s rynkom," protokol 11, 3 November 1929, in RGAE, f. 3915, op. 1, d. 342, ll. 162b–63. Archives of the VSS from 1929 contain extensive stenographic records of debates over financial, commercial, and organizational reforms.

[36] Ibid., ll. 161–62. Piatakov's comments are on l. 38.

that commercial credit was the lifeblood of industry. Any restriction of its flow would strangle the life out of the syndicates and halt the circulation of goods. He called the Fushman-Piatakov plan a "colossal bureaucratization of capital turnover." Sokolovskii wondered aloud how Piatakov and Fushman could present a plan of such "reasoned stupidity." If it were implemented, the plan would "destroy the final thread—credit—that connects industry with the consumer." Sokolovskii noted, however, that this was exactly what Gosbank and Rabkrin wanted. Going to the heart of the matter, he charged that debates about credit were not really about financial capital; the Fushman-Piatakov plan was one more tactic in the state's strategy to kill the market and undermine the syndicate system.[37]

P. Gavrilov, also of VSS, echoed Sokolovskii's remarks. Fushman, he noted, framed his arguments about credit centralization in terms of the unity of capital. Gavrilov unmasked this language, arguing that "discussions about the unity of capital mean the liquidation of NEP." He defended NEP relations and the syndicates' role in them: "Profit is a well-known criterion for the rational organization of an economy; there is nothing terrible in that, nothing antistate. Profit is one of the links of NEP." The syndicates, he claimed, were the organizations that had evolved to generate profit for the state and to regulate market and production relations. To deny them control over commercial credit would be to destroy simultaneously the syndicates and the state's ability to generate capital and stimulate the circulation of goods. Where in Gosbank, he asked rhetorically, was an apparatus technically competent enough in its understanding of markets and producers to replace the commercial networks painstakingly established by the syndicates?[38]

Fushman's replies reveal much about the mentality of Stalin's state-builders. The syndicates had failed to regulate industry financially, Fushman said, but worse was their failure to extend industry's influence into the market. To the extent that syndicates were successful, they had let the market influence industry too much. Sokolovskii interrupted to declare that Comrade Dzerzhinskii had created the syndicates to do just that. "No," replied Fushman, "now we consider it necessary to deliver a blow, to deliver a strong blow against the consumer."[39]

In the late spring of 1929, the All-Union Council of Syndicates proposed its own version of reform, which would have combined all commercial and production planning functions in the syndicates. At a congress of syndicate representatives in June, officials argued vigorously for their plan and against the Gosbank-Rabkrin plan. During the discussion, S. Ak-

[37]Ibid., ll. 149–51.
[38]Ibid., l. 159.
[39]Ibid., l. 161. Feliks Dzerzhinskii, founder of the Cheka, the Soviet secret political police, was also the head of Vesenkha until his death by heart attack in July 1926.

sel'rod, a member of the VSS presidium, spoke from prepared notes about the various practical flaws he perceived in the Gosbank plan. Yet some way into his analysis of prices and rates of commodity turnover, Aksel'rod hesitated, departed from his text, and delivered a short soliloquy on the rationalist mentality that motivated Piatakov and Rabkrin's reformers.

The Gosbank-Rabkrin plan, argued Aksel'rod, was a "utopian plan of dreamers." Theirs was "a schematized ideal of some new level of managerial organization." Gosbank's plan had no basis in reality, but that did not matter "in the least" to its creators. Piatakov and his colleagues, Aksel'rod charged, overvalued the efficacy of planning for planning's sake. "For Fushman and Piatakov it's enough to write an all-encompassing plan that by its own logic will resolve all questions. For Fushman and Piatakov, reform and rationalization exist for their own sake, somewhere entirely outside our real economy, outside the real tasks that lie before us. They can't tell you exactly how their reform will help us carry out the tasks of the five-year plan. They don't know; they don't ask such questions; they don't even think about it." The Gosbank-Rabkrin plan was a utopian masterpiece, Aksel'rod concluded, but if it were enacted it would leave the real economy in chaos.[40]

Syndicate officials warned repeatedly of the economically disruptive consequences of Gosbank and Rabkrin reforms. The syndicates' warnings went unheeded, however, even when their dire predictions turned out to be uncannily accurate.[41] Gosbank instituted its credit reform in January 1930 and the results were a disaster. Centralization of credit dispersal and accounting in Gosbank offices created a bureaucratic and financial nightmare. In the first weeks of the reform, the paper processed daily in Gosbank offices increased 50 to 60 times. According to a Rabkrin survey, at the end of May 1930, over 87,000 credit accounts remained unprocessed in Moscow alone. Thousands of claims lay in the dead file, improperly addressed or otherwise impossible to trace. Such a huge paper jam threatened to slow the rate of capital turnover. It also forced the bank to print large amounts of money to cover the immediate costs of producers and clients.[42] Moreover, bank officers, inundated with claims, ignored credit limits. Often bank officials had no way to determine when or if a client

[40]"Stenogramma zasedanii prezidiuma VSS, 17.6.29," ibid., ll. 56–58.

[41]Syndicate predictions about the effects of Rabkrin's proposed organizational reforms were quite accurate. Their predictions about the restriction of credit as the consequence of financial reform turned out to be wrong, but only because they assumed that the reforms would be administered as planned.

[42]GARF, f. 374, op. 7, d. 943, ll. 20–21. Sovnarkom, the Council of Commissars, initiated the survey by an order dated 7 July 1930. Rabkrin conducted the survey with help from Gosbank and Narkomfin. The survey covered the period January through early June 1930 and was submitted to Sovnarkom 8 August 1930. A copy of the full report is contained in Rabkrin archives, ibid., op. 1, d. 654, ll. 54–58. More detailed notes on irregularities caused by the reforms are in op. 7, d. 943.

exceeded its limits. Clients "commonly" falsified transactions or opened multiple accounts in various cities to obtain credit or cash. Enterprises "routinely" presented bills to the bank for payment on goods never sent, or created fictitious orders for which the enterprise obtained immediate credit.[43] The syndicates, with close ties to both producers and markets, had regulated transactions closely. Bank officers, however, had little contact with clients. They did not have the time, the means, or the expertise to check the validity of claims or accounts.

The dysfunctional effects of the reforms exacerbated the problems the reforms were designed to resolve. By the summer of 1930, commercial credit expenditures ballooned. Gosbank planned a ceiling of 437.3 million rubles for the third quarter of 1930, but actual commercial credit outlays reached 820.5 million rubles for the period. Printed money issues for the third quarter alone exceeded the planned limit for the entire year.[44] Nearly all regional offices of Gosbank reported severe strains on cash reserves by the early summer of 1930.

Contrary to the intention of the reforms, it became easy for enterprises to obtain credit from Gosbank. Moreover, in the chaos created by the reforms, it became commonplace for enterprises to use commercial credit illegally—to offset capital or production costs, or to pay wage bonuses or arrears. "More often than not," according to one report, when enterprises obtained commercial credit they did not apply it to finance the movement of goods. Thus, ironically, over the last two quarters of 1930 the growth of commercial credit in circulation grew "exponentially" over the increase in the amount of goods in circulation. The reforms added greatly to inflationary pressures, increased bureaucratization of the state's financial apparatus, and encouraged administrative irregularities and outright fraud. In the understated language of the Rabkrin report, the reforms "weakened rather than strengthened" financial and credit discipline in industry.[45]

Gosbank responded to the problems created by its reforms not by reversing them but by strengthening its administrative apparatus. In an effort to handle the flow of paper better, the bank added personnel. It also increased the number of accounting regulations that governed the use of credit. Sergo Ordzhonikidze, the head of Rabkrin, condoned these measures, as he did similar measures to strengthen administrative prerogatives in other state sectors. Following recommendations from Piatakov and Rabkrin officials, the Council of People's Commissars (Sovnarkom) sanctioned these further sets of reforms in October 1930.

These measures, however, did little to relieve the problems caused by

[43]Ibid., op. 1, d. 654, l. 54.
[44]Ibid., l. 56. Gosbank plans called for a limit of 415 million rubles for the year. Third quarter issues alone reached 578.5 million rubles. Issues for the half year ran at 200 million rubles. Thus by the end of the third quarter, printed money issues reached 779 million rubles, nearly double the limit for the year.
[45]Ibid, ll. 56, 54b.

the reforms. In a terse, tough memorandum to state bureaucracies in late November 1930, Rabkrin noted that financial discipline remained "at an extremely low level." The memorandum complained that the misuse of credit throughout industry was "crudely flagrant." Enterprises continued "completely unacceptable . . . and blatantly illegal" practices. The exaggerated demands for commercial credit by production associations had crippled the state's campaign to mobilize internal industrial resources through financial forms of rationalization. "Essential deformities" in the credit system had undermined "completely" any attempt to transfer factories and associations to cost-accounting (*khozraschetnye*) methods of financial discipline.[46] What had begun as a reform to enhance the state's control over the country's economic finances had rapidly turned into a nearly complete breakdown of that system.

Conclusions

Ordzhonikidze's actions and those of Gosbank seemed baffling and irrational to syndicate officials. In fact, the two sides spoke entirely different languages to express entirely different conceptions of how to construct the Soviet state's political economy. Advocates of the syndicate movement believed that trade knitted the economy and the society together. They conceived of the state as the facilitator of commerce, with syndicates playing a key role. To realize that role, syndicate officials strove to regulate trade relations within a commercial network that linked producers and consumers. Syndicate officials saw it as their function to create a viable commercial system and to integrate commercial relations with state economic planning. Koniukov, Veitsman, and other syndicate officials spoke in the language of trade and market relations. They employed metaphors of circulation and fluidity and conceived of capital accumulation, the heart of economic expansion, as a process of commercial exchange.

Rabkrin and Gosbank leaders, in contrast, saw it as their historical task to create a powerful, autonomous state. They systematically attacked market and commercial relations as a hindrance to the unrestricted exercise of state power.[47] Piatakov and his Rabkrin colleagues spoke in the language of control and mobilization, not of commerce and exchange. They understood capital accumulation to mean capital extraction and they conceived of the economy primarily as a source of wealth for the state. The financial reforms and organizational schemes put forward by Rabkrin and Gosbank

---

[46]"O narushenii gosorganami finansovoi distsipliny i pravoi kreditnoi reformy," protokol 11, 31 November 1930, ibid., d. 642, ll. 493–94.

[47]For more on Piatakov and his desire to create the "first industrial state in history," see Andrea Graziosi, "'Building the First System of State Industry in History': Piatakov's VSNKh and the Crisis of NEP, 1923–1926," *Cahiers du monde russe et soviétique* 4 (1991): 539–81.

officials set the institutional foundations of the Stalinist bureaucratic economy and undercut the syndicate movement. The growth of the syndicates posed a threat to the new industrial state, and the Stalinists fought hard and successfully to abolish them.

This interpretation of the syndicate movement runs counter to traditional interpretations. The story of rapid industrialization and the transition from NEP to a bureaucratically administered economy is often told as if the process had been inevitable. The history of the syndicate movement in Soviet industry shows that it was nothing of the sort. The syndicates' brief success in the last years of the 1920s opened up the intriguing possibility of a middle way, a way to combine commercial organization of the economy with planned industrial development. Destruction of the state's nascent commercial culture and the construction of a centralized, bureaucratic economy was not the inevitable consequence of rapid industrialization but the result of the Stalinists' political will to build a powerful state.

3

Rabkrin and the Militarized Campaign Economy

You *vesenkhovtsy* have fought us at every step, whether
here in Rabkrin's collegium, in Vesenkha's corridors, or in
front of Sovnarkom. For the last two years we have been
at war.

—Ia. A. Iakovlev, deputy chairman of Rabkrin,
August 1929

Sergo Ordzhonikidze believed in Stalin.[1] A stocky, solidly built Georgian, Ordzhonikidze first met the future Soviet leader in a prerevolutionary prison. The two found common cause and remained close comrades, especially during the revolutionary war years in Ukraine and the north Caucasus. During the early 1920s, as Stalin became deeply enmeshed in the work and intrigues of the Party's central apparatus in Moscow, Ordzhonikidze remained as regional Party head in the north Caucasus. In December 1926, Stalin brought him to the capital to become Rabkrin's new chief after the death of Feliks Dzerzhinskii and the transfer of Valerian Kuibyshev from Rabkrin to head Vesenkha.

In matters of dress and personal grooming, Ordzhonikidze emulated his mentor. Like Stalin, Rabkrin's *narkom* was distinguished by his bushy mustache and his penchant for a pipe. Like Stalin, Ordzhonikidze wore the jackboots and military-style tunic of the Civil War era to express the belief that the revolutionary struggle was not yet over, but was continuing in other forms on other fronts.

Whether as regional Party secretary or as chief of Rabkrin, Ordzhonikidze projected the zeal of a fighting Bolshevik. Those who met him spoke of his intensity, his expansive and volatile personality, and his single-mindedness. He evoked loyalty and admiration in his subordinates, wary respect, even fear in his opponents. Throughout the late 1920s, Or-

[1]See, e.g., Boris Souvarine's characterization of Ordzhonikidze in *Stalin: A Critical Study of Bolshevism* (New York, 1939), pp. 99, 113.

dzhonikidze wielded power as one of Stalin's closest and most loyal supporters.

As head of the RKI, Ordzhonikidze revitalized what had been a moribund institution, transforming it into a powerful political, administrative, and policy-making instrument. Under Ordzhonikidze's leadership, Rabkrin exercised much more than control over the state's executive branches. Rabkrin quickly forced the pace and direction of change in industrial organization and strategy. Charged to conduct surveys and recommend reforms, RKI's standing commissions and specialists' groups quickly became, in effect, a skeleton planning and operational administration within the government. The scandals that revolved around RKI reports and surveys defined the agenda of political-economic and industrial priorities in the late 1920s. Rabkrin's investigations shaped Party leaders' perceptions of the crisis in industrial administration. The agency usurped the administrative leadership functions of Vesenkha and the planning functions of Gosplan. In the last years of the 1920s, Rabkrin, not Vesenkha, became the center of the state's industrial policy-making and administrative system. By the end of the decade, Rabkrin constituted a state within the state.

That Rabkrin interfered in economic administration and came to wield decisive influence is well known. It was Rabkrin's officials, with their maximalist ideology, that pushed Vesenkha's bureaucrats to set ever more unrealistic targets for industrialization.[2] Yet it was not the specific character of Rabkrin's policies but the way Rabkrin went about its business that fundamentally shaped the Soviet industrial system under the first five-year plan. Rabkrin's reconstruction policies threatened both the trusts and the syndicates' influence in the Vesenkha system. Just as important, the agency's uncoordinated, piecemeal approach to industrial mobilization created much of the economic dislocation that characterized Soviet industrial administration in those years.

Rabkrin under Ordzhonikidze

Rabkrin gained so much power in the late 1920s in part because of its unique bureaucratic position. The agency reported directly to Sovnarkom, the highest governmental body, the state equivalent of the Politbiuro. Thus when Rabkrin's recommendations were approved, they carried the force of Sovnarkom decisions. Indeed, the agency's recommendations were considered governmental rulings even when Rabkrin officials issued

---

[2]For the most comprehensive discussions of Rabkrin, see E. A. Rees, *State Control in Soviet Russia: The Rise and Fall of the Workers' and Peasants' Inspectorate, 1920–1934* (New York, 1987); Fitzpatrick, "Sergo Ordzhonikidze"; Davies, *Soviet Economy in Turmoil*, pp. 240–42. One of the best monographs in Russian is S. N. Ikonnikov, *Sozdanie i deiatel'nost' ob"edinennykh organov TsKK-RKI v 1923–1934 gg.* (Moscow, 1971).

instructions and regulations under its own name, without Sovnarkom's official sanction. As one official noted, "When Rabkrin speaks, it speaks as the voice of the government."[3]

Rabkrin's recommendations also carried the weight of Party authority, both because of Ordzhonikidze's powerful political patronage and because of his position as head of Rabkrin and TsKK, the Party's Central Control Commission. Administratively, Rabkrin and TsKK were interrelated; they were joined in a single commissariat and shared key members of their collegiums. As head of both organizations, Ordzhonikidze occupied a position of power that was arguably second only to Stalin. It was because he was head of TsKK-RKI that Ordzhonikidze held a seat on Sovnarkom, but, as a close ally of Stalin, he was also one of the inner ruling circle. Late in 1930, Ordzhonikidze's position of influence was formalized by his election to the Politbiuro.

With Ordzhonikidze as Rabkrin's head, its recommendations were seldom successfully challenged. Yet, because of his other responsibilities, Ordzhonikidze left much of the daily conduct of Rabkrin's affairs to his deputy chairs, A. P. Rozengol'ts and Ia. A. Iakovlev. Both men also sat on the presidium of the TsKK, Rozengol'ts as a candidate member. Rozengol'ts first came to know Ordzhonikidze during the Civil War, when the two were on opposite sides of the political struggles between Trotsky and Stalin. In 1920 and 1921, at the height of that struggle, Rozengol'ts was a protégé and close friend of Georgii Piatakov, then closely allied with Trotsky and head of the coal "dictatorship" in the Donbass. Ordzhonikidze helped Stalin unseat Piatakov and drive him out of Ukraine, but he was impressed by Piatakov's "hard" methods. Ordzhonikidze was also deeply impressed by the discipline and loyalty of men who had worked with Piatakov, as Rozengol'ts had done.[4] Rozengol'ts distinguished himself as head of the Air Force's chief administration and as a diplomatic representative in Britain in the 1920s, and when Ordzhonikidze became head of Rabkrin, he brought Rozengol'ts with him into the agency.

As deputy *narkom* from 1928 to 1930, Rozengol'ts supervised the work of all of Rabkrin's survey groups. He issued specific instructions about what to investigate, how to organize the surveys, and when to make recommendations. Because of his former ties to Trotsky, Rozengol'ts was not included in Stalin's inner circle, but he was an energetic and competent bureaucrat. Rozengol'ts believed in authority and "iron administration," and Ordzhonikidze trusted him.[5] After Rozengol'ts recanted his ties to

[3]GARF f. 374, op. 1, d. 23, l. 38.
[4]On Piatakov and Ordzhonikidze, see Graziosi, "'Building the First System of State Industry,'" pp. 542–43.
[5]Alexander Barmine, *Memoirs of a Soviet Diplomat: Twenty Years in the Service of the U.S.S.R.* (Westport, Conn., 1973), p. 281.

Trotsky in 1928, he rose quickly in the Rabkrin hierarchy, and after Ordzhonikidze took over Vesenkha in November 1930, Rozengol'ts was appointed deputy and then head of the Foreign Trade Commissariat. There
he worked closely with Ordzhonikidze to secure foreign contracts and
financial underwriting for the Soviet industrialization drive.

Ia. Iakovlev, the other deputy head of Rabkrin, sat on the Central Committee and had been a Party member since 1913. In addition to his Rabkrin and TsKK duties, Iakovlev was assigned to report on the qualifications of Party personnel, and he helped administer the Party purge
commissions in 1929 and 1930. Like other allies of Ordzhonikidze,
Iakovlev had been active in Civil War military and economic administration, also in the Caucasus and Ukraine. The Civil War experience was an
important bond for all the major Stalinist leaders and it first brought
Iakovlev into contact with Ordzhonikidze. Iakovlev was trusted enough
within the Stalinist circle that he was appointed head of the reorganized
agricultural commissariat in 1929. There he directed Stalin's policies during the most intense period of mass collectivization. As deputy heads of
Rabkrin, Rozengol'ts and Iakovlev often chaired meetings of its collegium
and signed its directives. The two worked closely with Ordzhonikidze in
formulating Rabkrin policy, and both benefited from Ordzhonikidze's patronage. Along with Ordzhonikidze, these men gave energy and direction
to the RKI, turning it into a powerful instrument for the Stalinist assault
on Vesenkha and the NEP.

Several other prominent members of Rabkrin's collegium also shaped
the agency's administrative style and its industrial policies. Among the
most important were Mikhail Kaganovich and V. Ia. Grossman. Kaganovich, also a former ally of Trotsky, was the brother of Lazar Kaganovich, one of Stalin's confidants. In 1928 and 1929, Mikhail led important survey groups in the areas of machine building, engineering, and
metallurgy. He also headed a year-long survey commission on rationalization in the metal industries. Kaganovich was one of Rabkrin's most outspoken critics of Vesenkha. When Ordzhonikidze moved to Vesenkha, he
designated Kaganovich to head the newly reorganized machine manufacturing and engineering sectors of the economy. Grossman was in charge
of finance and state organization, and also worked on issues of rationalization. In 1930, when he moved to Vesenkha with Ordzhonikidze, Grossman became head of the rationalization bureau and a presidium member,
and in 1932 he produced a critical study of the need for rationalization in
Soviet industry.[6]

A. I. Gurevich and Abram Gol'tsman also sat on Rabkrin's collegium.
Gurevich, a former Menshevik and trade unionist, headed Rabkrin's sur-

---

[6]V. Ia. Grossman, *Sotsialisticheskaia ratsionalizatsiia promyshlennosti: Itogi i blizhaishie zadachi*
(Moscow, 1932).

vey of capital construction in 1928 and 1929, and he led the bitter public fight against Iugostal' in 1928. Gurevich's harsh criticisms of Vesenkha's lax administration led to centralizing reforms in the administration of long-term credit and earned him praise from Ordzhonikidze. After Rabkrin took over Vesenkha, Gurevich headed the council's planning sector and also took a seat on its presidium. In the mid-1930s, before his arrest and execution, Gurevich directed the country's metallurgical industries. He was, in the account of one memoirist, the consummate bureaucratic dictator.[7]

Gol'tsman had been a strong advocate of scientific management throughout the 1920s, and in the early years of the decade he had proposed to use scientific managerial training techniques to create a Soviet aristocracy of labor. Like other prominent *rabkrinovtsy*, Gol'tsman allied with Trotsky in the early 1920s. Although their efforts came to naught, the two had worked closely together to wed scientific managerial practices to a militarized labor force.[8] In the 1920s Gol'tsman helped develop many of the accounting methods used in central Vesenkha bureaucracies, but he became disillusioned by the muddle that Vesenkha made of the economy. By the end of the 1920s, Gol'tsman was convinced of the need to replace market mechanisms with an administrative and accounting "dictatorship" in order to bring discipline to the economy.[9]

After joining Rabkrin in the mid-1920s, Gol'tsman quickly moved to its top echelon. In 1927 and 1928 he led major survey groups on commercial and cost accounting policies, as well as on policies in numerous other areas of the industrial economy. In 1929 Ordzhonikidze appointed Gol'tsman to head the agency's commission to reorganize industrial administration. His proposals became the basis for the massive restructuring of Vesenkha in 1930. Gol'tsman became one of the most important of Rabkrin's officials. As much as any single individual, he shaped the organizational structure of the industrial system that emerged in the early 1930s.

The most famous of the group around Ordzhonikidze was G. L. Piatakov, another former ally of Trotsky. As head of the Donbass coal cartel in 1921, Piatakov had worked "demonically" to implement Trotsky's program for martial-law organization of industry and labor. There Piatakov refined many of the methods of military organization of the economy—armed grain procurements, labor conscription, sealed train transports, and graduated systems of food and commodities rationing—that successfully supplied coal to Moscow and to the Bolshevik industrial and military

[7]N. Valentinov [Vol'skii], *Novaia ekonomicheskaia politika i krizis partii posle smerti Lenina: Gody raboty v VSNKh vo vremia NEP* (Stanford, 1971), p. 85.

[8]Mark Beissinger, *Scientific Management, Socialist Discipline, and Soviet Power* (Cambridge, Mass., 1988), pp. 32–33.

[9]E. B. Koritskii et al., *Sovetskaia upravlencheskaia mysl' 20-kh godov* (Moscow, 1990), pp. 69–70.

centers essential to the war effort.[10] During the early 1920s, Piatakov worked in Vesenkha as deputy to Feliks Dzerzhinskii until he was expelled in 1926 for his Trotskyist affiliations. After his recantation in 1928, Piatakov was brought back into the Bolshevik fold as head of Gosbank. There he worked to consolidate state financial and administrative control over the largely decentralized commercial and trading infrastructure of the economy. Piatakov was not a member of Rabkrin but he maintained a close working relationship with the agency. He had been a close friend of Rozengol'ts since the revolutionary war, and, like Rozengol'ts, found a patron in Ordzhonikidze. As head of Gosbank, Piatakov worked closely with several of Rabkrin's commissions, particularly those headed by A. M. Fushman, which were concerned with credit, trade, and monetary reorganization.

Although they had been political enemies in 1921, Ordzhonikidze and Piatakov developed a close working relationship, and it continued until Piatakov's arrest in 1936. When Ordzhonikidze took over Vesenkha in 1930, he brought Piatakov into the council, and Piatakov took on duties as a member of the presidium. Indeed, during the crisis years of industrialization, Ordzhonikidze adopted many of the military-administrative methods that Piatakov had employed so successfully in the Donbass ten years earlier. In 1932 Vesenkha was disbanded, and when Ordzhonikidze became head of the newly formed Commissariat of Heavy Industry, Narkomtiazhprom, he made Piatakov his deputy. At Vesenkha and at Narkomtiazhprom, Piatakov, along with Rozengol'ts, Gol'tsman, and other former political allies of Trotsky, worked to construct what Piatakov called "the first system of state industry in the history of the world."[11]

Clearly, Rabkrin provided an institutional means for one-time supporters of Trotsky to influence industrial strategy and state organization. These individuals flourished in the intense working atmosphere of the agency under Ordzhonikidze's political patronage. Gol'tsman, Rozengol'ts, Kaganovich, Gurevich, and Piatakov had all publicly supported Trotsky's arguments for rapid industrialization in the early 1920s. Now the ideas formed in the revolutionary war years corresponded to Stalin's plans for large-scale industrialization. Moreover, all were committed to constructing a mighty state administrative system. They were core members of what the historian Isaac Deutscher described as the bureaucratic left that gathered around Trotsky in the revolutionary war and in the years of opposition during the early 1920s.[12]

[10]Graziosi, "At the Roots of Soviet Industrial Relations," p. 104. Graziosi elucidates many of Piatakov's Civil War measures that were revived in the early 1930s.

[11]Quoted in Graziosi, "'Building the First System of State Industry,'" p. 551.

[12]This is one of Valentinov's main points in *Novaia ekonomicheskaia politika*, pp. 65–86. Graziosi, citing Isaac Deutscher, has revived a discussion of the bureaucratic left tendencies in his work on Piatakov during the 1920s. See Graziosi, "'Building the First System of State

The so-called Left Opposition, which Trotsky led in the early 1920s, has generally been associated with the goals of rapid industrialization and with the struggle against the balanced economic policies of NEP. Encouraging the growth of the peasant and private sectors of the economy, argued the leftists, would quickly drain capital away from the state. This was a dangerous tendency, so the argument went, because it would create an investment crisis in the state's industrial sectors. At the same time, economic policies that favored private agriculture and trade would make the government vulnerable to the economic power of hostile social classes—the peasants and urban trading strata. Evgenii Preobrazhenskii, the well-known theoretician of the left, argued for a shifting of resources through price manipulations and other market mechanisms. The government should regulate prices and taxes, he believed, to force peasant producers and consumers to bear the burden of capital accumulation for the state's industrialization drive. When Preobrazhenskii articulated this well-known theory of primitive socialist accumulation in 1925, it was considered extreme, but it was nonetheless proposed within the framework of NEP market economics.[13]

Opposition to the policies of the Party's majority leaders centered on political as well as economic issues, and Trotsky publicly championed the cause of those who fought against Stalin and the growth of authoritarianism within the Party. Yet the Menshevik memoirist N. Valentinov argued that opposition leaders as a group were commited not to democracy but to building a strong dictatorship. According to Valentinov, few people in 1923 and 1924, when the opposition were at the height of their influence, believed their rhetoric about restoring democracy in the Party. Trotsky's martial law tactics all through the revolutionary war made the calls for Party democracy ring hollow. "We saw not a kernel of democracy in [the Left Opposition]," wrote Valentinov. "What kind of *demokratizm* could be nurtured by a mind-numbing little dictator such as Piatakov?" What the opposition "hammered" at constantly was not the need for greater freedom in the Party but the "necessity to subjugate the economy to planned leadership, 'to gather all enterprises into a unified system, obedient to a single powerful planning center.'" Regardless of what rank-and-file oppositionists may have believed, Valentinov reported, leaders such as Piatakov, Gurevich, and Rozengol'ts "talked much" about the need to create

---

Industry,'" p. 570. For Deutscher's discussion of this wing of the opposition, see his *Prophet Unarmed: Trotsky, 1921–1929* (Oxford, 1959), pp. 413–14. Whereas Deutscher characterizes Piatakov and company as "enlightened bureaucrats," Graziosi follows Valentinov's more critical assessment of them.

[13]Carr and Davies, *Foundations of a Planned Economy*, 1:26–27.

a mighty "'dictatorship of industry'" as powerful as possible and as quickly as possible.[14]

Oppositionists such as Preobrazhenskii argued for rapid industrialization, but, as we have seen, through policies that stayed essentially within the NEP framework. Other opposition leaders, however, never lost their taste for the martial law methods of the revolutionary war. Throughout his tenure at Vesenkha, Piatakov sought to revive those methods, either through proposals to reconstitute labor conscription for industry or through arbitrary allocations of resources to the state's heavy industrial sectors.[15] Rozengol'ts likewise sharpened his command methods of economic administration as head of the Air Force. Consolidating administrative powers in a central state system was not just the means by which Piatakov, Gol'tsman, and company wanted to move the country toward rapid industrial modernization; for them, state-building was a goal in itself. What they wanted, in their own words, was not just to industrialize Russia but to create an industrial dictatorship.

The military-economic dictatorship established under Piatakov in the Donbass between 1919 and 1921 did not survive the period of war communism. With the coming of NEP, Piatakov, Rozengol'ts, Gol'tsman, and others remained loyal to Trotsky, but by the mid-1920s, Trotsky's influence had been eclipsed. Fearful of the one-time commander of the revolutionary armies, Stalin and the Party's other leaders successfully isolated Trotsky politically, and by the end of the decade he was in exile. With their patron gone, men such as Gol'tsman, Rozengol'ts, and Piatakov saw in Stalin the one individual who had the will to pull the country through the process of modernization and who had the authority and vision to create a powerful industrial state. Unfortunately for them, their connections to Trotsky came back to haunt them, and all were swept away in the purges of the 1930s. In the late 1920s, however, all were willing to renounce their ties to Trotsky and to follow Stalin and his lieutenant Ordzhonikidze. The work of these former Trotskyites at Rabkrin provided the institutional means for their rehabilitation, and all quickly rose to prominence in the RKI's campaign against Vesenkha in the late 1920s.

For many of these men, the change in loyalty from Trotsky to Stalin was not just a matter of political calculation and survival. Their candid comments and correspondence reveal a deep sense of emotional conversion and renewal. In 1930, at the height of the first five-year plan—during the most intense and hectic period of industrial construction—Rozengol'ts confided to his assistant Alexander Barmine, the later diplomat and refu-

[14]Valentinov, *Novaia ekonomicheskaia politika*, pp. 79, 81.

[15]Piatakov was so blatant in his "highhandedness" that Dzerzhinskii finally despaired of his deputy. Shortly before his death in 1926, Vesenkha's chief accused Piatakov of betraying NEP and of being the "biggest disorganizer of industry": ibid., p. 106.

gee, that the path Stalin was taking was "the only possible one" for the country.[16] V. Feigin, a Rabkrin inspector also tainted with former opposition leanings, expressed similar feelings. During a tour to mobilize Party activists in Ukraine in late 1930, Feigin wrote to Ordzhonikidze about the reborn sense of "zeal and energy" among the Party cadre, himself included. "Stalin's power and authority," wrote Feigin, "are great and are felt everywhere, and derive from the fact that he, earlier than anyone, understood." Feigin was awestruck by the force of Stalin's power (*sila*), which gave him an authority that Feigin described as "already legendary . . . greater than that wielded by anyone, ever." It was Stalin's power and authority, and only Stalin's, that made it possible "to set millions of people to the tasks of [our] construction."[17]

Such passages can be found in numerous letters from activists during this period. And for many, and not just former allies of Trotsky, one of the places to be, if one wanted to be at the forefront of building the new state, was in Rabkrin. Party activists and specialists wrote often to Ordzhonikidze or to his deputies seeking their help in expediting requests for transfer to the agency. A letter from Feigin to Ordzhonikidze in mid-1929 reveals how complex the personal and bureaucratic politics could be in matters of administrative appointments, and how much time and energy such matters consumed. Feigin thanked Ordzhonikidze profusely for his assistance so far in securing a position at Rabkrin. He reminded Ordzhonikidze that Iakovlev had also intervened on his behalf, going so far as to speak with Viacheslav Molotov, Stalin's close ally and one of the most powerful of the Party's leaders. Feigin noted, however, that Molotov spoke against his appointment, presumably because of his past activities, although Feigin did not specify exactly to which activities Molotov might have objected. Molotov was not well disposed toward Feigin, but in view of Feigin's economic expertise, Molotov told Iakovlev that he could be put to good use in Zemplan, the agricultural planning section of Gosplan. Feigin informed Ordzhonikidze that when his appointment was discussed in the Secretariat, where all high-level appointments were approved, no one from Rabkrin was there to speak up for him. Feigin was now afraid he would be sent to work in Zemplan, and the prospect distressed him. Zemplan, he wrote, did nothing but carry out the orders of Gosplan, and he felt his capabilities would be wasted there. "Why did I specialize in . . . large-scale mechanized economies when Zemplan has no interest in such matters?" Feigin assured Ordzhonikidze that he would "follow the RKI line anywhere," would do any work for the RKI, no matter what or where. "In short," Feigin wrote, "I prefer working for RKI in Vladivostok than for Zemplan in Moscow." In draw-

[16]Barmine, *Memoirs*, p. 309.

[17]V. Feigin to Ordzhonikidze, 31 December 1930, in RTsKhIDNI, f. 85, op. 27, d. 206, ll. 7–8.

ing analogies to his potentially unfortunate situation, Feigin invoked the name of John Stuart Mill. "Mill once wrote that it is better to be a dissatisfied philosopher than a contented pig. But I prefer to be a contented pig in RKI than a dissatisfied philosopher in Zemplan."[18] Feigin eventually got his wish.

Rabkrin's Inner Workings

Soon after his appointment as Rabkrin's chief, Ordzhonikidze made his intentions clear. He laid out the Inspectorate's priorities and warned the state apparatus that the agency intended to fulfill its function to discipline and control. In December 1926 Ordzhonikidze told a Vesenkha gathering that in the coming years, Rabkrin would pursue two fundamental tasks: it would fight against bureaucratization of the state and economic apparatus and it would "review the whole complex of the state system . . . from top to bottom." Ordzhonikidze promised that Rabkrin's work would delineate clear boundaries of authority. It would strengthen planning functions at the top and operational independence at the lower levels of the state's administrative apparatus. It would eliminate unnecessary bureaucratic levels between planning and operational bureaucracies and, most important, it would free the lower levels of the state apparatus from petty operational interference from higher up. To accomplish these tasks, Ordzhonikidze was asking the government to bolster Rabkrin's staff and give the agency special powers. It was already preparing plans to investigate the textile, metal, and forestry industries. So that no one missed his point, Ordzhonikidze let it be known that these investigations would be only the beginning of a long process. Though Ordzhonikidze's message was couched in diplomatic terms, its meaning was clear. Rabkrin had declared war against the country's economic administrative system.[19]

Ordzhonikidze kept his promises. In the course of four years, from 1927 through 1930, Rabkrin conducted hundreds of investigations of the state industrial system. The agency baited, prodded, and probed into every aspect of industrial and economic administration, from finance and cost accounting to production and labor organization to administrative rationalization. Rabkrin's plan for the 1929–30 fiscal year, for example, anticipated at least 124 investigative surveys: 21 under a presidium member, Ia. Kh. Peters, to establish procedures and schedules for purging the state bureaucracies, plus 68 under the heading of industry, 7 under transport, 11 of agriculture, and 17 in the area of trade.[20]

---

[18]Feigin to Ordzhonikidze, n.d. (mid-1929), ibid., ll. 2–3, 5.
[19]TPG, 3 December 1926, p. 1. For a description of Vesenkha-Rabkrin relations as a state of war, see GARF, f. 374, op. 1, d. 616, l. 175.
[20]See GARF, f. 374, op. 2, d. 55, ll. 1–19, 30–56.

Almost weekly, the agency brought to light scandalous examples of mismanagement and malfeasance: the supposed misuse of equipment and capital funds, bureaucratic redundancy, conscious sabotage, or, almost as bad, the hoarding of vast material resources needed for the socialist construction drive. The agency's surveys in 1927 and 1928 focused on high production costs in industry. It was Rabkrin, through its surveys, that made public the so-called crisis of technical leadership that so dominated industrial policy discussions in the late 1920s. It was Rabkrin that initiated the infamous campaigns to mobilize internal industrial resources in the late 1920s. It was Rabkrin's relentless attacks that drove industry's economic administration into disarray and finally into complete paralysis.

Rabkrin developed its industrial surveys and plans through the activities of its "working groups." A working or survey group consisted of seven to ten people from the central administrative apparatus headed by a highly placed official. Though small, the survey groups had wide-ranging powers. A Rabkrin team had the authority to demand any documents it deemed necessary from Vesenkha offices, and they had to be supplied even at short notice. RKI officials could require agencies to produce summary reports, again often on short notice, or summon agency officials to attend investigative meetings to give evidence. Such demands disrupted normal activity, and Rabkrin inspectors became the bane of industrial managers. Indeed, managers had good reasons to fear a Rabkrin investigation. Rabkrin's surveys were often highly publicized affairs. They focused unwanted attention on an agency or enterprise and usually brought it scandal or worse. Many investigations ended in criminal indictments. Managers whose enterprises were targeted for a Rabkrin survey knew they were in for a difficult time.

By hiring consultants, Rabkrin extended its influence and expertise far beyond the ability of the agency's relatively small number of salaried operatives. In working up plans or conducting surveys of trusts, factories, or other state agencies, RKI groups consulted closely with appropriate specialists. Rabkrin's officials relied heavily on consultants from the engineering and production design bureaus Orgametall and Gipromez, for example, and from ORNOT, a scientific management consulting group that the RKI sponsored jointly with Vesenkha. When Rabkrin commissions surveyed financial institutions or the account books of a firm or trust, it drew on the expertise of accountants and financial experts from Narkomfin (the Commissariat of Finance) and Gosbank. According to Rabkrin's survey documents, the accountants who did much of the investigative work on Iugostal' in 1928 were Narkomfin officials. Piatakov and other Gosbank officials worked with a Rabkrin commission chaired by A. M. Fushman to develop and implement the credit and finance reforms of early 1930.

Rabkrin survey commissions also turned for help to local RKI and even

OGPU officials. E. M. Al'perovich, for example, headed Orgametall, the state engineering and rationalization bureau, but he was also employed by the Moscow office of the RKI. During the last years of the 1920s, Al'-perovich worked often with Rabkrin survey groups under the supervision of Mikhail Kaganovich. Al'perovich played an important role in Kaganovich's surveys of production and planning for the Soviet machine building and engineering industries.[21] So did OGPU investigators, who made up a significant proportion of the Rabkrin contingent that surveyed Iugostal' and its factories in 1928 and 1929. The Southern Trust had become a major focus of investigation into counterrevolutionary sabotage during this period, and police used much of the material gathered from Rabkrin's surveys. Throughout 1928 and 1929, both Rabkrin and police officials maintained a constant presence in the trust's administrative offices and in its factories.[22]

The survey groups may have comprised only a few people from Rabkrin USSR, but because of the agency's influence, its working groups could mobilize dozens of cadres at various governmental levels and in various agencies to do its work. Rabkrin extended its influence further by employing members of the Komsomol, the Communist youth organization, to collect material for inclusion in survey reports. Indeed, Komsomol groups fashioned themselves as the shock troops of the RKI in the factories. Rabkrin officials even tried, unsuccessfully, to extend their influence within the professional engineering strata. At a conference called by Rabkrin in July 1929, A. Z. Gol'tsman attempted to organize specialists "with the sanction of Rabkrin to treat issues not specifically within Rabkrin's purview." The journalist who reported on the meeting did not enumerate what issues Gol'tsman had in mind, but he noted that Gol'tsman compared this organization to the Komsomol movement. If the Young Communists were Rabkrin's "light cavalry," Gol'tsman offered, then this new organization of engineers and economists would be Rabkrin's "heavy artillery." Try as he might, however, Gol'tsman failed to move the meeting with his military metaphors. His resolution was formally approved, but the reporter noted that specialists' reactions varied from a polite lack of enthusiasm to open hostility.[23]

When one of Rabkrin's survey groups prepared to conduct its investigation, its members began by reading documentary "evidence": production and financial reports, memoranda, reports of previous survey groups, and any other material contained in an enterprise's files. This material helped

[21]The often low level of professional qualification of RKI consulting specialists is discussed in Davies, *Soviet Economy in Turmoil*, pp. 189–90, 198, 397.

[22]A copy of the OGPU report on counterrevolutionary activities in Iugostal' is in GARF, f. 374, op. 27s, d. 1536, ll. 10–14; Rozengolt's' report to the STO is on ll. 38–40.

[23]*TPG*, 18 July 1929, p. 2.

the survey group identify specific areas to review when it conducted its on-site investigations. In RKI parlance, survey leaders drew up a list of investigative "targets." Once it compiled its list of survey targets, the central group contacted local or republic RKI, police, and Party agencies to enlist help with the survey.

When Rabkrin conducted surveys of Ukrainian heavy machine building industries, for example, the agency mobilized a total of thirty-eight survey groups drawn from its central apparatus, Gipromez, the Ukrainian RKI, and local Party and Inspectorate offices. In all, these groups surveyed eight works. Nineteen of the teams descended upon the Lugansk locomotive works alone and stayed for a month, from 10 December 1928 through 12 January 1929. Their investigations covered twenty-four shops or offices, including the trust's administrative apparatus. Fifty-five of seventy-five factory technical personnel were interviewed or in some way participated in the survey. According to Rabkrin's report, close to 2,000 workers also "participated," in addition to Party, trade union, and Komsomol organizations in the factory.[24]

This was a typical scenario for a Rabkrin survey, and no major factory or trust was exempt from it. Moreover, a factory endured this kind of scrutiny not just once but as often as thirty times a year.[25] Most surveys, but not all, were conducted by Rabkrin. Vesenkha had its own inspectorate, as did Narkomtrud (the labor commissariat), NKTPS (the transportation commissariat), Narkomtorg (the state's trade organization), the OGPU, and numerous other agencies. And, of course, there were the numerous investigations conducted by special commissions of the Central Committee. Party surveys were not included in the listings of state agencies, so it is impossible to ascertain exactly how many surveys the Southern Metal Trust, for example, may have suffered. The number could have been close to thirty-five or forty for a difficult year such as 1928 or 1929.

Some of Rabkrin's survey reports ran to hundreds of pages. Questionnaires sent to factory personnel were voluminous and detailed. A Central Committee investigation in 1930 estimated that factory personnel spent five to six hours daily doing nothing but filling out survey questionnaires or participating in on-site inspections.[26] Industrial officials complained so often about such harassment that eventually the government reached the height of bureaucratic comedy by ordering a survey of surveys; that is, a series of investigations of the government's entire inspectorate system.[27]

As the state's primary control agency, Rabkrin took the initiative in this matter, even though it was Rabkrin that clearly initiated the greatest num-

[24]GARF, f. 374, op. 15, d. 45, ll. 1–2.
[25]This figure was given by I. I. Matrozov in TPG, 4 October 1928.
[26]RTsKhIDNI, f. 17, op. 113, d. 831, l. 27.
[27]See, e.g., "Issledovanie issledovanii" (A survey of surveys), TPG, 26 May 1928, p. 2.

ber of investigations of industrial enterprises. By the early spring of 1928, Rabkrin had completed its initial review. As expected, agency officials argued in April that since Rabkrin was the state's official inspectorate organ, it should regulate the number and kinds of surveys conducted in order to reduce bureaucratic overlap and a multiplicity of control functions.[28] Sovnarkom agreed, and on 30 May, after its own investigations, the government and Rabkrin issued a joint directive on the elimination of multiple control mechanisms.

Henceforward, Rabkrin required all commissariats and other governmental institutions to submit any plans for survey work to Rabkrin. These plans had to be completed on proper forms, which, of course, were drawn up by Rabkrin officials. After review of the various survey requests, Rabkrin would inform the agency whether it could proceed with its investigation or whether its surveys would conflict with its own. Vesenkha protested vigorously the loss of its right to survey its own factories without Rabkrin's express permission, but Sovnarkom upheld its earlier decision.[29]

To add insult to injury, Rabkrin also required Vesenkha to submit the forms it used for quarterly control figures for Rabkrin's approval before distributing them to the various industrial branches to be completed. In at least several cases, Vesenkha was forced to complain publicly that Rabkrin sat on the forms for up to ten months past the time for their distribution.[30] It was ironic that the agency designed to reduce bureaucracy created so much, and Vesenkha officials may have drawn some satisfaction from being able to accuse Rabkrin, for a change, of bureaucratic red tape. Still, in making such a public accusation, Vesenkha officials acknowledged the authority Rabkrin wielded over such a powerful governmental bureaucracy as the Supreme Economic Council. To acknowledge that Rabkrin second-guessed everything Vesenkha did must have cost Vesenkha officials a good measure of embarrassment.

Rabkrin's cavalier treatment of Vesenkha also aroused a great deal of resentment, which some Vesenkha officials were not shy about expressing. At an August 1929 meeting, one high-level official from the Russian Republic Vesenkha, Egorov, openly scolded Rabkrin officials for withholding accounting data: "We take careful pains to tabulate all these figures on production, labor, fuels, and you take it and say, 'No, comrade! We will not give this back to you for three months,' and we don't even see it then. How can we regulate and run industry this way? This is just one more example of our so-called Bolshevik 'flexibility,' which means that the state bank and Rabkrin can run industry any way they please." Egorov accused Rabkrin officials of treating him and other industrial managers "like dirt"

---

[28]*TPG*, 7 June 1928, p. 3, and 26 July 1928, p. 1.
[29]*TPG*, 7 June 1928, p. 3, and 10 January 1929, p. 1.
[30]*TPG*, 22 July 1928.

("Vy menia s graz'iu meshali"). Finally, he delivered what he must have considered the most stinging insult. In Germany, he declared, such a thing would not happen. There managers had access to accounting data on a daily basis. This was the secret of their success.[31]

Rabkrin's management of survey procedures and accounting materials carried serious implications. Vesenkha officials understood that these measures enabled Rabkrin to control the form and timing of the information Vesenkha received about its own industrial system. Serious doubts may have arisen about the accuracy of control figures, but these were the figures that officials used to make policy, and Rabkrin controlled access to them. Through its maneuvering, the Inspectorate became the gatekeeper to the information needed for industrial planning and administration.

This was only one of the means by which Rabkrin exerted influence and shaped policy; the RKI challenged Vesenkha in more direct ways. In July 1928, for example, on the basis of a preliminary series of production surveys headed by A. Z. Gol'tsman, Rabkrin recommended a 10 percent decrease in production costs for the operational year instead of the 3.9 percent targeted by Vesenkha. *Torgovo-promyshlennaia gazeta* reported the recommendation as Rabkrin's "opinion," but the government accepted the Inspectorate's arguments and ordered Vesenkha to find ways to reduce costs by at least 7 percent.[32]

In writing to Ordzhonikidze a month later, Gol'tsman pointed to the negotiations over industrial costs as a significant precedent. He informed RKI's leader that, while publicly trust leaders objected to the 10 percent figure, privately Iugostal' officials told Gol'tsman that such a goal was, "of course, feasible." "This means," wrote Gol'tsman, as if in surprise, "that RKI pays more attention to the details of production than VSNKh does." Vesenkha's "weak" preparation on the issue of costs "tells me that in the future we should make it our special task to conduct surveys, confirm all of VSNKh's figures, and insist on their inclusion [i.e., Rabkrin's figures] in industrial planning." Unable to trust Vesenkha's calculations, Gol'tsman recommended that from then on RKI "closely review" all decisions by the various trusts' production conferences. He further recommended that, starting in the autumn of 1928, Rabkrin begin a series of "much wider surveys" than the preliminary cost survey—at least one-third of all commissariats to start—and several local economic councils as well, "to expose their practices."[33]

Gol'tsman's letter reveals the kind of conscious strategizing in which Rabkrin's officials engaged in order to extend the agency's influence. Gol'tsman, for example, laid out a series of steps—specific administrative

[31]GARF, f. 374, op. 1, d. 616, l. 233.
[32]*TPG*, 27 July 1928.
[33]RTsKhIDNI, f. 85, op. 27, d. 205, ll. 3, 7, 11.

appointments, strategically placed and strategically timed political speeches, and the control of survey groups and information—to bring factory and shop production conferences under Rabkrin's direct control. Gol'tsman agreed with Ordzhonikidze's apparently earlier suggestion that any action by the RKI should be taken in coordination with the trade union organizations, which nominally administered the production conferences. Yet with well-placed people at various levels of the industrial system, he argued, Rabkrin could use the conference system to gain information and influence in factory shops. The conferences could be used to transmit recommendations and influence popular opinion, and thereby gain leverage over managers on a range of issues that affected labor productivity and work organization in industry.[34]

Gol'tsman also recommended deliberate obfuscation of the agency's intention to reorganize and administer the system of credit, monetary, and materials transactions within state industry. "Among ourselves," he wrote, "we will use the term internal industrial turnover. Publicly, however, we should formulate this in something like the following way: 'distribution of basic types of fuels and materials among state industrial enterprises, review of organizational forms of such distribution, and clarification of possibilities for its simplification.'" Gol'tsman argued that such a ruse was necessary to diffuse potential resistance from syndicates and financial institutions to any reforms that explicitly referred to credit, accounting, turnover, or money. Rabkrin had already clashed with the syndicates over credit issues, and Gol'tsman was wary of another public fight. "These are issues you don't want to rehash [*perechitat'*]." Finally, Gol'tsman recommended, apparently in response to Ordzhonikidze's query, that the agency "not yet make too many suggestions in the area of industrial reorganization. The novelty might frighten someone." Rabkrin was already beginning to push Vesenkha hard, and Gol'tsman felt it was too soon to raise questions of root reorganization. For the present, he suggested, Rabkrin should make only specific piecemeal recommendations.[35]

Gol'tsman's sense of strategy in the realm of bureaucratic infighting was matched by the agency's ability to manipulate its public image. By the late 1920s, the Stalinist faction had gained significant control over media outlets, but not yet a complete monopoly. Vesenkha still had a powerful voice, especially through its daily newspaper, *Torgovo-promyshlennaia gazeta*, and its editors did not hesitate to air their differences with Rabkrin policies. Still, the Inspectorate's officials were masterful in their use of the media. When Rabkrin completed a survey, it made its recommendations known in reports to Sovnarkom. Often the agency held open hearings as well, to which it invited relevant Vesenkha officials. These hearings were

[34]Ibid., l. 8.
[35]Ibid, l. 9.

covered by the press, of course, but they were also preceded and followed by Rabkrin's own highly orchestrated publicity campaigns. In addition to its own journal, *Za ratsionalizatsiiu* (For rationalization), Rabkrin publicized its findings in the two major state and Party organs, *Izvestiia* and *Pravda*. Often Rabkrin was also able to gain coverage in Vesenkha's own *Torgovo-promyshlennaia gazeta*. As Vesenkha's newspaper of record, it published Rabkrin's criticisms.

Typically Rabkrin built anticipation by releasing preliminary press reports suggesting wide discrepancies between its own and Vesenkha's calculations. Stories would often hint at the discovery of large-scale corruption and mismanagement or criminal negligence on the part of economic managers. Rabkrin officials were not at all averse to giving advance notice that its investigations, in whatever survey or campaign was being reported, would most likely end in serious allegations of wrongdoing for the agency under scrutiny.

The language of Rabkrin's press attacks was shrill and inflammatory, politically charged with innuendo and accusations of counterrevolutionary sabotage. In Rabkrin's accounts, whatever Vesenkha did was misdirected, consciously or unconsciously, and kept the Soviet economy mired in backwardness and hopeless tutelage to the powerful capitalist industrial states. Rabkrin's own recommendations, in contrast, were presented as models of modernization, efficiency, and socialist progress. Thus, by the time Rabkrin held its hearings, Vesenkha officials were already at a disadvantage. Tried and convicted in Rabkrin's press campaigns, Vesenkha officials appeared in the role of defendants at a revolutionary court of justice, not as official state representatives.

Planning the Parts but Not the Whole

Rabkrin's reports made detailed recommendations on every aspect of production and administration. In the autumn of 1929, for example, Rabkrin held a series of hearings, based on its surveys, dealing with the manufacture of diesel engines. In October the agency transmitted its directions for improvement in this area "to all the appropriate trusts, glavki, and factories." These instructions, as was usually the case with Rabkrin recommendations, represented direct orders from the government and were not open to discussion. Rabkrin advised the respective enterprises or organizations to "take appropriate action on the basis of these instructions and in accordance with Rabkrin's resolutions."[36]

Rabkrin began its instructions by requiring Vesenkha to establish what specific types of diesel engines would be needed for the whole of the five-

[36]GARF, f. 374, op. 1, d. 462, l. 325.

year plan period. Vesenkha was to keep in mind Rabkrin's already expanded plans for shipbuilding, construction of local power stations, and tractor output. These calculations were to be supplied to Rabkrin by 1 January 1930, a little over two months after the date of the request. By the beginning of April 1930, Rabkrin required Vesenkha to establish where the diesel engines were to be produced, "keeping in mind Rabkrin's directives on specialization of industrial production." Rabkrin suggested that no more than "several" factories be specialized for mass production of diesels. At the same time, the RKI enjoined Vesenkha to "ensure that no single enterprise specialize in more than four types of diesel manufacture." Rabkrin underscored that there should be no production overlap between factories.[37]

Rabkrin issued suggestions for specific types of diesel manufacture and asked Vesenkha to submit within two months a timetable for the manufacture of standardized parts. The Inspectorate gave further recommendations for specific types of specialty steels and aluminum alloys that Glavmashinstroi was to produce. Suggestions also included specifications for production of new types of oils, lubricants, and fuels. Rabkrin established a timetable for all this work and provided figures on the number of specialists and types of workers who would have to be transferred to work in this area. It reminded Vesenkha to make the appropriate adjustments in other areas of machine manufacture.

Rabkrin's recommendations for new diesel production amounted to fifteen pages of narrow-margin single-spaced typed script. Its final instruction was to S. K. Sud'in, head of the original survey team: he was to carry out a follow-up survey by the beginning of August 1930 to ensure that all measures were being fulfilled. The recommendations were signed by A. P. Rozengol'ts, deputy commissar.[38]

Vesenkha would have been hard pressed to carry out these instructions within the allotted time, even if diesel production had been an isolated case. Yet during this period, 1928–30, Rabkrin bombarded Vesenkha constantly with new production demands that created wrenching disruptions in normal administrative and production procedures. In September 1929, officials of the machine building administration protested that it was impossible to implement RKI's orders; they were simply overwhelmed. Trusts and factories were short of personnel as it was, and as soon as they would mobilize to achieve the goals of one campaign, they would receive instructions to gear up for yet another mobilization.[39]

Stepan Birman, the head of Iugostal', also complained about Rabkrin's

[37]Ibid., l. 327.
[38]Ibid., l. 330.
[39]Glavmashinstroi officials referred specifically to the campaign to implement one-man management and to reduce production costs in 1929. See RTsKhIDNI, f. 17, op. 74, d. 30, l. 99.

disruptive effect on industrial management. At Vesenkha's fourth plenum, in November 1928, Birman evoked sympathy by parodying the way Rabkrin officials "blithely" demanded root organizational changes "while we managers are locked in the midst of complex production tasks."[40] A year later, the tenacious Birman was sounding the same theme. In October 1929 he acknowledged that administrators often failed to cooperate with RKI surveys, because every Rabkrin survey resulted in higher production quotas or lowered targets for production costs. Such constant interference disrupted production, he complained, and he chastised Kuibyshev for acceding so easily to Rabkrin's every demand.[41]

Despite such complaints, Rabkrin continued its pressure on Vesenkha. Throughout 1928, 1929, and 1930, Rabkrin's groups made detailed recommendations in every sector of the industrial economy. Rabkrin's surveys always called for expansion of existing production or for new production and for corresponding changes in industrial administration. The Inspectorate called for centralized and expanded trust administrations in such branches as textile machine manufacture, turbine production, and the manufacture of machine tools and other equipment.

Here, in Rabkrin's relentless pressure on Vesenkha, was the origin not only of the constant recalculation of industrial targets but also of much of the disjointed, helter-skelter planning that so characterized the Soviet industrialization drive. Rabkrin issued its orders as revolutionary military commands. As the case of diesel manufacture shows, the RKI demanded increases in production, labor resources, and raw materials, yet it offered no suggestions as to how Vesenkha officials were to juggle already strained production schedules and labor resources to accomplish the tasks Rabkrin set before them. Rabkrin reports never indicated where Vesenkha was to obtain new materials or how it was to compensate for the transfer of labor or the disruption caused in production and delivery schedules. Recommendations simply ordered Vesenkha to compensate appropriately. Each new instruction from Rabkrin became a crisis for Vesenkha. What little economic planning and coordination had existed went for naught as officials responded to each new order. The problem, as one trust official put it, was not that there was no plan, but that there was a new plan every week.[42]

The disorder created by this campaign-cum-crisis style of management was exacerbated by the lack of coordination among Rabkrin's own economic working groups. RKI reports and the revisions that resulted from them were conducted in piecemeal fashion. Rabkrin officials rarely coordi-

[40]TPG, 1 December 1929, p. 2.
[41]S. P. Birman, "Osnovnie momenty raboty Iugostali, 1928–1929," Metall, October 1929, no. 10, p. 103.
[42]RGAE, f. 5716, op. 2, d. 2, l. 143.

nated or integrated the results of their various survey groups. The agency issued floods of detailed instructions in nearly every area of industrial and economic activity, yet it developed no overall industrial strategy beyond a sweeping but vague commitment to technological modernization and mass production. Despite the interdependence of production and supply, production plans developed in one sector, based on RKI criticisms and recommendations, were not coordinated with policies recommended in other areas. Rabkrin's orders and demands drove the industrial economy, but it was the haphazardness of these investigations, not any systematic planning, that defined the priorities and the style of Soviet industrial administration.

The consequences of Rabkrin's campaign style of administration were devastating. Managers at every level of the industrial system were forced into constant recalculations, based on the latest shift in production targets or the latest changes in organizational structure. The supposed discovery of vast unused reserves in metal-fabricating factories, for example, led to upward revisions in the production targets of the machine building industry. This move forced reassessment of metallurgical production, machine tool manufacture, and so on in numerous industrial sectors. The imbalances created by Rabkrin's surveys and orders rolled through the economy like shock waves, disrupting any attempt at systematic planning and administration. Here, in Rabkrin's campaign-style approach to economic management, was the origin of the Stalinist penchant for "planning without a plan."[43]

Rabkrin and the Campaign Economy

Ironically, the more Rabkrin interfered in Vesenkha's affairs, the more it fomented crisis in the state's administrative apparatus. Yet the RKI's officials always attributed that crisis to Vesenkha's incompetence or to political sabotage. Having helped create an administrative nightmare in the Vesenkha system, Rabkrin's surveys then confirmed the inability of economic and industrial managers to cope with the demands placed on them. Follow-up surveys nearly always showed that industrial officials had not implemented Rabkrin's or the government's recommendations, and further administrative action would be required. In this way, Rabkrin's highest officials moved inevitably from checking figures and making recommendations to direct and almost daily administration of the economy. Indeed, letters from Rozengol'ts, Gol'tsman, Kaganovich, Gurevich, and others to Ordzhonikidze and to one another are filled with the stuff of daily management: so many tons of sheet metal from this factory, so many

[43]Moshe Lewin, "The Disappearance of Planning in the Plan," *Slavic Review* 32 (June 1973): 271–87.

tons of pig iron to that enterprise.[44] Rabkrin officials attempted to supervise all reconstruction projects of the various industrial branches, often overturning plans submitted by local trust and regional authorities or by committees of the state's design agency, Gipromez.[45] Within a few years, Rabkrin displaced Vesenkha as the central authority in Soviet industry.

Rozengol'ts openly boasted of Rabkrin's takeover of the economy at the 11th Ukrainian Communist Party Congress in 1930. He also made clear the model on which Rabkrin based its administrative methods. Warning his audience that the "old" ways were over, by which he meant NEP, Rabkrin's deputy chief made a direct reference to the martial law administration of the revolutionary war period. "We achieved victory," he said, "only because we maneuvered material resources and cadre in the most expedient way."[46] Rozengol'ts, like his comrades in the RKI, had earned his reputation as a tough economic administrator in the Bolshevik army in Ukraine. His reference in 1930 to the militarized methods of that earlier period was not a casual one, especially to that particular audience. Those were the methods Rozengol'ts had in mind as most appropriate for the new civil war being fought over industrialization. He informed his listeners that the Party and state organs would revive those methods.

There was nothing subtle or secret about the return to militarized economic administration. "Mobilization of the population's funds" (*mobilizatsiia sredstv naseleniia*) was the official name given to the various campaigns to extract capital from the economy and the general public. Those campaigns encompassed the confiscation of everything from grain to commodities in warehouses and the money in savings banks to provide capital for the industrialization drive. All parts of the state administrative apparatus, all levels of the Party, and even the military and security organs were mobilized for these campaigns. Rabkrin played a key role in this drive because its extensive survey work had helped locate and identify economic resources and an extensive network of agents and activists to administer the military campaign economy it had helped create.

Nothing characterized Rabkrin's style of administration more than its campaigns to mobilize industrial resources. Rabkrin emphasized the importance of reducing industrial costs to create savings and accumulate capital, but the agency made its primary focus the other major source of capital extraction: direct mobilization of materials and labor. Vesenkha officials acknowledged the need to use resources effectively, but the two agencies differed fundamentally over how much was available to mo-

---

[44]See, e.g., RTsKhIDNI, f. 85, op. 27, dd. 200, 205, 206, 214, and op. 1s, d. 91. See also GARF, f. 374, op. 28s, d. 3547.

[45]For the metal industries esp. see GARF, f. 374, op. 28s, d. 3547, and follow-up suveys by Gurevich's group of southern metal industries ibid., d. 3449.

[46]Rozengol'ts, *Za sotsializm protiv biurokratizma*, pp. 27, 37. See his detailed discussion, pp. 6–34.

bilize and the way to go about putting those resources to work. Though clumsy and slow in their efforts, Vesenkha officials approached administration of resources in a methodical and measured way, combining administrative, tax, and commercial mechanisms. Rabkrin's methods corresponded more to the Bolsheviks' revolutionary sense of impatience with history. Rabkrin's various mobilization campaigns had all the characteristics of a Bolshevik project: the rhetoric of a Civil War military campaign, the administrative command style of execution, and the appeal to storm barricades, mobilize masses, and create immediate, visible, and huge results.

Rabkrin conducted several surveys of industrial resources in 1928, the largest in October. Under Gol'tsman's leadership, RKI teams surveyed twenty-eight trusts, including eight metal and twelve textile cartels. Rabkrin divided the rest of the surveys among the forestry, chemical, and paper manufacturing industries. The RKI reported to Sovnarkom in March 1929 that these trusts' undeclared reserves amounted to nearly half of all the materials they would need to fulfill their collective production programs for the current operational year. These reserves, the Inspectorate noted, far exceeded the three-month norms that Vesenkha allowed factories to maintain.[47]

According to Rabkrin, the state's metal factories were the worst offenders. The Inspectorate's surveys discovered that the Southern Machine Building Trust, IuMT, maintained an undeclared reserve of metal materials, fuels, and semifabricates for ten months of continuous production. The Leningrad Shipbuilding Trust had enough reserves to last for eighteen months, Lenmashtrest for fourteen months, Mosmashtrest for eight months, and Iugostal' for seven months. Rabkrin's group estimated that Vesenkha could mobilize 200 million rubles from the twenty-eight trusts in its survey and 850 million rubles' worth of reserve materials overall in the state's industrial system.[48]

Under pressure from Rabkrin, in December 1928 Vesenkha organized its own special mobilization commission under the dual chairmanship of A. B. Shtern, head of the financial department of the PEU, and G. Lakin, deputy head of Vesenkha's inspectorate. Though the commission expected an economic boost from the mobilization of reserves, it also warned against high expectations.[49] Vesenkha's caution was not surprising since Shtern, formerly of the Commissariat of Finance, was a fiscal conservative. He had been brought to Vesenkha by Feliks Dzerzhinskii in the early 1920s as one of the numerous Menshevik and nonparty specialists who were levelheaded administrators with expertise in industrial economics

[47]GARF, f. 374, op. 15, d. 596, l. 35.
[48]Ibid., l. 40.
[49]TPG, 11 December 1928.

and finance.[50] True to his training and temperament, Shtern opposed any measures that would radically upset what he considered the orderly administration of finance and industry.

On the one hand, Shtern's appointment made sense from the standpoint of officials who sought protection against Rabkrin's pressure. On the other hand, his strong Menshevik leanings and Kuibyshev's commitment to rid the economic council of just such influences made Shtern a curious choice. According to the memoirist Valentinov, Stalin placed Kuibyshev in the agency with specific instructions to "beat down" the non-Stalinist intelligentsia. This Kuibyshev did "without sluggishness," Valentinov reported, demoting Mensheviks such as Shtern and A. M. Ginzburg.[51]

Kuibyshev made it clear how the commission was to proceed. He told Shtern in no uncertain terms to "'forget about making a disgraceful counterrevolutionary mongrel out of the five-year plan. What we need is real industrialization . . . not a caricature of it.'" In effect, Kuibyshev told Shtern to extract any and all reserves from industrial enterprises and trusts, and that anything less would be regarded as counterrevolutionary. Shtern, however, refused to heed Kuibyshev's warning and continued to defend Vesenkha's interests, as he perceived them.[52]

In the meantime, Rabkrin officials, following their usual practice, leaked preliminary findings of their surveys to the newspaper during the last months of 1928 and the early weeks of 1929. These findings told of "huge" amounts of reserves being hidden by unscrupulous industrial managers, and of "ever new" discoveries of fuel and production material in various branches of the economy. Shtern responded that the figures were "greatly exaggerated," and that the government should proceed with caution in its policies of direct industrial mobilization.[53]

As expected, Vesenkha's preliminary report to Sovnarkom in late February differed considerably from Rabkrin's calculations. Because of the increasing strain on the economy, Vesenkha expected it could squeeze at most another 100 million rubles out of existing reserves. Sovnarkom noted the discrepancy between Vesenkha's figures and the 200 to 800 million rubles reported by Rabkrin. While not taking a position, the government urged Vesenkha to work with Rabkrin and Gosbank to find material and financial sources above those reported by the Shtern commission.[54] Rab-

---

[50]For more on Shtern as an "excellent" worker and on other nonparty specialists, see Valentinov, *Novaia ekonomicheskaia politiku,* pp. 127-36.

[51]Ibid., p. 140.

[52]Ibid., p. 140. Shtern died (committed suicide, according to Valentinov) just before he was to be arrested in 1931.

[53]E.g., *TPG,* 5 and 8 February 1929. In a meeting in January the syndicates' governing council also assessed the mobilization campaign as "incorrect," and as threatening to distort trade and supply balances in the economy. The council agreed, however, to remain part of the Shtern commission. See RGAE, f. 3915, op. 1, d. 241, l. 63.

[54]GARF, f. 374, op. 1, d. 596, ll. 37-38.

krin did not drop the matter, but dogged Vesenkha throughout the year. Rabkrin's other survey groups, especially the industrial branch and rationalization groups, maintained the pressure on Vesenkha and kept the issue of surplus resources in the public eye. In July, for example, *Torgovo-promyshlennaia gazeta* published an article that accused factories and trusts of falsifying inventories in order to avoid compliance with Rabkrin's order to mobilize resources. The next month Shtern responded, noting that in German industry, as inventory reserves increased over the course of the 1920s, so did capital turnover. Large amounts of reserve materials in stock, Shtern pointedly emphasized, allowed factories to respond quickly to shifts in consumer demand, thus "stimulat[ing] the business cycle." Conversely, during economic downturns warehouse inventories declined, "but so did turnover, even more."[55]

Shtern's economic logic may have been arguable, but his point was clear: the state would get more capital and productivity out of industry if it refrained from the extractive policies of the mobilization campaign. I. V. Kosior, a vice chairman of Vesenkha and one of its most influential presidium members, agreed with Shtern. Trusts, Kosior declared, should be allowed to keep the resources they generated and be left alone to use those resources to increase trade and production.[56] In a rare example of trust-syndicate agreement, syndicate officials also complained in January 1929 about Rabkrin's proposed tax increases on industrial and commercial enterprises. The proposed hike in taxes levied against the syndicates, from 2 to 17 million rubles a year, would restrict trade and slow capital turnover dangerously, they argued.[57]

Warnings about Rabkrin's tax and extract policies had little effect. In October 1929, Rozengol'ts once again publicly chastised Vesenkha for failure to do all it could to mobilize reserves, implement rationalization measures, maximize the use of equipment, and reduce costs to meet the government's ambitious industrial plans. As of 1 October, those plans required expenditures of an extra billion rubles over planned costs for the 1929–30 operational year.[58] As Rabkrin pushed for higher production targets, increasingly dramatic cost reductions, and higher taxes, Vesenkha was forced into the kind of crisis mobilization that characterized Rabkrin's own style of management. By forcing an economic crisis on Vesenkha, Rabkrin exaggerated the very shortages it was determined to eliminate and in doing so remade Vesenkha in its own image.

The first indication that a new push was under way came in late sum-

[55]*TPG*, 10 July and 8 August 1929.
[56]*TPG*, 1 December 1928.
[57]See the syndicates' discussion of RKI's tax proposals in RGAE, f. 3915, op. 1, d. 241, ll. 5–11. Syndicate leaders argued that on the basis of their yearly turnover of goods, they should be taxed no more than 2 to 3 million rubles. See also *TPG*, 30 September 1928, p. 2.
[58]*TPG*, 10 October 1929.

mer 1929, when Shtern was replaced by M. L. Rukhimovich as head of Vesenkha's mobilization campaign. Rukhimovich was also a member of Vesenkha's presidium and, from Rabkrin's point of view, well chosen for the task. Rukhimovich had been a close ally of Stalin and Ordzhonikidze since 1921, when he headed the executive committee of the Donbass regional Party organization. There he had been instrumental in mobilizing the local economy to supply the Bolshevik Tenth Army and had acted as one of Stalin's chief agents in the fight against Trotsky and Trotsky's ally Georgii Piatakov.[59] In February 1929, Rukhimovich was once again in Ukraine, applying the same methods to mobilize the economy for industrialization. As head of one of Vesenkha's mobilization commissions, Rukhimovich was finding "huge" reserves of fuels, raw materials, labor, and underused equipment.[60]

Rukhimovich's Civil War experience convinced him that the Soviet industrial economy should be organized by administrative rather than economic means. As the new head of Vesenkha's mobilization campaign, he adapted readily to Rabkrin's methods. In military fashion, Rabkrin gave the orders and Rukhimovich executed the instructions to form a "command staff" (komanduiushchii shtab) in each chief administration for the economic mobilization campaign. In Glavmashinstroi, Tolokontsev and V. F. Oborin "commanded" a campaign staff of forty specialists—engineers, economists, accountants—who were pulled from their regular assignments to work in the mobilization campaign. The "staff" received their "fighting orders" in the early autumn of 1929.[61]

The main problem for Tolokontsev and company was to find manufacturers for the thousands of new orders that flooded the chief administration as industrialization gathered steam. Throughout the last three months of 1929, Vesenkha's newspaper was filled with accounts of the frantic scramble by trusts and glavki to find unused or underused production capacity. Oborin's staff began with surveys of Glavmashinstroi's own factories, but quickly resorted to outright expropriation, despite sharp protest, of shops in republican and local-level factories to fill all-union orders.[62]

Throughout the autumn, survey teams with plenipotentiary powers were sent to major industrial centers. Their instructions were to place orders, regardless of circumstances. "Listen to no excuses . . . about 'objective conditions,'" Tolokontsev instructed them, "accept no arguments about the lack of labor, metal, or technical personnel. We're familiar with the deaf resistance of our factory directors, and it cannot be tolerated."[63]

[59]For more on Rukhimovich's role in the Donbass, see Graziosi, "At the Roots," pp. 16, 41.
[60]See TPG, 5 and 10 February 1929.
[61]TPG, 26 October 1929, gives a partial list.
[62]TPG, 31 October 1929.
[63]TPG, 5 November 1929.

Even powerful trust heads such as Birman of Iugostal' and Mikhailov of Lenmashtrest were forced to submit to the new strains imposed by Vesenkha and Rabkrin.

In the meantime, Oborin's mobilization staff created chaos out of Vesenkha's administrative system. To satisfy the crushing demands of the ever-changing control figures, the command staff shifted orders from factory to factory, regardless of specialization, production requirements, or production plans. They ordered machine tools from shipbuilding shops and boilers from locomotive factories. When directors protested, they were told to make do. The command staff forced the chief metallurgical administration, Glavchermet, to forfeit to Glavmashinstroi repair and auxiliary shops in the Urals and southern metal-producing factories. Glavmashinstroi commandeered twenty-two railroad repair shops belonging to the transport commissariat and "numerous undiscovered" auxiliary engineering shops at oil-producing and mining complexes. According to one engineer, these so-called repair shops were in fact fully outfitted factories containing, all told, close to 2,000 machine tools. The engineer estimated that Glavmashinstroi could squeeze out another 70 million rubles' worth of production from the railroad shops and additional tens of millions from auxiliary and repair facilities belonging to the oil trusts Grozneft and Azneft.[64]

The campaign to mobilize resources was not the only campaign forced on the industrial apparatus by Rabkrin. The creation of special *shtaby* or the dispatch of plenipotentiary commissions became routine in the glavki. Their formation disrupted normal operating procedure, and as commissions with special authority arrived in factories and trusts, all other activities stopped or were subordinated to the fulfillment of the commissions' task. Thus the institutionalization of this militarized campaign economy both resulted from and helped exaggerate the near-permanent state of crisis in industrial administration in the latter years of the decade.

Vesenkha's bureaucratic style of economic administration, though often ineffectual, should not be conflated with the campaign-cum-crisis style of management forced upon it by Rabkrin. Though it was abused and often had stultifying results, Vesenkha's administrative system was a classic bureaucracy, based on a drive for order, process, and stability. Rabkrin's military campaign approach, derived from the experience of its top officials in Civil War political and economic administration, distinguished it from the ponderous bureaucratic methods of Vesenkha on the one hand and the commercial culture of the syndicates on the other. In the late 1920s, as the country's economic crisis deepened, Rabkrin's officials revived and imposed a Civil War style of mobilization on the country's industrial system.

[64]*TPG*, 27 November, 23 October, and 25 December 1929.

Vesenkha fights Back

Valerian Kuibyshev offered no resistance to the RKI—understandably, since Stalin had placed him in charge of Vesenkha in order to bring the agency under the control of his own Party faction. Influential sectoral leaders and heads of regional industrial trusts, however, opposed the centralizing aspects of the RKI's strategy as well as its constant harassment of managerial officials. Stepan Birman of Iugostal'; S. S. Lobov, the caustic and energetic head of the Russian Vesenkha; and Mikhailov of Lenmashtrest were among the most outspoken of officials who clashed with the RKI. Tolokontsev, the head of Vesenkha's machine building sector, also publicly defended his administration and often criticized Rabkrin. These industrialists controlled the administrative apparatus against which RKI officials aimed their attack. They had helped construct the industrial system and had a vested interest in seeing it work. They understood, correctly, that Rabkrin's strategies and its arbitrary interference would wreck the existing market, technological, and administrative organization of industry. While favoring reform, Vesenkha's industrial managers and economists argued that the existing system was tried and tested and adequate to the tasks of industrialization.

Rabkrin had no more outspoken critic than Stepan Birman.[65] He treated even high-level RKI officials with polite contempt, and he gave at least the impression that even the OGPU could not intimidate him.[66] On several occasions during Rabkrin's major investigation in 1928, Birman refused to supply materials on short notice or to appear at meetings to answer allegations of mismanagement. In one reply to A. I. Gurevich, the head of a survey group and a Rabkrin presidium member, Birman wrote that he was simply "too busy with the affairs of the trust and Vesenkha" to accede to Rabkrin's "constant" demands. When three of the six members of the trust's board of directors were arrested on charges of wrecking and mismanagement, Birman vigorously defended them, even to the Central Committee plenum.[67]

Because of his outspoken views, Birman and Iugostal' became favorite targets, and some local Party and Rabkrin officials did not wait for higher authority to act against the trust. In 1928 several local officials conducted their own investigations of nearby Iugostal' factories, and went so far as unilaterally to dismiss directors and technical staff. Such action went beyond their administrative authority and Birman wasted no time seeking redress. In a fourteen-page single-spaced letter to Lazar Kaganovich, then

[65] See Davies, *Soviet Economy in Turmoil*; Fitzpatrick, "Sergo Ordzhonikidze"; Rees, *State Control*; Lampert, *Technical Intelligentsia*; Azrael, *Managerial Power*.

[66] A special report prepared by the OGPU for high Party officials confirmed Birman's reluctance to cooperate with police investigations. See RTsKhIDNI, f. 85, op. 1s, d. 129, l. 68.

[67] GARF, f. 374, op. 15, d. 484, ll. 82–84; RTsKhIDNI, f. 17, op. 2, d. 441, suppl. I.

the Ukrainian Party chief, Birman complained that local Party and Rab-krin organs ran smear campaigns in local newspapers, and that even the Ukrainian Republic organs of Rabkrin made unfounded public accusa-tions of sabotage against the trust. Birman was sure that many of the slanderous allegations originated with an accountant who had been fired from Iugostal' for incompetence. "Now," wrote Birman, "the former em-ployee is working as a Ukrainian RKI 'expert.'" He appealed to Ka-ganovich to regulate Rabkrin's "wild" behavior and emphasized the "in-tolerable" situation in which the trust found itself, forced to compensate for numerous arrests "at a time when the government presents tasks to industry that [could] be described only as grandiose." To suffer the aggra-vation of "petty-minded" interference from Rabkrin and other govern-mental and Party organs "played on the nerves" of overstrained industrial officials.[68]

Birman was not the only official to try to stand up to Rabkrin. Iosif Kosior defended Iugostal' as "a model trust," and he pleaded for all con-trol agencies, Vesenkha's inspectorate as well as Rabkrin, to stop harass-ing the industrial trusts and let them take the risks appropriate to the state's industrial entrepreneurs.[69] Kosior also convened a special Vesenkha commission in June 1929 to investigate Rabkrin's purge of the Dneprostroi project earlier that year. Tolokontsev, too, complained to a Central Com-mittee plenum meeting in November 1929 about the "constant pressure" from Rabkrin.[70]

Despite Kuibyshev's attempt to Stalinize Vesenkha, the agency took a strong institutional stand against Rabkrin. *Torgovo-promyshlennaia gazeta*, for example, ran a scathing editorial on the front page on 1 January 1928 suggesting that Rabkrin was out of control. The editors criticized the In-spectorate for "always being ready to bring factory administrative person-nel to trial, often with the flimsiest of evidence, even hearsay." They charged that the attacks on trusts and industrial officials were often moti-vated by personal rivalries, either by Rabkrin officials themselves or by disgruntled managers seeking to use the RKI to settle old scores. Just as often, industrial managers exploited Rabkrin surveys to blame their mis-takes on previous administrations. The editors criticized the hastiness of Rabkrin investigations and the lack of qualified staff in the agency.

Occasionally industrial officials managed to embarrass Rabkrin into an admission of error. In July 1928, S. S. Lobov, the head of the Russian Ve-senkha, categorically denied Rabkrin's accusations of improprieties and

---

[68]RTsKhIDNI, f. 17, op. 15, d. 8, ll. 34–47. Birman does not name the former employee, but he was most likely B. Bakumenko, who wrote several articles critical of Iugostal''s accounting practices. Birman, of course, did not let the criticism pass, and the two exchanged charges and countercharges in *TPG*, 1 and 17 June and 13 and 19 July 1928.

[69]See *TPG*, 2 December 1929, p. 2.

[70]See RTsKhIDNI, f. 17, op. 15, d. 8, l. 186, and op. 2, d. 441, l. 53.

charged in turn that the republic-level RKI based its criticisms on thin and hastily assembled evidence. Lobov warned that he would press the matter with the appropriate Party and state organs until Rabkrin withdrew its accusation or was properly disciplined. A month later, *TPG* reported, without comment, that Rabkrin RSFSR had retracted its charges. The Inspectorate explained that its investigations had been blown out of proportion and that its charges concerned "only a few Russian enterprises."[71]

The ever-energetic Birman finally won his fight against Rabkrin. Birman recalled in a memoir in 1937 that on "several occasions" he was able to appeal directly and successfully to Ordzhonikidze to halt Rabkrin harassment.[72] Finally, after several years and numerous entreaties, the Central Committee ordered Rabkrin to cease its investigation of the trust. Ordzhonikidze signed an instruction to that effect on 6 February 1930.[73] Birman's was a symbolic victory, however. Ordzhonikidze signed the instruction on the very eve of Iugostal's dissolution and its incorporation into the nationally organized steel cartel, Stal'.

Some of the most rancorous exchanges occurred at the 16th Party Conference in April 1929 and at the 16th Party Congress in June and July 1930. Rozengol'ts's attack on Birman at the 1929 conference is well known; Gurevich and Mikhail Kaganovich continued the assault at the Party congress a year later.[74] Birman's outspokenness gave his critics plenty of ammunition. So did Birman's strong regional bias and his aggressive policies of technological reconstruction of Iugostal'. Rozengol'ts, for example, attacked Birman and Vesenkha not only on the issue of tempos but, like his RKI colleagues in other forums, on the "crisis" of technical leadership. It was Vesenkha's passivity, he charged, that had allowed the trusts to "run amok" (*v putanitsu*) and bring the government's programs (that is, Rabkrin's programs) of technological reconstruction and rationalization to a standstill.[75]

Ordzhonikidze's speech to the Party congress proved the most devastating. Ordzhonikidze was reluctant to attack Kuibyshev openly, and in the weeks before the congress he vacillated on the question of how blunt to make his criticisms. Receiving assurances from Kliment Voroshilov, another of Stalin's close allies, Ordzhonikidze decided that he should, in fact, proceed with a critical speech. At the same time, in view of

[71]*TPG*, 28 July and 21 August 1928.
[72]F. B. Seiranian, ed., *O Sergo Ordzhonikidze: Vospominaniia sovremennikov* (Moscow, 1981), p. 76.
[73]GARF, f. 374, op. 15, d. 484, l. 94.
[74]See, e.g., descriptions of these attacks in Azrael, *Managerial Politics*, pp. 92, 226. See also Fitzpatrick, "Sergo Ordzhonikidze," p. 159; Lampert, *Technical Intelligentsia*, pp. 98–99.
[75]See Rozengol'ts report in *XVI konferentsiia VKP(b), Aprel' 1929: Stenograficheskii otchet* (Moscow, 1962), pp. 552–60. For other attacks against Birman and Vesenkha see the speeches by Ia. Iakovlev, pp. 444–88; A. I. Gurevich, pp. 505–10; and V. P. Zatonskii, pp. 527–29.

Kuibyshev's long friendship and his stature as one of Stalin's close allies, Ordzhonikidze apparently decided to refrain from personal attacks.[76]

The substance of Ordzhonikidze's address has been analyzed numerous times, but the style of his speech was just as important as its substance in winning over the audience. The speech lasted nearly 3 hours and struck a masterful balance between conciliation and condemnation.[77] Ordzhonikidze demonstrated his rare ability to mesmerize an audience as he systematically criticized every aspect of Soviet state bureaucracy and industrial performance. He drew his audience in by asking rhetorical questions, by joking, and by inviting answers and dialogue. He riveted his listeners with story after story of scandal, incompetence, and even collusion to hinder maximum industrial output. He openly discussed the OGPU's role in ferreting out corruption and wrecking, and he hinted at foreign powers moving behind the scenes.

Time and again Ordzhonikidze provided his listeners with figures that supposedly proved the capacity of factories and whole industries to produce at two to three times the current rate of output. In each case, Ordzhonikidze left his audience with no doubt that the deficiencies he described resulted from the shortsighted pursuit of local and individual trust interests, combined with a lack of central state authority and coordination of the economy. He was careful to give Vesenkha's leaders credit for acting on problems brought to its attention by the RKI and the police. He lauded Vesenkha for revising its five-year plan figures upward. At one point he even apologized for usurping part of Kuibyshev's speech on the economy. But he made it clear that in every instance of proceedings against corruption, wrecking, or incompetence and of revisions in plans, action was taken only after pressure had been brought to bear by the RKI and the OGPU. Ordzhonikidze spoke in tones of reasoned criticism. Nonetheless, his attack amounted to a withering and humiliating onslaught against the competence of Vesenkha's leadership and its lack of control over the economy.

Kuibyshev, by all accounts, was stunned. He acknowledged the criticisms leveled at Vesenkha under his leadership and pledged, among other things, to redouble efforts to relieve the machine goods famine. Still, the congress's resolution on the five-year plan was critical of Vesenkha and the trusts, and it represented clear acknowledgment that Rabkrin, not Vesenkha, set priorities and strategies for the industrial economy. The resolution stressed the need to force development of all industrial branches of

---

[76]Reported by Oleg Khlevniuk in conversation. For Kuibyshev's submissive attitude after the congress see Fitzpatrick, "Sergo Ordzhonikidze," p. 161, and Davies, *Soviet Economy in Turmoil*, pp. 335–36.

[77]*XVI s"ezd Vsesoiuznoi Kommunisticheskoi Partii(b), 26 iiunia–13 iiulia 1930: Stenograficheskii otchet* (Moscow, 1935), pp. 536–80.

the economy, but particularly the machine tool, metallurgical, and metal fabricating industries. The congress also called for further industrial modernization through greater specialization of factory production and the widespread introduction of mass-production techniques. Finally, the resolution approved the trend, also advocated by Rabkrin, toward branch reorganization of industries under centralized corporate administration.[78]

Many of Vesenkha's officials could sincerely endorse the fundamental provisions of the congress's resolution. Tolokontsev embraced the goals of modernization and the move away from traditionally divisive regional units toward national reorganization of the economy. In the political context of the congress and of the preceding years, however, the outcome of the congress represented a clear victory for Rabkrin. It was a blow from which Vesenkha did not recover.[79]

Conclusions

For well over a year, throughout 1929 and into the first half of 1930, Vesenkha officials attempted to hold their own against Rabkrin. They gave as good as they got, but in the end they could not save themselves from the RKI's onslaught, backed as it was by the Party and the OGPU. The constant and bitter wrangling with the RKI sapped morale and disrupted administration. Yet the political beating that economic officials suffered at the 16th congress did not end their troubles. The summer and autumn of 1930 brought massive arrests, between 3,000 and 7,000 in the economic bureaucracies. In November the first public indictments were brought against high-level officials in what came to be known as the Industrial Party conspiracy. Newsreel, newspaper, and radio accounts of the trial riveted the country in December. The trial coincided with Ordzhonikidze's reorganization of Vesenkha; indeed, newspapers reported his appointment and the Industrial Party indictments on the same day.[80]

As is well known, Party backing and police involvement played important roles in Rabkrin's takeover of Vesenkha in late 1930. But it was not just Rabkrin's policies or its use of political pressure that overwhelmed Vesenkha; the agency's style of management had much to do with the outcome. Production, cost, resource mobilization, and rationalization campaigns descended on trusts and factories one after another in the wake of Rabkrin surveys. Rabkrin's fragmented operations created a culture of crisis within the industrial administration, which was reinforced by Rab-

[78]Ibid., pp. 988–96, 1354–56.

[79]Though Rabkrin won a clear victory, Oleg Khlevniuk has suggested in conversation that Ordzhonikidze did not. Ordzhonikidze's appointment to head Vesenkha several months after the congress, Khlevniuk reasons, was a step down from his position as head of both TsKK and Rabkrin.

[80]See *TPG*, 11 November 1930.

krin's own military campaign approach to economic management. The numerous mobilization campaigns that the Inspectorate imposed on Vesenkha disrupted normal bureaucratic and economic routines and finally paralyzed the industrial apparatus. Rabkrin's plans were the antithesis of planning, not just because their production targets were unrealistic but because of the lack of coordination in the way the agency developed its sectoral strategies and because of the managerial crisis it fostered within the state's industrial administration. The severe economic strains caused by the five-year industrialization drive stemmed as much from administrative collapse brought on by Rabkrin as from overly ambitious planning.

Rabkrin officials never remedied the problems caused by their piecemeal approach to planning and their campaign style of administration. Late in 1928, however, the Inspectorate's leaders began talking about the need for systematic reorganization of the state's industrial system. By the end of the year, several branches had already undergone administrative restructuring, in part as a result of Rabkrin's proddings, and Vesenkha officials were debating the appropriateness of a general reform. The controversies over reorganization lasted well into 1930. Those debates became the focal point for the bureaucratic and political-economic struggle to control the new industrial state.

PART II

The Struggle for a New State, 1928–1930

4

What Kind of State?

Comrades, even barbershops will be centrally planned,
even barbershops!

—S. S. Lobov, 1929

In early October 1928, I. I. Matrozov, a Vesenkha economist, described the organizational crisis that faced the Soviet industrial system at the beginning of the first five-year plan. Industrial administration no longer had a center, he declared; there was no authority that could enforce discipline in Vesenkha's various "kingdoms." Relations between trusts and syndicates continued in a tangle of contested and overlapping jurisdictions. There was no clear delineation of authority between all-union, republic-level, and local bureaucracies or between glavki and trusts. Glavki interfered in trusts' affairs and trusts interfered in their factories. Rabkrin, wrote Matrozov, interfered in everybody's business.[1]

Trust authority, once the center of industrial administration, had been eroded by the rise of the syndicates, by Vesenkha's own policies, and by the increasing role of Rabkrin, Vesenkha's chief inspectorate, and the Party's various commissions. Trusts, Matrozov argued, had been reduced to mere executive agencies trying to meet the demands of competing administrative bureaucracies. Authority over construction, sales, supply, and export and import rights had all been parceled out to other administrative bodies. Worse still, the various functions of the industrial system "were no longer connected to the trust or to each other in any commercial or administrative way." Matrozov warned that the centrifugal tendencies at work in Vesenkha created a chaotic lack of direction in planning, a "paralyzing complexity" in industrial management, and a "real rigidity and bureaucratization of the whole economic apparatus."[2]

[1]*TPG*, 4 October 1928, p. 3.
[2]Ibid.

Matrozov did not exaggerate. Government and Party officials admitted that the state's economic administration was in chaos. With no commercial or administrative center, the state's industrial system was breaking apart; the various sectors of the economy were disengaging. By late 1928, as the economy strained under the increasing demands of industrialization, Vesenkha faced an organizational crisis of immense proportions.

Government economists and high Party officials recognized the seriousness of the economy's problems. Issues of economic and administrative organization were complicated. Chief among them was the central task formulated by the Party's 16th Conference in April 1929: to centralize and coordinate economic planning, but decentralize operational functions of economic administration.[3] How, practically, could the government accomplish this? Would not centralization of planning rob the lower levels of the industrial bureaucracy of operational initiative? What would be the function of the trusts, already under attack by Rabkrin, within this new organizational framework? Would they be disbanded altogether, or play an increasingly diminished role in the new system?

A second set of issues revolved around the conference's resolution to strengthen "technical leadership" (tekhnicheskoe rukovodstvo). According to the Party's resolution, this was to be the primary task of the trusts. But what did technical leadership mean? Would the trusts be merely institutionalized engineering consultants to their factories and to Vesenkha? If, as most delegates agreed, technical leadership were more broadly defined to mean production leadership, would not trust activities overlap those of the syndicates and the chief administrations? It sounded clear in theory to separate the functions of planning, production leadership, and commercial activities, but trusts, syndicates, and glavki had been fighting inconclusively for years over practical authority in these areas. And what of Rabkrin? Should it, as some argued, act as a superagency, combining all planning, administrative, and control functions?[4] If so, what was to become of Vesenkha, not to mention Gosplan?

As complicated as these issues were, they involved another level of debate, at times made explicit, often not, about the character of the state and its economic goals. In a capital-starved economy, how would the government generate enough investment for its industrialization drive: by promoting commercial exchange or by extractive methods such as direct mobilization of resources and high taxation? Which of the competing economic and administrative cultures would form the basis of the new state industrial system: the bureaucratic economy of Vesenkha, the syndi-

[3]Kommunisticheskaia Partiia Sovetskogo Soiuza v resoliutsiiakh s"ezdov, konferentsii i plenumov TsK, vol. 2 (Moscow, 1954), pp. 597–98.
[4]See M. Artamonov's article in TPG, 11 November 1929, pp. 2–3.

cates' commercial system of organization, or Rabkrin's direct military-style mobilization?

Officially, resolution of these issues found expression in a governmental and Party order of 5 December 1929. That order, establishing the formal organization of the state's economy for the rest of the first five-year plan, had a profound influence on Soviet industrial organization. Yet the evolution of Soviet industrial administration bore little resemblance to its formal incorporation. The debates that led up to the December 5 order and the alternatives that were proposed reveal much about the political and social forces at work in the formation of the Soviet industrial state during the crucial final years of the 1920s.

The Struggle over Organizational Reform

Throughout 1928 and 1929, Vesenkha's officials enacted piecemeal organizational reforms, but they began to discuss publicly the need for a complete administrative restructuring only in late 1928. As expected, discussions of organizational reform divided along factional lines. In late September, Kosior published the first set of proposals on the organization of industry. He intended his proposals as a strong plea to restore the trusts' authority, but he damaged his credibility by singling out Iugostal' for special mention. At that time Iugostal' was embroiled in one of its biggest fights with Rabkrin over the latter's survey of the trust. Accounting procedures were at the heart of a series of heated and very public exchanges between the trust and the control agency. In his theses, Kosior lauded Iugostal' as a model to be emulated in the way it established financial and accounting relations with its factories.[5] His reference to Iugostal' was clearly intended as a public defense of his old and close "Ukrainian" comrade Stepan Birman. The connections between Kosior and Birman were well known, however, and Kosior's comments about Iugostal' gave a partisan flavor to his general argument. Many in Vesenkha regarded his proposals, not as a plan for organizational reform but specifically as an attempt by the "South" to reassert its influence in the central industrial apparatus.

Kosior's proposals provoked a flood of vituperation from syndicate leaders. At an October 8 meeting of the VSS, the syndicates' governing board, one presidium member dismissed Kosior's proposals as the trusts' final and desperate effort at bureaucratic survival. "They are afraid of their fate," he declared. Kosior's proposals, noted another official, might be appropriate for 1924, when economic and commercial mechanisms

---

[5]*TPG*, 28 September 1928, p. 3; 30 November 1928, p. 3.

were not well developed in the economy, "but not for 1928." Another called them a "dangerous step backward" to the glavkism of the early 1920s, and received unanimous agreement. Kosior's proposals had "no basis in any economic reality" and were "wholly useless" (*iavno ne prikhoditsia*).[6]

In October, Vesenkha's trade department published a set of counter-proposals that favored an increased role for the syndicates in planning.[7] Other departments and individuals followed suit with their own versions of reform, and it soon became clear that no consensus existed within Vesenkha's hierarchy over how to reorganize industry. Even Vesenkha's presidium was divided on the issue. Iosef Khodorov, the syndicate councils' trade expert, told his fellow syndicate leaders that Kuibyshev and M. L. Rukhimovich supported "only parts" of Kosior's plans. Moreover, Kuibyshev was more inclined toward the syndicate's view than he was commonly thought to be. Khodorov quoted Kuibyshev to the effect that Vesenkha had "mistakenly underestimated" the usefulness and experience of the syndicates in organizing industry. Khodorov encouraged his syndicate colleagues to take heart in the hope that officials at the highest level of government were beginning to see the importance of the syndicate movement.[8]

A Vesenkha commission attempted to find a compromise between trust and syndicate positions in a set of proposals, also published in October 1928.[9] As with most compromises, however, the commission's theses brought no clarity to the organizational debates and did little more than muddle the issues. Exchanges continued in meetings and in the press right up to the beginning of Vesenkha's fourth plenum meetings, which started on 30 November 1928. The plenum produced no breakthrough. Trust supporters made a strong showing, but so did officials sympathetic to the syndicates. The plenum's resolutions did nothing to change the status quo or to clarify lines of authority.

Rabkrin entered the debate on industrial organization in early January 1929, not long after the close of Vesenkha's fourth plenum. Until then, the RKI had taken an active role in the survey and reorganization of individual branches of industry but had made no proposals for fundamental reform. Neither did Rabkrin officials commit themselves in the trust-syndicate debates. They supported the creation of the textile trade syndicate, for example, merging the glavk with the VTS and subordinating trusts to

[6] RGAE, f. 3915, op. 1, d. 241, ll. 118, 160, 166, 108.

[7] *TPG*, 19 October 1928, p. 3.

[8] RGAE, f. 3915, op. 1, d. 241, l. 158. Rukhimovich did oppose Kosior's proposals, but Khodorov was wrong in assuming that he therefore supported the syndicates. Rukhimovich was in Rabkrin's camp and supported centralizing reorganization that would usurp the roles of both syndicates and trusts.

[9] *TPG*, 23 October 1928, pp. 3–4.

the single organization, yet they took no principled line in Vesenkha's organizational debates. Ordzhonikidze, when pressed to endorse or criticize the textile syndicate's experiment, equivocated, giving a wait-and-see answer.[10]

Finally, in early 1929, Rabkrin established a commission to investigate organizational issues and named A. Z. Gol'tsman to head it. From the beginning, Gol'tsman made it clear he would not continue the piecemeal approach taken by Vesenkha and Rabkrin to questions of administrative reform. He believed in root reorganization. In a memorandum to Ordzhonikidze that spring, Gol'tsman stated the need to create an industrial structure "entirely new," a system that "will mold the economy to our ends, whatever it is we wish to accomplish."[11]

What Gol'tsman and his Rabkrin colleagues wished to accomplish was to turn the USSR into an "industrial power." To favor industrialization was not unusual; strengthening the Soviet Union through industrialization was a widely accepted goal. But the word Gol'tsman used for power was *derzhava*, which called forth memories of autocratic state power, the *samo-derzhavie* of the tsarist regime.[12] Gol'tsman's apposition of the words *industrial'naia* and *derzhava* created provocative images of an "industrial autocracy," a term that linked the processes of industrialization, state-building, and great-power status.

Such language and the images it created shaped the way many economic planners thought about industry and state power. M. N. Falkner-Smit, member of the collegium of the Central Statistical Bureau and head of its section on industrial statistics, cited only two people, Gol'tsman and Lenin, in her introduction to the 1929 statistical survey of industrial capital in the USSR. This was the first Soviet survey of its kind to describe statistically the distribution of capital and labor in industry. Falkner-Smit credited Gol'tsman with providing the organizing principle behind the survey, which was to measure the "capital capability" or "capital power"—*kapitalovooruzhennost'*—of Soviet industry. The term was Gol'tsman's, as Falkner-Smit indicated by setting it off in quotation marks. Quotation marks also drew attention to the word and its military connotations. *Vooruzhenie* most often referred to capability or power in the sense of military armament. The implication of a military-like mobilization of the economy reinforced the autocratic image evoked by Gol'tsman's *industrial'naia derzhava*.[13]

Like Gol'tsman, Falkner-Smit defined the goal of industrialization as

[10]GARF, f. 374, op. 1, d. 616, ll. 227, 233.

[11]Ibid., d. 598, l. 90.

[12]A. Z. Gol'tsman, *Upravlenie promyshlennost'iu v Germanii i v SSSR* (Moscow, 1930), p. 3.

[13]*Kontsentratsiia fabrichno-zavodskoi promyshlennosti*, p. 4. Robert Tucker emphasizes the militarized, almost feudal character of Stalin's state system in "Stalinism as Revolution from Above," in *Stalinism: Essays in Historical Interpretation*, ed. Tucker (New York, 1977), p. 95.

world-power status. She emphasized the connection between the two by comparing the process of capital concentration in Soviet Russia to the same process in the two most powerful capitalist nations, Germany and the United States. For her authority on industrial concentration under capitalism, Falkner-Smit quoted at length from a work that was familiar to her readers, Lenin's *Imperializm kak poslednii etap kapitalizma* (Imperialism as the highest stage of capitalism). Lenin argued that it was the concentration of capital in large-scale industrial development that made the imperial nations of Europe and North America great world powers. Drawing on the works of the Austrian economist Rudolf Hilferding and the British economist John Hobson, Lenin referred to the transition of capitalism from its Manchesterian stage to the stage of organized or monopoly capitalism. The former was small-scale and individualistic; the latter was organized on a massive national and international scale and was directed toward the world aggrandizement of capitalist state power. Falkner-Smit favorably compared the processes of industrial concentration in Soviet Russia with the levels already achieved in Germany, Britain, and the United States.[14]

Falkner-Smit's linking of Gol'tsman's vision with Lenin's analysis created a compelling image of Soviet industrial power acting on the world stage. At the same time, that image carried implications of industrialization for the sake of state power, not for the sake of social improvement. In fact, Gol'tsman's ideas about the state and the economy had little to do with socialist principles. Neither his nor Falkner-Smit's language evoked images of industrialization as a means to raise standards of living; neither fostered images of the state as a mechanism to ensure social justice, foster commercial exchange, or achieve an equitable distribution of wealth. Gol'tsman and his Rabkrin colleagues favored state monopoly control over industry and economy, but not because they considered planning a better way to distribute economic goods than the capitalist anarchy of the market.[15] For Gol'tsman, as for many of his Rabkrin colleagues, the economy served as a source of wealth for the state. Centralized administration served as the best means to extract that wealth. Like his friend Georgii Piatakov at Gosbank, Gol'tsman set out to create the mechanisms that would maximize the state's ability to manipulate the economy and mine capital and other resources from it. For Gol'tsman, industrialization amounted to an extension of state power and was part of the process of state-building.

[14]*Kontsentratsiia fabrichno-zavodskoi promyshlennosti*, pp. 3–4. For a discussion of organized capitalism and the transition from "Manchesterian" capitalism, see the essays in *Organisierter Kapitalismus: Voraussetzungen und Anfänger*, ed. Hans August Winkler (Göttingen, 1974). For Germany in particular, see the Introduction to Robert Brady, *The Rationalization Movement in German Industry* (Berkeley, 1933).

[15]Gol'tsman, *Upravlenie promyshlennost'iu*, p. 8.

Gol'tsman's ideas about the state evolved, in part, from his work in the "scientific organization of work" movement, or NOT (*nauchnaia organizatsiia truda*). During the Revolution and Civil War, Gol'tsman had been a prominent member, along with Aleksei Gastev, of the Taylorist faction that dominated the metal workers' union. In 1918 this group was instrumental in forcing the reintroduction of piece rates and production norms. Using methods developed by the American Frederick Taylor and other scientific management experts, Gol'tsman also helped Gastev pioneer military-like methods for training new labor recruits. In fact, Trotsky proposed to incorporate these ideas into his own plans in 1919 and 1920 to create a militarized labor army.[16]

Gol'tsman's vision of the state reflected the ideas behind scientific management projected onto a grand scale. According to Gol'tsman, scientific and technological mastery, harnessed in the service of the state, was the key to power (*vlast'*) in the modern age.[17] Gol'tsman believed that a certain level of commercial activity was necessary, but he excoriated the "anarchy of production" that allegedly ran rampant in NEP Russia.[18] The messiness of markets and trading confounded Gol'tsman's obsession, which he shared with Georgii Piatakov, to systematize, discipline, and order. The restructuring of industries into branches controlled by central cartels represented, in theory, a triumph of administrative efficiency over the chaotic regional and commercial market structures that characterized Russia's economy. Gol'tsman's proposals complemented Piatakov's efforts at Gosbank to centralize and streamline control over financial and credit transactions. Both men were committed to a vision of state power unconstrained by social and market demands.

Gol'tsman looked to Germany for practical models, drawing on an extensive study of the German industrial cartel system. He became interested in the German system for several reasons. By the late 1920s, Germany was the Soviet Union's major trading partner among Western industrial nations and one of the most powerful capitalist industrial economies. More important, cartelization in German heavy industry had created monopoly market conditions that closely resembled the conditions of state trading in Soviet heavy industry. Moreover, the relation of production trusts to trade and planning cartels in German heavy industry approximated the Soviet relation of trusts to syndicates and glavki. Gol'tsman examined the American corporation system, but quickly concluded

---

[16]Beissinger, *Scientific Management*, p. 27. Gastev recalled that to persuade the union to accept these measures he and his group, members of the union presidium, had to have their proposals put to a vote five times and then threaten to resign: A. K. Gastev, *Kak nado robotat'* (Moscow, 1924/1972), pp. 22, 32–33.

[17]A. Z. Gol'tsman, "Problemy upravleniia promyshlennost'iu," *Problemy ekonomiki*, 1929, nos. 7–8, p. 3.

[18]A. Z. Gol'tsman, *Voprosy planirovaniia narodnogo khoziaistva* (Moscow, 1927), p. 6.

that market competition and the subcontracting relationship of suppliers and producers did not provide a model on which to base Soviet reforms.[19]

Gol'tsman studied the German system firsthand as head of a Rabkrin delegation in the winter, spring, and early summer of 1929. They visited nearly all the major capital industry associations and examined operations of firms in the giant petrochemical conglomerate I. G. Farben. Gol'tsman held working discussions with the steel industrialist Fritz Thyssen and examined the structure of the steel cartel, Vereinigte Stahlwerke A.G. The Soviet commission also examined the organization of the Ruhr coal producers' syndicate and the German machine tool and engineering consortium, the Verein Deutsche Werkzeugmaschine, or VDW.

The Soviets took particular interest in the way the German cartels organized production and commercial relations. Gol'tsman examined in detail how the cartels contracted with consumers and how they distributed orders among consortium members. The commission studied the production specialization of member firms and how costs and prices were assessed. The Soviets interested themselves especially in how German cartels organized the division of administrative tasks at the various levels of the industrial bureaucracy and how they managed the flow of orders and information from one office to another, from one factory to another, and from administrative and commercial offices to production offices. The Soviets examined German accounting methods, and Gol'tsman even noted where cartels located their business, production, and engineering offices in physical relation to production sites.

Similarly, the Rabkrin commission examined how cartels balanced commercial and engineering factors that affected the organization of production. The tension between commercial and engineering demands was particularly troublesome in the Soviet industrial economy. Soviet trusts and factories resisted specialization and mass production for reasons of commercial flexibility. The German cartels, Gol'tsman found, protected their member enterprises from the uncertainties of the business cycle by guaranteeing them a certain percentage of the cartel's market influence. Market protection, in turn, encouraged firms to specialize and introduce new technologies and production systems with little commercial risk.[20]

Gol'tsman was particularly impressed by this monopoly approach to innovation. He was convinced, as were others, that cartelization was the key to the enormous technological and productive power of German industry in the late nineteenth and early twentieth centuries.[21] He believed it

[19]See Gol'tsman's report on his survey of German and American managerial systems: GARF, f. 374, op. 1, d. 616, ll. 182–210.

[20]GARF, f. 374, op. 1, d. 616, ll. 194–201.

[21]P. Savchuk makes the same argument in TPG, 19 October 1929, p. 3. Steven B. Webb confirms this interpretation of the rise of German industrial power in "Tariffs, Cartels, Technology, and Growth in the German Steel Industry, 1879–1914," Journal of Economic History 40 (June 1980): 309–30.

was only under monopoly conditions—either through market monopolies, as in Germany, or through outright state ownership and organization, as in the Soviet Union—that industry could overcome the "distortion" caused by market demands. Only through monopoly conditions, Gol'tsman believed, could the state free production to achieve its full technological and therefore highest productive potential.

Gol'tsman's reports from Germany make for arcane reading, but the mass of detail they conveyed was the stuff of administration. The information Gol'tsman and his colleagues gleaned from their trip was vital to Rabkrin's efforts to replace a market economy with an administered one. Gol'tsman called for a sharp expansion in the sphere of centralized, planned regulation of the state's industrial economy, but he did not call for the wholesale elimination of a market economy. He distinguished between two types of economic exchange: exchange within the socialized sector, which he defined as trade turnover within the state industrial system, and exchange, or trade, in the private market sector.[22] According to Gol'tsman, production should be planned and trade regulated within the state industrial system, while market forces should operate within the private sector. Gol'tsman saw in the syndicate system the organizational mechanism to regulate trade and turnover within the state sector. He saw Narkomtorg, the state's commercial trade commissariat, as the agency best suited to facilitate trade between state and private sectors.

Gol'tsman claimed that his organizational plans placed the syndicates at the center of the industrial system. In fact, syndicate officials understood that if Gol'tsman's plans were implemented, the syndicates' role would be significantly diminished. The syndicates' influence was based on their function as trade organizations. State industry, Gol'tsman argued, should not be subjected to the operation of trading and market forces. In Gol'tsman's scheme, state trade was to be conducted on the basis of planned industrial expansion, not on the basis of consumer demand. That trade should be regulated by the syndicates, but Gol'tsman preferred to describe their function as distribution (*raspredelenie*) rather than trade (*tovar'*). Gol'tsman regarded trade as a rudimentary form of capitalist market organization.[23] Stripped of their trading role, then, syndicates would be reduced to mere executive offices of higher planning bureaus.

Gol'tsman's proposals threatened the syndicates in one other way. In accordance with plans then being discussed by Rabkrin and Gosbank officials, financial transactions among industrial trusts and branches would be regulated by Gosbank, not, as they had been, by the syndicates. Gol'tsman argued that the new syndicates, indeed all of Vesenkha, should concentrate on the organization of production, not on the organization of exchange. Exchange was to be the business of Narkomtorg. To highlight this

[22]Gol'tsman, "Problema upravleniia promyshlennost'iu," p. 10.
[23]GARF, f. 374, op. 1, d. 616, ll. 183–84.

shift in emphasis, Gol'tsman suggested for a brief period in 1929 that Vesenkha be renamed the Commissariat for Organization of Production (Komissariat Organizatsii Proizvodstva).[24]

Within this new commissariat, Gol'tsman proposed to unify planning and commercial administration by merging the glavki with the syndicates to form powerful associations, or ob"edineniia, of state-owned manufacturers. These ob"edineniia would concentrate all the functions that previously were divided among Vesenkha's various administrative bureaucracies. The ob"edineniia were to combine the functions of technical and production planning and design; functions of distribution, by which Gol'tsman meant sales and supply; export and import planning; capital construction; and cost accounting. The new super-ob"edineniia were the center of Gol'tsman's reforms. They were to be the mighty organizational engines of state industrialization.

When critics charged that he was reviving the worst features of glavkism, Gol'tsman argued that the ob"edinenie system would in fact advance the struggle against bureaucratism. He assured the Central Committee that concentration of all administrative functions in a single association would enforce economic accountability. No longer, he said, could an office at one level pass off responsibility to another at a higher or lower level. Moreover, the concentration of functions in the ob"edineniia would allow the state to realize huge savings by eliminating redundant and competing structures. Gol'tsman anticipated, for example, that by creating one sales and supply office at the ob"edinenie level, the state could eliminate the welter of analogous structures that currently operated at both the trust and syndicate levels.[25]

Gol'tsman's plans were often misinterpreted as a call for the elimination of the trusts and the overcentralization of authority in the new ob"edineniia. Overcentralization is in fact an apt description of what happened, but it is not what Gol'tsman intended. To him centralization did not mean that ob"edinenie leaders would sit in their offices in Moscow and never set foot in a factory. To counter this image, he often cited the German steel cartel: its offices were not in Berlin but in the major production complex at Düsseldorf.[26] Krupp's main offices, he noted, were in Essen and those of the metallurgical trust in Oberhausen. Gol'tsman proposed that ob"edineniia offices, too, should be close to the major centers of factory activity.[27]

Gol'tsman did not call for the outright elimination of the trusts, but he proposed that ob"edineniia would organize factories and trusts not by re-

[24]See Koritskii et al., Sovetskaia upravlencheskaia mysl', p. 71.
[25]RTsKhIDNI, f. 17, op. 2, d. 441, ll. 126–27.
[26]Gol'tsman, "Problema upravleniia promyshlennost'iu," p. 9.
[27]GARF, f. 374, op. 1, d. 616, ll. 281–82.

gion, as was currently the case, but by industrial branch. Within the branch organization, some local trusts might remain, he conceded, but they would manage only factories specialized for the same type of production, and they were to be stripped of their old commercial and supply functions. The new branch-organized trusts were to be the technical-production centers of the industrial system, the link that would translate the planning functions of the ob"edineniia into the reality of production at the factory level.[28]

In accordance with Party directives, Gol'tsman described the task of the new trusts as that of "technical leadership," a phrase that was often and falsely interpreted in its narrowest form. In fact, Gol'tsman conceived of the trusts' role as much broader than that of an institutionalized kind of engineering consultant. The trusts should be responsible for ensuring the most effective operation of all factors affecting production in their factories. Trusts were to ensure that each factory operated at its maximum output level, with technologically advanced equipment and a rationalized form of production organization, and within the cost-accounting figures of the industrial-financial plan, the so-called *promfinplan*, established by the parent ob"edinenie.[29] In the various debates about reorganization, trust officials often voiced the fear that the Gol'tsman plan would either eliminate their trusts altogether or turn them into mere executive offices of the ob"edineniia. Gol'tsman insisted that the trusts were to play an important role in the new system. The impression persisted, however, with justification, that Rabkrin's plans certainly meant the end of the once mighty trusts.

Rabkrin officials had celebrated each step of Gol'tsman's trip to Germany with great fanfare. Periodic press releases recounted his progress through Germany and anticipated his return to Moscow. Upon his arrival in early July, Rabkrin scheduled a colloquium for 11 July to hear his preliminary report and issued several hundred invitations. In addition to Rabkrin officials, eighty-six people attended—high functionaries and factory directors from Vesenkha, officials from Gosbank, Gosplan, Narkomfin, the trade union organizations, and other economic and industrial agencies.

Gol'tsman did not present a systematic outline, but in a two-hour informal talk he compared German and Soviet industrial organization. He used his descriptions of the former to highlight shortcomings in the latter, and made clear where he and his commission would focus their attention in developing specific proposals. Although Gol'tsman was vague on many points, it quickly became clear that Rabkrin's initiative was not going to be another variation of earlier Vesenkha plans. Gol'tsman em-

[28]Ibid., l. 284.
[29]Ibid., ll. 194, 281, 293.

phasized several times that he was preparing nothing less than a complete overhaul of the country's industrial administrative system.[30]

Rabkrin officials moved quickly to capitalize on the initiative provided by Gol'tsman's trip and his report. At the conclusion of his talk, Iakovlev, the chair of the meeting, announced the formation of an interagency commission to elaborate Gol'tsman's presentation into a set of specific theses. Gol'tsman, naturally, was named to chair the commission. Rabkrin personnel were to dominate the commission, but Iakovlev presented a list of other officials whom the RKI would recommend for inclusion. Among them were N. D. Koniukov, the head of the engineering syndicate; Stepanov, the director of the Serp i Molot (Sickle and Hammer) metallurgical complex in Moscow; and A. M. Ginzburg, Vesenkha's representative. Iakovlev publicly charged the commission, in the name of Rabkrin and Sovnarkom, to prepare a set of working theses for general discussion within one month.[31] The publicity surrounding Gol'tman's trip, his talk, the public formation and charge of Rabkrin's commission—all created an aura of expectation and allowed Rabkrin to seize the initiative from both Vesenkha and the syndicates. For several weeks Rabkrin received requests for transcripts or a summary report of the 11 July proceedings. Debate about industrial organization now focused on the Gol'tsman proposals.

Gol'tsman's call for sweeping centralization of administration aroused considerable concern. Many officials argued that Vesenkha should address questions of reorganization in each branch as problems arose. One scheme, they argued, could not be applied to all industrial branches. For a while, even Kuibyshev endorsed the idea of organizational flexibility.[32] Others argued that Gol'tsman's theses failed to clarify the relationship between local economic organs and Vesenkha. Regional economic representatives complained bitterly that the emphasis on centralized state industry left no authority to republic or local economic councils.

Local officials from the major industrial regions were outspoken in their criticisms of Rabkrin's proposals. Indeed, they formed the most highly organized and articulate bloc of opposition to the Inspectorate. An official of the Ukrainian Vesenkha pointed out that as of 1928, over 50 percent of Soviet industrial production fell within the jurisdiction of republic or local councils, yet Gol'tsman's proposals had nothing to say about that level of organization. An official of the legal department of the Russian Vesenkha, went so far as to demand that only a few branches of heavy industry—heavy metallurgy, heavy machine building, and petrochemicals—be cen-

[30]Ibid., l. 295.
[31]Ibid., l. 171.
[32]*TPG*, 10 August 1929, p. 3. See the headline and discussion in *TPG*, 11 September 1929, p. 1: "An individual approach is needed in the reorganization of the industrial managerial system."

tralized in all-union administrations. All the rest, he declared, should be administered by republic or local-level bureaucracies and cooperatives.[33] A factory director wondered why reorganization was not proceeding in the opposite direction. In view of the government's decision to decentralize operational control in industry, he argued, the glavki should be pared down to skeleton size. Local trusts and economic organizations should be reinforced with personnel and greater authority. If Rabkrin's proposals centralized commercial and technical leadership even more than they were at present, "we in the trusts and factories will sit around like little boys with our hands in our pockets."[34]

A. I. Ivanov, deputy head of Vesenkha RSFSR, concurred. He pointedly reminded Vesenkha and Rabkrin officials that the Party's resolution on reorganization, adopted in April 1929, called for centralization of planning but decentralization of administrative control.[35] Some officials called for all industries, both all-union and local, to be subject to the jurisdiction of regional economic and governmental executive councils. Others argued that Rabkrin's call for elimination of many trusts would strand local enterprises. "These can't all be run from the center," a factory director said. "It's ridiculous to think so, and to try this under the current conditions of shortages will be disastrous."[36]

Stepan Birman, too, argued that it would be "completely senseless" to administer metal production in such disparate areas as the Urals, Siberia, and Ukraine from one superassociation. It would make even less sense, he said, to undertake a root restructuring in the middle of the five-year plan. It would take years for a new administrative structure to acquire the "organic" ties to industry that had grown up within the existing trust system. Centralization of all functions, especially central control over profit, would blatantly contradict the government's policy of strengthening factory autonomy.[37]

S. S. Lobov, chair of the Russian Vesenkha, emerged as one of the most vigorous critics of the Gol'tsman plan. He ridiculed and parodied it in every public forum. Like other local officials, Lobov demanded that reorganization decentralize the administrative system to local control, with "only a very few exceptions."[38] At the sixth Vesenkha plenum in October 1929, Lobov warned against trying to construct a universally applicable

---

[33]*TPG*, 11 September 1929, p. 1; 13 August 1929, p. 2.

[34]GARF, f. 374, op. 1, d. 1055, ll. 45b–46.

[35]*TPG*, 13 August 1929, p. 2.

[36]GARF, f. 374, op. 1, d. 1055, ll. 45b–46. These comments were echoed in the presidium of the Russian Vesenkha: *TPG*, 10 August 1929, p. 1.

[37]"Ukrainskie khoziaistvenniki protiv reorganizatsii upravleniia promyshlennost'iu" [Ukrainian managers against reorganization of industrial administration], *TPG*, 8 September 1929, p. 1.

[38]*TPG*, 1 November 1929, p. 1.

organizational scheme for all industrial branches. With heavy sarcasm he emphasized Rabkrin's intention to centralize and plan every detail of economic life: even barbershops would be planned. Three times he repeated "even barbershops" to impress upon his colleagues the absurd lengths to which Rabkrin would go to centralize economic administration.[39]

In late October 1929, Vesenkha RSFSR outlined its own proposals for reorganization, which emphasized decentralization and local control. In his opening remarks at a meeting to discuss the proposals, Lobov tried to play down the differences between the RSFSR and the RKI plans, claiming that Rabkrin was on the right track and that his proposals differed only in degree. This statement was clearly a rhetorical diversion, however, to mask what amounted to a renewed attack against Rabkrin. The editors of *Torgovo promyshlennaia gazeta* were not fooled. On 1 November they gave the meeting front-page coverage under the headline "Vesenkha RSFSR proposal diverges from those of Vesenkha SSSR and NK RKI."

Rabkrin's plan, argued Lobov, "concentrates on structural changes, but gives no attention to actual methods of management." Lobov did not develop this thought, but it was one of his most telling criticisms. Other critics described this flaw as a lack of administrative process (*planovost'*) or coordination (*administrativnaia koordinatsiia*). However the problem was described, officials who were forced to work in the new system quickly discovered that there was little substance to Gol'tsman's grandiose schemes. Once cartels were established, Gol'tsman believed, administration would take care of itself. On the contrary, as we shall see, the new system was an administrative nightmare with no established lines of communication, authority, or information flow. Syndicate officials had noted the utopian quality of Piatakov's plans for financial centralization. Lobov saw the same quality in Gol'tman's proposals.

Even Rabkrin's supporters cautioned against overcentralization. V. Ia. Chubar' worried at the November 1929 Central Committee plenum that centralization of planning (*planirovanie*) could too easily turn into centralization of administration (*upravlenie*)—in fact, was already doing so—and that "too much hope" was being placed in centralization "as the salvation of industry." Vesenkha's higher administrative bodies were already alienated from the factories they governed, he warned. The creation of super-production associations could result in "paper plans" with no basis in reality. Moreover, with so much talk of reorganization and detrustification, factory directors were beginning to ignore instructions from their immediate administrative superiors. Southern metal factories, for example, were looking more to Moscow for answers to production problems than to themselves or to their trusts. There was a real danger, Chubar' declared,

[39]RGAE, f. 3429, op. 6, d. 197, l. 405.

that centralized production associations, far from strengthening technical leadership in industry, would "suction" people into the central apparatus.[40]

If Gol'tsman's plans failed to address questions of administrative process, neither did they speak to problems of capital formation and commercial organization of the economy. Gol'tsman often referred to the merger of syndicates and glavki as the combination of commercial and regulatory functions of industrial administration; yet by divesting the syndicates of their commercial and trading function, he left the state no entrepreneurial mechanisms to reproduce capital. State industry could generate capital by trading through Narkomtorg, and Vesenkha's rationalization campaign was designed to generate capital through more efficient organization of production and labor; but neither of these arrangements held the same potential for capital accumulation as entrepreneurial trade. As syndicate officials realized, Gol'tsman was not interested in creating the mechanisms of a commercial state. His plans fitted integrally with—in fact, created the mechanisms for—mobilization of the economy in a military manner.

As charged, Gol'tsman's commission submitted its recommendations within a month of the 11 July presentation; they were published first in *Izvestiia* on 1 August 1929. The next day, Vesenkha, in order to regain initiative, announced the organization of its own commission to review and recommend administrative changes, under the leadership of V. N. Mantsev, a member of Vesenkha's presidium and head of the All-Union Council of Syndicates. On 8 August *Torgovo-promyshlennaia gazeta* reported at length on a meeting of Leningrad industrialists in which Mantsev staked out Vesenkha's organizational position. It was clear from the review, however, that Mantsev's remarks were defensive, offering less a constructive plan than a piecemeal response to Rabkrin's proposals.

Mantsev strained to reassure and regroup the conflicting interests in Vesenkha's economic bureaucracies. He promised, for example, that Vesenkha's proposals would not go to such extremes as Rabkrin in dismantling the trusts' administrative system. Coming from the head of the syndicates' governing council, however, the statement undoubtedly brought little comfort to the state's industrial producers. To counter the administrative emphasis in Rabkrin's plans, Mantsev asserted the primacy of commercial organization of the economy through the work of the syndicates. This point, too, can hardly have reassured trust officials. Mantsev also attempted, without success, to appeal to local economic interests. He said confidently that Vesenkha's proposals would redress Rabkrin's over-emphasis on central authority, yet he acknowledged the need for better coordination in the administrative system and posited the formation of

---

[40]RTsKhIDNI, f. 17, op. 2, d. 441, l. 87. Chubar's assessment was uncannily accurate.

what he called *kontserny* (concerns) that would unify the functions then dispersed among the glavki, trusts, and syndicates. He neglected to explain how these *kontserny* would differ from Rabkrin's ob"edineniia.

Mantsev's talk to the Leningraders failed to reassure or regroup Vesenkha's fragmented bureaucratic lobbies. Officials, mostly trust and factory personnel, reacted "coolly" and with "outright skepticism." Each speaker criticized Mantsev's presentation for its lack of specifics and its emphasis on centralization. It was, as one disappointed delegate phrased it, "no different than Rabkrin's proposal." A representative of the chemical trust claimed not to understand the tendency toward centralized reorganization. The existing system, he argued, was not bad. "We need to fix it, not scrap it." Creation of powerful all-union associations "will only add to our bureaucratic illness." What they should do, he argued, was restore full financial, commercial, and production authority to the regional trusts.

The tendency toward creation of all-union specialized associations, agreed Gurevich, technical director of Leningrad's Karl Marx factory, was "all wrong . . . completely backward." Like his fellow Leningrad industrialists, Gurevich asserted the "primacy" of locally organized industrial administration as the only way to cope with problems of supply and commercial and technical leadership. Yet the industrialists sensed that the trend toward centralization was irreversible. Gurevich agreed that little separated Vesenkha's proposals from those published by Gol'tsman. Under either plan, he said, the trusts would be eviscerated. Still, the Leningrad trusts should fight back. Declaring that "in essence" all economic administration was local, the Leningraders voted to establish their own commission to propose a system governing regional industrial and economic relations, and relations of the Leningrad region with the Russian and all-union levels of Vesenkha.

The next day the editorial board of *Torgovo-promyshlennaia gazeta* expressed the jaded feelings of many officials. The front page of the 9 August 1929 issue displayed a rare editorial cartoon depicting an evil-looking dragon, labeled "Kontsern," devouring syndicates and trusts. *Kontsern* was a transliteration of the German word used to describe a corporation or a military base. Gol'tsman never used the word; he preferred the more prosaic Russian *proizvodstvennoe ob"edinenie*, or production association. Mantsev and other Vesenkha officials, however, used the German word often, especially when they were attempting to distinguish their proposals from Rabkrin's. Unfortunately for Mantsev, the term quickly became associated with the worst features of bureaucratism and with things foreign. Ironically, it was Gol'tsman who made explicit references to German models of organization, but it was to Vesenkha's proposals that the foreign stigma came to be attached.

When it became known that Vesenkha's commission, too, favored cen-

Кого он раньше слопает?

"Who has it already gobbled up?" A "concern," one of the unifying organizations proposed by Vesenkha, devours syndicates and trusts. *Torgovo-promyshlennaia gazeta,* 9 August 1929, Hoover Institution Library.

tralized administration, other regions followed the lead of the Leningraders. Republic, regional, and local-level economic councils in the major industrial areas began to draw up their own proposals, some patterned after the Gol'tsman or Mantsev model but many incorporating some measure of regional or local autonomy.[41] The pressure by local and regional councils and interest groups was so strong that Mantsev felt compelled to remonstrate against it publicly. At a meeting on 23 August 1929 to discuss reorganization, the issue of local control arose again. This time the attack against the center was led by one of the main sponsors of the meeting: the Moscow regional economic council.

At the time of the debate, the Moscow council was fighting to keep control over its last prize factory, the Krasnyi Proletarii machine building complex. The Krasnyi Proletarii was slated to be included in an all-union

[41]See, e.g., the proposals of the Russian Vesenkha and government in *TPG,* 1 November 1929, p. 1. See also GARF, f. 374, op. 15, d. 1056, ll. 1–145.

trust and the Moscow Machine Building Trust, the factory's parent organization, was scheduled to be reduced to a local organization of repair shops. The Muscovites lost the fight, and in October the factory was reorganized into the all-union Stankotrest under the direct control of Vesenkha's chief administration for machine building, Glavmashinstroi. In August, however, the council was in the midst of its vain struggle with Vesenkha and this situation gave a sense of urgency to local criticisms of *Rabkrin's* and Vesenkha's reorganization plans.

Delegates at the meeting offered the same arguments that had been raised in previous forums and showed no signs of willingness to mute their criticisms. Both Gol'tsman and Mantsev gave presentations, but their bickering only confirmed the audience's worst suspicions. One local trust representative declared that he saw no difference between the two presentations; both were "muddled" (*tumano*). Neither addressed issues of local concern, and the only point on which they were clear was that both favored extreme centralization. Both plans, therefore, violated the government's instructions to decentralize operational control in industry. "Everyone knows," another delegate said, that central organs were "rotten through and through." A third delegate criticized the plans as nothing more than a legitimation of the centralizing trends that had been paralyzing industry for years. Either plan would return factories and local organs to the state of "vassalage" they had endured at the end of the Civil War.[42]

Mantsev was not prepared for such vigorous criticism from Vesenkha's own organs. As he began to name the industrial branches that should come under central control—metallurgy, machine building, ferrous and nonferrous metallurgy, mining, oil—someone called out, "What will be left for us!?" Mantsev, clearly caught off guard, replied that he didn't know, exactly, but he thought "there must be a lot left—light industry, and the processing of agricultural raw materials."[43] The stenographer who was recording the exchange used punctuation marks to reproduce Mantsev's verbal floundering, and one gains a strong sense from the transcript that Mantsev was not adept at thinking quickly on his feet. To the Moscow delegates, about to lose a major industrial enterprise, such a reply must have served only to heighten frustration.

Recovering his composure, Mantsev launched into a criticism of what he described as a widespread local movement toward organization of the economy in the form of regional communes (*oblastnye kommuny*). He acknowledged that this term was used by many people who favored full decentralization of the economy. Mantsev also noted its origin in Lenin's writings on the state and revolution, and he acknowledged that "many comrades" were using this authority to attack the move toward centraliza-

[42]GARF 374, op. 1, d. 616, ll. 301, 287, 297.
[43]Ibid., l. 268.

tion. He cautioned, however, that the communal system Lenin described was to come about at the end of the period of socialist construction. In current circumstances, Mantsev argued, centralization was required to ensure the "coordination" (*sochetanie*) of all interests, local as well as all-union. Local officials, however, understood what talk of coordination meant. Coordination, declared one delegate, was another word for centralization.[44]

Vesenkha's revolt against its own leaders culminated at the agency's sixth plenum meetings in October 1929. Most of the thirty-five delegates who attended were hostile to Mantsev's proposals. I. V. Kosior tried to clarify aspects of the proposals: "How is the relationship between union and republic levels formulated?" he began. Before he could continue, however, S. S. Lobov cut in: "It's not formulated in any way at all!" Lobov led the plenum's delegates in their resistance to the presidium. When he pleaded in defense of local interests, he received extended applause. One delegate shouted, "You keep them from laying their hands on us!" (Ty za to, chtoby ne trogali nas!). Lobov likened the Rabkrin-Vesenkha plans to Trotsky's Civil War schemes to militarize economic and labor organization. "Schematically," Lobov said, "this is all very beautiful, but Trotsky also drew pretty pictures that turned out to be useless. With forty-two industrial branches plus subbranches planned, we'll have hundreds of ob-"edineniia, and all of them will sit on Vesenkha's shoulders." Republic- and oblast-level bureaus would just sit and "waste their people." Under the ob"edinenie system "we'll no longer have a republican union, but the geography, once again, of an undivided Russia. We got rid of that during the October Revolution. We don't need to go back to it."[45] Lobov's comments were greeted with cheers and applause. They exposed the real purpose behind Rabkrin's plans: not to resolve economic problems but to build a powerful Russian industrial state, the state dreamed of by Trotsky, Piatakov, and others of the bureaucratic left during the Civil War and early NEP years.

Despite strong resistance, it was clear that the old system was doomed when even Kosior, the staunchest defender of trust and regional rights, refused to champion the cause of the southern regional bloc. In a surprising turnaround, Kosior identified himself with Vesenkha's centralizing plan by presenting it to the sixth plenum meeting. As one of Vesenkha's vice chairs, Kosior was a logical choice for the assignment, but Kuibyshev could just as well have given it to Mantsev, chair of Vesenkha's organizational commission, or to Rukhimovich, the other vice chair and a supporter of centralizing reforms. Tapping Kosior to be the presidium's spokesman was no doubt a conscious decision to demonstrate the unity of

[44]Ibid., ll. 268, 269.
[45]RGAE, f. 3429, op. 6, d. 197, ll. 234, 405–6.

Vesenkha's leaders. In outlining the plan, Kosior was forced to defend it over the strong objections of the delegates.

The presidium members must have placed a great deal of pressure on Kosior, but his turnabout may also have had something to do with Rukhimovich's speech to the plenum. Rukhimovich began with a scathing attack on the southern regional bloc: in resisting the Rabkrin-Vesenkha plan, the "southern comrades" were interested only in what served their own narrow interests. They were "divisive . . . selfish . . . parochial"; they wanted reform only so long as it "all lay in their own hands." To highlight the narrowness of their interests, Rukhimovich presented a bizarre picture of a united industrial Europe. Whether this would be a Soviet Europe he did not say, but he held out (in words that were "not for print") a vision of a Europe-wide "metal" cartel with headquarters in Berlin and branch offices from Alsace to the Urals. This, he declared, was very likely the future of Europe, "possibly in the next few years." In that context, Rukhimovich argued, the Ukrainian interests seemed small indeed. It was time, he said, for them to rise above their petty local concerns.[46]

It is impossible to know whether Rukhimovich concocted this image to make a rhetorical point or whether he believed in the future he predicted. Such a belief may not have been as improbable in 1929 as it appears in retrospect. It is quite possible that Gol'tsman's negotiations in Germany involved topics of mutual cooperation, even discussions about organizational consortium. Such agreements would have looked beneficial to the Soviets, starved for capital at the beginning of their industrialization drive. The prospect of consortium agreements may also have looked promising to German industrialists. By the middle and late 1920s, German heavy industry was overcapitalized and actively seeking new markets in Soviet Russia. In late 1929, especially, German capitalists faced the first slowdowns that presaged the onset of the Great Depression.

Discussions about consortium arrangements would have fitted easily into the articles of secret industrial and military cooperation already established between the two countries. Gol'tsman was certainly not high enough in the government to negotiate any agreements, but the status of his commission was certainly high enough to permit him to broach the subject and have it taken seriously by his German counterparts. Both Rukhimovich and Kosior, as Central Committee members, were in a position to hear of such discussions, even if they were still at an informal stage. The possibility of such an international consortium might have been enough to effect Kosior's turnabout on the issue of reorganization.[47]

[46]Ibid., ll. 384–86.
[47]Rukhimovich's slip and what it may have revealed about ongoing negotiations by the Soviet government may have been the reason these stenographic records were classified "secret" and placed in the "special" Vesenkha files of RGAE. They were declassified in 1992.

If Vesenkha officials expected a vigorous syndicate-led or Vesenkha-led campaign against Rabkrin's proposals, they were disappointed. Vesenkha established the Mantsev commission with great publicity, but little came of it. Throughout August and early September, the Vesenkha and Rabkrin commissions met several times for public debate, but Mantsev's commission never formulated a coherent set of proposals. As a result, Vesenkha officials were placed on the defensive, able only to criticize Rabkrin's plans. On several occasions Gol'tsman even ridiculed Mantsev and his commission for having no plan.[48] At best, the Mantsev commission suggested amendments to Rabkrin's plan. Its most substantive recommendations were efforts to protect their own republic-level and local interests. The commission suggested decentralization of some of the administrative authority that Rabkrin proposed to concentrate at the state level, but these were minor matters; otherwise, the Vesenkha commission took little initiative.[49]

In joint meetings held on 9 and 13 September, Kuibyshev announced that Vesenkha would make no substantive recommendations, only minor alterations to Rabkrin's basic proposals.[50] To give the appearance of unity, a joint Rabkrin-Vesenkha commission was established to make final recommendations for organizational restructuring. Rozengol'ts chaired the commission, whose findings were due in early November. Recommendations of the joint committee did little to change Rabkrin's basic formulas. These recommendations became the basis for the order, issued on 5 December 1929, that abolished the old regionally organized Vesenkha system. In its place, Vesenkha's officials established branch organizations dominated by the all-powerful production ob"edineniia.

Conclusion

Gol'tsman intended the new production associations to form the basis of a unified administrative and planning system to replace the hodge-podge of chief administrations, trusts, and syndicates that had evolved over the course of the 1920s. The ob"edineniia were to reintegrate the functions of investment planning, commercial organization, and accounting control that had been dispersed among the state's different economic and administrative bureaucracies. Through centralizing reforms, Gol'tsman and his Rabkrin colleagues also hoped to overcome regional divisions in the country's trade and commercial networks, and they believed that the new system would finally break the hold of local councils and powerful regional trusts on the economy.

[48]See, e.g., *TPG*, 10 August 1929, p. 1; GARF, f. 374, op. 1, d. 616, l. 295.
[49]GARF, f. 374, op. 1, d. 616, l. 154.
[50]Ibid.

Gol'tsman's organizational reforms laid the foundation for a new industrial state system. Ironically, however, his plans had little to do with organizing an effective economy to accomplish the tasks of industrialization.
In fact, Rabkrin's reforms threatened to exacerbate the two most serious
problems facing the Soviet economy in the late 1920s. A severe shortage of
capital hampered the regime's ambitious plans for new industrial investment and placed a tremendous strain on operating budgets and production programs. And despite expansion throughout the 1920s, the industrial economy at the beginning of the first five-year plan was plagued by
increasingly serious shortages of goods and resources and by an inability
to coordinate supply and demand between industrial producers and consumers. Vesenkha's various rationalization campaigns had failed to generate the kind of savings necessary to finance large-scale industrialization.
Rabkrin's numerous mobilization campaigns, while extorting some supplies, disrupted normal industrial administration and strained already
scarce factory and trust inventories.

As many participants in the organizational debates observed, Rabkrin's
proposals not only threatened the state's commercial economy but violated Party and government instructions to decentralize economic administration. To some it may have seemed curious that Gol'tsman never acknowledged the economic flaws in his proposals or addressed the charges
that his organizational schemes contradicted government directives. Yet
these lapses were curious only to those who assumed that Gol'tsman's
proposals were designed to resolve the salient economic problems affecting the Soviet industrial system. Solving the economic problems of industrialization was not Gol'tsman's principal concern. His primary goal was
to enhance the state's power. He saw centralization of industrial administration as the most effective means to achieve that goal. That state power
might come at the cost of severe economic, social, and financial dislocation
was a point made numerous times and quite forcefully by syndicate
leaders, as well as by other economic officials. Gol'tsman was not moved
by those arguments. Nor was Piatakov, the architect, with Rabkrin's assistance, of the centralizing financial reforms of 1930. The reforms put forward by Rabkrin and Gosbank were designed to create the financial and
organizational mechanisms by which the state could most directly and
effectively extract and use social and economic resources. They were designed to mobilize the economy and society in the service of the state.

Syndicate, trust, and local economic leaders were appalled by those
plans and fought a bitter but losing battle against them. Yet these were not
the only battles to be fought over Rabkrin's policies. Those policies held
implications for other groups in the Soviet industrial system. Many production managers, engineers, labor economists, trade unionists, and workers' organizations opposed Rabkrin's plans for modernizing the industrial

economy, but many others supported and helped shape the RKI's policies on issues of technological reconstruction, productivity, labor organization, and managerial strategies. Their struggles to influence policies contributed as much to the formation of the Soviet industrial state as the organizational battles fought at the level of Vesenkha's central administration.

5

The Politics of Modernization

We were fascinated by mass production . . . infected with
the idea that technology would save us.
—Engineer A. I. Gorbunkov, 1933

The campaign against Vesenkha and the NEP culminated in November
1930, when Sergo Ordzhonikidze and the Rabkrin group that surrounded
him took over Vesenkha.[1] The takeover consolidated the Stalinists' hold on
the country's economic and industrial apparatus and ended the bitter disputes over industrial reorganization and production priorities. It also formalized the radical left turn in the state's economic strategies toward centralized administration, large industrial investment, and ever-increasing
production rates.

The assault on Vesenkha and the trusts was closely linked to the virulent attack by the Stalinist-dominated Party apparatus, the OGPU, and the
RKI against professionals' opposition to the state's program of crash industrialization. Many in the technical and managerial intelligentsia, especially the older, nonparty "bourgeois specialists" who had dominated industrial and economic administration during the NEP years, considered
Rabkrin's plans overambitious, and said so publicly. The Stalinist-dominated Party, believing they faced a revival of class war from the bour-
geoisie, turned on the *spetsy* and suppressed specialists' opposition
through intimidation and arrest. The arrests of *spetsy* demoralized the
country's professional strata and sanctioned a wave of popular assaults
on all professional groups. The sensational trial of mining engineers in the
spring of 1928 inaugurated the Party's antispecialist offensive, which culminated in the Industrial Party trial and purge of the state's economic
administrative apparatus in 1930.[2]

These events—the turn toward maximalist production strategies, the

[1] Fitzpatrick, "Sergo Ordzhonikidze."
[2] For accounts of the antispecialist campaign and trials see Azrael, *Managerial Power*; Bailes,
Technology and Society; Lampert, *Technical Intelligentsia*; Fitzpatrick, "Sergo Ordzhonikidze."

reorganization of Vesenkha, and the antispecialist campaign—have traditionally been viewed as the defeat of rational economic planning and industrial management and the subordination of industry's professional elites to political control by the Communist Party. All the major accounts of Party-professional relations during the 1920s and 1930s agree that there existed an inherent conflict between Communist Party control of the economy and the threat, perceived by the Stalinists, of control by technocratically minded, non-Party specialists.[3] Certainly, tension existed between the Party and the professionals, and Party officials jealously guarded control over economic decision making. As Kendall Bailes observed, "Stalinist wills continued to be the final arbiters of all important policy decisions."[4] So they did, but by emphasizing the conflicts between politicians and specialists, historians have tended to fix their attention on the fates of specialists who opposed Stalinist policies. Most acknowledge that some specialists were loyal, but few examine the extent of professional support for the Stalinists' left turn, or the role specialists played in designing Stalinist industrial strategies.

It is not clear why this aspect of Party-professional relations should remain unexplored. Perhaps because Stalinist policies were so economically irrational, we assume that trained specialists could not have designed or supported them. Whatever the reason, most historians have assumed that since politicians had the final say in matters of industrial strategy, they were the primary initiators of those policies. Specialists, in other words, either quietly acquiesced in the regime's policies or had the courage to question them and suffered the consequences.[5]

In fact, specialists exerted considerable influence over the views of Party and government officials responsible for the formulation of industrial policy. Politics was certainly "in command," as Nicholas Lampert argues, but the issues that politicized industrial policy in the late 1920s did not cut neatly along the lines of Party vs. specialists.[6] Conflict arose not just between politicians and professionals but also among the various occupational strata of engineers and managers, between generations of specialists, and between specialists in different bureaucracies and different regions. Those disagreements heightened political and ideological ten-

[3]Lampert and Bailes show that the interaction between Party and professions was complex and contingent, not a relationship of simple hostility, yet even Lampert accepts the basic premise that tensions were "endemic . . . between the agencies of the state and technical intelligentsia": *Technical Intelligentsia*, p. 157. See also Kendall Bailes, "The Politics of Technology: Stalin and Technocratic Thinking among Soviet Engineers" *American Historical Review* 79 (April 1974): 445–69.

[4]Bailes, *Technology and Society*, p. 413.

[5]Many writers cite the famous economist S. G. Strumilin's line about standing for high targets rather than sitting for low ones as generally characteristic of Party-professional relations. See, e.g., Davies, *Soviet Economy in Turmoil*, p. 119.

[6]Lampert, *Technical Intelligentsia*, p. 149.

sions between professionals and Party officials. Indeed, conflicts among engineers and managers helped polarize debates over industrial policy and pushed thinking about production and technological possibilities to extremes.

As conflict between Vesenkha and the RKI sharpened in the late 1920s, so did differences in strategies among professional organizations that aligned with one or the other agency. This was especially the case in the area of machine building, one of the most important industrial sectors of the economy. Some of Vesenkha's leading specialists opposed Rabkrin's naive mass-production strategies and fought for a balanced approach to industrial modernization. Specialists in the syndicates and in the trusts advocated moderation and a mix of technological and commercial reforms to stimulate production. Other specialists, however, especially engineering experts in design bureaus and central state administrations, encouraged Rabkrin's planners to disregard economic constraints and pour resources into technology. Engineers and other specialists who worked in production and in factory administrations also supported Rabkrin's modernization policies, and all had their own reasons for doing so: because those policies promised to change occupational or production relations, or because modernization, they hoped, would solve problems in the labor market. Whatever the reason, for the many specialists who supported the regime's industrial drive, politics did not mean interference by Party or police in their sphere of professional authority; just the opposite. The industrialization drive and the regime's determination to modernize the economy opened up new professional opportunities and promised to resolve long-standing professional and occupational problems. It was not just the unrestrained hubris of Stalinist planners that accounted for the utopian character of the state's industrialization strategies during the first five-year plan. The modernist vision of technological salvation that mesmerized Party leaders also mesmerized many engineers and other specialists. Those specialists not only supported but helped shape the state's strategies for transforming Soviet industry.

Rabkrin and the Politics of Mass Production

As we have seen, Rabkrin officials challenged the adequacy of the Vesenkha system to mobilize the economy on a scale adequate for rapid industrialization. They charged that weak central leadership throughout the 1920s had resulted in loose financial control, an orgy of spending, and a system of interregional rivalry that threatened the state's control of the economy. They were convinced, rightly, that the cause of Vesenkha's weakness lay in the decentralized commercial, technological, and administrative structures that allowed regional interests to dominate and distort the state's economic policies. The industrial trusts were the key representatives of those interests. Thus Rabkrin's officials were determined not to resolve the economic difficulties of the industrialization drive but to break the regional trusts' power over the economy.

Rabkrin's leaders set out their industrial strategy in a summary report edited by A. P. Rozengol'ts for the 16th Party Congress in the summer of 1930. Almost all of their recommendations involved technological reconstruction, especially the introduction of mass-production methods. RKI planners believed that industry could eliminate shortages not by market or pricing adjustments, as many specialists in Vesenkha and Narkomfin advocated, but by maximizing production capabilities. Mikhail Kaganovich, in particular, called for the "emulation" of American methods of mass production, which he claimed would open up vistas of nearly unlimited production capacity.[7] Rozengol'ts claimed that the introduction of flow and mass production techniques promised such a revolutionary increase in production capacity that shortages would disappear.[8]

Rabkrin officials intended that the country would literally produce its way out of crisis. At the same time, through centralized reorganization of industrial administration by branch or sector, Ordzhonikidze and RKI planners hoped to eliminate regional divisions within Vesenkha's administrative system and build a nationally integrated state industrial system.[9] Articles critical of regional trust organization of industry appeared frequently in *Za industrializiatsiiu* and *Za ratsionalizatsiiu*, both RKI journals. *Izvestiia* and *Pravda* gave the RKI criticisms prominent coverage. A typical article, signed by the RKI worker L. Lipovetskii, appeared in *Za ratsionalizatsii* in June 1929. Writing about the machine building industries, Lipovetskii asked rhetorically, "What kind of trusts do we need?" He described the existing regionally organized trust system as "backward," a "hindrance to full utilization of modern mass production technologies and engineering practices within a socialist system of centralized planning." He chastised trusts for resisting specialization and mass production technologies and charged that the narrow, regional interests of the trusts blocked the kind of modernization so desperately needed. Lipovetskii went so far as to suggest that trust practice bordered on open sabotage of the socialist construction program. He referred to the much-deplored crisis of technical leadership and called for centralized administration of the various machine building and engineering sectors of the economy.[10]

[7]See Kaganovich's early 1930 letter to Ordzhonikidze reporting on his tour of American machine plants: RTsKhIDNI, f. 85, op. 27, d. 214, ll. 9–13.

[8]Rozengol'ts, *Promyshlennost'*, p. 16.

[9]Ibid., p. 17.

[10]L. Lipovetskii, "Kakie mashinotresty nam nuzhny?" *Za ratsionalizatsiiu*, 1929, no. 6, pp. 18–19.

Vesenkha and the Politics of Modernization

Numerous specialists, of course, opposed Rabkrin's plans. They included some of the most distinguished engineers and economists in Vesenkha, among them N. F. Charnovskii, head of the Rationalization Bureau. Charnovskii had been a distinguished engineer-economist since before the Revolution and had written several theoretical works on the relation of economic principles to engineering practice.[11] In the mid-1920s he headed Vesenkha's Scientific-Technical Section before his appointment as head of its Rationalization Bureau. Charnovskii belonged to no professional union and was not a Party member, but he worked loyally for the Soviet regime and attempted to separate his political views from his work as a professional engineer. All the same, Charnovskii became a prominent defendant in the Industrial Party trial in late 1930. It was the price he paid for opposition to Rabkrin's line.

L. Ia. Shukhgalter was another of Vesenkha's leading engineer-economists who publicly criticized Rabkrin's industrial policies. S. Veitsman and B. N. Dobrovol'skii worked as chief engineers in the state's design office, Gipromez, one of Rabkin's favorite targets in 1928 and 1929. M. L. Kheifets and M. F. Orentlikher worked for VMTS, the engineering syndicate. Kheifets was a leading industrial economist and a frequent contributor to the journal *Metall*, a syndicate journal and key organ of anti-Rabkrin professional opinion. He often wrote substantive reviews of current developments in engineering practice and the economics of machine building industries in foreign countries. Orentlikher was the syndicate's chief engineer and also a well-known contributor to *Metall*. He used the journal and his position at VMTS to promote development of an indigenous engineering tradition and criticized Rabkrin's enthusiasm for the latest Western technologies.

These specialists favored modernization, as did Vesenkha officials in general, but not Rabkrin's overambitious plans for large-scale mass production and centralized administration. Although Vesenkha and syndicate officials had their quarrels with the trusts, economists and engineers in those bureaucracies united in their opposition against the RKI's strategies. Their criticisms focused mainly on what they charged was an uncritical adaptation of American production methods. Ford-style mass production technologies, Charnovskii wrote, should not be introduced simply because they promised greater production capacity. They were appropriate for automobile and tractor production, he acknowledged, but the nature of the product and its market requirements also had to be considered, even within a planned economy.

[11]E.g., N. F. Charnovskii, *Tekhno-ekonomicheskie printsipy v metallopromyshlennosti* (Moscow, 1927).

In fact, Charnovskii wrote, mass production methods in some areas of machine building required a flexible, individualized style of production in other areas. Charnovskii did not explain the reasoning behind his argument, but it was well known to his readers. For mass production to work properly, the manufacturing process had to be broken down to single-task operations, and machines had to be developed that could perform each of these operations in a repetitive, standardized manner. Operations for this kind of manufacture could number in the hundreds or even the thousands. Each operation required either a specialized machine or special tools that could be adapted to machines used for similar operations. Thus mass production of automobiles or tractors required machine tool factories to supply a broad range of specialized cutters, shapers, and other kinds of instruments. Those machines and instruments could not themselves be mass produced; each had to be individually designed and machined for its intended purpose. Clearly, as Charnovskii argued, mass production of machine tools was inappropriate, even as mass production methods were being introduced in other areas of machine manufacture. Without mentioning the RKI by name, Charnovskii cautioned that those who advocated mass production technologies without regard to economic constraints and consumer needs were ill advised.[12]

Kheifets echoed Charnovskii's criticism in a review of the German and American machine tool industries. The American engineering industry, he wrote, consisted of nonspecialized, small to medium-sized shops. Employing highly skilled workers, these shops maintained a broad product range to satisfy the specialized needs of a variety of industrial customers. The secret of their success, Kheifets argued, was that they not only produced machines to their customers' specifications but acted as engineering consultants. American companies supplied advice and equipment for tooling up and integrating their equipment with existing production processes. Such flexibility and sensitivity to the client's needs resulted from the close relations the machine builders maintained with their clients, a collaboration that was possible mainly because the industry was not centralized. An American machine tool shop maintained its own sophisticated design and research facilities; it had no need to deal with a faraway national design bureau. This arrangement stimulated new technical ideas "at the crucial juncture of design and production."[13]

In Germany, Kheifets noted, though the average size of machine tool works was not large, production was dominated by a consortium of man-

---

[12]N. F. Charnovskii, "Ekonomicheskie i tekhnicheskie predposylki 'Fordizatsii' proizvod-stva," *Metall*, 1927, no. 6, pp. 61–64. Charnovskii's article amounted to a defense of the flexible production strategies favored by Soviet industrial trusts in the 1920s.

[13]L. M. Kheifets, "Mashinostroitel'nye promyshlennosti Germanii i SASSh," *Metall*, 1929, no. 12, p. 99.

ufacturers. By controlling market competition, the consortium could coordinate the specialization of factories in the production of two or three basic types of machines. Such specialization permitted the use of long-run production methods hitherto considered inappropriate to machine tool building. These techniques increased the productive capacity of particular types of machinery enormously, but they reduced the industry's ability to adapt to the increasingly specialized and rapidly changing technological structure of the domestic and world engineering market. Kheifets produced statistics to show that German firms were having trouble selling their machinery both at home and on the world market. As a result of their extreme rationalization policies, Kheifets wrote, German machine building firms now found themselves overcapitalized with conservative technologies, burdened with high amortization costs, and losing profits to American firms.[14]

Kheifets extracted the lessons from his review tactfully but clearly. Whether the economy was planned or capitalist, he argued, most manufacturing firms had to respond to the specialized and changing needs of their industrial consumers. The Americans' nonspecialized, decentralized, medium-scale production strategy provided the flexibility needed to do so. Kheifets distinguished this style of production from the *Fordizm* of the popular imagination: large-scale, single-type, integrated mass production technologies. Like Charnovskii, Kheifets did not specifically mention Rabkrin, but the implications of his review clearly amounted to a criticism of the RKI campaign to convert Soviet industry to mass production.

Charnovskii and Kheifets focused on the economic constraints to developing mass production; Shukhgalter emphasized Russia's cultural limitations. He insisted that continuous flow and mass production methods were appropriate only in "rare cases," not only because of market considerations but also because of the need to concentrate the country's scarce technical and labor talent. The relatively simple tasks of mass production might be appropriate for Russia's vast semiskilled working population, Shukhgalter argued, but the need to coordinate primary and auxiliary production processes required a "highly advanced economic, technological, and organizational culture." Such characteristics were hard to find among Russia's few professional engineers and skilled workers. Shukhgalter and like-minded labor economists considered the training of managerial and technical cadre to deal with the organizational problems of mass production to be the single greatest hindrance to the introduction of this type of manufacture. It would require, Shukhgalter declared, at least a generation to overcome Russia's backwardness in this area.[15]

[14]Ibid., p. 94.
[15]*TPG*, 23 May 1928, p. 5. See also A. Sipachev, "Dva goda piatiletki Mosmashtresta," *Metall*, 1930, no. 1, p. 108. In practice, attempts to introduce mass production exploded the myth that such production required only unskilled labor.

Orentlikher, Kheifets, and other syndicate engineers and economists played central roles in shaping Vesenkha's five-year plan for machine building, adopted in the spring of 1929. They worked closely with a group of specialists around A. F. Tolokontsev, the head of Glavmashinstroi, which included Shukhgalter and Charnovskii. The Vesenkha-syndicate proposals called for an increase in manufacturing capacity through greater specialization, but Vesenkha's specialists stopped short of calling for the introduction of mass production methods. "Realization of specialization in this branch," they wrote, "requires great circumspection in view of the diversity of types, the large number of models, and the vast assortment of machines required by Soviet industry."[16] While it called for greater specialization in all areas of machine building, the plan advocated production flexibility, especially in the area of machine tools.

The five-year plan produced by the Vesenkha-syndicate engineers did not provide for any radical break with current trust practice. Rabkrin officials characterized it as conservative—indeed, as "backward" and therefore politically suspect—because it did not envision the kind of instant modernization that supposedly would bring Soviet technology up to German or American standards. Yet the politics of backwardness was a tricky game, and what appeared conservative from one point of view could look radical from another. Rabkrin officials always cast themselves in the light of radical modernization and Vesenkha in the gloom of stagnation and conservative backwardness. Occasionally, however, Vesenkha officials were able to point up the conservative underside of Rabkrin's boasts. I. I. Matrozov, a Vesenkha economist, responded to Rabkrin's accusations in *Torgovo-promyshlennaia gazeta*: The RKI's strategies, which Matrozov equated with bureaucratization and detrustification, "are rejected by all industrialists. They lead to extreme complications in planning and administration, to the dissipation of economic experience, a demand for huge increases in circulating capital, and the loss of production advantages through narrow specialization and standardization of factories."[17]

Trust leaders understood that, despite Rabkrin's claims to being the true revolutionary modernizers of industry, mass production and centralization would have an ultimately *conservative* effect on production. Specialization threatened to lock factories into the manufacture of a narrow range of items, thereby reducing trusts' production flexibility and limiting producers' ability to respond to trade and market fluctuations. Just as important, Rabkrin's drive toward administrative centralization and massive industrial reconstruction threatened to undermine the network of economic, technological, and commercial structures that had formed the basis of the trusts' autonomy. No single trust could amass resources for industrialization on the scale Rabkrin anticipated. Only the combined resources of

[16]See "Obzor piatiletnogo plana razvitii mashinostroenii," *Metall*, 1929, nos. 5/6, p. 18.
[17]*TPG*, 4 October 1928, p. 3.

powerful central bureaucracies could mobilize society and the economy on that scale. Rabkrin's plans required complete reconstruction of the state and the end of the regional trust system.

E. M. Al'perovich and Orgametall

In contrast to Vesenkha's specialists, engineers in Orgametall, the state design consulting bureaucracy, allied themselves closely with Rabkrin. The engineer E. M. Al'perovich, head of Orgametall during the mid- and late 1920s, stated the bureau's position on machine tool production clearly in the autumn of 1930. He agreed with the RKI that the machine tool industry fell short in both quantity and quality and must be reconstructed to take advantage of the newest technologies and production techniques.[18] Al'perovich advocated the use and reproduction of foreign, especially German, production models and designs. He pleaded that it "should not be a crime" to use imported equipment if it was of a higher quality than domestic equipment. He cited the recent experience of German firms in the application of cutting instruments made from special carbide alloys. These instruments, he claimed, increased cutting speed up to 200 percent.[19] In the short run, A'lperovich argued, the judicious use of foreign equipment and expertise could only help Soviet industry to meet the targets set for the industrialization drive. To lend his case the appropriate credibility, he cited RKI's statistics to show that domestic cutting equipment was only 7 to 25 percecnt as efficient as foreign machines. German machinery, adapted with interchangeable cutting heads and other attachments, would allow large increases in productivity while maintaining the necessary flexibility in production range and scale.[20]

Specialists in both Orgametall and Vesenkha advocated greater factory specialization and centralized control as a means to standardize materials and reduce the number of types of manufactured products. These were classic rationalization measures designed to raise productivity and lower costs. At the same time, specialists in both organizations stressed the need to develop an innovative design tradition, and both groups urged development of an engineering industry that provided ongoing technical assistance to factories. Syndicate and Orgametall strategies diverged on the matter of centralized administrative control. More important, they took different approaches to markets and consumer conditions. Syndicate engineers and economists cautioned against overspecialization and overcentralization. Orentlikher, the VMTS's chief design engineer, warned re-

---

[18] E. M. Al'perovich, "Stanok i instrument: Osnovnoe zveno mashinostroeniia," *Izvestiia*, 9 September 1930, p. 2.
[19] Ibid.
[20] Ibid.

peatedly that the engineering and organizational potential for increasing production had to be balanced against the need to respond to industry's demands.[21] Here he agreed with Charnovskii, Vesenkha's chief engineer-economist, and with the leading trust specialists.[22] Orentlikher advocated greater specialization and standardization, but the syndicate's market and labor orientation kept him from fully adopting the radical RKI position of an undifferentiated mass production strategy based on the sole criterion of increased productive capacity. Vesenkha and VMTS officials had their quarrels, but their common market orientation made sense of the engineering strategy they advocated.

Orgametall's function as an engineering design bureau and its role as a foreign liaison led its specialists to be concerned primarily with advances in the engineering field. Thus Orgametall envisioned a centralized design and engineering bureau for the whole country, one with close ties to foreign engineering developments. It would function much as Orgametall was supposed to function already, but it would have more than mere consulting powers. Existing trusts would be consulted on their needs, but their only decisive function would be to ensure the execution of production plans developed by higher economic and industrial organs. All design, commercial, and production functions would be centered in an all-union association. Centralization, Al'perovich argued, would promote better use of scarce engineering personnel and would ensure rapid progress in modernizing Russia's machine manufacturing industries.[23]

Orgametall officials acknowledged that the most modern equipment and techniques were not always suited to Soviet conditions, and they conceded that adaptations would have to be made. Thus the state's central engineering association needed to work closely with its industrial clients.[24] But Al'perovich was adamant that in general, and contrary to the opinion of Vesenkha and syndicate engineers, it would be better to train workers to work on new technologies than to design machines "down" to the relatively unskilled levels of Russia's workforce. Vesenkha's plan, he charged, would sentence both Russia's labor force and its engineering industries to perpetual backwardness.[25]

Orgametall's engineering orientation explains why its specialists actively endorsed Rabkrin's strategies. For both groups, state-sponsored industrial expansion provided an unlimited market in which constant technological modernization became an end in itself. Whereas syndicate

[21]See M. F. Orentlikher, "Sostoianie i perspektivy stankostroeniia SSSR," *Metall*, 1927, no. 6, pp. 74–81, and "Problema stankostroeniia v SSSR," *Metall*, 1928, nos. 3/4, pp. 123–28.
[22]Charnovskii, *Tekhno-ekonomicheskie printsipy*, p. 19.
[23]Al'perovich, "Stanok i instrument."
[24]Ibid.
[25]Ibid.; E. M. Al'perovich, "Stankostroenie v Germanii i v SASSh," *TPG*, 31 December 1927, p. 3.

policies were designed to encourage a balanced and gradual evolution of technology, skill levels, and industrial consumer needs, Rabkrin and Orgametall proposed to force modernization onto industry and labor.

The memoirs of a young engineer reveal how committed both Rabkrin and Orgametall officials were to aggressive modernization. The young specialist A. I. Gorbunkov, who worked in the Krasnyi Proletarii machine tool factory in Moscow in the early 1930s, recalled the debates that arose when the factory proposed to adapt a German lathe design. Al'perovich, by then head of the machine tool consortium that supervised the factory, opposed the plan to simplify some of the lathe's operations to accommodate the level of Soviet workers' skill. In keeping with his commitment to aggressive modernization, Al'perovich argued that the factory should reproduce the machines as they were manufactured in Germany. Ordzhonikidze, already head of Vesenkha, attended a meeting to discuss the Krasnyi Proletarii plans and concurred with Al'perovich, stating that "it isn't worth it" to buy the latest designs and then make them into "inferior" Soviet equipment. According to Gorbunkov, Ordzhonikidze argued that "it was time the Soviet worker became accustomed to working in modern industry."[26]

That the strategies of the Rabkrin and Orgametall were similar was no coincidence. Al'perovich and his group were well situated to influence Rabkrin's policies. Al'perovich not only was head of Orgametall but served on the collegium of the Moscow RKI. As an RKI specialist, he toured machine building works in both the United States and Germany in 1927 and 1928. Al'perovich became an expert on industrial survey methods and published several works on the subject.[27] Few of the major RKI functionaries involved in the survey work of the machine building industry were trained engineers. Thus Kaganovich, the head of Rabkrin's machine building strategy group, drew on the expertise of Al'perovich, the engineers in Orgametall, and Moscow's RKI bureau.[28] The coincidence of views between the two groups was striking, as was Al'perovich's highly public alliance with Kaganovich and the RKI against Vesenkha, the engineering syndicate, and the trusts.

Al'perovich did more than court favor with a powerful state inspectorate. He pursued the campaign against Vesenkha and the trusts more aggressively than Rabkrin's officials did, even as Vesenkha's managers attempted to accommodate Rabkrin's demands. Indeed, the more Vesen-

[26]GARF, f. 7952, op. 3, d. 94, l. 123.

[27]*Vsia Moskva*, 1926, 1928. See his *Osnovnye polozheniia po metodike obsledovanii* (Moscow, 1927).

[28]B. G. Rubinshtein, "Orgametall," *Metall*, 1928, no. 10, pp. 119–26. See also Julian Cooper, "The Development of the Soviet Machine Tool Industry, 1917–1941" (Ph.D. thesis, University of Birmingham, 1975), p. 56.

kha's officials compromised, the more vociferous and radical became Al-
'perovich's criticisms. He insisted, for example, that the machine tool
branch be given first investment priority among the various machine
manufacturing sectors of the economy.[29] Although Kaganovich supported
the demand that more attention be given to machine tool production, he
never advocated that it be given first investment priority. In May 1929,
Kaganovich welcomed Vesenkha's initiative to create Stankotrest, the all-
union engineering cartel, yet Al'perovich continued to criticize Vesenkha
policy as if the new trust did not exist. Throughout the late months of
1929 and into 1930, Al'perovich reiterated his call for the forced development of the machine tool industry as a separate branch of machine building administered under a specialized administration. It did not seem to
matter to him that Vesenkha had created Stankotrest to do precisely that.[30]

In the summer of 1930 Al'perovich achieved part of his goal. In the
general reorganization of that year, Vesenkha's chief administration for
machine building, Glavmashinstroi, was replaced by a new production
association, Mashinoob"edinenie. Stankotrest was disbanded and the
VMTS was absorbed into the new machine building cartel. In June a new
all-union association, Soiuzstankoinstrument (SSI), was set up to administer the machine tool and instruments industries. Unlike Stankotrest, the
SSI combined all engineering, production, and commercial functions,
as Al'perovich had demanded. Al'perovich was named to head the new
association and he brought seven of his assistants with him from
Orgametall. Together this group dominated the ten-member collegium of
Soiuzstankoinstrument, and they used their new positions to press the
attack against Vesenkha.

Under constant pressure, Vesenkha finally endorsed Al'perovich's
plans, which he presented to Vesenkha's presidium on 9 September. Vesenkha's resolutions did not, as Al'perovich had urged, give machine tool
building first investment priority, but they did call for forced development
of the machine tool and instruments industry under the SSI. The resolutions also concurred in the need for a fundamental effort to renew equipment and machine designs, and to make the transition to production of
modern, Western-style machine models by 1932. They foresaw the development of a central design office and the construction of new experimental factories, and they sanctioned the use of foreign technical assistance.
Finally, the resolutions restated the need to rationalize the engineering

[29]*Izvestiia*, 9 August 1930, p. 2.
[30]See Al'perovich's criticisms in *Za industrializatsiiu*, 24 July 1930, p. 3, and 9 September
1930, p. 2; *Izvestiia*, 5 August 1930. The strategies advanced by the Orgametall group differed
from those advocated by the VSNKh group in other ways, but most of these differences
concerned the timing of investment strategy and how best to use foreign expertise and equipment.

industries through strict factory specialization and the consequent introduction of large-serial and mass production methods of manufacture.[31]

The resolutions of Vesenkha's presidium meeting set policy for the machine tool industry for the next two years and marked a significant turn
from Vesenkha's original plan of 1929. Kaganovich and the Rabkrin group
had triumphed, but the victory of Al'perovich and the Orgametall specialists was greater. Al'perovich took the lead in formulating Rabkrin's policies and pushed the hardest for the changes that eventually led to establishment of Soiuzstankoinstrument. As its head, Al'perovich set Soviet
engineering policies throughout the 1930s.

A. I. Gorbunkov and the Krasnyi Proletarii Factory

If Rabkrin's plans appealed to engineers in central state design bureaucracies, those plans also appealed, for different reasons, to a growing
number of production engineers. Such was the case of the young Komsomol engineer A. I. Gorbunkov and his co-workers at the Krasnyi Proletarii
machine factory in Moscow. Gorbunkov's story and that of his comrades
at the Krasnyi Proletarii comes from a series of unpublished memoirs
transcribed in the early 1930s. These memoirs were part of Maxim
Gorky's project to compile a history of Soviet factories. Gorbunkov's account candidly describes the often ugly politics of reconstruction and the
conflicts that arose at the Krasnyi Proletarii during the late 1920s.

Formerly the Bromley works, the Krasnyi Proletarii squatted in a near
southeast suburb of Moscow. It was a medium-sized plant that produced
precision lathes and diesel engines. In 1928 the factory employed 1,500
workers, but reconstruction promised to double its output and require
twice as many employees. Gorbunkov was part of a cohort of young engineers, freshly graduated from the Moscow Technical Academy in 1926. He
went to work at the Krasnyi Proletarii the same year.

Gorbunkov and his colleagues uncritically embraced Rabkrin's modernization strategies. They were, by their own accounts, "enthusiastic" about
the opportunities presented by industrial expansion and by the prospects
of working with new technologies. As committed Communists and young
professionals, these men saw themselves as playing important roles in the
reconstruction of Soviet industry. They followed the strategy debates between Rabkrin and Vesenkha closely and kept up with current developments in foreign engineering industries in technical journals, especially
Orgainformatsion, Orgametall's official journal. Gorbunkov recalled that he

[31]The resolution is summarized in *Za industrializatsiiu*, 12 September 1930. It is also printed
in *Direktivy i postanovleniia KPSS i Sovetskoe pravitel'stva po khoziaistvennym voprosam* (Moscow,
1962), pp. 455–57.

and his colleagues were much influenced by a newly published translation of a work on rationalization by the German professional engineering association, the Verein Deutscher Ingenieur, or VDI.[32]

Gorbunkov felt strongly that the RKI's plans would allow Soviet Russia to adopt the latest German and American engineering advances. He felt also that the fragmented, local control of industry in Soviet Russia hindered engineering development. He identified trust interests as too narrowly regional and market-oriented to allow full use of new technologies and production techniques. Only an all-union organization of the machine building industries, he believed, could mobilize and concentrate the technical, financial, and material resources necessary to propel the industry out of its "backward" state and into the modern engineering era.[33]

Despite their enthusiasm, Gorbunkov and others in his cohort felt deeply frustrated in their efforts to realize their professional and political goals. New on the job, low in the professional hierarchy, and often with little formal training, young specialists bitterly resented what they referred to as an industrial caste system. They felt excluded by the older, mostly noncommunist professional strata that dominated management of the Krasnyi Proletarii and its parent organization, Mosmashtrest.[34] Throughout the 1920s, this older cadre of engineer-managers maintained control over production planning and engineering design decisions at the Krasnyi Proletarii. Older engineers with broad prerevolutionary training occupied authoritative positions in the factory and trust and socialized in the prestigious All-Union Association of Engineers, the VAI. Many had held factory leadership positions before the Revolution. The Krasnyi Proletarii was one of the few works lucky enough to have several top engineers stay on after the Revolution. One of the leading trust engineers, Nikolai List, was the son of the former owner of the Krasnyi Proletarii works.

Gorbunkov began work as an assistant engineer in the production control department. Many of his young colleagues worked as shift engineers directly in production. Younger engineers were more narrowly trained than their older colleagues, and because of the pressing need for technical staff, many of them started work before they had completed their training programs. While older managers and engineers lunched together in their

---

[32]GARF, f. 7952, op. 3., d. 94, l. 91. The publication of this three-volume work in 1928 appears to have been a major event in the Soviet engineering world. Numerous engineers and economists made reference to it. Gorbunkov referred to it as *O kulture vzaimozameniaemogo proizvodstva, o sovremennykh rezhushchikh instrumentakh, i o kulture prisposoblenii*, but I find no listing for a work of that title or of a literally translated title in German.

[33]Ibid., l. 84.

[34]Ibid., l. 94.

A Komsomol meeting at the Krasnyi Proletarii factory, c. 1930. GARF.

offices, younger colleagues tended to gather at breaktime in the office of the factory Party or trade union committee. There they would socialize, drink tea, and discuss the latest political events.[35]

Though all technical staff were part of the same professional strata, the two generations of engineers inhabited very different social, political, and occupational worlds. Young communist specialists associated professionally in the engineering-technical section of the metallists' union rather than in the prestigious VAI. Moreover, the commitment of younger engineers to the Party appeared "very strange" to their older colleagues, who conceived of their relation to the state in traditional professional terms of an exchange of services for financial remuneration and social status.[36] Younger engineers identified personally and enthusiastically as well as professionally with the regime's industrialization goals, and felt that the older men were robbing them of their rightful place at the head of the great socialist construction offensive.

The differences that separated engineering groups translated into dis-

[35]Ibid., ll. 107, 89.

[36]See the memoir of the engineer Gil'debrand ibid., l. 75a, and the discussion of ethics and professional values by the engineer Bobrov in the spring of 1929, ibid., d. 82, ll. 150–85, esp. 150–53.

putes over engineering and production strategy. Younger specialists criticized factory and trust leaders for their resistance to new designs and mass production methods. Moreover, they charged factory and trust managers with conspiratorial intent in making production and engineering decisions in secret, without consulting lower personnel or the factory workforce in general. Trust officials doggedly explained that market conditions prevented the factory from specializing. Managers defended their authority to make decisions and argued that older, simpler machines were more appropriate and cost-effective than new sophisticated tools in the relatively underdeveloped conditions of Soviet industry.[37]

Social and political tensions in the factory mounted in 1928 and 1929, as they did throughout Soviet industry. Denunciations of oppositionists became routine in Party meetings at the Krasnyi Proletarii and fistfights broke out daily between Stalinist agitators and workers sympathetic to political opposition groups in the city. Rabkrin was pressing its attack against Vesenkha during these years, and the Party's antispecialist offensive was gaining momentum after the sensational trial of mining engineers in the spring and summer of 1928. In such an atmosphere, the Krasnyi Proletarii's Party cell began to pressure the factory's director, Stepanov, to take action against the noncommunist specialists. Though Stepanov was himself a Communist, he defended the factory's "bourgeois" specialists and cautioned Party activists not to construe differences over production strategy as political sabotage. Political tensions in the works were already running high, and Stepanov pleaded that Party members not inflame workers' resentment against the older engineering strata. Good engineers were difficult to find, he argued, and it was already hard enough to maintain production schedules in the face of increased economic strains and rising social tensions.[38]

Political reporting by outside newspapers, especially by *Komsomolskaia pravda* and the RKI journal *Tekhnika upravleniia*, heightened tensions by focusing the city's attention on the factory. So did intervention by the Moscow Party committee. Two of Stalin's close allies, Anastas Mikoyan and Viacheslav Molotov, had once worked at the factory and they lent their considerable political weight to the factory Party committee's fight against the "old *Bromleevshchiki*." Both Molotov and Mikoyan visited the factory often during these troubled times. They toured the shops and gave speeches at political rallies. They criticized the "conservatism" of the trust

[37]Gorbunkov summarizes the differences in strategy ibid., d. 94, ll. 84–85. E. A. Satel', technical director of Mosmashtrest, argued that too much specialization "is extremely risky": ibid., d. 82, ll. 11–11a, 12a–13.

[38]Stenographic records of the factory Party committee session of 23 February 1929, Protokol no. 13, "O rukovodiashchik kadrakh zavoda," are ibid., d. 94, ll. 22–26.

management and openly warned factory officials that their secretive (*ka-binetnye*) methods of management would no longer be tolerated.[39]

In the spring of 1928, a Party purge relieved Stepanov of his position as director. Mozgov, his replacement, also found himself trapped between the political demands of the Party committee on the one side and the engineering and managerial staffs of the factory and trust on the other. Mozgov was a weak leader and did not have Stepanov's resolve in opposing the Party committee. Mozgov vowed to create a loyal Communist engineering cadre at the works, but he was reluctant to take action against Tugarinov, the chief engineer, whom the Party committee singled out for harassment. Although Mozgov proved a reluctant ally, demographics was on the side of the Party committee. Throughout 1928 and 1929, Mozgov brought in young engineers to fill positions in the recently expanded functional and production departments. Most of these recruits were Communists and graduates of the Moscow Technical and Engineering Academy, and they found common cause with Gorbunkov and his colleagues.

Tensions between professional groups erupted in late 1929 over a relatively minor issue. At a stormy factory engineering meeting, Gorbunkov led a group of young specialists who challenged the decision to purchase diesel engine designs from the Deitz engineering firm in Germany. The designs were outdated, Gorbunkov claimed; Deitz was producing engines far more advanced than the ones Krasnyi Proletarii had ordered. Tugarinov and his assistant Bobrov were guilty of intentional sabotage at worst, of gross incompetence at best. Gorbunkov produced evidence, gathered with the help of the factory's Party committee, that managers had made serious mistakes in the design and instrumentation work for manufacture of the Deitz engine, and he was ready with counterproposals that he and his young colleagues had drawn up.[40]

Gorbunkov's group, with the help of the Party committee, had planned the confrontation with senior managers for some time. Faleks, the committee head, called several closed strategy meetings, which Molotov and Mikoyan attended. Some of these sessions ran through the night. According to Gorbunkov, the issue was considered so sensitive that the meetings were kept secret even from Party members who were part of the factory administration.[41]

Bobrov defended the decision to purchase the Deitz motor designs and justified the production plans drawn up at the factory. The two sides traded charges that went far beyond the original issue of diesel manufacture. Bobrov claimed that he had acted with the best professional judg-

[39]Gorbunkov reports Molotov's warning that if management policies should continue as in the past, "it might end quite sadly" for them: ibid., l. 114.
[40]Ibid., ll. 96–98.
[41]Ibid., l. 96.

A Party cell at the Krasnyi Proletarii factory, c. 1930. GARF.

ment, and he failed to understand why his younger colleagues were attacking him. Gorbunkov reiterated the charges of elitism and anti-Soviet-
ism. The meeting, which had begun in the early evening, wore on into the
early hours of the morning.[42]

The next day E. A. Satel', technical director of the Moscow Machine
Building Trust, called Gorbunkov into his office. Satel' was furious. He
swore at Gorbunkov and accused him of slanderous and unethical behavior by making unfounded charges of sabotage. He accused Gorbunkov of
demagogy and of violating professional standards by creating an open rift
between colleagues. Satel' reminded Gorbunkov that such behavior demoralized the workers by encouraging them to mistrust the judgment of
factory and trust managers.[43]

Gorbunkov replied that factory managers had ignored the younger specialists' suggestions. Deficiencies in the work of the engineering staff
needed to be exposed. His actions were not only justifiable but necessary
within the bounds of the Party's instructions on self-criticism, or *samo-*

[42]Ibid., d. 82, ll. 150–85.
[43]Ibid., l. 97.

kritika. Samokritika was the policy, begun in the late 1920s, by which institutions and individuals endured public censure, usually in collective gatherings, for political or professional failings. It was supposed to be a constructive process of reeducation and rededication, but it was often the Party's way of breaking down authority by legitimating popular resentment. In refering to *samokritika*, Gorbunkov was telling Satel' that the rules of professional behavior had changed, that Satel' now had to play by Gorbunkov's rules. Satel', however, continued to be guided by the old code of professional behavior. When Gorbunkov asked Satel' to review his group's criticisms, the trust director refused. If he accepted Gorbunkov's criticisms, Satel' replied, he would sanction the rift that Gorbunkov had created and further undermine the authority of the factory's management. Satel', Gorbunkov noted, did not yet "appreciate" the new Soviet ways.[44]

Gorbunkov's challenge accomplished only part of what he had intended: it drove a political wedge between occupational groups in the factory. It also revived the charges of sabotage. *Komsomolskaia pravda* and *Tekhnika upravleniia* published the charges, and a Vesenkha commission led by Charnovskii investigated them. While the commission questioned some aspects of the contract with Deitz, it found no reason to bring disciplinary action against factory management. That decision, Gorbunkov was sure, was undoubtedly part of the wreckers' conspiracy. Charnovskii, he noted, was a defendant at the Industrial Party trial in late 1930, along with most of the management of the Moscow trust.[45]

Thwarted in the state's channels of administrative review, Gorbunkov turned again to the Party. Over the course of several months in the summer and autumn of 1929, Gorbunkov's group gathered material against the trust and factory management. These materials charged that refusal to adopt new engineering designs for machine tool production was a conscious decision to perpetuate Soviet technological backwardness; that trust management drew out reconstruction at the works as part of a deliberate plot to hinder production; and that the trust's decision in 1927 to destroy the factory's foundry, ostensibly to rely on other sources for metal, was designed to cripple production.[46]

As the split widened within the Krasnyi Proletarii's professional staff, Komsomol specialists such as Gorbunkov became active in agitation work. According to Faleks, the factory's Party head at the time, Gorbunkov in particular spoke to workers in the various shop cafeterias.

---

[44]Ibid.

[45]Ibid., l. 90.

[46]Ibid., ll. 87–90. The charge of wrecking was, of course, untrue. Trust officials were following Vesenkha's orders to consolidate foundry work. Gil'debrand's version of the story is ibid., ll. 77–79.

A socialist competition display outside a Moscow factory, 1931. GARF.

Komsomol specialists were often at the head of socialist competition and rationalization brigades and initiated many of the officially sponsored campaigns to master new technologies during the late 1920s and early 1930s. Those campaigns provided a way for young specialists to gain promotion and recognition, sometimes on a national level, and professional work experience beyond the scope of their usual production duties. Because of its political and populist tendencies, however, the movement to master new technologies often exacerbated tensions among professional and managerial groups in the factory.

In late 1929 Gorbunkov organized at least one of these campaigns at the Krasnyi Proletarii to set up production of a German automatic lathe. Through a combination of Party pressure and public newspaper campaign, the young engineer and a group of Komsomol specialists quickly gained control over the lathe project, called the VDW.[47] The group established itself in one of the auxiliary buildings of one of the smallest machine shops at the factory, and this out-of-the-way building became the

[47]For Verein Deutscher Werkzeugmaschine, the German engineering consortium that originally produced the lathe.

focal point of Komsomol activity at the works. Red-and-gold Komsomol banners draped the entrance to the newly dubbed "experimental" shop, and the weekly Komsomol meetings were held there. Placards appeared over the entrance and inside the shop proclaiming it the "Eksperimen-tal'naia masterskaia 'komsomol udarnik'" (experimental Komsomol shock workers' shop). Other placards identified Komsomol youth with the spirit of technological progress and socialist construction and with the campaign to master new technologies. The Komsomol group inside produced its own manifestos and pledged to turn out twenty-five prototypes of the new machine.[48]

Gorbunkov alone cannot be credited with the campaign that made the VDW project a popular issue and a matter of national priority. Intervention by Komsomol and eventually the Moscow Party Central Committee transformed the project from a contained issue of production strategy in a local factory to a national cause of industrial and technological importance. Still, Gorbunkov's participation was crucial. Once the Komsmol Udarnik group was established, it proved difficult for factory managers to dislodge it from its "experimental" shop. Even the respected "Red" director Izakov, appointed in the spring of 1930, failed to persuade Gorbunkov to give up the project. The young engineer recalled that in the course of the public campaign around the lathe project, a "common language" developed which made opposition to the project increasingly difficult—in fact, a matter of political sabotage. Through this campaign, mastery of the VDW became such a popular symbol that it gained a national following. Both the Moscow and the national press followed the story of the Komsomol shop. Placard photographs of Gorbunkov's group hung in Red Square, and even the Soviet Writers' Union passed a resolution endorsing the VDW project.[49]

Tensions over issues of technology, production, and professional behavior at the Krasnyi Proletarii played into the growing conflict at the national level between Rabkrin and Vesenkha. In the early months of 1930, on the partial basis of evidence collected by the factory committee, the police arrested Satel', List, and other members of the MMT and its factory administrations. At Krasnyi Proletarii several engineers, including Bobrov, were arrested. The OGPU detained Tugarinov for questioning but brought no charges against him and later released him to continue work at the newly formed Stankotrest. In the spring of 1930, the Krasnyi Proletarii's director, Mozgov, was removed by request of the city's Party organization, and a new director, Izakov, was appointed. The arrest of the "wreckers" prompted a significant exodus of the older engineering staff from the

[48]GARF, f. 7952, op. 3, d. 94, l. 125.
[49]Ibid., ll. 126, 128, 123. In 1931, even Ordzhonikidze and Al'perovich, by then the heads of Vesenkha and Soiuzstankoinstrument, toured the shop (ibid., l. 130).

works. Ganriu, however, remained as chief engineer, and another older engineer, Gil'debrand also remained. As a result of the changes, a number of younger specialists moved into higher positions. Gorbunkov was named assistant chief of the production preparation department and left almost immediately for a several-month work tour of the Deitz motor factory in Germany. Upon his return, he was appointed head of the production preparation department, and in this capacity was in charge of factory teams assigned to work up production specifications for lathes and other machine tools.

Rabkrin's policies provided a focus for the frustrations and aspirations of the Krasnyi Proletarii's young engineers. In turn, their kind of activism gave broad social momentum to RKI's campaign against Vesenkha. Certainly the Party and police played important roles in the affair at the Krasnyi Proletarii. Molotov and Mikoyan were such powerful figures that their intervention and guidance were crucial to the successful outcome of the campaign. Yet much of the initiative came from the factory's Party committee and the specialists around Gorbunkov. Their involvement contributed significantly to the success of the RKI campaign and the sweep of arrests in the Vesenkha system in 1929 and 1930. As a result of that campaign, several thousand state employees lost their jobs. Many of these so-called wreckers eventually returned to work, but in the meantime, their positions were filled by younger personnel such as Gorbunkov.

The Politics of Modernization at the Klimovsk Machine Factory

Like many factories, the Klimovsk textile machine building works underwent reconstruction and technological modernization during the last years of the 1920s. The factory was expanded and several production lines were reconstructed for the mass production of new looms. Plans for the reconstruction were developed jointly by Gipromez and Rabkrin. It is not clear to what extent Rabkrin specialists actually participated in engineering and design work, but the agency did oversee the factory's reconstruction plans. The factory's chief engineer, N. G. Stremlianova, lauded Rabkrin's role in the reconstruction campaign. Like Gorbunkov, she saw in Rabkrin's policies the promise of modernization, and in modernization she saw the means to resolve social and occupational conflicts in her factory. Yet the conflicts that preoccupied Stremlianova differed from those that concerned Gorbunkov. In 1931 she described the effects of technological modernization and the organization of mass production at the Klimovsk works.

According to Stremlianova, reconstruction enhanced productivity in the factory and resolved one of its most costly labor problems. With the new machinery and standardized manufacturing processes, Stremlianova claimed, operators no longer needed the skill that the old processes required. By 1928, a year after reconstruction, average skill levels had dropped from 4.4 to 3.2 on a scale of 1 to 8. In fact, skill levels might have dropped for a number of reasons, but Stremlianova believed they fell as a result of technological reconstruction and mass production. She still recognized an important role for skilled craft machinists in the toolrooms, repair shops, and production design and instruments departments, but it was clear to her that further modernization could reduce the factory's labor needs and costs considerably.[50]

Stremlianova no doubt exaggerated the smoothness with which the factory made the transition to mass production and the effectiveness of the new manufacturing processes. Stremlianova discussed workers' difficulties in adapting to new technologies and routines, but she did not dwell on those problems. The chief engineer also mentioned workers' initial skepticism of the new methods but she did not describe their resistance in the language of class conflict. Whether she viewed such problems in class terms is impossible to determine, since it was politically impermissible to acknowledge working-class resistance to state policies. Yet whatever Stremlianova believed about workers was incidental to what she described as the most important social changes to arise out of her factory's reconstruction. Those changes had little to do with class relationships. For Stremlianova, modernization focused occupational conflict in the spheres of factory life most directly related to her work and status; that is, in the relations of authority between shop administrations and central factory departments.

Stremlianova took pains to describe how reorganization of production and management stripped shop managers and foremen of their traditional authority. As Stremlianova explained, the degree of standardization, specialization, and precision engineering required in mass production demanded factorywide coordination of manufacturing and assembly processes. This level of coordination could be accomplished only by central factory production and managerial departments, not by individual shop administrations. At the Klimovsk works, central departments became responsible for supervising the functions of labor organization and wage determination, routing and distribution of parts and supplies, engineering specifications and machining standards, production rationalization, and technical norming of equipment. Each department had complete authority over its area of expertise; it gave orders directly to shop administrators and foremen, who then saw to their proper execution.[51]

This type of systematic, or functional, management was not unique to

[50]N. G. Stremlianova, *Organizatsiia truda na mashinostroitel'nom zavode: Opyt Klimovskogo zavoda* (Moscow, 1931), p. 38.
[51]Ibid., pp. 9–12.

the Klimovsk factory. By order of Vesenkha, many factories reorganized in the 1920s under functional lines of authority. More to the point, Stremlianova, like many of her professional colleagues, saw in mass production and systematic management the means for engineers to gain the upper hand over shop personnel in the decades-old struggle for control of the factory. Using language evocative of revolutionary slogans, Stremlianova proclaimed that modernization at the Klimovsk works was what "finally broke" the hold of the foreman over production. Modernization heralded the end of the "outmoded, archaic, and arbitrary" system of shop and foreman management. From now on, the foreman would be "merely an executor" of orders handed down from the engineering and central factory departments.[52]

Stremlianova, like many advocates of mass production and systematic management, believed that this kind of modernization benefited workers as well as administrators. To her, mass production and systematic management promised not only high productivity and greater authority but socialist progress. Stremlianova conceded that adjustments still needed to be made in production relations, but she claimed that Klimovsk workers welcomed modernization of the factory.

This claim was neither naive nor entirely disingenuous. Many workers at first welcomed systematic management and mass production methods as means to curtail the traditional power of the shop foreman. Before the Revolution, foremen exerted extraordinary and often arbitrary authority over conditions of work. Acting as semi-independent contractors, foremen had the power to hire and fire workers, set wages, and distribute work orders. Rejected by managers and engineers because of their lower social and professional status, foremen were also despised by workers as the most visible and immediate manifestation of arbitrary managerial power. Foremen came to stand for capitalist oppression, and they were workers' favorite targets during and after the Revolution.[53]

In the mid-1920s, before the failings of functional management became apparent, workers often found common cause with engineers and managers in support of the systematic management movement.[54] Although functionalism increased managers' authority in the organization of production, it did so, in theory at least, in an evenhanded way, by the uniform application of standardized regulations and work routines. Workers, though wary of managers of any kind, often deemed the routinizing consequences of systematic management a more egalitarian approach than

[52]Ibid., pp. 10, 39.

[53]See Heather Hogan, *Forging Revolution: Metalworkers, Managers, and the State in St. Petersburg, 1890–1914* (Bloomington, 1993), esp. chap. 2.

[54]Gil'debrand of the Krasny Proletarii factory discusses the conflict between central administrative and shop groups in the factory: GARF, f. 7952, op. 3, d. 84, ll. 89–92.

the older arbitrary system of shop management. Workers were opposed less to the bureaucratization of work than to the arbitrariness of managerial authority.[55]

Workers throughout Soviet industry eventually rebelled against the kind of functional management Stremlianova attempted to introduce. Yet Stremlianova was convinced that centralized, functional management was more productive and socially progressive than the older practice of shop and foreman control. Stremlianova was, as she phrased it, for the "new" ways and against the "old."[56] To her the new meant modern, which in turn meant all that was technologically advanced, highly productive, and socially progressive. This is the context in which she framed her narrative of changes at the Klimovsk factory, and she connected the positive aspects of those changes with Rabkrin's policies. To Stremlianova, Rabkrin fought for modernization and socialism as she understood them, and for that reason she supported its policies.

Modernization and the Social Politics of Support for Stalin

Specialists such as E. M. Al'perovich, N. G. Stremlianova, and A. I. Gorbunkov were not alone in their support of Rabkrin's policies. The vision of revolutionary modernity that characterized the Stalinist industrialization drive appealed to specialists across the spectrum of groups in Vesenkha's industrial administrative apparatus, the trade union organizations, the professional engineering and managerial strata, and Party functionaries. Indeed, Rabkrin's call for aggressive technological modernization did not stifle but culminated a strong technocratic tradition within the Soviet managerial and technical strata.[57] In the course of the 1920s, technological modernization and the implementation of systematic forms of management had become something of a panacea. Many specialists, managers, and even trade unionists came to believe that new technologies and systematic managerial methods would bring both unbounded productivity and social peace.[58] This was Stremlianova's vision of socialist modernity. It was also the vision of scientific management, as developed by the American efficiency expert Frederick Taylor, transplanted into the Soviet context as *nauchnaia organizatsiia truda*, or NOT, the scientific organi-

[55]Workers promoted to foreman complained that workers "conspired" to undermine their authority: "Protokol soveshchaniia vydvizhentsev na zavode 'Krasnyi Profintern,' 16.12.1926," ibid., op. 6, d. 63, ll. 31–32. Gil'debrand also tells of workers seeking the help of engineering staff against favoritism displayed by foremen in the distribution of well-paid piecework: ibid., op. 3, d. 94, ll. 74–75.

[56]Stremlianova, *Organizatsiia truda*, p. 10.

[57]Bailes, "Politics of Technology," argues that Stalinist policies were designed to stifle technocratic thinking among Soviet professionals.

[58]David R. Shearer, "The Language and Politics of Socialist Rationalization: Productivity, Industrial Relations, and the Social Origins of Stalinism at the End of NEP," *Cahiers du monde russe et soviétique* 32 (October–December 1991): 581–608.

zation of labor or work. NOT proponents believed that the principles of scientific management, skewed and distorted in capitalist production relations, could be realized finally in their full potential in a socialist planned economy, which they believed they were creating in the Soviet Union.[59]

NOT groups enthusiastically endorsed the RKI's strategies, and the RKI provided an institutional center for the development of the NOT movement. Some of the country's leading NOT experts, such as E. F. Rozmirovich and A. A. Gofman, sat on the RKI presidium. The journal *Tekhnika upravleniia*, a leading NOT journal, was published under Rozmirovich and the RKI. A. Z. Gol'tsman was a close associate of Rozmirovich and was much influenced by her in the development of his organizational ideas.[60] The Organization of NOT Specialists (Organizatsiia Rabotnikov NOTa, or ORNOT), a managerial consulting group, developed many of the RKI's proposals for functional reorganization in factory management. These groups linked technological modernization with scientific management and defined both as the essence of socialist forms of rationalization.

The NOT movement flourished under Rabkrin's patronage, especially in the early 1920s, when Kuibyshev headed the Inspectorate. Rabkrin continued to support the movement after Ordzhonikidze took over in 1926, although Ordzhonikidze eventually distanced himself from functional organization and other scientific managerial initiatives.[61] After 1930, as head of Vesenkha and its successor, Narkomtiazhprom, Ordzhonikidze worked to reverse many of the functional management reforms implemented earlier. Still, the NOT movement was strong in Rabkrin in the last years of NEP. The movement's technocratic vision of industrial relations informed nearly every aspect of the agency's technological and managerial policies.[62] Emphasizing maximization of production capabilities and centralized bureaucratic control, RKI plans were based on the logic of engineering and administrative rationality. Rabkrin's policies represented the triumph of rationalist, technocratic forms of planning.

We are not accustomed to thinking of Stalinist policies as having any appeal to rationalist, technocratic sensibilities. Traditionally, we associate social support for the Stalinist industrial revolution primarily with disaffected and radicalized segments of the Soviet working population. Certainly, the language of class dominated the official rhetoric about socialist construction and industrialization. Determined to turn industrialization into class war, Stalinist leaders encouraged workers to challenge established industrial relations in the name of new kinds of socialist labor organizations. In the last years of the 1920s, managers and engineers especially

[59]See Beissinger, *Scientific Management*; Ikonnikov, *Sozdanie i deiatel'nost'*; Rees, *State Control*.
[60]Beissinger, *Scientific Management*, pp. 112–13.
[61]Ibid., p. 117.
[62]Many of the agency's proposals for work norming, labor classifications, piece-rate and bonus quotas, and reconciling shock work with other forms of rationalization came out of the ORNOT group. See GARF, f. 5286, esp. op. 1.

fell prey to political suspicion, harassment, and physical violence—the infamous *spetseedstvo* or specialist-baiting campaigns of 1928–30. Many workers formed shock brigades, the *udarniki*, and engaged in work competitions, so-called *sotsialisticheskoe sorevnovanie*, to improve production quality or voluntarily to lower wage rates and raise work tempos. These groups were motivated by a complex mix of ideological enthusiasm and economic and political pressures. Yet when they had the support of Party activists, they sought to wrest control of production from established managerial hierarchies and to fulfill the revolutionary goal of worker self-management. The official press trumpeted the success of shock groups in reducing waste, increasing productivity, and raising working-class political consciousness. Political leaders greeted the new labor organizations as historically unprecedented, their methods uniquely socialist forms of work organization.

Rabkrin officials were in the forefront of those who supported the idea of socialist rationalization as workers' control. Ordzhonikidze's speeches, for example, reveal the fervency of his belief in socialist rationalization from below as a kind of populist check on managerial bureaucratism.[63] At the same time, Ordzhonikidze and other Rabkrin officials demanded that industrialists modernize their factories through sophisticated technological restructuring of production, accounting reforms, functional reorganization of administrative offices, and mass production. These and other such measures were supposed to bring order and greater productivity to Soviet industry. Yet such measures required precise coordination, routinization, and an overall increase in managerial control over production processes. These qualities—order, precision, control—did not integrate easily with populist revolution and the Bolshevik penchant for storming barricades. Rabkrin's modernization policies contradicted the revolutionary and populist goals of shock work and socialist competition, which Stalinist leaders also supported.

That Stalinist policies were contradictory should not surprise us. More important is that the incoherence of the regime's industrial policies inadvertently encouraged support across a wide spectrum of social and occupational groups. The call to industrialize the country and build socialism drew support not only from the working class but also from the supposedly middle-class professional strata of specialists, administrators, and planners in the state apparatus. To make this argument is not to deny the political character or scope of the regime's antiwrecking campaign. There is no doubt that the struggles to define industrial policies during the late 1920s reflected a strong ideological bias and a deep-seated suspicion of

---

[63]See, e.g., the description of Ordzhonikidze's visit to the Kolomenskaia factory in *V bor'be s proryvom: Itogi rabot obshchzavodskoi proizvodstvenno-tekhnicheskoi konferentsii udarnikov kolomenskogo mashinostroitel'nogo zavoda* (Moscow, 1933).

specialists among high Party officials. There is also no doubt that the state's professional strata bore the brunt of the antiwrecking campaign as collective scapegoats for the overambitiousness and chaos of the regime's industrial and economic policies. Specialists lost their jobs, were arrested, even shot for having the wrong social origins or for supporting a politically unacceptable professional position. Specialists not directly charged with wrecking offenses also suffered harassment and political suspicion. While the Gorbunkovs were attacking their colleagues in 1929 and 1930, other specialists were openly expressing skepticism about the purportedly widespread wrecking activities. Many specialists tried in vain to understand how the regime could pursue policies of industrial modernization and yet encourage a populist backlash against the professional groups needed to carry them out. They pleaded with high officials of the regime to realize their "mistake," to "put an end to intolerable work conditions," and to return to the policies of systematic management. Only those policies, they argued, would ensure both productivity and social peace.[64]

Yet, regardless of what particular individuals thought about the antiwrecking campaign or the inconsistency of industrial policies, many specialists did not find it inconsistent with their professional interests to support the Stalinists' goals of industrial modernization. Specialists such as Al'perovich, Gorbunkov, and Stremlianova did not experience Party-professional relations as historians have since come to define them. For many specialists, support for industrialization and modernization did not imply surrender of professional integrity or autonomy. On the contrary, Rabkrin's commitment to revolutionary industrial modernization opened up new opportunities for promotion and expanded professional authority and activity.

The Inspectorate's strategies appealed especially to a growing number of younger engineers, such as Gorbunkov, who were just beginning to work in factory production jobs. These young specialists had little economic training, felt professionally excluded by older engineers, and often had little tolerance for the economic aspects of engineering and production design. Their enthusiasm was unbounded, and they responded wholeheartedly to Rabkrin's vision of a modern and powerful industrial state. Indeed, young specialists' groups formed the shock troops of the RKI's assault against Vesenkha. They, and not just radicalized workers or Party activists, were responsible for much of the hostility and specialist baiting directed toward managers and senior engineers. Yet the revolt of

[64]For reference to "intolerable" work conditions, see B. Iu. Mirskii, "Ratsional'noe ispolzovanie oborudovanii i rabochei sily v metallopromyshlennosti," in GARF, f. 5286, op. 1, d. 16, ll. 33–34, 36. See also comments by a norming expert in "Stenogramma disputa o normirovanii truda v epoku sotsialisticheskoi rekonstruktsii, 17.12.1930," ibid., d. 14, l. 17; and B. G. Iashchenko, "Normirovania truda v periode Sotsialisticheskoi rekonstruktsii," ibid., d. 18, ll. 56–65.

these young specialists was intended not to destroy managerial hierarchy but to ensure advancement within it. Although they used the language of shock work and class war, young Communist specialists also rallied around the slogan "Ovladenie tekhnikoi!" (Mastery of technology!).[65] Some of the most ardent and active supporters of Stalin and industrialization came from this professional strata of Soviet industry.

Conclusions

It is in the contradictory character of Stalinist industrial policies that we find the key to the broad social support for the Stalinist regime. Stalinist leaders gained support not because of the coherence of their policies or because those policies were directed toward the mobilization of support within a particular class. Stalinist policies drew support because of the many social and ideological cross-currents they encompassed.[66] Some people understood industrialization and socialist construction in the language of class war, a call to complete the revolutionary struggle. The language of class war drew support not only from many workers but also from many young production engineers who heard a more complicated message than simple anti-managerialism or worker control. The rhetoric of anti-bureaucratism and military mobilization appealed to many managers who had gained their leadership and organizational experience as Civil War commanders. By 1929 and 1930 this group made up nearly 48 percent of the managerial strata in Soviet heavy industry.[67] At the same time, the language of modernization appealed to NOTists, engineering design and consulting specialists, supporters of systematic managerial techniques, and many other specialists.

Different groups heard different meanings in the often grandiose but vague rhetoric of industrialization and socialist construction. That rhetoric legitimated class war and working-class mobilization. Yet the major conflicts that arose over policies and spheres of authority did not reflect the alignment or resolution of conflict along clear-cut class lines, or between easily identifiable camps of Stalinists and non-Stalinists. The class rhetoric of socialist construction and industrialization masked a more complex struggle for hegemony in the state's economic and industrial apparatus. Certainly tensions existed between Party officials and professional groups. Yet here, too, no clear-cut line of conflict can be drawn. Party officials were the final arbiters of industrial strategy. Specialists, however, were not

[65]Among biographical works of this kind are K. Shuvalov, *Shturm tekhniki* (Leningrad, 1931), and V. Ol'khov, *Za zhivoe rukovodstvo sots-sorevnovaniem* (Moscow, 1930).

[66]The argument I make here is analogous to that about the contradictory appeal of National Socialism in Germany. See Thomas Childers, *The Nazi Voter: The Social Foundations of Fascism in Germany, 1919–1933* (Chapel Hill, 1983).

[67]*Sostav rukovodiashchikh rabotnikov i spetsialistov soiuza SSR* (Moscow, 1936), p. 16.

the passive victims of a politicized process of industrialization. Conflicts among occupational groups and professional strata drove policy conflicts at the highest levels. The active, even aggressive participation of key individuals and professional groups decisively influenced the formulation of industrial policies and the character of social relations throughout the Soviet industrial system in the late 1920s. Conflict among occupational and professional groups shaped strategy and social relations in Soviet industry, despite the Party's attempt to bring planning and administration under its control.

PART III

Working in the Madhouse, 1930–1934

6

Daily Work in the *Apparat*

I think working in the apparat must be like living in a madhouse.

—S. B. Sandomirskii, January 1930

Nineteen-thirty, the second year of the first five-year plan, was a year of economic crisis. The strain of forced industrialization was beginning to show in the breakdown of supply networks and production facilities and in rising rates of work accidents, breakage, and labor turnover. Real wages and living standards plummeted as money became scarce, and the country experienced the shock of a severe shortage of capital. The relentless pressure on production also created such severe shortages of raw materials and fuels that rational planning was impossible. As the country's leaders intensified the pace of industrialization, the economy began to break apart.

The crisis was made worse by disorganization in the state's industrial bureaucracies. The year began with the wholesale restructuring of industrial administration. According to the plans developed by Abram Gol'tsman's commission at Rabkrin, reorganization was to be based on the model established in the Party and government directive of 5 December 1929.[1] Centralized associations of state producers, the proizvodstvennye *ob"edineniia*—a separate ob"edinenie for each major branch of the economy—were to replace Vesenkha's complicated regional system of production trusts. No longer were factories with different kinds of production to be directed by a trust simply because they were located in the same area. Now, one central association managed factories with the same type of production no matter where they were located. All steel-producing plants, for example, were to be administered by the association Stal', with head-

[1] *Direktivy KPSS i Sovetskogo pravitel'stva po khoziaistvennym voprosam*, vol. 2, 1929–1945 (Moscow, 1957), pp. 126–33.

167

quarters in Moscow; all machine building works were to be subordinated to Mashinoob"edinenie, also headquartered in Moscow. Each association was to be further divided into sectors that administered the various sub-branches of an industry. Thus Mashinoob"edinenie was to establish individual sectors to coordinate shipbuilding, textile equipment manufacture, turbine production, machine tools and engineering instruments, and so forth. Eventually many of these sectors were split off from Mashino-ob"edinenie and reconstituted as separate associations. Initially, however, all came under the purview of the one association of machine building factories.

Ob"edineniia were supposed to coordinate all production planning, sales, supplies, and accounting functions of their factories. Previously these operations had fallen within the overlapping jurisdictions of the trusts, the syndicates, and the glavki. Under reorganization, these bureaucracies were to be eliminated and their operations consolidated in the branch associations. The reform allowed for some regional trusts to continue operation, but most factories and enterprises were to be administered directly from subbranch or sectoral departments in the various associations. Trusts that remained were to be reorganized according to the same branch principle as their parent associations. In other words, a trust would administer factories in its geographic area, but only those that belonged to the same parent association. The reform cautioned against the proliferation of trusts and envisioned the need for them only in areas where a large number of similar types of factories were concentrated. Under reorganization, trusts were regarded as executive offices of their governing associations. They were not supposed to be the powerful industrial cartels they had been throughout the 1920s.

Republic and local levels of industrial organization reproduced the same branch and sectoral schemes as the all-union level of administration. Some combines, or *kombinaty*, such as the scattered metal and mining manufactories in the Urals, would still be administered through regional trust organizations. For the most part, however, the schematic diagram of the new system looked orderly. Industrial branches were categorized neatly in separate boxes, their factories lined up below (Figure 2). Lines of authority and responsibility ran straight or at right angles from box to box. There was no overlap, no duplication. It was an idealized scheme.

Formation of Associations and Problems of Administration

In contrast to the order of 5 December, actual reorganization of industry turned out to be an ill-conceived and protracted process, and it could not have come at a worse time. With the industrial system already strained to fulfill the Party's economic goals, central administrative au-

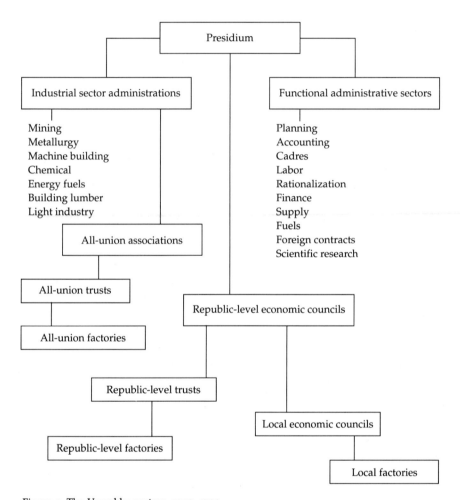

Figure 2. The Vesenkha system, 1930–1932

thority broke down entirely with the added confusion of reorganization. In fact, reorganization did not occur with the promulgation of the order of 5 December, but proceeded in a piecemeal fashion over the course of the entire year. The net effect was to disable the existing administrative system before a new system could be established in its place.

Delays hampered the reorganization effort even before the order was issued. Thirty-five Vesenkha-Rabkrin subcommissions were established in September 1929 to organize the new associations, but by December, when reorganization was to begin, their work was far from complete. These subcommissions had to decide the criteria for specialization of each association and to choose which factories to include in which association. This painstaking task was made more difficult by bureaucratic politics. The officials who worked on these commissions also worked in the institutions that were to be reorganized—the trusts, syndicates, glavki, departments of Vesenkha, and various republic and local economic councils. Thus the people in charge of the reform process had a vested interest in its outcome.

Administrative groups lobbied hard to protect their interests. Representatives of the Southern Machine Building Trust (Iumashtrest), for example, lobbied to bring their factories into the powerful all-union association of general machine building, Mashinoob"edinenie, or Moob, rather than see them relegated to republic or local associations. Directors of the gigantic southern metallurgical conglomerates of Iugostal' pleaded to keep the machine building parts of their factories under their own supervision, rather than have them split off and subordinated to the Mashinoob"edinenie. The same directors opposed inclusion of their steel-producing plants in the same ob"edinenie as small steel and iron manufactories in Siberia. The differences in production, scale of organization, and degree of modernization were so great, the southerners argued, that it made no sense to try to administer these works in the same ob"edinenie.

Goodwill was in short supply for the once powerful Iugostal', however, and the southerners were not granted their requests. Iugostal' was abolished and its metallurgical works were incorporated in Stal'. Their machine building sections went to Moob. Uralmet, by contrast, was allowed to remain intact as a regional trust organization overseeing the Urals metal factories. Unfortunately for the Moscow city economic council, it lost its struggle to retain the key Krasnyi Proletarii machine tool works, which was transferred to Soiuzstankoinstrument. After 1930, Mosmashtrest sank into obscurity as a local machine tool producing and repair trust.

Members of the reorganization commissions jockeyed for positions that would determine their personal fate as well as the fate of their institutions. Stepan Birman, though he lost Iugostal', was promoted to a seat on the Vesenkha presidium. A. F. Tolokontsev, who had feared for his position as head of the much-maligned Glavmashinstroi, was made head of its successor, Mashinoob"edinenie. In the end, most of the collegium of Glavmashinstroi joined him there. N. D. Koniukov and Ia. M. Gendin, heads of the engineering syndicate VMTS, were also transferred to the governing board of Mashinoob"edinenie when the syndicate was absorbed by the new association.

It was difficult to keep negotiations at the top levels secret. Rumors flew through the bureaucracy, disrupting work and lowering morale. According to one disgruntled factory director, people at the enterprise level were kept in the dark. Director Kurnosov of the Tver railroad car factory complained that rumors abounded, "first, that we'd be incorporated into a separate railroad trust, then into an association for diesel and locomotive construction, then into the supertrust Mashinoob"edinenie, then we'd have this or that department or not, depending on what day it was." As early as August 1929, hearing rumors of the impending reorganization, the personnel of many trusts began to "flee in all directions." Those who had the right connections "leaped" to safety in Gosplan, the most secure of the high planning and administrative organs. Many sought positions in the central apparatus of Vesenkha. Others fled to the glavki and syndicates in the mistaken belief that there they would be safe.[2]

The managerial turnover in late 1929 and early 1930, a kind of frantic musical chairs, only added to the chaos of reorganization. Officially, in contrast, personnel were reassigned so slowly that a rolling paralysis spread through the industrial administrative system. The creation and staffing of the new associations took months, not the weeks called for by the reorganization order. Though the Vesenkha-Rabkrin commissions began work in early September, formation of the first associations was not announced until the end of November. The first all-union associations, established on 28 November, were the ferrous metallurgical association and the corresponding metallurgical construction association. V. I. Mezhlauk was appointed head of the former and I. V. Kosior of the latter. V. V. Osinskii was chosen to head a new all-union association for automobile and tractor manufacturing.[3] On 1 December *Torgovo-promyshlennaia gazeta* announced formation of several more major associations in coal, oil, and chemicals. Mashinoob"edinenie was included in this list. New announcements continued well into the new year.

Most associations existed in an administrative limbo for months. Vesenkha's newspaper announced the creation of Mashinoob"edinenie in December 1929, for example, but the association was not officially incorporated until 29 January 1930. In the meantime, the old trusts, glavki, and

[2]RGAE, f. 5716, op. 1, d. 50, l. 140; f. 3429, op. 6, d. 197, l. 270.
[3]*TPG*, 29 November 1929.

syndicates continued to function. For several crucial months, old glavki and new associations existed side by side, literally in the same office buildings. This duplication and confusion so blurred lines of authority that "no one knew where to send documents or who had authority to sign which documents."[4] Bureaucrats found themselves in a muddle over who was in which organization and which organization had what authority.

When Vesenkha's newspaper announced formation of a new association, it noted that the new head was given two weeks to report on staffing and progress in the administrative transfer of its factories; yet many of the major associations continued to operate for weeks and months with only skeleton staffs. By late January 1930, only the board of directors and a "few" department heads had been appointed to Mashinoob"edinenie. By early March its central apparatus had only 250 people, about a quarter of Glavmashinstroi's old staff and only a quarter of its own full complement of staff.[5]

Appointments to new positions were slowed considerably because Rabkrin was conducting a purge of the industrial apparatus at the same time that Vesenkha and Rabkrin were reorganizing it. No appointment could be made until an individual's professional and political profile, or *kharakteristika*, was updated and he or she was cleared for work in the new apparatus. As a result, many administrators sat idle, sometimes without pay, in their old offices. Others sought employment elsewhere if connections could expedite or bypass Rabkrin's vetting procedures. S. B. Sandomirskii, of the planning department of Mashinoob"edinenie, complained to Rabkrin's purge commission in January 1930 that he was so short of staff that he had to lock the office door when he went to the bathroom. The only alternative was to fetch someone to sit at his desk while he was away from it. But he could not leave the office, so he had to wait for someone to happen by in the hallway. Normally the planning department would have had ten specialists with technical assistants and a staff of secretaries, but staff had begun to leave Glavmashinstroi as early as mid-1929, when rumors of reorganization had started to fly, and for nearly two months Sandomirskii had been left almost alone. Only he and, at best, three other people were responsible for planning and administering construction and operations for the whole of the Soviet machine manufacturing industries. "I don't even have anyone to help me keep the mountains of files from falling on the floor," he declared.[6]

Sandomirskii's situation was not unusual. Throughout the last two months of 1929 and the first two months of 1930, the import department of Moob was staffed by only one qualified engineer and two assistants.

[4]RGAE, f. 5716, op. 2, d. 2, l. 12b.
[5]Ibid. and op. 1, d. 29, ll. 50–59.
[6]Ibid., op. 2, d. 2, l. 13b.

"We handle millions of gold rubles through that office," reported M. M. Ianovskii, head of the department. "If our engineer's arithmetic is off only three percent, it can amount to tens of millions of rubles." Zertsalov, of Glavmashinstroi's machine design department, reported that positions remained vacant for months in his office, even after several appeals to the personnel department, as staff left for other jobs or were arrested on charges of wrecking. When M. A. Khrennikov (brother of S. A. Khrennikov, one of the alleged Industrial Party conspirators) left the machine design department, no one replaced him, and two months later the work loads of fourteen branches of machine design were still piling up on his desk. Glavmashinstroi's rationalization department had a similar problem. In December 1929, A. S. Chernov was transferred to become the interim last head of the machine design department, leaving the rationalization department with one lone secretary. The rationalization department ceased to exist in practice, but as of the end of January it still had not been reconstituted in the new association.[7]

Political vetting was only one of many ways Rabkrin contributed to the strains placed on Vesenkha. Problems of reorganization were compounded by new demands. In December 1929, Vesenkha ordered Glavmashinstroi, by then nearly defunct, to increase machine building production targets 100 million rubles over the original figures. The increase resulted from one of Rabkrin's many investigations, this one of surplus capacity in machine building and repair shops. At the same time, Vesenkha was ordered to launch yet another campaign to reduce industrial costs. Unless immediate and drastic action were taken, Rabkrin had reported to Sovnarkom, industry would not meet its goal of a 7 percent cut in production costs by the end of the year.[8]

Rabkrin's campaigns disrupted administrative routines even under normal working conditions, but the cost reduction campaign coincided with the confusion and strains caused by reorganization, purges, and forced industrialization. Chernov complained in late January that only a few weeks after taking over at the machine design department, he was forced to send over half his meager staff to factories as part of the cost-reduction campaign. Those left in the office had to work nineteen- and twenty-hour days to keep up with the work. A. V. Astashev, head of Glavmashinstroi's general administration department, concurred that mobilizing staff for the cost-reduction campaign seriously disrupted work routines. He acknowledged, however, that the lack of any systematic planning in Vesenkha had led to the crisis and the consequent need for mobilization. "Of course, Vesenkha sent instructions about cost reduction," he said, but "no directives were ever distributed about priorities or where to reduce. Nothing

[7] Ibid., ll. 11, 19, 12b.
[8] *TPG*, 6 and 15 December 1929.

was ever done, there was no follow-up. As a result, we needed a mobilization."[9]

Comrade Didukh, of the accounting department, was more straightforward in his criticisms. "It's not normal," he said, "to take dozens of people from each department and send them out to the field for two months at a time." The accounting department had only four specialists, each of whom was paid between 150 and 200 rubles a month. At such low wages, the government could hire a whole stable of accountants, and "we could be spared the expense of mobilizing all these people to go helter-skelter all over the country." If authorities paid attention to proper and regular accounting procedures, the higher organs wouldn't have to engage in such disruptive campaigns.[10] Didukh's comments provide striking evidence of at least one way in which Rabkrin's campaign style of management disrupted normal administration.

One of the main purposes of reorganization was to cut the size of the bureaucracy, yet nearly everyone complained about the lack of staff. B. N. Dobrovol'skii, former chief engineer of Glavmashinstroi and head of Mashinoob"edinenie's construction department, told the purge commission that all glavki and their successor associations were understaffed. In his opinion, Glavmashinstroi had been the most understaffed, but the situation at Mashinoob"edinenie was worse still.[11]

Chernov echoed this sentiment, noting that only twelve people were working in the machine design department when he took it over in late 1929. Nine of those twelve were engineers, but their support staff was so inadequate that they could not keep up with the work load. The department's burden was eased somewhat by the work of the engineering syndicate while it still existed, but the load was still "crushing." Each engineer was responsible for handling correspondence and planning for anywhere from ten to sixteen industrial branches. Engineer Shchepkin, for example, serviced fourteen branches alone. Engineer Kupsko had responsibility for eight large branches, which had twenty to twenty-five subbranches. When Chernov tried to hire more engineers, he found his efforts stymied. "It's true," he said, "that the best way *not* to get someone hired is to send their file to our general [personnel] department." The delays in hiring caused by the combination of bureaucratic processing and political vetting was "absolutely intolerable. . . . Of course we need to check people, but we shouldn't be twisting their arms." Other officials reported that it was common to try to bypass the general department, but, as Astashev noted, this practice led to "all manner" of abuses. Staff selection was "entirely arbitrary," so that the lengthy process of professional and political

[9]RGAE, f. 5716, op. 2, d. 2, ll. 12b, 10.
[10]Ibid., l. 17.
[11]Ibid., l. 16.

vetting defeated its own purpose. G. F. Davydov, the former head of Glav-mashinstroi's Party organization and also head of its personnel department, made the same point in more direct language. "Leaders," he declared bluntly, "have already wasted months."[12]

Many officials pleaded with the purge commission to reduce the "insane" amount of paperwork and relieve the "fundamental administrative disorganization." I. S. Dotsenko, a member of Mashinoob"edinenie's presidium, said that so far, reorganization had not reduced but increased the paperwork and duplication. "Even Vesenkha leaders admit they don't know how the system is supposed to function." Many orders that came down from Vesenkha and requests from factories lacked signatures and were so vague as to be unintelligible; many of them had nothing to do with Mashinoob"edinenie. There were no standardized administrative procedures. In this respect, Dotsenko claimed, nothing had changed from the old glavki system.[13]

Neplanovost'

Dotsenko pointed to one of the basic problems that reorganization had failed to address: *neplanovost'*, the lack of ordered administrative process. Nearly every witness before Rabkrin's purge commission spoke about *neplanovost'*. The difficulty of getting anything accomplished, according to Sandomirskii, was only partly a result of understaffing. Even after reorganization, there was still no order to departmental relationships. "We've undergone a structural change," Sandomirskii said, "but no administrative reform. There are masses of departments, and all demand information and correspondence from us"—not through normal procedures but always "at a moment's notice."[14]

One official noted that it could take anywhere from twenty days to five months for a piece of paper to "swim" its way through the bureaucratic system, if it made it at all. There was no organization or hierarchy of information flow. Dobrovol'skii complained that Vesenkha demanded data and information only days before it was due, and requests or orders often arrived days after they were to have been executed.[15]

The difficulty of gaining access to responsible officials compounded the problem. M. M. Ianovskii, of the import department, reported that it could take hours, even days of effort to see V. F. Oborin, a member of Mashinoob"edinenie's collegium. When he finally got an appointment, Oborin

[12]Ibid., ll. 12b, 10b, 19.
[13]Ibid., l. 17.
[14]Ibid., l. 13b–14. Note that this had been the substance of Lobov's criticism of Rabkrin's reorganization plans.
[15]Ibid., ll. 14, 18.

would "see us for two minutes only, to decide a million questions that involved millions of gold rubles." Ianovskii exaggerated to make his point, but it elicited an empathic response from other officials. Dobrovol'skii confirmed it could take days to get the signature of someone in authority. "Even when I leave a document overnight," he said, "it still doesn't get signed." Presidium members "sit in meetings until midnight, sleep, and then they're gone again at seven in the morning." According to Dotsenko, the need to get signatures led many staff members to corner anyone on a higher committee they could find in the hallways, whether or not that person had the requisite authority. "People are constantly running up to me, quite out of nowhere. They try to sneak a signature from me, often for paperwork marked 'extremely urgent.' Who knows what I'm signing?"[16]

Sandomirskii, a former member of the engineering syndicate and always an astute critic, placed *neplanovost'*, in a broader context. According to him, *neplanovost'* stemmed from an "unacceptable" lack of clarity in the orders and instructions issued by higher authorities. Directives from PEU (Vesenkha's economic planning administration) especially were vague and unclear. Sandomirskii mocked the form of PEU instructions: " 'Implement the five-year plan directive and the directive on control figures.' This isn't a directive. They give orders in the most general terms . . . and then try to tell you you're an idiot if you don't carry them out." As if vagueness were not enough, "the orders come in masses," and all are urgent or extremely urgent." It was typical, he said, "to receive a demand from Vesenkha's finance department for figures on the number of trucks, fuels, and materials that will pass through the Volzhske *gosparkhodstvo* in '32 and '33. Then, before I can [turn around], I'll get a phone call from Kuibyshev—'We need this information immediately.' How are we supposed to work like this, especially when we still have to spend over half our time working on problems of coordinating and integrating the work of the old glavki and syndicates? Everything comes at once. I think working in the apparat must be like living in a madhouse."[17]

As testimony before the purge committee revealed, organizational reforms restructured the administration of industry but failed utterly to address the problems of administrative process. Even as authoritative a figure as M. G. Ostrovskii, on the presidiums of both Mashinoob"edinenie and Vesenkha, admitted that *neplanovost'* continued to be "the greatest weakness" of the economic bureaucracies. Astashev pleaded with the commission to resolve these problems quickly, for they "tie everyone's hands [*u vsekh ruki otnimaiutsia*]."[18]

[16]Ibid., ll. 16, 18.
[17]Ibid., l. 13b. See also the comment by A. V. Astashev: "In general, there's no plan, no rational procedure to our work" (l. 10).
[18]Ibid., ll. 21, 12b.

The coming months brought little improvement. A Vesenkha report in late May concluded that reorganization had so far yielded no significant improvement in the agency's ability to plan, administer, or regulate industry. A Sovnarkom resolution prepared in response declared that the problems of reorganization were much more fundamental than even the Vesenkha report implied. Sovnarkom charged that the internal organization of the associations was still "extremely unsatisfactory," that no defined structure for the associations existed; they had become "bloated grandiose facades." Relations between union and republic levels of industry were not just "unhealthy"; they were nonexistent. Instead of simplifying the organization of industry, the reforms had made industrial relations far more complicated and unsystematic than they had been before.[19]

Some of these complications were logistical and temporary. Transferring thousands of people through the bureaucratic vermicelli was a slow and tedious task, made no easier by Rabkrin's purge. Other logistical problems went unnoticed. As Ia. M. Gendin, a member of Mashinoob"edinenie's collegium, pointed out, hundreds of telephones had to be moved or installed. File boxes went missing so that staff members sometimes did not know which factories were in their jurisdictions. Once settled in an office, departments might be moved again at short notice. Paper was so hard to get that many departments used old stationery bearing the seal of the old glavk or trust, and factory and trust administrators were sometimes confused about the trust or association to which they were subordinate. The machine association was promised a new building, but in July its offices were still scattered in five locations across Moscow.[20]

Short-term difficulties notwithstanding, fundamental contradictions arose between the means and ends of reorganization. Centralization, the cornerstone of reorganization, was supposed to simplify and unify planning, operational, and regulatory functions, but it exacerbated economic disruptions and led to a loss of control. Consider the crucial area of supplies and sales. The intent was to close all regional offices and networks of sales and supply activities and to centralize the allocation of goods and equipment, thus "freeing" trusts and factories to concentrate on fulfilling their production and cost plans. But the worst fears of syndicate critics were realized. Throughout the year, central offices of the associations were overwhelmed with complaints, demands, and urgent pleas from disgruntled factory and trust administrators.[21] Managers vented their criticisms at numerous meetings called to deal with supply problems. One manager, Dushkin, from the Karl Marx machine building works in Leningrad, expressed the thoughts of many people in May 1930 at a meeting of factories that had transferred from Lenmashtrest to Mashinoob"edinenie. Noting

[19]GARF, f. 374, op. 1, d. 616, l. 16.
[20]RGAE, f. 5716, op. 1, d. 50, l. 235.
[21]GARF, f. 374, op. 1, d. 616, l. 19.

that many factories had not left Lenmashtrest by choice, Dushkin castigated Mashinoob"edinenie for its inability to supply the materials they desperately needed. Factories had had to fight a lot with the trust, but "when it took on the responsibility, Lenmashtrest delivered the materials. If you want us to get our own materials, why do you take our orders and then do nothing?" Mashinoob"edinenie's irresponsibility "goes beyond this or that excuse; it pervades your whole organization." Bureaucratism was worse in the new association, he declared, than in the old glavki system.[22]

Under the old trust and syndicate system, factories had had a "certain flexibility" to find their own materials, especially in cases of shortages or late deliveries. Factories, according to Comrade Klochko, director of the Kriukovsk railroad car repair works, had not been so dependent on an association that was "far too large and too far away. When a factory in our trust appeals to the association, it gets lost in your huge departments," said Klochko. Mashinoob"edinenie may decide something, "but we won't know about it or see anything tangible till the end of the five-year plan."[23]

Comrade Ginzburg, of the Railroad Car Manufacturing Trust, noted another difficulty: the trust no longer had access to its own internal source of metal. The metallurgical parts of some of its machine building factories were now under the jurisdiction of Stal', so the trust found itself in the absurd situation of being unable to get metal supplies from contiguous parts of its own factories. It had to appeal to Mashinoob"edinenie in Moscow to appeal to Stal' to ship steel out of its factory to a central distribution point and then back again. So far, according to Ginzburg, the trust had woefully underfulfilled its plan for the year because of such problems. "We depend now entirely on the association," Ginzburg said. "Wouldn't it change the picture if we could put supply activities in the hands of the trust instead of in the hands of the association? Of course, it wouldn't increase the amount of metal in the country, but it would give our work a little more flexibility."[24]

Informal Networks and Remnants of the Old System

Despite the complaints, factories that operated under the railroad car construction trust were fortunate to have an intervening layer of bureaucracy to pursue their interests in Mashinoob"edinenie. Other factories and enterprises were not so fortunate. For much of the year, the association attempted to administer most of the hundreds of enterprises under its jurisdiction directly out of its Moscow offices. As soon as the association

[22]RGAE, f. 5716, op. 1, d. 35, l. 127.
[23]Ibid., d. 50, l. 238.
[24]Ibid., l. 237.

was created, Vesenkha officials realized it was far too large and encompassed too many types of manufacturing to be effective. In January Mashinoob"edinenie supervised as many as 40 trusts and 327 enterprises.[25] As a result, it underwent several reorganizations in the course of the year. Vesenkha split tractor and turbine manufacture off into two cartels, then organized machine tool and instrument manufacture as an independent association, and in May Mashinoob"edinenie spawned several more independent associations. Through further subdivision the association streamlined its structure so that by mid-August it administered 7 trusts and 120 factories. Where there had been one association in January 1930, by the summer's end thirteen ob"edineniia administered the country's various machine building industries.[26]

Subdivision created smaller, more manageable organizational units at the center, but as associations divided and divided again, jurisdictional confusion increased. By the summer of 1930, lines of authority over supplies, sales, and production were in disarray. "When Mashinoob"edinenie was created," noted one official, "We thought all products, equipment, and material supply orders would go through the single association. It turns out everything has gone to hell. We don't know where our orders are . . . [they're] scattered everywhere . . . or who is responsible for them. . . . No one knows who or what belongs where."[27]

Mashinoob"edinenie tried to compensate for the confusion by developing informal networks of contacts. Of course the reorganization was supposed to eliminate intermediate trusts, but in March the Central Committee bowed to pressure from numerous associations, Mashinoob"edinenie among them, and issued a finding that allowed associations to decide whether trusts should be organized as exceptions to the general association model. The association quickly found that it needed the intermediate layer of bureaucracy to handle its hundreds of factories.

What was to be an exception became the rule. By the summer, the machine manufacturing association had established multiple trusts for nearly every sector under its jurisdiction: a railroad car and repair shops trust, a trust for diesel and light motor manufacture, a locomotive manufacturing trust, an armature trust. . . . These branch trusts combined with the remaining few regional trusts, such as Uralmet, to create, once again, a large middle administrative stratum. By August, Mashinoob"edinenie supervised only seven factories directly, without any intervening trust organization. And the new trusts were not content to be mere executive organs. Trusts were financially and administratively accountable for overseeing

[25]S. B. Sandomirskii, "O reorganizatsiia upravlenii mashinostroeniem i metalloobrabotkoi," *Metall*, 1930, no. 1, p. 5.
[26]RGAE, f. 5716, op. 1, d. 50, ll. 231–36.
[27]RGAE, f. 3429, op. 3, d. 2555, l. 1.

successful completion of their factories' production programs, so they demanded all the sales, accounting, and other staffs needed to carry out their tasks. Despite Vesenkha's intention to centralize operational and regulatory functions in the associations, by summer it had returned many of the financial, sales, and supply mechanisms to the trusts. In a resolution dated 23 July 1930, Vesenkha pledged to negotiate all sales transactions with trusts rather than directly with factories. Trusts were also given responsibility, again, to disperse capital construction funds to their factories as they deemed appropriate. Finally, trusts were given full responsibility to maintain financial discipline in their factories, and they had the right to maintain full-fledged accounting and commercial-financial offices so they could do so.

Decentralizing these functions to the trust level, necessary though it was, defeated the purpose of the reorganization. Functions and staffs were once again duplicated and the trusts regained the financial and commercial functions that supposedly had distracted them from providing technical leadership to their factories.[28] Far from being eliminated, the new trusts became mini-ob"edineniia. Although not organized as regional cartels, they fulfilled most of the same commercial and managerial functions as their predecessors.

Other remnants of the old system also survived or were revived. The factories and personnel of Gomzy, for example, the large central Russian machine building trust, were supposedly assimilated into Moob or parceled out to other associations in January, but as late as March the *ekonomkomissiia* (economic commission) of the supposedly defunct Gomzy issued an assessment of Moob's shortcomings. The association, claimed the report, was too large and unwieldy to deal flexibly with all the factories under its control. The report urged Moob to decentralize control of sales and supplies to the trust (to Gomzy?) and even to the factory level.[29]

A letter to Abram Gol'tsman from the Party cell bureau of Gomzy dated 3 April 1930 made many of the same criticisms. It noted further that Mashinoob"edinenie violated the goals of the reorganization—to create specialized managerial units to administer specialized production processes. Mashinoob"edinenie, the letter argued, should be disbanded and re-formed as several separate associations. This had already been done, the letter concluded, for machine tools, tractors, and automobiles.[30]

The engineering syndicate, VMTS, also ceased officially to function on 29 January 1930, the day Mashinoob"edinenie began administrative life. Yet, like the biblical Jonah, the VMTS continued to live inside the belly of

[28]RGAE, f. 5716, op. 1, d. 50, ll. 233, 78, 116.
[29]GARF, f. 374, op. 15, d. 1057, ll. 7–7b.
[30]Ibid., ll. 1–4.

the bureaucratic whale. When the syndicate was "disbanded," its organizational structure and eventually most of its staff were swallowed intact and reconstituted as the sales administration of Moob, yet the VMTS continued to operate under its own name. In March, stenographic records of the sales office were still listed under the heading "VMTS." Regional offices remained staffed throughout the summer, and officials of the association's sales department continued to identify their affiliation as *mashino-sindikat* or VMTS.[31]

Despite restructuring, the VMTS proved difficult to kill off as an institution. The rudimentary commercial mentality fostered by years of syndicate work proved equally difficult to expunge. At a meeting on 30 May 1930, Moob officials tried to explain to staff members how operations in the association would differ from those of the syndicate. Ironically, the meeting was chaired by Koniukov, the former head of VMTS, now on the board of directors, or collegium, of Moob. In a further irony, Koniukov introduced Ia. Gendin, the former operations manager of VMTS, reincarnated also as a member of Moob's collegium. Moob's task, Gendin declared, was to supply (*snabzhat'*) specific industrial branches with machinery, not to sell (*prodat'*) products through regional offices to local industrial consumers. The staff should now think in terms not of consumers but of clients. Gendin emphasized that "the newly formed central state associations are our only clients." Since Moob no longer "sold" machinery to a broad market of "customers," there was no reason to maintain the old regional offices of the VMTS. Genden announced that these would be closed within two weeks.[32]

After his talk, Gendin answered written questions, passed to the lectern during his presentation. He noted with exasperation that they reflected the persistence of the old ways of thinking. There were, Gendin said, "too many managers who are still thinking in terms of markets and commercial relations." Gendin read several questions in quick succession: "'How will we develop the market?' 'How will we monitor and regulate production?' 'If we close regional offices, how will we carry out market surveys and our tasks of technical consultation with local customers?' 'To whom will customers turn if not to local sales and consultation offices?'"

Gendin answered the first question with a question: "How can we develop a market if there is no market to develop?" Moob's task, he repeated, was not to sell machinery on a market but to supply equipment to other central industrial associations according to specific state orders. Moob's supply department did not need to engage in market surveys or in technical consultations, or to be concerned about production organiza-

[31]E.g., RGAE, f. 3429 op. 3, d. 2555, ll. 3b, 6.
[32]"Stenogramma soveshchaniia upravliaiushchikh kontor Moob, 30 maia 1930," in RGAE, f. 5716, op. 1, d. 223, ll. 33–34.

tion in factories. These were no longer its functions. There was no longer any need for local representatives.[33]

Former VMTS officials, especially those still working in regional offices, reacted angrily. Transcripts of the meeting report noise in the auditorium as Gendin spoke. A Urals official identified only as Golovko remarked that this meeting marked not a new beginning but a "wake." He bristled when Gendin characterized people who thought in terms of markets and commercial relations as backward. "Yes, those of us who think in those terms live in the past because we live in the real world, from which you have taken flight in your administrative fantasies." Golovko noted the deluge of telegrams from all over the Urals to his supposedly nonexistent regional office—"telegrams from Zlatoust about the lack of this, from Izhorsk about the failure of that. All these telegrams are going to end on your desk, Iakov Moiseevich, and you won't be able to answer them, because—excuse me—you'll be buried in a mountain of telegrams." All these problems, Golovko argued, could not possibly be solved administratively by central authorities, they needed the commercial intervention of the old VMTS structure. Instead of closing offices, Moob should be opening new ones to handle all the problems that would arise in connecting producers and consumers.[34]

S. Korenevkin, of Khar'kov, concurred that dismantling the regional networks of commercial representatives would end in chaos. "How can it not?" Korenevkin reported that it took, on the average, fifteen telegrams to Moob to get a reply, and then the reply did not answer the original inquiry, or it raised more questions than it answered. Korenevkin pleaded that, despite reorganization, a network of the sort that had existed under the syndicate was needed to determine market needs, move goods, connect buyers and sellers, and serve technical and service functions. "You can't solve these problems," he declared, "by simply pretending they don't exist—by closing up all the offices and saying it has nothing to do with me [moia khata s kraiu, nichego ne znaiu]." Administrative centralization would only exacerbate the very problems the reforms were designed to resolve.[35]

The syndicate's regional networks were supposed to be closed when all sales and supply activities were centralized in the main offices of the association, but in the haste of reorganization, most of these regional offices were incorporated intact into Moob along with the central syndicate structure. As a result, local trade networks continued to function in an informal capacity throughout much of the year. At the meeting of 30 May, the Leningrad and Khar'kov officers of VMTS read telegrams from large

[33]Ibid., ll. 40–42.
[34]Ibid., l. 47.
[35]Ibid., l. 53.

trusts in their areas refusing to submit to the new system and making clear their intention to continue their commercial relations with suppliers and customers unchanged. Other trusts and factories, fearing that reorganization would disrupt established supply routes, hired local syndicate representatives ostensibly as administrators but actually as commercial agents, to continue in semilegal ways the commercial relations established under the old syndicate system.[36]

Before reorganization, the syndicate's commercial networks made up the sinew of the state's industrial sales and supply apparatus. They provided the commercial contacts that linked industrial producers and consumers. The syndicate system accounted for about two-thirds of all commercial transactions within Glavmashinstroi. After January 1930, commercial activities by regional offices were restricted to materials and equipment not covered by supply and distribution agreements made at the association level—some 15 percent of all the new association's transactions.[37] Thus the syndicate network had lost the commercial leverage it had before reorganization, but its offices continued to perform a crucial service. The existence of the regional offices was particularly valuable at a time when centralized supply channels rarely functioned properly. Some factories continued to rely primarily on these old networks for most of their supplies, and most trusts turned to them for emergency help in the frequent instances when they ran short of materials, equipment, or fuel.[38]

Eventually Vesenkha officials saw the wisdom of reconstituting independent trade and sales organizations for the various industrial branches, but these were not the powerful commercial syndicates of the 1920s. The new trade associations maintained commercial relationships with trusts and production associations, but only for materials and equipment not already covered in the planned system of allocations. Despite the arguments of former syndicate officials, the new sales associations had no real power over the trusts; they had lost the financial and commercial leverage that the old syndicates had wielded. The new sales associations played an important auxiliary role, but the new industrial system remained bureaucratically controlled and attuned to producers, not consumers.

Something Old, Something New

By refusing to heed the urgings of former syndicate officials, Vesenkha's leaders retained the essential element of their reforms: centralized

[36]Ibid., ll. 59–60.

[37]RGAE, f. 5716, op. 1, d. 229, l. 4.

[38]Nearly all the representatives at the May meeting acknowledged this, and they did so again in August. For transcripts of the latter meeting, see esp. RGAE, f. 3429, op. 3, d. 2555, ll. 1–6.

bureaucratic control over the economy. Yet the industrial system that emerged at the end of 1930 bore little resemblance to Vesenkha's original blueprint for reorganization. In many ways, Vesenkha officials found themselves back where they had started. On the one hand, large, centralized associations could not manage their far-flung and diverse empires effectively. The attempt to centralize all trade and distribution in the Moscow offices of all-union associations created bottlenecks of nightmare proportions. On the other hand, as associations subdivided into trusts and other associations, Vesenkha lost the advantage in administrative coordination and control that was supposed to have accrued from centralization. Administrative structures replicated themselves at every level of the system and in every new association. As a result, sales offices not only competed across association lines but duplicated efforts and competed with offices at all levels of an association.

Such developments were entirely unplanned and therefore often unregulated. Few rules existed to govern the increasing proliferation and jurisdictional confusion of overlapping bureaucracies. This was exactly the situation that had prompted officials to set about reforming the old system. Throughout 1930, officials spent an enormous amount of time in attempts to patch the system. They devoted whole conferences to sorting out the lines of bureaucratic process. Large-scale meetings in January, in March, at the end of May, and in August revisited the same problems, and each time officials had to adjust to and incorporate new complexities.

Reorganization was supposed to replace the old industrial system with a new one, but the haphazard way it evolved reproduced the old four-tiered system of associations, trusts, sales associations, and factories. Trusts were now organized largely by branch and were less powerful than the old regionally organized trusts, but most factories remained unspecialized, so most trusts still ruled over a mixed conglomerate of industrial enterprises. Reorganization was also supposed to unify and centralize trade, planning, and regulatory functions, yet by the summer of 1930 those functions were once again dispersed and duplicated throughout the bureaucratic system. Administrative reforms, in fact, failed to resolve the major problem of integrating the economy. Expanding the sales associations enlarged the industrial bureaucracy but did not address the essential task of linking industrial producers with consumers in an effective manner. Reorganization created a mammoth bureaucratic economy, but it had no commercial engine. Soviet officials tried to free themselves from commercial and market constraints, yet the very process of bureaucratization hampered the apparatus's efforts to cope with problems in the economy. As the regime's officials quickly discovered, highly centralized administrative structures could not replace decentralized and semi-autonomous forms of commercial exchange as a means to regulate and integrate economic activity.

Neither did reorganization resolve the problems of *neplanovost'*. Nothing was done to systematize the flow of information through the bureaucracy or to resolve the piecemeal approach to planning that had so characterized Rabkrin's control over the economy. Trusts continued to complain that their production quotas were raised, their allocations of supplies and labor were not. The plan remained a myth, a "joke," as Comrade Klochko of the Kriukovsk rail car repair works bluntly described it.[39]

Centralizing reforms and the substitution of bureaucratic for commercial mechanisms overwhelmed the administrative apparatus.[40] Decrees and instructions poured out of Vesenkha by the hundreds and were ignored by the hundreds. Meanwhile, lower-level officials, deprived of authority, appealed in vain for instructions and then found their own often devious ways to cope with the crises that came upon them. Faced with such chaos, industrial and Party officials turned to Rabkrin's tried and true methods of military-style mobilization to meet production and cost targets. In March the Central Committee became so concerned about the situation that it dispatched high-level plenipotentiaries to spend two months, if necessary, working with officials in key industrial regions to reestablish order in factory production schedules and ensure that the governments orders were followed. Kuibyshev, then still head of Vesenkha, and Tolokontsev went to Leningrad; V. V. Shmidt, a Central Committee member, traveled to the industrial center of Nikolaev; Rozengol'ts was sent to Dneprostroi, the huge dam construction site in Ukraine; S. Kosior went to the metallurgical center at Taganrog; Ordzhonikidze spent two months in Ukraine; Lazar Kaganovich settled for the same period in the middle Volga area; and Anastas Mikoyan went to the north Caucasus region. In all, the Central Committee dispatched twenty-four of the highest ranking government and Party officials to provincial centers.[41] Their absence from Moscow for such a long time testified to the seriousness of the crisis.

The intervention of high-ranking officials was typical of the crisis management style that became a permanent characteristic of the Soviet industrial system. The way the Central Committee dealt with the March crisis was, in essence, a reprise of Rabkrin's periodic campaigns to lower production costs, to mobilize industrial resources, or to meet monthly and

[39]RGAE, f. 5716, op. 1, d. 50, l. 239. Similar comments were made by a representative of the rail car construction trust (l. 242) and all the other factory representatives (ll. 238–68).

[40]B. Klimov-Verkhovskii, a member of Vesenkha's presidium, acknowledged these problems in a long article, "Piatiletku mashinostroeniia nado peresmotret'," *TPG*, 15 December 1929.

[41]See the list in RTsKhIDNI, f. 17, op. 113, d. 831, l. 127.

quarterly production targets. These campaigns operated outside the normal administrative process and were always characterized as extraordinary measures to cope with emergency situations. In fact, these mobilization campaigns exacerbated administrative problems by drawing off scarce resources and personnel. As Vesenkha became increasingly mired in the problems of reorganization, military-style mobilizations came to substitute for regular economic administration.

Conclusion

Reorganization of industrial administration in 1930 was supposed to replace Vesenkha's cumbersome multilayered administrative infrastructure with a centralized system that concentrated major planning and commercial functions in the powerful industrial associations. Centralization was supposed to increase economic control, flexibility in planning, and efficiency of administration. As officials quickly discovered, however, centralization actually reduced control over the economic administration of industry. No sooner did Vesenkha's leaders create the highly centralized production associations than they dismantled them, dispersing administrative functions to smaller associations and trusts. Once the process of subdivision began, it mushroomed out of control. The unplanned evolution of Mashinoob"edinenie was typical of that process. In fact, by the end of August 1930, Moob's system of trusts and subbranch administrations had become so complicated that Vesenkha's presidium abolished the association and established three associations, one each for heavy, medium, and light machine building. Each of these associations in turn replicated a complex system of trusts and departments whose overlapping jurisdictions created further confusion and bureaucratic conflict. Vesenkha's administrative apparatus went on dividing and multiplying, largely unregulated, in response to unforeseen circumstances. This was not planning, but its antithesis.

7

Purge and Patronage

Comrades, we are here to purge your organization.
—I. Z. Gokhman, 28 January 1930

One of the major goals of administrative reorganization in 1930 was to reduce the size of the industrial bureaucracy. Administrative cutbacks not only had economic benefits but were a political priority as part of the antibureaucratic campaign of the late 1920s. In numerous directives, Rabkrin warned Vesenkha that the staffs of the ob"edineniia should, "at a minimum," not outnumber the employees of the old organizations that were to be abolished.[1] Thus in 1929, when Vesenkha drew up blueprints for Mashinoob"edinenie, it gave special attention to the savings that would result from a decrease in personnel.[2]

Vesenkha targeted commercial sections of the old bureaucracy for the most significant reductions. According to its figures, 1,406 people worked in the combined financial and sales bureaucracies of Glavmashinstroi, the various trusts under its control, and the engineering syndicate, VMTS. By concentrating financial and sales functions in the central association departments, Vesenkha calculated it could reduce the number of employees in this area to 1,035, a reduction of 371 people (about 26 percent), for a 19 percent savings in salaries, from 367,350 to 216,095 rubles a month. As for salespeople alone, VMTS employed 108 in its central apparatus, with expenditures of 21,924 rubles per month. The trusts, combined, had 180 people in their sales departments, costing 24,600 rubles per month. Mashinoob"edinenie was scheduled to employ 145 people in its sales apparatus at 29,510 rubles per month. In all, Vesenkha planned for 1,121 positions to be filled in the central Moscow apparatus of the new machine building

[1] Rozengol'ts, *Za sotsializm protiv biurokratizma*, p. 50.
[2] RGAE, f. 5716, op. 1, d. 76, ll. 1–60.

association. Vesenkha compared this figure favorably to the 1,406 staff positions in the glavk, syndicate, and central administrations of the machine building trusts.[3]

Contrary to government directives, reorganization of the industrial apparatus during 1930 dramatically increased the numbers of staff positions. In the early summer of 1930 Rozengol'ts described an "unbelievable" bureaucratization of administration. All of the associations experienced significant increases in staff over the numbers employed in the old glavki: a 51 percent increase in agricultural machine manufacturing, with a 71 percent rise in wage expenditures; a 36 percent increase in personnel in the oil production association; a 41 percent rise in employment for the paper industry.[4]

Rozengol'ts repeated the often-heard criticism that these increases provided evidence of a "mechanical" rather than an "organic" integration of the bureaucracies. He accused Vesenkha, in other words, of simply combining administrative units of the old chief administrations with those of the new associations. Stal', for instance, simply incorporated the whole apparatus of Iugostal'. In figuring costs, Rozengol'ts added, Stal' officials did not even count the enormous amount of money needed to transport all of Iugostal''s people to Moscow and find them apartments. According to Rabkrin surveys, most of the staff increases occurred in the areas of clerical and office help rather than "operational" personnel—engineers, economists, and other specialists. "The bureaucracies continue to live in extreme luxury," Rozengol'ts said. "We live by the bureaucracy."[5]

Rozengol'ts's charges should have been reversed. As syndicate officials pointed out in 1929, it was the Rabkrin-Vesenkha models of industrial organization that were mechanistic. Their schemes for centralized reorganization were based on simplistic administrative criteria that bore little relation to the complexities of production and commercial trading in the country. Moreover, as we have seen, the industrial system that evolved during 1930, though unwieldy, developed in response to existing contingencies. It was more "organic" in its responsiveness to real conditions than the schematized models concocted by Rabkrin officials. The staff increases that Rozengol'ts so scathingly criticized reflected Vesenkha's attempts to respond to the desperate pleas of trust and association members for clerical and accounting help in the work that daily overwhelmed them. Harried industrial administrators may well have listened in amaze-

[3]Ibid., ll. 59–60, 3, 40.

[4]Rozengol'ts, *Za sotsializm protiv biurokratizma*, p. 51. A Central Committee survey taken on the eve of the 16th Party Congress confirmed that in almost every instance, associations had used reorganization not to streamline their operations but to increase the number of employees over the combined totals that had worked in the corresponding trusts, syndicates, and chief administrations. See RTsKhIDNI, f. 17, op. 74, d. 8, l. 97.

[5]Rozengol'ts, *Za sotsializm protiv biurokratizma*, pp. 51, 52.

ment as Comrade Rozengol'ts informed them that they were living in the lap of luxury.

Amazed or not, every industrial official understood the political import of Rozengol'ts's words. He was, after all, deputy *narkom* of Rabkrin and a high Party official. His criticisms of bureaucratism were not idle words; they held a clear political warning. The fear of bureaucratism had always been an obsession of the Bolsheviks, but since the sabotage trial of Donbass mining engineers in 1928–the famous "Shakhty affair"—Party officials viewed the bureaucracy as a hotbed of political criminals. Loyal Soviet administrators were shocked to learn that in their midst were not just bourgeois specialists but whole networks of wreckers, saboteurs, spies, and agents of hostile powers. As the hunt for political opposition gained momentum, administrators were forced to habituate themselves to the frightening banality of state-sponsored political terror. When S. B. Sandomirskii likened work in the industrial bureaucracy to the idiocy of a madhouse, did he suspect that the keepers of the madhouse were more insane than its inmates?

The Police and Party Investigations: Spring and Summer 1929

Political investigations were both frightening and routine because, ironically, the police campaign against enemies in the state's bureaucracies was itself highly bureaucratized. Three bodies, the OGPU, Rabkrin, and the Central Committee, had the authority to conduct such investigations. These organs engaged in at least three major purges of Vesenkha's industrial apparatus from the autumn of 1929 until the autumn of 1930. Political investigations came on top of the normal scourge of economic inspections and surveys, and involved many of the same kinds of tedious activities. Industrial officials were constantly harassed to fill out surveys, attend purge meetings, answer investigators' questions, provide facilities, and amass data for the numerous commissions that descended upon them. Political investigations were closely monitored by a special Central Committee commission, established at the time of the Shakhty affair, to fight bureaucratism and to ensure the development of a Soviet technical and administrative cadre. Lazar Kaganovich headed the commission, and he reported regularly on its activities to Central Committee plenum sessions. Occasionally, and then with increasing frequency, officials had to accustom themselves to the absence of comrades who ran afoul of the official organs and were dismissed and arrested.

In the summer and early autumn of 1928, at the request of Kaganovich's commission, police conducted a social and political survey of 9,000 engineers and other specialists in the state's economic apparatus. OGPU administrators used this survey to target priorities for an investigation of

sabotage and other anti-Soviet activities. After a year of "hard" investigation, Kaganovich reported preliminary results to the Central Committee in
November 1929. The breadth and depth of anti-Soviet activity uncovered
by the latest investigations, Kaganovich said, made the Shakhty conspiracy pale in comparison. The OGPU was finding nothing less than an organized war against Soviet power. As of November 1929, five hundred specialists had been arrested on wrecking charges. Former "big" capitalists
and landholders accounted for 29 percent of that number; former nongen-
try intelligentsia made up 70 percent. Of the 106 arrested so far in the area
of transport, 62 percent came from the ranks of the old honorary nobility,
trading class, and clergy. In these numbers, Kaganovich declared, was
proof that the bureaucratic war was coordinated by the "commanding
elite of the old capitalist order."[6]

Clearly, the OGPU was not working behind the scenes, waiting to make
their arrests all at once. So many arrests over fifteen months made police
involvement a matter of common knowledge in the bureaucracies. By
early 1930, regional Party bureaus and the Central Committee's Control
Department were already receiving frequent letters from disgruntled
managers pleading that no more transfers or arrests be made from their
factories.[7]

In his TsK report of November 1929, Kaganovich named twenty-three
well-known specialists in various areas of industrial administration and at
various levels of the apparatus who were under arrest. S. A. Khrennikov
and V. I. Zhdanov, former heads of the metal trust Gomzy and later high
specialists in Glavmetall, had already been arrested by November 1929. So
had D. N. Shvetsov, former head of the Leningrad shipbuilding trust and
then head of Gipromez. Chief engineers Gaude and Gartman in the industrial section of Gosplan had been arrested, as had several prominent members of the collegium of Iugostal', most notably the technical director, A.
Svitsyn.[8]

These specialists, Khrennikov chief among them, figured as key defendants in the Industrial Party trial a year later. Interestingly, Shvetsov came
to the attention of the police through a second and overlapping series of
investigations, carried out in the spring and summer of 1929 under the
authority of a purge commission made up jointly of Party officials and
members of the economic commission of Glavmashinstroi. The purge
commission must have been convened in February or early March and
gathered its materials in March and early April. G. F. Davydov, head of
the Party cell organizations in Glavmashinstroi, chaired the commission

[6]RTsKhIDNI, f. 17. op. 2, d. 441, l. 94.
[7]See, e.g., the collection of such letters gathered by the Central Committee's Department of
Personnel Control, the Uchraspred bureau, ibid., op. 74, d. 8, ll. 50–65.
[8]Ibid.

and called its first hearing on 2 April 1929. Davydov's commission conducted weekly hearings throughout April and May, at least, and perhaps on into the summer.[9]

Shvetsov's troubles began in April 1929, when Davydov's commission investigated what were thought to be serious production problems in the shipbuilding industry. The commission found that while Shvetsov was head of the Leningrad trust, he and his staff were responsible for breakdowns in supplies, loss of materials, damaged parts, and a host of other catastrophies that forced a two-month shutdown in several of the major Baltic shipyards during the latter part of 1928.[10] Although Davydov's hearings took place in April, it was not until 7 May that the commission recommended Shvetsov's category I removal, as well as the category I removal of Shvetsov's assistant B. I. Shostakovskii. Category I dismissal identified Shvetsov and Shostakovskii as alien and hostile social elements, and indicated that their activities were the result not of incompetence but of willful sabotage. In other words, category I dismissal identified the pair as political enemies. Unless successfully contested, it virtually ensured their arrest.[11]

V. A. Medvedev, a high official in Glavmashinstroi, spoke against the category I sanction at the 7 May meeting, arguing for censure, but not removal under political suspicion. Medvedev cited Shvetsov's long history of loyal work for the regime. Shvetsov's background, however (his father had been a tsarist government official), and his participation in the White army during the Civil War weighed heavily against him. The official police summaries, or *kharakteristiki*, of both Shvetsov and Shostakovskii described their work as "formal" and "bureaucratic," their attitude toward work and comrades as "uncooperative and antisocial," and, most damning of all, their attitude toward the Soviet regime as "hostile."[12] Still, no action was taken against the men for several months. Shvetsov's official release from Vesenkha was not registered in Glavmashinstroi's personnel records until 16 August, Shostakovskii's not until 20 November. Their dismissals, like those of all who were removed under a category I sanction, were noted as *bez ukazaniia prichin*, "without specified reason." It is not clear whether these men continued to work until their officially registered dismissal or whether they were removed or resigned only when they were arrested. In any case, by the time the *kharakteristiki* were written, sometime in September or October 1929, Shvetsov was already in Solovki prison.

[9]RGAE, f. 5735, op. 2, d. 24. The dates of this first purge are not precisely given in the archives.

[10]Ibid., ll. 49–73.

[11]The other two criteria for removal were professional incompetence (category II) and inappropriate assignment (category III).

[12]RGAE, f. 5735, op. 2, d. 23, ll. 79–82.

Interestingly, Shvetsov's *kharakteristika* also noted that he was removed from work at the specific request of Rabkrin. Such a notation was unusual and certainly shows that that agency's officials were involved in the purge commission's work. In fact, it was Rabkrin, through one of its own surveys, that brought the situation at the shipbuilding yards to the attention of Davydov's commission.[13] The reference to Rabkrin in Shvetsov's *kharakteristika* could also have indicated a division of opinion about his removal. Davydov may have cited Rabkrin's request to add weight to the recommendation for a category I dismissal.

The length of time it took to effect the removal of the two officials, four and six months respectively, is curious. That time gap very likely reflected attempts by Shvetsov and Shostakovskii to appeal the recommendation for their dismissal. Many officials appealed formally, in writing, to the Party commissions and to the head of their chief administration for reconsideration or reinstatement in good professional standing. Most of these appeals went unheeded. A politically damaging *kharakteristika* by the local Party secretary was a serious matter, and appeals were nearly always denied. But not always. Powerful patronage could protect a specialist, at least for a time, even from middle-level Party officials.

The Case of G. A. Spektor

G. A. Spektor served as assistant head of Glavmashinstroi's planning department in 1928 and 1929. In his early fifties, Spektor was a highly qualified engineering economist who had worked in the pre-Soviet and Soviet industrial bureaucracies for thirty years. Before his appointment to Glavmashinstroi's planning department, Spektor had served as a high official in Glavmetall. He was also a respected and prolific author, publishing often in the journals *Metall* and *Puti industrializatsii*. Spektor knew French, English, and German, and wrote most often about problems and prospects in the domestic and foreign metal manufacturing industries.

Spektor's qualifications did not spare him from political troubles. The *kharakteristika* written by Davydov's purge commission described him as extremely hostile toward Soviet power and personally insulting to Party comrades. Hostility toward Soviet power was the first of the Bolshevik deadly sins. The second was opportunism, and Spektor was accused of that, too. Spektor received payment for published articles, to which he allegedly devoted too much attention, so he was also guilty of personal aggrandizement. Writing for remuneration supposedly distracted him from his administrative duties. Finally, Davydov's commission noted that

---

[13]Ibid., d. 24, l. 52.

Spektor had been a member of the Menshevik Party's Central Committee and had been "high" in the White resistance to Bolshevik power during the Civil War. Spektor's Menshevik sympathies supposedly continued and he had allegedly surrounded himself with Mensheviks in his various positions of responsibility in Soviet industry.[14]

Surprisingly, Spektor was not removed from his post. He voluntarily resigned in July 1929, no doubt under pressure, but he resumed work in late September in the prestigious economic planning administration (the PEU) of Vesenkha's central apparatus. In the meantime, Spektor and Davydov engaged in a political sparring match that lasted several months. Davydov's attempts to have Spektor removed eventually involved the regional Party secretary, the Party apparatus at several levels of the Vesenkha bureaucracy, the OGPU, and no less a figure than V. I. Mezhlauk, deputy head of Vesenkha and a Central Committee member. In a secret memorandum written in February 1930, Davydov recounted his efforts and the efforts of other Party officials to have Spektor removed and arrested as a class enemy.[15]

Davydov noted that the Party committees of both Glavmetall and Glavmashinstroi recommended Spektor's dismissal on political grounds on at least two occasions, in 1927 and 1928. Those recommendations were forwarded to the appropriate offices of the OGPU. "Apparently," Davydov wrote, "a strong hand," whom he believed but could not prove was Mezhlauk, defended Spektor. In each instance, a separate and presumably higher Party review commission overruled the local Party purge commission, and Spektor was "left in his position." Even though the review commission recommended that Spektor not be given a leadership post, he was appointed assistant head of the planning department of Glavmashinstroi in early 1928. Still a third Party review commission recommended Spektor's removal, as did Davydov's purge commission, and still Spektor remained at his post. In the last instance, Davydov recounted, the collegium of the glavk openly defied the purge recommendation and refused to dismiss Spektor.[16]

Spektor finally resigned in July 1929, when he learned about the Party committee's actions against him. Deliberations of Party committees were regarded as confidential until the information was made public, and despite Davydov's best efforts, no official action had been taken against Spektor as of July. Supposedly, then, Spektor was in ignorance of the machinations behind his back. Yet Spektor knew. According to Davydov,

[14]Ibid., d. 23, l. 82.
[15]This remarkable four-page, single-spaced typed document is marked "completely secret": ibid., d. 24, ll. 152–53b.
[16]Ibid., l. 152.

Spektor had gained this information from Smelov, the former Party secretary of Glavmashinstroi. Davydov noted that he would bring this breach of Party discipline to the attention of the next purge commission.[17]

When Davydov discovered that Spektor had already arranged to work at the PEU before he left Glavmashinstroi, he and another Party official in the glavk, P. P. Lapidus, attempted to block Spektor's appointment by appealing to the heads of the PEU, Mantsev and Ianishevskii. Ianishevskii was also the Party cell leader in the PEU. Both Mantsev and Ianishevskii supported Spektor's appointment. In September, Davydov and Lapidus appealed to the regional Party secretary for that part of Moscow, Skorniakov, and requested an interview with the assistant head of the OGPU for the Moscow region. Both Skorniakov and the OGPU office refused to take action. Skorniakov had already approved Spektor's posting at PEU, and the OGPU officer had agreed conditionally to Spektor's appointment, at least until Mezhlauk reviewed the case after he returned from vacation.[18]

Davydov recalled that during this period, early September 1929, he met Spektor several times by chance in the corridor at Vesenkha, once just as the specialist was entering Mezhlauk's office. "I asked him how things were going," wrote Davydov, "and he replied, 'You [*ty*] know better than I.'" Spektor said he had had several job offers, but had refused them because he did not want to cause trouble for his supporters. "You've cut me both ways," Spektor reportedly said to Davydov. "If I'd been fired from GUMS [Glavmashinstroi], you could use all the laws against me, but I left voluntarily and still it doesn't matter. You still hinder me from getting work, and I'm still left in the position of a useless person with no rights." Spektor named others in the Party collective at Glavmashinstroi who he knew were against him. He had "put them on their feet" and taught them how to work, but "instead of thanking me," Spektor said, "they betray me." After this exchange, Spektor went into Mezhlauk's office.[19]

In this exchange we see Spektor's awareness of the trap he was in and his maneuverings to extricate himself. He had left Glavmashinstroi under pressure from Davydov's purge commission, but also to protect himself. If he had waited to be fired, he would have been unemployable as a political pariah, and then he would have been subject to arrest under Soviet anti-parasite social laws. Willful unemployment was a criminal offense, and authorities often harassed political undesirables under this charge, even though the offenders usually lost their jobs as a result of political stigma rather than any antisocial behavior. Spektor preempted this process by resigning rather than waiting to be dismissed. Legally he was still employable. More important, Spektor bought himself time. If he accepted a

[17]Ibid.
[18]Ibid., l. 152b.
[19]Ibid.

position in an agency other than Glavmashinstroi, he would come under the jurisdiction of another Party committee. If Davydov's charges were to be pursued, they would have to be brought again under the new committee, which would conduct its own review and might overturn the *kharakteristika* issued by Davydov's commission. Spektor understood these bureaucratic implications. As his exchange with Davydov shows, his concern was to avoid the catch-22 of dismissal and also to protect friends who were willing to offer him the life-line of a job in another agency.

Davydov also understood the implications of Spektor's actions. He was aware that Spektor had outmaneuvered him at least temporarily; that was why he reported the encounter with Spektor in the hallway. Spektor's remarks revealed that he knew more than he should have known. It was disturbing, Davydov wrote, that Spektor knew the names of Party officials who had worked against him. Even more alarming was Spektor's apparent knowledge of the details of the measures taken against him. Davydov reiterated his belief that Spektor had defenders in high places. His reference to the exchange at Mezhlauk's door made it clear who he believed one of those defenders was.

Despite Davydov's machinations and Spektor's concern about his friends, Spektor decided to take the position at PEU, and he began work there in late September 1929. This was not the end of the affair, however. Davydov and several other Party officials at Glavmashinstroi filed an official protest. A hearing was held by the so-called Party Committees' Bureau—the top Party officials from both the glavk and the central administration of Vesenkha—and officials high in the city's regional Party hierarchy. Skorniakov, in Davydov's account, continued to defend Spektor as a "quick, creative, and accurate" worker who was attentive to his coworkers. At one point Skorniakov lost his temper. "It would be good for us Communists," he was reported to have said, "if we had comrades who worked as hard as Mensheviks such as Spektor." Davydov noted laconically that "the Bureau decided to discuss Skorniakov's attitude in a separate gathering."[20] After a long and rancorous meeting, a resolution was passed declaring that it was dangerous for Spektor to work in Vesenkha. But Vesenkha Party officials refused to sanction any action against Spektor and none was taken. Spektor remained at his post.

Davydov was still not deterred. He prepared his secret report and submitted it to yet a third purge commission organized by Rabkrin in January and February 1930. Unfortunately, Davydov's report ends with Spektor's move to the PEU in September 1929. No further information about Spektor is available in the archives, but as late as January 1931 he was still publishing articles under his own name.

[20]Ibid., ll. 153–53b.

Though we do not know Spektor's eventual fate, his story reveals much about how the purge process worked in the late 1920s. Clearly, there was little coordination and much disagreement between levels of the Party bureaucracy over the fate of individual specialists. Resolutions to censure Spektor adopted at one level of the Party hierarchy were ignored or overturned at another level. Party officials disagreed with OGPU officials, and the OGPU refused to be bothered with Davydov's insistent accusations. Most important for Spektor was Mezhlauk's patronage. Mezhlauk held an important position in the state's economic system, and he sat on the Central Committee. Davydov was not privy to information at Mezhlauk's high level, and was powerless to overcome his influence. There was no effective legal protection against political repression. But jurisdictional confusion and disputes sometimes acted as an unintentional check on the unrestrained exercise of power by an agency or an official. Spektor's story reveals how an individual could move in and out of political danger, and how bureaucratic politics arbitrarily could decide an individual's fate. In Spektor's case, bureaucratic politics allowed him to slip through the purge process, at least for a time.

Rabkrin's Purge

The purge commission to which Davydov submitted his report on G. A. Spektor began its work in late 1929 and ran at least through the early spring of 1930. Rabkrin initiated this purge as a result of the resolution on cadres and specialists issued by the 16th Party Conference in the spring of 1929. Ordzhonikidze placed Ia. Peters, a member of Rabkrin's presidium, in charge of the purge commissions, and it was Peters who coordinated and supervised the investigations.

Rabkrin's involvement in matters of political criminality and industrial sabotage was not surprising. The agency's leaders—Ordzhonikidze, Iakovlev, and Peters—were all members of the Party's special purge commissions administered by the Central Committee. Rabkrin also doubled as the Party's Central Control Commission and was deeply involved in the Party purge of the late 1920s. As a result, Rabkrin was regularly consulted by the Party's personnel department and by the OGPU when appointees were considered for high-level positions in the industrial apparatus. Rabkrin's working relationship with the OGPU was so close that several high-ranking OGPU officials sat on Rabkrin's collegium or on that of the Central Control Commission. OGPU officials cooperated with Peters in organizing Rabkrin's purge hearings on Vesenkha in late 1929 and 1930.[21]

Rabkrin's purge commissions focused on the major financial, economic,

---

[21]See Davies, *Soviet Economy in Turmoil*, pp. 115–20, for a general discussion of Rabkrin's role in the purge of the Soviet economic and industrial apparatus.

and trade bureaucracies in the state apparatus. Mashinoob"edinenie was one of the first to come under scrutiny. Peters appointed I. Z. Gokhman to chair the purge commission that reviewed Mashinoob"edinenie; Andriadis served as his deputy. Gokhman divided his commission into subgroups, one for each of Moob's departments. Some member of these subgroups came from Rabkrin, but most were minor officials in their departments. P. P. Lapidus, for example, worked as an "economist" in Moob's scrap metal section; P. P. Kiskeev was an "economist" in the construction and design department; A. V. Tyrin was an assistant economist in the production sub-department of the machine building office; M. M. Ivanov held a politically more sensitive position as head of the legal bureau of the personnel control (*uchraspred*) department.

As members of the purge commission's investigative staff, these men had more authority than they normally enjoyed. Except for the most secret Party files, all materials of the departments they investigated were open to them. They gained access to personnel records, could and did request work-related materials from colleagues, and had access to all records of the association and its predecessor organizations. Commission members were authorized to ask any question or read any file they deemed pertinent to their task. That task, of course, was not just political. The purge was also intended to review the professional qualifications of personnel working in the bureaucracies. Thus minor administrative officials suddenly acquired official sanction to judge the political and professional capabilities not only of their colleagues but also of their superiors.

Inverting the hierarchy of authority, as the purge investigation did, must have made for very uncomfortable working relations. The reaction to these investigations was predictable. After several weeks of work, Andriadis openly complained about lack of cooperation from the various departments. Personnel files and materials requested by the commission often arrived late and incomplete. He noted incidents of hostility to investigators, unwillingness to talk to purge officials, and "overall, a not very cooperative and forthcoming [*dobrozhelatel'noe*] attitude."[22] One official who came under investigation expressed his "antisocial attitude" in a particularly inventive and insulting manner: despite a ban on travel when under investigation, he left Moscow for vacation at the time his case came before the commission's tribunal.[23]

Many showed their hostility by not attending the hearings. The commission began open hearings in late February, and at the second session on 3 March, Gokhman noted that only 60 of the 250 association personnel were in attendance—and 20 of them were members of the commission's investigative brigades. This, he declared, was not a "stunning" (*blestia-*

[22]RGAE, f. 5735, op. 2, d. 24, l. 138.
[23]RGAE, f. 5716, op. 2, d. 2, l. 85.

A shop-level purge commission at the Krasnyi Proletarii factory, c. 1930. GARF.

shchee) turnout. He warned his audience to take the purge more seriously and declared ominously that the commission would note the attitude indicated by failure to attend. Gokhman also complained that only certain people were "talking to and cooperating with" the commission. This situation would have to change if the commission was to conduct its business in an orderly manner. Gokhman did not explain what a disorderly investigation would entail.[24]

Moob's distinct lack of enthusiasm was due partly to the curious purview of the commission's charge. At its opening session, 28 January 1929, Gokhman stated that the commission was investigating not Mashino-ob"edinenie but its predecessor, Glavmashinstroi.[25] When persons were brought before the commission, the charges against them dealt with their activities in the old glavk, not in Moob. Still, the investigations and hearings were conducted on an institutional level. Members of the association were pressured to attend the nearly nightly hearings of the commission, whether or not their activities were under discussion. When questioning people about their activities, commission members used the past tense, but when they made general criticisms, they often confused past and pres-

[24]Ibid.
[25]RGAE, f. 5735, op. 2, d. 24, l. 138.

ent. It was as if the institutional guilt of the glavk carried over to the association. Indeed, in the minds of the commission members, it did. Gokhman's opening sentence at the 28 January meeting made his intention clear. "Comrades," he said bluntly, "we are here to purge your organization."[26]

For several weeks, from early January to late February 1930, the various subcommissions conducted their reviews, and the commission drew up its list of charges. In late February, Gokhman reconvened the general commission to begin hearings. From late February through mid-May, the commission met nearly every evening to hear charges against individuals or groups. Sessions lasted from 7:00 to 10:00 or 11:00, and sometimes they ran as late as midnight. Gokhman opened each session by reading the decisions reached in previous cases, then read charges against the people to be vetted that evening. Charges usually focused on economic mismanagement and involved two to five officials at a time. Each of the persons charged presented a biographical sketch and answered the accusations against him. The hearing proceeded as a free-for-all, commission members asking questions or making statements in no particular order. Much attention was given to an individual's activities during the Revolution and Civil War. Commission members often presented evidence allegedly proving that officials had tried to hide anti-Bolshevik activities committed between 1917 and 1922. Commission members did their preliminary work thoroughly and were prepared with detailed information about the backgrounds of the accused.

No one managed to clear himself of the charges against him. Charges of mismanagement were read as a proven fact. The explicit purpose of the hearings was to assess the extent of the person's responsibility, not to determine his guilt or innocence. Thus the hearings functioned as a political morality play, not as a trial. Gokhman repeatedly and impatiently interrupted the accused, telling them that their protestations and explanations were irrelevant. "That has nothing to do with the matter. Speak to the matter of your responsibility," he said when V. F. Oborin declared that he and his colleagues had nothing to do with the charges against them. "We are not asking you to place blame on someone else. We are asking you for an explanation of your own bureaucratic bungling [*volokita*]." In this instance, Oborin was attempting to explain that pricing policies established by the state and administrative procedures at other administrative levels caused underproduction of tractor parts in late 1928. "What other agencies did or did not do does not interest us," Gokhman scolded. "Speak to the matter."

"I am speaking to the matter," replied Oborin.

[26]RGAE, f. 5716, op. 2, d. 2, l. 1.

"Stop all this childish talk," Gokhman demanded. "Every day our newspapers cry for spare parts; we may loose the harvest. You are powerful leaders of industry and you give childish explanations."[27]

M. N. Poliakov, another official charged in the tractor parts scandal, explained that there had been a misunderstanding in the charges brought against him and his comrades. Gokhman broke in. "We don't care whether we're talking about 10,000 parts more or less; we're interested in the fact that localities won't have the parts for the harvest campaign." When Poliakov protested that in fact 10,000 parts made a significant difference, Gokhman cut him off. "Get to the heart of the matter," he snapped. "Tell us in what ways you are to blame."[28]

Some exchanges were truly bizarre. A third official charged in the tractor parts affair, one Popov, readily declared his responsibility in the matter, but Gokhman was not satisfied. In response to prompting from the chair, Popov attempted to find an acceptable formulation for the degree of his guilt.

"You answer for the whole affair?" asked Gokhman.

"We're all responsible," replied Popov.

"You answer for the affair. What is your monthly salary?"

"Four hundred rubles."

"To what extent do you accept responsibility in the matter of the tractor parts?"

"It's difficult to say. We all dealt with important questions in these matters."

"Well . . . how . . . what did you not foresee?"

"I said . . . in this regard . . . I didn't make sure that we had back-up factories we could turn to in case we . . . if our main contracts didn't work out."

"Only that?"

"Yes, apart from general responsibility."

"For that, then, you are held responsible."[29]

At times commission members questioned accused officials closely about activities and decisions as much as several years before the hearings. They reviewed in detail the timing of contract negotiations, financial transactions, even telephone and telegraph exchanges between the glavk and other organizations. These hearings provided the purge commission with valuable information about how the administrative process could be improved. Testimony of industrial officials made it clear that in every case investigated, disruptions in production schedules or underfulfillment of contracts arose largely as a result of breakdowns in the bureaucratic pro-

[27]Ibid., ll. 27–28, 34.
[28]Ibid., l. 34.
[29]Ibid., l. 41.

cess or an absence of administrative control mechanisms. Yet, as these exchanges demonstrate, purge officials were not interested in resolving administrative problems or in recommending changes in procedures. Commissioners did not even discuss the obvious structural problems that led to the economic disruptions they were investigating. Such matters did not fall within their purview. That responsibility belonged to other Rabkrin commissions, but there is no evidence that the purge commission communicated its findings to any committee or agency other than the OGPU and the Central Committee. Rabkrin's purge commission was a victim of its own ill-conceived mission. The commission diligently carried out its charge to assign personal blame and to root out suspected sabotage, and that was all.

This was not the last of Rabkrin's investigations. Nor were its purges the most ruthless, despite the impression that they were harsher than those conducted by the Party apparatus. Both the Rabkrin and the Party purge commissions passed over officials who only a few months later were arrested and tried as part of the Industrial Party conspiracy. The Party commission, for example, noted the Menshevik past of N. F. Charnovskii, yet his *kharakteristika* gave him high praise for his professional achievements and his willingness to work loyally for the Soviet regime. That was in August 1929. The Rabkrin commission found no fault with Charnovskii and it completed its work in May 1930. By November, however, Charnovskii was listed as one of the leading defendants in the Industrial Party group.[30] Clearly, the OGPU proceeded with its own investigations apart from the Party and Rabkrin commissions. The OGPU used information gathered in the other purges, but it had its own criteria for arrest and indictment.

Many of the trials for sabotage during the late 1920s resulted from both local and national Rabkrin investigations. Trials of less prominent persons were handled by local courts, but the indictments often reached up to the level of factory director and sometimes higher. K. I. Portenko, former head of the Krasnyi Profintern works in Briansk, testified as a codefendant in a local trial of the factory's administration and twenty-three specialists. The trial lasted for several weeks during September and October 1929. *Torgovo-promyshlennaia gazeta* reported crowds of up to a thousand people attending the hearings or milling about outside the palace of culture in Bezhitsa, where the trial was being held.[31] The charges, stemming from an investigation conducted by local Rabkrin and Komsomol activists, ranged from mismanagement to illegal speculation to outright wrecking. The newspaper reported that, of the twenty-three defendants at the Briansk trial, three were sentenced to ten years' imprisonment, three were given five-

[30] *Za industrializatsiiu*, 11 November 1930, p. 1.
[31] *TPG*, 6 October 1929, p. 2.

year sentences, one received three years, and several were publicly cen-
sured. For his mismanagement of the factory, Portenko was suspended
from work in any high industrial position for two years. In November
1929 Lazar Kaganovich, reporting to the Central Committee plenum, singled out Portenko as one who had "gotten two years," and he noted that
a special Central Committee tribunal had approved the sentence.[32] Yet
Portenko's censure was apparently not taken seriously, for his name appeared on the active roster of Moob's board of directors in January 1930.
The roster did not note the assistant director's censure.[33]

Iugostal' was especially hard hit by Rabkrin and police investigations,
as was, among other enterprises, the Dneprostroi engineering and dam
construction project. A secret report of the Party's organizational bureau
revealed that over 400 people were purged from Dneprostroi. They included about 2 percent of the workforce (117 workers), nearly 20 percent
of all clerical staff (183 slushashchie), and a little over 25 percent of all the
technical and engineering cadre (107 inzhenerno-tekhnicheskie kadry).
Whether all of these people were arrested is not clear, but the designation
"purged" (ochistili) indicated that at the very least they were dismissed.[34]

Conclusion

The purges of Glavmashinstroi and Mashinoob"edinenie were typical
of the process carried out in every one of Vesenkha's production associations. It was a humiliating and disruptive process to which specialists reacted with a mixture of anxiety and anger, or in some cases indifference.
Under the threat of investigation and possible arrest, paranoia and fear
pervaded the chief administration. But most specialists experienced the
purges as a bureaucratic process. They spent inordinate amounts of time
filling out surveys, answering questions, and attending the endless rounds
of meetings and hearings. The purge process hindered the administrative
restructuring of the industrial economy more than any other single factor.
It created emotional stress and distracted the attention of specialists at a
time when their efforts were most needed to deal with the pressures of
industrialization and administrative chaos.

The purges were designed to break opposition to Stalinist policies, and
they also functioned to redirect blame for the failings of those ill-consid-
ered policies. But the purges served yet another function as a deadly form
of Stalinist morality play. In the absence or abeyance of clear administrative procedures and political processes, the purges articulated new rules
of professional and political behavior. This didactic purpose explains why

[32]RTsKhIDNI, f. 17, op. 2, d. 441, l. 106.
[33]RGAE, f. 5716, op. 2, d. 4, l. 1.
[34]See, e.g., RTsKhIDNI, f. 17, op. 74, d. 8, l. 60.

purge hearings were public spectacles and officials were required to attend. These hearings were not designed to get at the truth, or even to
assess blame for specific crimes. Forcing specialists to admit responsibility
for mismanagement or wrecking was only part of the process. The purge
hearings conducted in Glavmashinstroi were entirely unrehearsed. Purge
commissioners and accused officials alike struggled to get the language
right, to establish the correct formulation of culpability and subordination.
Reading the transcripts of the various purge commissions, one can see the
participants groping for the proper way to play their roles, the refusal of
some to play the roles assigned them, the blatant attempts by others to
coach defendants. Certainly the purges served up scapegoats, but the
reader receives a strong impression that establishing the vocabulary of
blame and submission was one of the main purposes of the hearings.

If proceedings of the purge tribunals clarified nothing about criminal
culpability, they reaffirmed in the crudest way the primacy of politics in
professional culture. At the most basic level, the purges demonstrated that
there were no longer any clear distinctions between professional and political behavior. The purge of the industrial bureaucracies reestablished a
professional and political culture not seen in the Soviet state since the
revolutionary war years. Politics was once again in command in a way it
had not been during the relative social peace of the 1920s.

8

The Pathologies of Modernization

The situation remains as bad as it ever was. . . . Factory
shops lack even the most rudimentary order, and so far
we've seen almost no improvement.
  —Sergo Ordzhonikidze to Stalin, August 1931

In May 1933, Sergo Ordzhonikidze, then commissar of heavy industry, convened a small conference of managers and technical personnel from Moscow-area metal factories. Most of the participants were lower-level supervisors—work brigade leaders, production foremen, and shop heads. The *narkom* invited engineering department chiefs but no factory directors. Ordzhonikidze opened the meeting with what must have been a startling admission: he and the other heads of industry did not know how their factories worked, how anything was accomplished. "I'd like you to tell me what you all actually do. What does the shop head do? The brigade leader? The foreman especially, in the factory, in his own shop? What authority does he have in respect to workers? To brigade leaders? In respect to wages? In respect to deciding the production program?"[1]

As Ordzhonikidze and other presidium members asked questions, it became clear that the organization of work and authority differed significantly from factory to factory, from shop to shop in the same factory, and even from brigade to brigade in the same shop. In some works, foremen determined piece rates and wage levels and hired and fired workers. In other factories, foremen had little authority in contrast to central factory administrative departments. Some representatives insisted their shops maintained accurate accounting records; others declared "categorically" that their factories had no serious accounting system. Some spoke of close working relations with central factory departments; others declared that their shops were left "pretty much on their own." Ordzhonikidze asked

[1] RTsKhIDNI, f. 85, op. 29, d. 38, l. 1.

how work orders were issued and how workers knew exactly what to do. Iu. P. Figatner, head of the commissariat's labor sector, asked how piece rates and wages could be determined if one brigade was paid collectively while others worked at individual piece rates. All of the questions revealed the commissariat's genuine confusion over the organization of Soviet factories. The answers revealed the confusion within those factories.[2]

Ordzhonikidze's small conference revealed more than speeches and statistics how little managers knew about what went on in industry. Despite several years of concerted efforts by Party, police, and government agencies, the development of the Soviet industrial system was more spontaneous than planned. This is not to say that all was simply chaos. Patterns of work and organization emerged, but they bore little resemblance to a formal organization chart. This was an industrial system that defies easy categorization. It was a system in constant motion, evolving in multiple and contradictory ways, driven by forces only partly controlled by central state and political authorities.

Factory-Association Relations: The Drive to Expand

In the administrative hierarchy of the industrial state, factories were supposed to have considerable scope for independent action. Reorganization in 1929–30 was intended to strengthen the factory's autonomy. According to the order on reorganization of 5 December 1929, the factory was the "fundamental link" in the management chain of industry. Its director was to have "a necessary degree of independence" in the technical outfitting of the factory, in organizing supplies and labor, hiring qualified engineering and administrative personnel, and "in general creating the most optimal conditions of . . . production." The order did not spell out the legal regulations on which the factory director's authority was to be founded, but the factory was supposed to operate on the basis of full cost accountability, *khoziaistvennyi raschet*—a stipulation that implied control over production management and over the capital and supplies needed to operate.[3]

The reorganization order was never officially superseded and was frequently cited as the legal basis for the autonomy of the factory as the fundamental administrative unit of industry. Yet factory autonomy was a fiction. Industrial associations constantly interfered in factory operations, routinely usurping the factory's authority in nearly every aspect of production and management. Association personnel often intervened directly in matters of labor and production organization in its factories' shops. Associations sequestered factory funds, controlled the use of working cap-

[2]Ibid., ll. 11, 18–19, 34.
[3]*Resheniia Partii i pravitel'stva po khoziaistvennym voprosam* (Moscow, 1967), 2:136.

ital, monitored inventories and account books, and decided questions of factory reconstruction. Associations retained the authority to hire and fire engineering and managerial staff in their factories, and intervened in the hiring and distribution of personnel even at the lower echelons of factory administration.

At a 1931 conference of industrial leaders, Sergo Ordzhonikidze expressed his concern over the state of affairs that allowed production associations to usurp functions that were supposed to lie within the factory's sphere of authority. In many enterprises, he complained, directors had "almost no direct participation" in the ordering and distribution of materials and equipment for the factory, or in the establishment of production schedules. Many factory directors were managers in name only. Operational control of their factories remained in the offices of the cartels, "almost to the exclusion of directors and their staffs."[4]

The aggressiveness and initiative of middle-level industrial managers during the 1930s belie the traditional image of the passive and fearful Soviet bureaucrat, bound and besieged by political pressures and production targets. Administrators were besieged, and many sought protection in anonymity and passivity, doing only what was required and no more, or avoiding what was required and hoping it would not be noticed. Ironically, however, the goal of stability, on which the image of passivity and avoidance is based, drove many administrative officials to take initiative and risks. Industrial leaders were forced into aggressive bureaucratic and quasi-entrepreneurial behavior in an effort to gain some control over the erratic commercial and production system. In response to pressures from above and below, those who sat in leadership positions—whether in the trusts and syndicates of the 1920s or later in the ob"edineniia—fought to establish and expand their spheres of activity and authority. In the chaotic world of Soviet industry in the 1930s, aggressiveness was the key to stability.

Interference by the association in day-to-day factory operations evolved gradually, often in response to financial crises and increasingly numerous production breakdowns. Minutes, stenographic records, and reports of the Soviet machine tool cartel Soiuzstankoinstrument, or SSI, and its predecessor, Stankotrest, exist for the whole of their brief lives, 1929–32, and they reveal the patterns of interference that developed during this period.[5] These were years of severe strain in the Soviet industrial economy and work stoppages and breakdowns occurred frequently, even in a relatively

[4]*Pervaia vsesoiuznaia konferentsiia rabotnikov sotsialisticheskoi promyshlennosti: Stenograficheski otchet* (Moscow, 1931), p. 11.

[5]See RGAE, f. 7880, op. 1, d. 2, "Materialy i protokoly zasedanii pravlenii Stankotrest i Soiuzstankoinstrument, 1929–1930"; d. 3, "Materialy i protokoly zasedanii pravlenii Stankotrest i Soiuzstankoinstrument, 1929–1930"; and d. 41, "Materialy i protokoly zasedanii pravlenii Stankotrest i Soiuzstankoinstrument, 1930–1932."

well run association such as the SSI. When a breakdown persisted more than a few days, SSI leaders convened an extraordinary (*upolnomochnaia*) commission of inquiry made up of engineering and managerial personnel from the association. This group was dispatched to the factory to determine the causes of the breakdown and to recommend ways to get production moving again.

During the inquiry, the line between investigation and management became fuzzy. More often than not, the commission would stay on at the factory anywhere from two weeks to two or three months—until production lines were again operating regularly. Association departments took over the work and functions of corresponding factory departments. They drew up supply and labor requirements on the basis of the commission's recommendations. They also had the authority to allocate extraordinary funds. Normally the commission worked with factory management and engineering staff, but commission members had authority to reorganize labor, mobilize technical staff, reroute supplies, alter inventories, and remove and reorganize machinery and production processes. Commissions often by-passed the factory production and planning departments and worked directly with shop heads. As the frequency and severity of production stoppages increased, the work of these special commissions became institutionalized as a semipermanent system of crisis management.

Some commissions went so far as to establish quarterly and yearly production quotas. When production broke down at the Krasnyi Proletarii works in September 1930, for example, a commission from the SSI's production planning and labor organization departments developed measures for the factory to fulfill the production program for the final quarter of 1930 and worked up a plan for the whole of the 1931 production year. A group from the technical department and from the rationalization sector of the association supervised reorganization of some of the basic and auxiliary production processes at the factory to ensure fulfillment of the manufacturing schedule worked out by the planning commission.[6]

Frequent directives from higher administrative organs, usually Vesenkha, delineating new forms of economic and work organization also forced associations to encroach on the factory's prerogatives. Directives required factories to provide detailed reports on the preparation and implementation of new methods of work organization such as the seven-hour day, the continuous workweek, and the four-brigade system. Orders were typically sent to the ob"edinenie, which was responsible for ensuring compliance by its factories. Assessing production capabilities was often beyond the capability of the factory staff, and reports on preparation and implementation were often required in "the shortest possible time" (*do*

[6]Ibid., d. 2, ll. 5–7.

srochno). As a result, the ob"edinenie had to mobilize its own departments and send them to the factories to carry out the accounting and production surveys required by Vesenkha. Between 1930 and 1932, the association was forced to conduct major production surveys and forecasts of its factories almost every quarter.[7] Since the surveys were often associated with reorganization of production, association departments were actively drawn into detailed management of factory operations.

To ensure their own economic accountability, associations audited factory accounts, sequestered factory funds, and performed other supervisory activities that interfered directly in factory financial administration. This kind of interference occurred so frequently at the Sverdlov machine building plant that by mid-1930 the SSI had taken over the work of its commercial accounting and production planning departments all but permanently. At times even a well-organized plant such as the Krasnyi Proletarii found itself in arrears to the SSI and overwhelmed by accounting tasks. In late January 1931, a commission from the SSI's accounting department was sent there to investigate a growing discrepancy between the growth in wages and labor productivity. The commission found that the discrepancy reflected a lack of systematic technical and work norming and a lack of control over forms of wage payments. On the commission's recommendation, the appropriate association departments sent representatives to reorganize the structure of wage dispersal and technical norming at the factory. They made "significant" changes in the work organization of the main machine shops and advised the SSI's labor and economics department to survey the workforce. That department was authorized to reorganize work groups; release superfluous workers, especially clerical staff; establish hiring quotas in individual shops; and "create general methods of work distribution in both production and auxiliary areas of the factory."[8]

Hidden Market Forces and Competition among Associations

The association was forced not only to regulate factory affairs but also to try to control hidden market forces and competition from other ob"edineniia. This kind of competition arose as a result of contradictions between industrial policy and practice. Despite official instructions to specialize, most machine building factories in the 1930s continued to manufacture a wide range of products.[9] The blatant market considerations

[7]Ibid. See also d. 41.

[8]Ibid., d. 2, ll. 20–22a.

[9]Although many factories had been reorganized for mass production, by 1933 only 21 percent were specialized for production of just one item. See Ia. Kvasha, "Mashinostroenie i vosproizvodstvo oborudovaniia v narodnom khoziaistve," Planovoe khoziaistva, 1933, nos. 5/6, pp. 38–39.

that had led trust officials to resist specialization in the 1920s no longer existed, but the vicissitudes of the supply system still gave factories an incentive to make a variety of products. Resistance to specialization was especially strong in metal supply and machine tooling and instrumentation. As of 1932, nearly 37 percent of Soviet machine building plants continued to maintain their own smelting capabilities. Machine building factories accounted for 25 percent of all Martin furnace production in the country, and they supplied about 17 percent of their own metal needs.[10] This practice continued despite the state's massive construction efforts in the metallurgical industry, and despite stated policy to separate metal work from metal supply.[11]

Similarly, many machine building works continued to maintain their own tool and instrument making shops. Only 42 percent of Soviet machine tool needs were satisfied by domestic production in 1930–31 and only 20 to 21 percent of those machine tools came from SSI factories. Thus nearly half the domestic production of machine tools in 1931–32 came from factories not under SSI's control. A significant number of those tools were made by machine building factories for their own needs. All of the new auto and tractor factories of the period, for example, were constructed to supply their own machine tools.[12] Although the SSI was supposed to administer all domestic production and supply of machine tools, other machine building factories and associations threatened SSI's control of that branch.[13]

Such overlapping jurisdiction created tensions that looked very much like market competition. To standardize production of machine tools along lines dictated by the SSI, its head, E. Al'perovich, fought hard and successfully to extend SSI control over design and production planning of machine tool types in factories under the jurisdiction of other ob"edineniia.[14] The drive for control also led the SSI, like its predecessor, Stankotrest, to seek authority over all machine tool production, even in factories under other associations. Like Stankotrest, SSI started life with only three factories—the flagship Krasnyi Proletarii, the Sverdlov, and the Dvigatel' Revoliutsii. Within a few months Al'perovich reported the takeover of three more works. And the SSI did not stop there. Over the two years of its existence, it gained authority over eight entire factories and

[10]Dzh. Pepper, "Itogi pervoi piatiletki v oblasti spetsializatsii, kooperirovaniia i kombinirovaniia mashinostroeniia," *Planovoe khoziaistva*, 1932, no. 3, pp. 123–24.

[11]E. S. Perel'man, *Mashinostroenie v SSSR* (Moscow, 1931), p. 91.

[12]Kvasha, "Mashinostroenie," pp. 51–52. See also Perel'man, *Mashinostroenie v. SSSR*, pp. 8–9.

[13]E. Al'perovich, "Sovetskoe stankostroenie na novom etape," *Planovoe khoziaistva*, 1933, nos. 7/8, p. 52.

[14]Postanovlenie VSNKh, SSSR, no. 1396, 1930, quoted in RGAE, f. 7880, op. 1, d. 3, ll. 56–57.

twelve machine tool shops, the latter located in either automobile factories or metallurgical complexes.

Such crossing of association lines was common practice in the early 1930s. At times administrative overlap approached the level of bureaucratic comedy. All the major older factories that remained unspecialized suffered under divided authority. These factories included some of the largest machine building plants in the country: the Krasnoe Sormovo machine building works, the Krasnyi Profintern in Briansk, the Kramatorskii works in southern Russia, and the Krasnyi Putilovets in Leningrad. By 1934 the Krasnyi Putilovets labored under the authority of four specialized production conglomerates: the turbine building association, Turboostroenie; the auto-tractor conglomerate, GUTAP; the ob"edinenie for specialized machine building, Spetsmashinostroenie; and the metallurgical production association, GUMP.

Such a situation made for chaos. Factory production meetings were attended by inspectors from as many associations as had jurisdiction in the factory. According to the director of the Krasnyi Putilovets, T. Ots, there was little or no cooperation among them. Each year the factory received drafts of four separate and often incompatible production plans from the four associations with jurisdiction over some aspect of its production. Each association aimed to use the Krasnyi Putilovets to further its own interests against those of the others. Ots complained in particular that the associations used the various shops under their control to fill back orders in other factories or "on the side" and small-batch orders unrelated to the production profile of the Krasnyi Putilovets.[15]

This was an extreme case. Not all factories labored in such a labyrinth of confusion. Yet the problem was serious enough that administrators in Vesenkha expressed public concern over the consequences of competition among ob"edineniia and their tendency to treat factories and shops as feudal fiefdoms. Industrial writers complained especially about the "hoarding" of experience resulting from mutual hostility, arguing that the cost in duplicated and wasteful effort was nearly incalculable. One author claimed to have found numerous instances in which knowledge gained by practical experience in one shop was withheld from workers and engineers in another shop in the same factory because the two shops worked under the authority of different associations.[16] Vesenkha and other state organs intervened often in conflicts between ob"edineniia, but hidden

[15]Z. Shkundin, "Voprosy upravleniia promyshlennost'iu na sovremennom etape," *Planovoe khoziaistva*, 1934, no. 3, pp. 85–86, 94. Ots expressed his complaints in a letter to *Za industrializatsiiu*, 14 January 1934.

[16]S. G. Sandomirskii, "O reorganizatsii upravleniia mashinostroeniem i metalloobrabotkoi," *Metall*, 1930, no. 1, pp. 5–14. See also G. A. Spektor, "Balans oborudovaniia na 1931 g. i zadachi mashinostroeniia," *Metall*, 1931, nos. 2/3, p. 4. The practice of socialist competition exacerbated these problems.

forms of market competition continued to foster aggressive bureaucratic behavior that worked against the kind of order associations were supposed to bring to the industrial system.

Reconstruction and Changes in Production and the Labor Market

Rapid expansion and overall change in the period of forced industrialization aggravated factory managers' problems. Between 1929 and 1932, nearly two-thirds of machine building factories underwent major reconstruction. By 1933, less than one-quarter of domestic machine production was carried out in what were designated as unreconstructed works. Reconstruction meant expansion as well as replacement of equipment, and during the first five-year plan period, the amount of capital stock in individual machine building works increased anywhere from 150 to 400 percent.[17] The number of machine stocks doubled and the total amount of capital stock nearly tripled during the first five-year plan.[18] The average number of machine production shops in machine building plants also tripled, as did the numbers of production and clerical workers in factories. By the end of the period, some factories had fifty to sixty major machine production shops, each with its auxiliary shops.[19] The production and organizational structure of the factories in the early 1930s changed so rapidly from year to year, and even from month to month, that "more than a few" directors never knew at any one time how many shops they had in their works, who headed them, or exactly what they produced.[20] High turnover of personnel added to the confusion.

The rapidity and scale of change bewildered many managers. But the increase in size of factories and the quickness of change did not account for all of the problems associated with industrial reconstruction. When production capacity expanded, many factories specialized work processes in some shops but continued to manufacture a variety of goods. Specialization of individual production lines with no narrowing of the overall product range complicated rather than streamlined management. In the

[17]Ia. S. Rozenfel'd and N. N. Klimovskii, *Istoriia mashinostroeniia SSSR* (Moscow, 1961), p. 216. Most of the increase in production capacity was achieved by renewal and expansion of machine stocks in factories. Interestingly, despite the priority and publicity given to new factory construction, nearly 53 percent of all new machines installed between 1929 and 1933 went into factories founded before the Revolution. See Kvasha, "Mashinostroenie," pp. 39–40.

[18]*Perepis' oborudovanii promyshlennosti, 1932–1933: Metaloobrabatyvaiushchee oborudovanie SSSR* (Moscow, 1933), p. 99. See also *Sotsialisticheskoe stroitel'stvo SSSR* (Moscow, 1935), p. 35.

[19]Kvasha, "Mashinostroenie," p. 40. See also Shkundin, "Voprosy upravleniia," p. 85.

[20]Mikhail Kaganovich acknowledged this in a speech to the First All-Union Production Planning Conference for the Metal and Electro-technical Industries, held in Moscow in January 1931. See Shkundin, "Voprosy upravleniia," p. 85. The most complete summary of the conference is S. M. Kovartsev, "Planirovanie proizvodstva," *Metall*, 1931, no. 1, pp. 3–9.

1920s, machine work had been organized by the kind of operations a shop performed, regardless of where in the factory the pieces it produced were destined. By 1932, 70 percent of machines had been regrouped in specialized shops according to the type of product being manufactured. In other words, factory managers separated machine work for production of one item from similar work done for another product. Such reorganization had started in the 1920s, and by the early 1930s it was as far advanced in older reconstructed factories as in the new, highly specialized works.[21] Reconstruction of the Krasnyi Proletarii works in Moscow was typical of this process. By the end of 1930, as its reconstruction program neared completion, the Krasnyi Proletarii works separated its complement of lathes into two machining shops: the original shop was converted for construction of diesel engines and a new shop was constructed for machine tool production. The two machine shops had many of the same kinds of tools and their workers performed many of the same kinds of operations, but management administered the shops separately.[22]

Specialization of machine work according to the type of product manufactured made sense as a means to rationalize production and lower costs. Yet some managers worried that such trends would enhance the autonomy of individual shops and threaten the managerial cohesiveness that made the factory an integrated production organization. Others worried that such specialization would further encourage the ob"edinenie to bypass the factory director and interfere directly at the shop level.[23] At a conference on industrial management in Moscow in 1929, Comrade Livait, an engineer in the textile machine building trust, contended that shop specialization was inimical to the development of mass-production culture. "Specialization should proceed according to similarities in the technical aspects of the work being performed [tekhnicheskaia obrabotka]," Livait argued, "not by product. That latter type of specialization will only strengthen the shop. We could end up with a situation in which each shop has its own labor bureau, its own planning bureau, etc. This would encourage varying wage policies in a single factory and less integration and order in production. We can't let different kombinaty operate in a factory,

---

[21]Perepis' oborudovanii promyshlennosti, 1932–1934: Oborudovanie metalloobrabatyvaiushchei promyshlennosti (Moscow, 1935), p. 74. Note that grouping of machinery by type was not the same as differentiation by flow arrangement. Only about 21 percent of machine stocks were organized in flow arrangement (ibid.).

[22]"Istoriia zavoda 'Krasnyi proletarii,'" in GARF, f. 7952, op. 3, d. 94, l. 76, describes the reconstruction of the factory.

[23]The problems of shop specialization are discussed in "Doklad M. P. Rudakov, 'Funktsional'naia organizatsiia upravleniia promyshlennost'iu i sotsialisticheskoe sorevnovanie,' 16.VIII.1929," in "Protokoly Organizatsii rabotnikov NOTa," GARF, f. 5286, op. 1, d. 6, ll. 75–102. On balance, such reorganization did lower production costs. See O. M. Kuperman, "Mashinostroitel'naia promyshlennost' na putiakh rekonstruksii," Puti industrializatsii, 1930, nos. 11/12, p. 83

Unmechanized transport at a Moscow factory, early 1930s. GARF.

each with its different policies for the same kind of production processes and the same kind of workers. This would only return us to the old arti-san way." As it turned out, Livait's prediction was uncannily accurate.[24]

If specialization threatened factory cohesion, so did patterns of techno-logical reconstruction. New investment favored reconstruction of basic production processes, but modernization of internal factory transport sys-tems and other auxiliary processes received a low priority during the first five-year plan period. The largest share of new equipment in the economy, 65 percent, went into the main production shops of machine building and metal plants. Only about 17 percent of new machinery was installed in repair shops or other auxiliary areas.[25] The lack of cranes and conveyer systems, both mechanized and hand operated, caused the most acute problems.

[24]Ibid., l. 99. Differentiation of work processes by product and shop also had an interesting effect on workers' perceptions of themselves. In factory and Party cell meetings workers identified themselves not just by their occupations, such as "machinist Shevrev," as they had done when all machine work was done in one shop, but by the shop they worked in. Identi-fication with and pride in working in a particular shop could be reinforced by such things as official sanction of intrashop socialist competitions. A worker's identification with his or her shop was reinforced by the increasing autonomy of shops.

[25]*Perepis' oborudovanii promyshlennosti, 1932–1933*, p. 45.

Unmechanized pouring of molten steel at the Serp i Molot factory, early 1930s. GARF.

Factories also experienced a severe lack of intershop rail transport and a lack of mechanized loading and unloading machines.[26] A survey done in 1931 found that only about 47 percent of such work was mechanized in machine building factories. This was by far the lowest figure for any branch of the national economy save the food industries, in which only 44 percent of such systems were mechanized. On average, mechanization of factory transport and loading facilities reached 75 percent for all branches of the economy.[27] According to one assessment, lack of reconstruction of factory transport systems proved "a decisive block to factory production integration." Inattention to mechanization in such a vital area was "the single most important cause" of bottlenecks and production breakdowns in factories, more important than the oft-cited poor quality of materials, poorer quality of planning, and disruptions in the state's factory supply system.[28]

The lack of adequate dispatching systems contributed significantly to the isolation of shops and to the general absence of production integration. A 1931 Vesenkha commission noted that even when the destination of pieces was known, they often could not be moved because adequate transport was not available, and machine parts never got to the machines for which they were clearly labeled. "Pieces pile up in the shops," wrote the commission's head, E. S. Perel'man, "sometimes for months." They created hazards and even blocked the routes of the equipment necessary to clear them away. "Decisive" and "immediate" action was needed to facilitate the flow of materials through the production process. At the very minimum, the commission called for triple the number of all types of mechanized cranes, hoists, mono- and birail transport trolleys, and automated off-loading equipment. Machine shops had a "desperate" need for mechanized mid-sized overhead cranes with lifting capacities of 5 to 10 tons. A dearth of such equipment crippled the productive capacity of shops engaged in large-batch and serial output. Sorting shops of factory foundries lacked heavy cranes and hoists capable of lifting 50 to 60 tons. In "more than a few" works, even in works with newly reconstructed and expanded oven production capabilities, materials were still being lifted and loaded by hand with chains, pulley hoists, and mules.[29]

[26]Perel'man, *Mashinostroenie v SSSR*, p. 18.

[27]Spektor, "Balans oborudovaniia," p. 3.

[28]Perel'man, *Mashinostroenie v SSSR*.

[29]Perel'man, *Mashinostroenie v SSSR*, pp. 19, 28, 31, 32. Attention to auxiliary processes and an alleged inattention to basic production processes was considered a major strategy of industrial wreckers in 1929–30. See M. G. Ostrovskii, "Vrediteli v metallopromyshlennosti," *Metall*, 1930, nos. 10/12, p. 6. In 1934, 75 percent of iron foundries in machine building works were still not equipped with conveyor systems for the processing and handling of castings. The great majority of handling was done by cranes "on the ground" (*na platzu*) from spot to spot. See *Izderzhki proizvodstva i proizvoditel'nosti truda v promyshlennosti* (Moscow, 1935), pp. 90–91.

Without simultaneous introduction of specialized flow arrangements and adequate transport systems, expansion in the size, production capacity, and complexity of work in factories contributed to an exorbitant increase in overhead costs and auxiliary labor requirements. As factories expanded, the distances that pieces had to travel between shops and work stations increased significantly. Pieces often had to traverse six to seven buildings, distances of two to three kilometers, and could require frequent transfer by hand from wagons to mules to carts. The expenditure for labor to transport a piece could amount to 30 percent of the cost to manufacture it.[30] Because of the lack of attention to such requirements, between 1928 and 1934 general overhead costs increased from 28 percent to a full 50 percent of manufacturing costs in the machine building industries.[31]

The commission noted that in the capitalist West, factories intensively mechanized their internal transport systems during the Great War because industrialists found this the most expedient way to maintain and increase production levels as workers were conscripted into the armed forces. Russian factories had also developed a fairly advanced "technical culture" by the end of the war with Germany, but much of it had then been destroyed during the Civil War. The relatively labor-rich Soviet economy in the late 1920s allowed industrialists and managers to ignore the need for mechanization in auxiliary processes, at least until factory expansion overtook the labor supply. By 1931, however, extensive reconstruction of production processes and a lack of attention to auxiliary processes had created an "exhausting hunger" for labor to do heavy hauling work. This was work, the commission noted, fit mainly for beasts of burden.[32]

In fact, the pattern of technological reconstruction created heavy demand for unskilled labor for hauling and transport. Shop managers and production foremen paid big bonuses for such work, especially during intense campaigns to meet production quotas. In an increasingly tight labor market, this practice drove up the wages of temporary and day workers and unskilled laborers generally. According to Z. Mordukhovich, a specialist in the Commissariat of Labor, this practice contributed to the collapse of wage differentials in the middle and at the lower end of the scale of skill levels. Workers, especially younger ones just starting out in main production shops at low or moderate skill levels, realized they could make money quickly by doing temporary heavy labor in auxiliary areas. In a period of inflation, such as the late 1920s and early 1930s, the tempta-

[30]O. Gaposhkin, *Potochnyi metod v promyshlennosti SSSR* (Moscow, 1946), p. 19.

[31]*Izderzhki proizvodstva*, pp. 30–31. The average for all group A industries in 1934 was 24.7 percent. O. M. Kuperman, "Sebestoimost' produktsii VOMT," *Metall*, nos. 5/6, 1931, pp. 34–41 discusses rising production and overhead costs in machine building factories.

[32]Perel'man, *Mashinostroenie v SSSR*, pp. 8–9. The engineer Gil'debrandt confirms wartime destruction of advanced technology in his account of the Krasnyi Proletarii works in GARF, f. 7952, op. 3, d. 94, ll. 73–80.

tion was strong to leave low-paying professional jobs and do just that. According to Mordukhovich, such pressures contributed to the general trend in wage leveling and to the decline in skill levels in production shops.[33]

Examination of wage structures confirms Mordukhovich's observations. In 1934 the average loader (*gruzchik*) of skill grade 1 in machine building and metal factories made 78 kopecks an hour when piece-rate earnings and bonuses were added to the base wage. For all other jobs in metalwork, grade 1 earnings amounted to 69 kopecks an hour. Out of sixty listed professions, only six had average earnings in the first skill level higher than 78 kopecks. In two professional categories, carpenters and pressers (*davil'shchik*), workers took home 79 kopecks, only one more than unskilled loaders. The remaining four categories listing higher earnings were for jobs in hot shops. Three categories that listed 81, 84, and 85 kopecks were for laborers in foundry work; boiler room workers earned 99 kopecks. The average hourly pay for loaders in the lowest skill category was also equal to or higher than earnings for the second skill grade in twenty-nine of the sixty listed professions.[34]

Shop managers and foremen had control over sums of money, often large, for discretionary wage payments, and they hired unskilled day labor at the factory gates each morning. In fact, according to a Rabkrin survey, this form of spot hiring had already become a "common" practice in the late 1920s. Shop managers, pressed to fulfill production quotas, began temporary hiring as a way to get around labor regulations and the slow process of hiring through official labor exchanges.[35] By the early 1930s, the practice was widespread. Workers came to a factory for several days, made good money, especially during production campaigns, and then left. Mordukhovich identified this practice as a major factor in increasingly high rates of labor turnover and in seasonal variations in the labor market that corresponded to quarterly factory production campaigns.[36]

Mordukhovich discerned a causal relationship between patterns of reconstruction and labor market difficulties. He acknowledged that both economic incentives and outright administrative measures had failed to regulate an ungovernable labor force. Mordukhovich did not openly dispute the argument, then common, that much of the industry's labor ills stemmed from lack of discipline and from the peasant and petty bour-

[33]Z. Mordukhovich (Mokhov), *Ispol'zovanie trudovykh resursov i podgotovka kadrov* (Moscow, 1932), pp. 95–96. It is interesting that Mordukhovich stressed production factors as more important than egalitarian wage policies in the leveling of wages in the early 1930s.

[34]*Zarabotnaia plata rabochikh krupnoi promyshlennosti v oktiabre 1934 g.* (Moscow, 1935), table 3, pp. 164–67.

[35]GARF, f. 374, op. 15, d. 484, l. 19.

[36]Mordukhovich, *Ispol'zovanie trudovykh resursov*, p. 96.

geois social origins of the millions of new labor recruits swelling factory work rolls. He argued, however, that modernizing and mechanizing internal factory transport systems could go far toward stabilizing the workforce, raising productivity, and allowing a more rational organization of labor and production in the shops.[37]

Ia. Ia. Ossovskii, also a labor economist, advanced similar arguments in 1930, but he made it a point to distinguish between the production and social factors in industry's productivity problems. Too much attention was being paid to workers' social origins, Ossovskii argued. In fact, administrators would be "surprised" at how many times workers moved from machine to machine and shop to shop without any supervision. High labor turnover, discipline problems, and poor productivity, wrote Ossovskii, resulted from poor production planning and "a complete disregard for labor organization by both shop and general factory administrators." As a result, worker turnover inside shops—that is, movement from machine to machine and shop to shop—reached as high as 5,000 percent in some Moscow factories. A worker changed jobs inside his shop and factory at least as often as 100 times a year, and this figure did not take into account the number of times a worker left the factory and then returned to it. It was management's fault, Ossovskii claimed, that "our factories present a picture of a working mass in constant motion, a mass entirely out of control."[38]

Ossovskii provided fascinating details about how production and labor were actually organized (or not organized) in factories, but he left himself open to political criticism. Editors of the journal *Metall*, which published his article, took Ossovskii to task for his implicit criticism of the current policies on productivity and labor discipline. Mordukhovich made his bow to current political wisdom and was careful to disassociate himself from Ossovskii's way of thinking, but his arguments against the social-origin thesis of labor's troubles were essentially the same as those made by Ossovskii.[39]

The problem of nonproductive labor became chronic and widespread in the early 1930s. The lack of mechanized equipment to support basic production processes lowered productivity and required workers to perform numerous tasks not related to the actual working of a piece. Inattention to

[37]Ibid.

[38]Ia. Ia. Ossovskii, "K voprosu ob organizatsii rabochei sily kak faktora proizvodstva," *Metall*, 1930, nos. 10/12, pp. 15–28.

[39]Ossovskii also had the audacity to imply that wages were too low and that one of the major causes of high labor turnover was that workers were in constant search for higher pay ("a natural progressive striving": ibid., p. 23). The journal's editors agreed that many workers sought higher wages, but they attributed the practice to the "greedy . . . anarchistic . . . petty bourgeois" influences of the new workers: ibid., p. 15.

routing and dispatching systems contributed to the disorder that reigned in shops. Skilled machinists often fetched materials or scarce instruments from stores rather than wait for them to be delivered to the work site. This could take an inordinate amount of time since long lines tended to form at shop stores. In addition, machinists often had to hunt up shop administrators or dispatchers to confirm work orders or fill in incomplete machining specifications. And they had to spend considerable time and energy setting up pieces on their machine, work that could have been done by automated feed bars.[40]

Because of the amount of time lost in such activities, machine use remained low and probably dropped considerably in the early 1930s, despite technological modernization.[41] To avoid delays, managers often organized brigade systems, usually shock brigades of unskilled laborers and semiskilled setup men, to assist skilled workers at the bench. A brigade usually consisted of four men, more often boys, to set up the machines and fetch tools and materials. This practice left more time for actual machine use, but gains in productivity were often offset by the costs associated with the enormous numbers of laborers in the shop.[42] The ratio of workers to machines nearly tripled during the first five-year plan period.[43]

The state had expected technological modernization to compensate for declining skill levels in the labor force, but modernization of basic production technologies at the expense of auxiliary processes produced the opposite result: the demand for brute labor increased to compensate for the effects of technological reconstruction. Managers relied increasingly on the carrying, hauling, pushing, and lifting strength of the huge numbers of raw recruits coming into the factories. Factories "soaked up" labor like a "huge sponge," in the words of I. P. Bardin, chief engineer of the giant Kuznetskstroi metallurgical complex.[44] According to the Vesenkha commission in 1931, the lack of mechanization in auxiliary areas was one of the major reasons why Soviet industry lagged behind capitalist factories in labor productivity.[45]

[40]B. Iu. Mirskii, "Ratsional'noe ispol'zovanie oborudovaniia i rabochaia sila v metallopromyshlennosti," in GARF, f. 5286, op. 1, d. 16, l. 14.

[41]Typical estimates ranged between 25 and 40 percent—lower than the 50 percent agreed on in the mid- and late 1920s, before technological reconstruction. See ibid., ll. 24–26.

[42]Ibid., l. 15.

[43]Between 1928 and 1932 the number of workers per machine on the main shift rose from 3.4 to 9. See V. F. Oborin, "Stankostroitel'naia promyshlennost' v Anglii, Germanii, i SSSR," Vestnik metallopromyshlennosti, 1932, no. 10, pp. 56–64. For 1928 figures, see Rabochyi den' v fabrichno-zavodskoi promyshlennosti v 1928 (Moscow, 1928).

[44]GARF, f. 7952, op. 5, d. 69, ll. 46–47.

[45]Perel'man, Mashinostroenie v SSSR, p. 19. Conveyor and mechanized transport systems were not widely used in Soviet machine building factories until World War II. See Gaposhkin, Potochnyi metod, pp. 13–19.

Workers in the mechanical repair shop of the Serp i Molot factory, early 1930s. The young boys in the top row probably set up the machines and fetched tools and materials. GARF.

From Systematic Management to Shop Contracting

As factories grew and production became more complex, the functional departments of the central factory administration began to atrophy. Planning and control departments, wage, technical norming, and rationalization and instrument departments remained strong in highly specialized works and in small or medium-sized works that had only a few major production shops, but in large unspecialized factories the central departments became increasingly alienated from actual operations. Factories suffered from a lack of trained clerical staff and engineering personnel, and still more from a lack of attention to systematic accounting methods. As a result, in "all but a very few" enterprises systematic financial accounting methods were never implemented.[46] In factories that maintained accounting departments, outdated practices proved inadequate to the task of

[46]Ordzhonikidze to a gathering of industrial managers in *Pervaia vsesoiuznaia konferentsiia*, p. 12. Ordzhonikidze demanded to know "if any one of you factory directors or shop heads . . . work on the basis of *khozraschet* [financial autonomy]." Replies ranged from "few" to "none" to "on paper." Grossman offers similar criticisms in *Sotsialisticheskaia ratsionalizatsiia promyshlennosti*, pp. 41–42.

managing the growing complexity of production.[47] Labor, financial accounting, and production planning departments kept statistical records for the several associations with jurisdiction over the factory, for Rabkrin, and for the police, but little use was made of them for management of shop-floor operations.[48] The factory's central administrative departments became more adjuncts of the state statistical apparatus than a system of production management.

By 1932, industrial leaders openly acknowledged that central factory administrations had lost control over their factories.[49] Some writers feared the imminent demise of the factory as an integrated economic and production organization.[50] Vladimir Grossman, member of Vesenkha's presidium and head of its sector on rationalization and industrial management, wrote that there was "no systematic central factory administrative organization that could be called characteristic of the whole of the various industrial branches." According to Grossman, a Vesenkha survey found that inter- and intrashop planning was "different in nearly every factory." In "many" factories, such planning "simply did not exist at all." The majority of factories exercised "no central control over technological processes and equipment, or over labor and wage organization." In many plants, second and third shifts worked with no responsible shift engineer. In general, control over production was left "almost entirely" to the shop administration, or to no one at all.[51]

As systematic managerial and engineering techniques broke down, control over work, labor, and wage organization devolved into the hands of increasingly powerful shop administrators and production foremen. These were the real *nachal'niki*, the bosses or chiefs of production. In the Krasnyi Proletarii plant, for example, regulations issued in April 1931 gave the shop head, the *nachal'nik tsekha*, or *nachtsekha*, and the foreman, literally the master of production, rights and responsibilities "commensurate with

---

[47]See *Industrializatsiia SSSR, 1929–1932: Dokumenty i materialy* (Moscow, 1970), pp. 258–60. At a production meeting of the Kuznetskstroi metallurgical and machine building complex in October 1934, the director, B. Butenko, blamed continuous production stoppages on a "complete lack of central factory organization and production cost accounting": GARF, f. 7952, op. 5, d. 69, l. 6.

[48]In 1929 a management expert complained that RKI and OGPU policies made industrial statistics increasingly difficult to obtain. "How can you expect us to correct mistakes," he asked an RKI official, M. P. Rudakov, "if you don't allow us access to the statistics we need to assess trends in industry and labor?" Rudakov replied that one didn't need statistics to see how conditions were: GARF, f. 5286, op. 1, d. 6, l. 23

[49]See Vesenkha's "Postanovlenie o vnutrizavodskom planirovanii," 12 August 1931, in *Industrializatsiia SSSR, 1929–1932*, pp. 258–60.

[50]See, e.g., A. A. Gofman, "Reorganizatsiia promyshlennosti po priznaku tekhnologicheskikh protsessov," in GARF, f. 5286, op. 1, d. 15.

[51]Grossman, *Sotsialisticheskaia ratsionalizatsiia*, pp. 24–25, 40. Ordzhonikidze made much the same kind of criticism at the January 1931 industrial managers' conference. See *Pervaia vsesoiuznaia konferentsiia*, pp. 17–18.

[their] vital place in the production process." Foremen had wide leeway in setting output quotas and technical norms, in allocating work, and in determining the skill level required to perform it. Foremen and shop heads were responsible for ensuring proper labor discipline and economic organization of work, so they had the right to hire, fire, and discipline workers. They also had discretion over the distribution of bonuses and "other forms of work encouragement."[52]

Changes in the structure of piece rates and bonuses especially enhanced the authority of shop chiefs. Official policy encouraged individually and progressively determined piece rates and bonus systems in the hope of stimulating productivity, improving quality, and eliminating wage leveling.[53] By 1932, slightly less than two-thirds of all work hours in the machine building and metal industries were paid under some system of progressive piece rates and bonuses. By 1934 that figure had reached 70 percent.[54] Piece rates in themselves did not threaten factory authority, but in many factories they were regarded as discretionary and so came under the control of the administrator and foreman of each shop. Thus, as piece rates and bonuses made up an increasingly large proportion of the wage bill and applied to an increasing proportion of workers, a concomitant proportion of the system of wage determination fell within the discretionary power of the individual shop administration.

Many factory directors condoned shop authority over wages. The director of the Kuznetskstroi works, B. Butenko, boldly asserted in an October 1934 production meeting that the task of setting wages and enforcing wage policy belonged primarily to the shop administration. When queried about the function of the factory's labor organization department and the rate and norming bureaus, Butenko replied that "their task is to study the labor process, not to set wage policy." According to Butenko, central departments at the factory functioned "by order [po zadaniiu] of the shop administrator and production foreman." The shop nachal'nik was now "the undisputed master in his realm of the factory." He was responsible directly to the factory director, and to no one else. In practice, Butenko

[52]"Polozhenie o pravakh i obiazannosti mastera proizvodstva, tsekha," in "Istoriia zavoda 'Krasnyi proletarii,'" GARF, f. 7952, op. 3, d. 84, ll. 22–25. See also "Organizatsiia truda i sistema zarabotnoi platy," in Industrializatsiia SSSR, 1929–1932, pp. 263–64. For a discussion of the position of foremen in industry during this period, see Lewis H. Siegelbaum, "Masters of the Shop Floor: Foremen and Soviet Industrialization," in Social Dimensions of Soviet Industrialization, ed. William G. Rosenberg and Lewis H. Siegelbaum (Bloomington, 1993), pp. 166–93.

[53]Industrializatsiia SSSR, 1929–1932, p. 267.

[54]Trud v SSSR: Statisticheskii spravochnik (Moscow, 1936), p. 156. Lewis H. Siegelbaum discusses workers' response to piece rates through collective work organization in "Production Collectives and Communes and the 'Imperatives' of Soviet Industrialization, 1921–1931," Slavic Review 45 (Spring 1986): 65–84.

explained, this meant that the orders of the shop head and foreman were final; they superseded all other instructions.[55]

Butenko invoked Sergo Ordzhonikidze's name to confirm that this formulation of managerial command authority had the approval of the highest leaders of the government and the Party. Ordzhonikidze himself, stressed Butenko, had emphasized the importance of *nachal'stvo* in a recent gathering of industrial leaders in the capital. And indeed he had. Ordzhonikidze, now head of the Comissariat of Heavy Industry, ridiculed the methods of systematic management as ineffective and bureaucratic. He repeatedly emphasized the command authority of the factory and shop *nachal'nik* and encouraged his industrial "commanders" to take charge, to "use the authority and rights you have to run your factories as they should be run."[56]

The emphasis on *nachal'stvo* signaled the end of systematic management and strengthened the responsibility of those managerial groups most directly involved in the production process. Often, however, it did so at the cost of overall factory integration and in flagrant violation of labor and work codes. Decentralization of wage controls, for example, played havoc with the wage system and encouraged increasingly high rates of turnover among workers. At the Kuznetskstroi complex, even as Butenko emphasized the *nachal'nik*'s responsibility for determining wage structures, he complained that shop heads and foremen adjusted wage differentials to steal workers from other shops during shock production campaigns and encourage workers to quit during slack periods.[57] And these practices were in addition to the shop bosses' use of wage funds to hire spot labor for heavy work.

According to the chief engineer of the Kuznetskstroi complex, I. P. Bardin, the unregulated wage strategies of shop administrators represented a reversion to "barbarian . . . colonial" attitudes. Shop wage policies thwarted any attempts at rational organization of labor. Like Butenko, Bardin charged that shop administrators purposely varied discretionary wage levels as a way to regulate labor. It was easier to force excess workers out through wage adjustments than to fire them and endure trouble from the trade union. This practice was particularly unethical, Bardin explained. A worker who quit because the piece rate was reduced was registered as having left voluntarily. Thus turnover that resulted from wage finagling appeared to strengthen the argument that turnover was a problem not of managerial disorganization but of poor work discipline.[58]

[55]GARF, f. 7952, op. 5, d. 69, ll. 10, 17.
[56]RTsKhIDNI, f. 85, op. 29, d. 67, l. 98.
[57]GARF, f. 7952, op. 5, d. 69, l. 2.
[58]Ibid., ll. 46–47.

Neither Bardin nor Butenko drew the obvious conclusion that the chaos in wages and work conditions resulted from the unchecked authority granted to shop foremen. It seems likely that Bardin understood this, and perhaps was trying to make the connection plain without directly criticizing the principle of *nachal'stvo*. Butenko, however, seems not to have grasped the point. His complaints about wage variations and labor disruption came right on the heels of his diatribe against bureaucratic management and his glorification of *nachal'stvo*. Yet Butenko's priorities were clear. Like other industrial officials, he was willing to tolerate gross inefficiency and blatant violations of labor and work codes so long as his shops fulfilled their production quotas.

As systematic management atrophied, factories revived prerevolutionary shop contracting practices in the guise of socialist shop competitions. Shop administrators contracted directly with each other, with the factory management, and even with sources outside the factory. The competitive aspect of socialist shop contracting originated with the challenge of one shop to another to lower costs or increase productivity. Challenges were issued and accepted supposedly on a voluntary basis, without consultation through the vertical chain of central factory planning departments. Soon, however, the practice of competitive contracting broadened to encompass all aspects of production. As before the Revolution, shop administrators became subcontractors to their factory directors and to the trusts and associations that governed them.

As shops became increasingly involved in contract negotiations, they developed their own expertise. To coordinate supplies and operations with other shops, managers set up production accounting departments (*khozraschetnye proizvodstvennye otdely*). These departments were supposed to be ad-hoc organs subordinate to the functional departments of the central factory administration, but in fact they acquired a semipermanent status. They "clearly usurped and duplicated" the production planning, supply, and even financing work that was supposed to be done by the central departments. Under control of the shop administrator, these departments contracted with other shops in the factory for supplies and semifinished materials, and they often bypassed the factory's central departments to work directly with production association staff in planning production and supply for their shops.[59]

The contracts the shop administration drew up and signed were legally binding documents, based on total cost estimates supplied by the shop and verifiable by the factory administration. They stipulated the amounts, prices, and delivery dates of materials the administration was to supply

[59]Shkundin, "Voprosy upravleniia," pp. 84–85, quoting Mikhail Kaganovich.

and of the products the shop was to deliver. Though contracts varied in particulars, questions of wages, labor organization, and hiring and firing were often left specifically to the discretion of the shop administration. Though hailed as a unique form of socialist industrial organization, shop contracting amounted to another admission that central authorities had lost control over their factories.

Social and Economic Corporatism

Shop heads and production foremen enhanced their authority in ways not directly related to production and work organization. As normal commercial and social structures began to break down during the years of rapid industrialization and collectivization, the factory took on social roles never intended by industry's leaders. Shop heads quickly realized that supplying workers' social and material needs had a direct effect on their productivity, and they worked hard to wrest these functions from the trade unions and Party. By 1934, shop administrators at the Kuznetskstroi works routinely oversaw the housing, food, and even hygiene of their workers. Each shop maintained its own cafeteria, to which workers were admitted only with ration cards distributed by the shop. Each shop built and maintained its own baths and took responsibility for the upkeep of its workers' barracks.[60] Shop heads also allocated shock-work awards, which gave workers access to more material privileges. In the early years of the shock work movement, trade union and Party organs distributed the awards but now this function, too, belonged to the shop heads.

The better material and social privileges a shop could provide, the better its chances of holding a skilled and stable workforce. Some shops set up stores, and one enterprising administrator even added an occasional dress department. Workers and their spouses could use the shop's food ration cards as currency. Discussion of workers' social and material well-being occupied considerable amounts of time at production meetings and provoked heated exchanges when a shop head felt his authority challenged or believed some other shop had an unfair advantage. In 1934 a *nachal'nik* at Kuznetskstroi complained that when the central administration had allocated money for expanding showers, his shop had gotten less than it needed. His workers had nowhere to shower but the shop, and his facilities were so inadequate that some of his workers had not been able to

---

[60]During one particularly heated exchange at a factory production meeting in October 1934, the head of the Kuznetskstroi trade union committee berated the head of one shop for the "disreputable" condition of the workers' barracks. When the shop head demanded to know why the trade union had not bothered to become involved in the workers' welfare, the union official replied, apparently without irony, "That's the shop head's responsibility." GARF, f. 7952, op. 5, d. 69, l. 63.

shower for a week. The *nachal'nik* noted wryly that "if the director wants us to keep our machines clean and productive, then he should first give us the facilities to keep ourselves clean."[61]

Another *nachal'nik* reported in outrage that the trade union and Party cell functionaries in his shop had somehow gotten hold of shock worker certificates and bread cards and were distributing them without his consent. He demanded that the factory administration and Party committee put a stop to it. Otherwise, "we *nachal'niki* will lose our influence over the workers." That a shop administrator could make such a complaint about Party interference in 1934 reveals how much production and social relations had changed since the late 1920s. Director Butenko expressed astonishment that the shop administration had permitted the situation to arise in the first place ("Razve! Vy eta razreshali?"). Other speakers expressed similar surprise. Butenko made it clear that Party functionaries had no business interfering in policies affecting shop productivity. He promised to discover who was responsible and to put a stop to it.[62]

Forced to supply at least the basic needs of their workers, factories relied to a large extent on the state's distribution system. Yet this system proved so inadequate that many factories sought local solutions. Factories leased land and paid local farms to produce exclusively for them. Others contracted for a percentage of the produce of a particular farm. The Kolomenskii factory contracted with the state to buy the land on which a cooperative farm stood, so that the farm and its village became in effect the property of the factory. The factory's accounts include expenditures for the farm as a part of its yearly budget, and farm laborers are listed on the factory work rolls.[63]

In most factory-farm relationships, informal barter arrangements developed. A factory regularly sent a mechanic to the farm to repair machinery or sent workers to help with the harvest and planting; in return, the farm sent temporary workers to the factory and supplied it with produce. Arrangements of this sort became indispensable to the survival of many factories and to their ability to feed their workers. Such relationships encouraged the growth of local economies outside the boundaries of state-run industry and agriculture.

The factory-town aspect of industrial life in the 1930s was especially characteristic of new complexes such as Kuznetskstroi and Magnitogorsk.[64] Across the breadth of the Soviet Union, industrial centers and factories, rather than towns and cities, became nodal points for a seminomadic pop-

[61]Ibid., l. 54.

[62]Ibid., l. 22.

[63]See, e.g., a description of arrangements made by the Krasnyi Proletarii: "Stat'ia o snabzhenii rabochikh v 1933," ibid., op. 3, d. 96, ll. 92–94.

[64]See John Scott, *Behind the Urals: An American Worker in Russia's City of Steel* (Bloomington, 1989).

ulation in constant search for work, shelter, and food.[65] Factory shops were always crowded with workers "who came and went" and whom foremen had never seen before. Workers "smoked, conducted business, played cards, slept, and listened to the radio." They did not even "start" when the foreman approached on his rounds through the shop.[66]

The increased social role that factories were forced to play was no less prominent in major cities. The description quoted above comes from a manager at Moscow's Serp i Molot metallurgical works. Even urban factories had no choice but to involve themselves in agricultural and housing management and in barter relationships within their local communities. Such arrangements were never a part of any formal organization chart. Elaborate plans existed to supply factories from central distribution points, but enterprising managers relied as much on informal ties to the local economy and labor market to survive. The social role that factories acquired and the ties that came to bind them to their surrounding communities gave the Soviet factory system an intensely local focus. Modernization was supposed to break down local ties. Instead, it strengthened those ties and produced in industry elements of social and economic corporatism that were as much feudal as modern.[67]

Factories' social role extended even to police functions. The resources of the civil police were so meager that factories were forced to employ their own police forces, which worked as adjuncts to the regular city police. The *vedomstvennaia militsiia*, or *vedmilitsiia*, as the administrative police force was called, patrolled the factory grounds, but was also responsible for keeping order in the surrounding streets and in the workers' village (*rabochii selok*) associated with their factory.[68] Often these *vedmilitsii* provided the only police presence there. They were supplemented by civilian volunteer police organizations (*obshchestva sodeistviia militsii*), organized usually by shop. These vigilante units were armed, with weapons supposedly supplied by and registered with the regular police, and had the authority to use deadly force if necessary to keep order.[69]

Just as supply problems forced factories onto the local economy, so the collapse of systematic management accentuated the local character of pro-

[65]Lewin, *Making of the Soviet System*, p. 221, quotes Ordzhonikidze's comment that Russia was becoming a country of vagrants.

[66]Mirskii, "Ratsional'noe ispol'zovanie oborudovaniia," l. 12.

[67]For more on the role of factories in supplying food and other commodities, see E. A. Osokina, *Ierarkhiia potrebleniia: O zhizni liudei v usloviiakh stalinskogo snabzheniia, 1928–1935* (Moscow, 1993), pp. 32–36.

[68]For the number of *vedmilitsii* operating in the early 1930s, see GARF, f. 1235, op. 2s, d. 910, ll. 40–42. In the Russian republic, the number of regular police increased only gradually during the first five-year plan period, from 42,500 in 1929 to 47,612 by mid-1932, while the number of *vedmilitsii* more than doubled, from 37,606 to 82,000.

[69]On regulations governing the volunteer police organizations, see GARF, f. 5446, op. 13a, d. 1314.

duction and work organization. Despite the pretense to planning and standardized manufacture, the organization of work in most factories came to depend largely on the vicissitudes of the local labor market and on the specific technological and production culture of an individual shop. The jerry-rigging of cutting instruments and holding fixtures and the cannibalizing of even new machinery became so commonplace that there was no such thing as standard operating procedure. A skilled worker entering a shop for the first time had to be trained on that shop's machinery even if he or she had operated the same sort of equipment elsewhere.[70]

The 1932 Soviet industrial census showed how heavily production depended on unique local conditions rather than on standard procedures. According to the census, about 25 percent of metal-cutting machines in machine building factories were consistently being used without attachments to hold the pieces that were worked on them. In other words, many of the pieces to be worked by lathes and drills and other cutting tools were held by hand, or were otherwise propped up for machining. More often than not, the hands that held pieces belonged to some of the homeless or unsupervised boys who swarmed at the factory gates every morning, hoping for a temporary job. In 26 percent of the factories surveyed, pieces were held in place with jerry-rigged attachments (*sluchainaia dlia dannoi mashiny*). Thus, at a conservative estimate, fully half of Soviet machining equipment was being operated under conditions "disruptive of a proper technical regimen."[71]

Census officials noted that they had expected a different picture. The proportion of machines using specified cutting fixtures and holding attachments was supposed to be higher in the new mass production works constructed or re-constructed during the five-year plan period than in works not suited to large-scale manufacturing processes. Yet only about 26 percent of metal-cutting machines used to make parts for mass-produced goods were equipped with specified cutting and holding fixtures to ensure standardized work.[72] On the day of the census, 46 percent of the metal-cutting machines in the Sormovskii locomotive plant near Moscow, supposedly organized for standardized production, were being operated without proper fixtures.[73]

As machine work expanded but standardized machining practices lagged, an acute need arose for universally skilled and experienced laborers to work as fitters, joiners, and all-around machine operators. Moreover, because of the often unique character of work organization and tech-

[70]*Perepis' oborudovanii promyshlennosti, 1932–1934*, p. 19.
[71]Ibid., pp. 34, 19.
[72]Ibid., p. 36.
[73]Kvasha, "Mashinostroenie," p. 63.

nical culture that evolved in shops, experience in one locale and even on particular machines became as valuable to the maintenance of production lines as either formal skill or engineering knowledge. Lacking proper technical data about machines and with many machines cannibalized and jerry-rigged, managers valued workers who could set machine speeds by the pitch of the sound, or who knew by the feel of the machine as they operated it whether it could perform the task required.[74] And what was true of operating machinery was also true of working materials. A production *nachal'nik* considered himself fortunate if some of his workers had been in his shop long enough to know the kinds and composition of materials likely to be supplied to the shop's workplaces. Materials and pieces to be worked often arrived with no precise instructions for machining, and most materials consisted of bastardized composites of alloys that did not meet standard specifications for strength and flexibility. It took skill and experience to judge how to work such pieces without damaging or breaking them.[75]

Conversely, workers could use their knowledge to abuse the wage system in an effort to stay ahead of inflation and wage cuts. At a conference in Moscow in October 1920 a technical normer named Korovin, who had been a machinist for twenty-three years, described how easy this was to do. As Korovin's audience knew, workers' wages were made up of several components: the basic hourly wage plus graduated bonuses or rates for the number of pieces or units worked in a shift. Under pressure to raise productivity and eager to raise their wages, many workers were tempted to run machines beyond normal limits. "Any worker at the bench knows how to do it," Korovin declared. "Basically, you don't consider the problem of damage to equipment or pieces. You set the gear ratio high and force the machine. Doing this, I can break any technical norm or rate you set by at least 35 percent and no [one] here can help it if I want to overwork." In theory, if technical norms were set correctly, piece rates based on those norms would limit overproduction and runaway earnings; but as long as piece rates existed, workers would be tempted to abuse work and machine norms. And there was no technical norm that could not be broken. "Naturally, workers measure their work by the ruble," Korovin said, "and the ruble is the basis on which we must establish proper work norms and rates." Where workers were encouraged to overfulfill norms, "that's where technical normers function only as furniture."[76]

[74]So said the engineer B. Iu. Mirskii of the AMO automobile plant, 17 November 1930: GARF, f. 5286, op. 1, d. 16, l. 11.

[75]Workers were aware of the problems caused by nonstandardized machining but shrugged them off; the assemblers "always manage somehow": ibid., l. 28.

[76]"Stenogramma disputa o normirovanii truda v epoku sotsialisticheskoi rekonstruktsii, 17.10.1930," ibid., d. 17, ll. 30, 33.

By 1934 the situation had improved little; in some factories it was worse. The head of the labor organization department at the Kuznetsk-stroi offered a 1934 production meeting his assessment of work organization at the complex: "We have no technically literate instruction for workers. In most production areas we have no technical standards whatsoever. . . . For the vast majority of equipment . . . we have no idea what their possible production range is or their optimal work regimen. We're probably operating far below possible productivity levels. But we really have no way to know or estimate this." His colleagues confirmed his exasperated assessment with shouts of "Yes, yes!" and "That's the way it is."[77]

To many engineers the shop became a black box, "a wild place," a "very different and strange world." They seemed to understand little of what went on there; they knew only that whatever was going on, they had lost control of it. Astute observers, such as the prominent engineer I. P. Bardin, remarked on the increasing alienation of engineers from production. Bardin took ironic note of the revival of "primitive" forms of work organization concurrent with the most massive campaign ever undertaken to modernize the technological structure of machine manufacture. He spoke of the increasing gap between engineering knowledge and factory work culture, and he warned that a way had to be found to reestablish technical control over production.[78] M. P. Rudakov, member of both the RKI and Vesenkha, pointed out that in fact the one process exacerbated the other; the reconstruction that had modernized industry had accentuated its backwardness. Modernization, Rudakov said, "has thrown into sharp relief [iarko vyrazhaet] our inability to master new forms of production."[79]

The breakdown of systematic engineering and managerial supervision undermined attempts to introduce routinized forms of work organization and standardized manufacturing practices. In most Soviet factories, successful production strategy became contingent on specific knowledge of local conditions and on the skills and experience of workers. Shops and factories guarded their production secrets jealously. Managers paid high wages and bonuses and offered other inducements to retain workers who combined skill with experience. Such workers commanded respect and high social status wherever they were employed.[80]

---

[77]"Stenogramma proizvodstvenno-tekhnicheskoi konferentsii rabotnikov zavoda i stroitel'stva 'Kuznetskii metallurgicheskii i mashinostroitel'nyi kombinat,' 11.10.1934," in GARF, f. 7952, op. 5, d. 69, ll. 41–42.

[78]Ibid., l. 47.

[79]Rudakov's comment is part of the discussion in Mirskii, "Ratsional'noe ispol'zovanie oborudovaniia," l. 24. On accentuating backwardness see Lewin, Making of the Soviet System, pp. 293–94.

[80]Donald Filtzer, among others, has described the kind of status and prestige that such workers enjoyed in his Soviet Workers and Stalinist Industrialization.

Conclusions

Industrial officials never resolved the tension between systematic and shop management. Despite official repudiation of functionalism by the Seventeenth Party Congress, functional bureaucracies continued to operate in the industrial administrative apparatus. Occupational conflicts continued between central factory authorities and shop administrators over wage policies, work organization, and output quotas. Resurgent trade union and Party activism in the mid-1930s aggravated these conflicts and confused lines of managerial authority. The rise of the Stakhanovite movement complicated and politicized an already chaotic system of factory management.

Just as the structure of authority in the factories suffered from a lack of clear definition, so did the organization of industry at the national level. Reconstruction altered patterns of bureaucratic and economic organization but in ways Stalinist leaders neither anticipated nor controlled. Industrial bureaucracies expanded rapidly, not by design but haphazardly, in response to a host of unforeseen production crises, administrative pressures, and hidden market forces. Hoarding of resources, barter exchange, and tremendous waste characterized a system bereft of money and commercial incentives to trade. Officials continued to reorganize and reform, exhort and even threaten, but to little avail. Stalinist leaders built a powerful industrial system, but they ultimately failed to create a state that was somehow above or immune to the social and economic forces they tried to subdue. They commanded vast resources but were nearly powerless to manage the day-to-day economic affairs of their empire.

Conclusion: Socialism, Dictatorship, and Despotism in Stalin's Russia

In the 1920s, German observers used the term *grosser Kleinbetrieb* to capture the contradictions of modernity and backwardness in their industrial system.[1] Literally, this oxymoron means "gigantic small shop." *Kleinbetrieb* referred not to a factory of a certain size but to the managerial and organizational techniques that traditionally were used to run small businesses and artisans' workshops. In the Germany of the early twentieth century, these techniques were still being used to operate large production conglomerates equipped with new and complex manufacturing technologies.

The phrase grosser Kleinbetrieb succinctly describes the kinds of factories that populated Soviet Russia's industrial landscape in the 1930s. The reconstruction and reorganization of the first five-year plan were supposed to have resulted in a nationally integrated, centrally controlled command economy. Reality looked different. The social, institutional, and economic dynamics that drove the industrial system defied attempts by Stalinist leaders to impose their own order, either through administrative and technological rationalization or through outright social repression. The Soviet industrial system was shaped and reshaped by social and economic forces that the country's leaders could alter, even remake, but ultimately could not control.

At the factory level, the skewed pattern of modernization exacerbated the problems in production, the labor market, and social relations which modernization was supposed to remedy. Throughout the early and mid-1930s, most factories operated in a web of relations only partly deter-

[1]"Rationalisierungsbestrebungen im Ruhrbergbau," *Bergarbeiterzeitung*, June 1924, p. 37. I am grateful to John Shearer for this reference.

mined by national planning and administrative organs. Despite constant intervention by higher political and governmental bodies, most factories and trusts were forced to rely on their own devices to get supplies, secure labor, and actually produce something. Networks of traders, recruiters, and subcontractors arose out of and reinforced remnants of older commercial and administrative practices. Government policies exaggerated the local character of production and bound factories more tightly than ever before to their local economies. Indeed, as normal trade and commercial relations collapsed or were destroyed by state policies, the social role of factories increased and became inextricably tied to their production obligations. During the early 1930s, production was only one of a factory's functions, and in some ways not the most important one. Whether administrators liked it or not, they had to attend to all the details that their factories' increased social role entailed: forms of land tenure, farm production, food storage, housing, retail commercial activity, commodities rationing, and a host of other activities.

What evolved in the typical industrial plant was not a system of integrated production shops but a patchwork of semi-autonomous factories within a factory. In the vast production cities that factories became, numerous subcultures coexisted, sometimes in conflict and rarely integrated socially or administratively. Some subgroups had little contact with or knowledge of one another. A near-artisanal work culture continued to dominate many machine and repair shops, while a modern engineering stratum emerged in the central administrative departments of factories and production associations. Youth gangs, protected by the mantle of socialist competition, roamed the factories challenging the authority of both older workers and managers and engineers.

For a time, shock work and other socialist competition gangs were the only groups that successfully threatened the hold of the older generation of worker-princes on shop-floor culture. Wage and piece-rate reforms, scientific management, even attempts to militarize labor had failed in the 1920s to break down traditional hierarchies in factories and force workers to increase productivity. The Stalinist regime sanctioned the activities of shock work gangs because they held out the promise of a new labor hierarchy and more intensive work methods. Even this movement, however, was absorbed into the factories' labor culture. After initial resistance, workers joined socialist competitions in increasing numbers. By the early 1930s, the socialist competition movement had not brought about more workers' control, as some Party activists had hoped, or significantly affected productivity, as many managers had hoped. Managers used shock work to relieve the constant production bottlenecks, and workers joined in for their own ends: to increase their earnings, to protect themselves against inflation and the perceived consequences of rationalization, to secure a niche in the social and economic hierarchy of the shop. Workers thus blunted the intended political and economic effects of the socialist competition movement. Whether ruled by a traditional or new labor hierarchy, the shop floor remained an unruly place. It was a world the regime could terrorize politically but could not control economically or administratively.[2]

The administrative subculture that arose in the late 1920s also persisted and grew, despite official repudiation of functional management in 1934. By the mid-1930s, technical normers, rationalization experts, accountants, labor statisticians, quality control technicians, and a host of other systematic management specialists were still drawing salaries. In fact, central factory departments became dumping grounds for people of undesirable social origins. Many thousands of these "former people" had been purged from higher administrative organs and transferred to factory work, ostensibly to bolster factory administrations. Despite attempts to cut back bureaucracies at the higher levels, factory administrative offices swelled with the ranks of displaced people. And all these thousands of administrators kept themselves busy. Central factory personnel still conducted labor studies and experiments. They continued to produce graphs, flow charts, and plans. They held conferences and published articles. Yet they had little contact with the engineering and planning departments that were supposed to manage the factories. Administrators in the functional offices had even less contact with the director's office, or with the shop managers, foremen, and workers who actually controlled production.

As systematic management broke down, authority devolved into the hands of increasingly powerful shop administrators, foremen, and skilled workers. These people controlled wages, work assignments, the disbursement of ration and travel cards, and hiring and firing. As before the Revolution, shop administrators and foremen could run their shops much as they pleased, so long as they produced. With the revival of shop autonomy, such traditional practices as shop contracting and unskilled work gangs for heavy labor reemerged. Yet the organization of work and authority that evolved in the early 1930s was not simply a revival of old ways. Soviet officials maintained a brutal pace of production, in keeping, so they thought, with the technical possibilities of modern industry. The results—in breakage, labor turnover, outright sabotage, and accidents— were staggering. Soviet officials attributed many of the problems to the "socially unhealthy," nonproletarian influence of the peasant workers who streamed into the factories in the early 1930s. Others dared to point out, to their political peril, that industry's problems resulted less from the social

[2]Most social histories of the 1930s make this point, but see esp. Filtzer, *Soviet Workers*, and Andrle, *Workers in Stalin's Russia*. See also Siegelbaum, *Stakhanovism and the Politics of Productivity*, chap. 1.

origins of the workforce than from the state's poorly conceived policies of modernization.

Industry's modernizers took as their models the West's most advanced industrial sectors. In practice, this strategy translated into German equipment and American mass production methods. Yet the Soviets fundamentally misunderstood what made the American system workable. Like many others they believed the Ford myth that the essence of mass manufacture was the production system. Consequently, they concentrated their efforts on the modernization of primary production technologies and facilities and ignored auxiliary systems, such as internal factory transport, and managerial and organizational infrastructure, such as accounting and routing systems.

What made the American system successful was the welter of auxiliary processes that grew up to support the production system: mechanized transport systems, extensive service facilities, a phenomenal growth in managerial and accounting staffs, and a new place in the factory hierarchy for highly skilled workers who worked in the toolrooms, filing and machining the mass-produced, "standardized" parts to fit the pieces they were supposed to fit.[3] The Soviets' lack of attention to such auxiliary processes was one of the major causes of their "backwardness." It was the single most significant reason for the huge number of laborers required in Soviet production shops. The explosion in the size and complexity of factories, the massive influx of new machines, and the invasion of millions of labor recruits overwhelmed the still primitive managerial, transport, and engineering infrastructure. Initial attempts to implement systematic forms of management and accounting were feeble at best. Those attempts collapsed with the onslaught of forced modernization.

At the national level, the administrative apparatus of Soviet industry was also beset by contradictions. Relations among the Soviet industrial bureaucracies bore little resemblance to the formal structures and hierarchical processes that supposedly governed them. Suppressed market forces and administrative pressures created competitive relations between associations and encouraged aggressive bureaucratic behavior among association leaders. Yet, as bureaucratized as the Soviet system was, bureaucratic rationality remained underdeveloped throughout the 1930s. Few formal procedures governed administrative relations in industry. The organizational reforms of 1930 supposedly restructured the bureaucracies in a new hierarchy of authority, but those reforms never addressed the important issues of procedures and processes within and between bureaucracies. Many officials did not know what was and what was not in their

---

[3]For this assessment of American manufacturing, see David Hounshell, *From the American System to Mass Production: The Development of Manufacturing Technology in the United States, 1800–1932* (Baltimore, 1984), esp. chaps. 4–6.

jurisdiction. To justify their actions, harried bureaucrats garnered signatures and stamps from as many higher officials as they could find. Documents and authorizations circulated for months through the bowels of the administration, not in slow inevitable progress toward resolution but almost in random passage until someone finally took the initiative to act. This lack of established procedure, this *neplanovost'*, gave administrators wide leeway for either passive avoidance or aggressive entrepreneurial behavior. By 1934 the situation had changed very little. Ordzhonikidze acknowledged that *neplanovost'* was still the single most serious problem in the Commissariat of Heavy Industry.[4]

Crisis management continued throughout the 1930s. Each organization had its contingent of "responsible officials," the *otvetrabotniki*, who could be empowered to circumvent normal procedures. Party and industrial officials relied increasingly on these "authorized" individuals and commissions, the *upolnomochnyikh*, for everything from ensuring grain collections to quelling labor trouble to restoring production in factories. The military-command methods that characterized their administration grew out of the shock and mobilization campaigns that Rabkrin imposed on Vesenkha during the crisis years 1929 and 1930. Styled after the military campaigns of the Civil War, command administration emphasized rapid shifts of personnel and resources from one crisis "front" to another.

In the short run, this style of administration was effective in mobilizing the state's administrative apparatus to deal with shortages and unforeseen problems. Direct and extraordinary intervention was also the way the Politbiuro managed the major construction projects during the industrialization drive. Shock campaigns, socialist competitions, economic mobilizations, and other forms of direct and extraordinary intervention were even raised to the level of socialist managerial principles. Ultimately, however, these methods contributed to the chaos of industrial management. They disrupted serious attempts to establish normal administrative and commercial procedures.

What emerged in the 1930s, then, was a command-administrative economy, but not a planned one. Centralization of administrative mechanisms and the elimination of the commercial economy enabled Party and government leaders to shift massive resources from one economic sector to another at will. In the absence of market mechanisms or at the very least proper accounting methods, however, centralizing reforms created no systematic administrative process by which to manage those resources.[5] The military command style of management that grew out of Rabkrin's mobilization campaigns formed the basis of a crude crisis management system,

[4] RTsKhIDNI, f. 85, op. 29, d. 67, l. 99.
[5] Moshe Lewin has also pointed out this contradiction in "On Soviet Industrialization," in Rosenberg and Siegelbaum, *Social Dimensions of Soviet Industrialization*, p. 278.

but it was a poor substitute for systematic forms of planning and administration.

Sergo Ordzhonikidze personified the contradiction between systematic and command methods of management. This man combined Max Weber's contradictory types: the charismatic leader and the rational bureaucrat.[6] Throughout his career, Ordzhonikidze was the sworn enemy of bureaucratism. Rather than demanding subservience from his subordinates, he ridiculed managers for timidity and passivity, always waiting for orders from higher up.[7] He constantly exhorted his industrial leaders to take charge and to cut through bureaucratic red tape.[8] *Nachal'stvo*, Ordzhonikidze's word for leadership, was borrowed from military usage as a designation of command rank. It conveyed Ordzhonikidze's belief in a strong, even charismatic style of management. Ordzhonikidze distinguished *nachal'stvo* from the pedantic bureaucratism he hated and fought against. Despite his frequent clashes with Stepan Birman, the feisty chief of Iugostal', Ordzhonikidze respected Birman as the kind of industrial leader the country needed. Though Birman fought bitterly with Rabkrin, Ordzhonikidze kept him in Vesenkha, even promoted him to the presidium after he took over Vesenkha in 1930. Birman, in Ordzhonikidze's view, was no mere industrial manager; he was an industrial commander, a true *nachal'nik*.

Despite Ordzhonikidze's antibureaucratism and his emphasis on *nachal'stvo*, Rabkrin's centralizing reforms, which were supposed to reduce bureaucracy, resulted in its nearly unchecked proliferation. The sophisticated production technologies that Ordzhonikidze hoped would revolutionize Soviet industry required ordered procedure and precise coordination. These were not qualities that integrated easily with populist revolution and the Bolsheviks' penchant for storming barricades. At the same time that Rabkrin officials were urging greater attention to accounting procedures and other forms of systematic management, they were forcing Vesenkha into disruptive mobilization campaigns that undermined orderly administration. Ordzhonikidze and those around him never came to terms with the basic contradiction inherent in their policies.[9] The tensions between command and systematic styles of management were never resolved. Those tensions became institutionalized in the Soviet

[6] See Max Weber, *The Theory of Social and Economic Organization*, trans. A. M. Henderson and Talcott Parsons (New York, 1947).

[7] See, e.g., Ordzhonikidze's scolding of industrial managers for bureaucratism in *Pervaia vsesoiuznaia konferentsiia*, pp. 10–12.

[8] RTsKhIDNI, f. 85, op. 29, d. 67, l. 98.

[9] See, e.g., Ordzhonikidze's angry rhetorical demands to know why the bureaucratic apparatus continued to grow, despite attempts to trim, merge, and purge it, in *XVI s"ezd vsesoiuznoi kommunisticheskoi partii(b), 26 iiunia–13 iiulia 1930* (Moscow, 1935), pp. 227–29. See also the comments of Ordzhonikidze's deputy A. P. Rozengol'ts in *Za sotsializm protiv biurokratizma*, pp. 48–54.

industrial system and continued to disrupt industrial administration throughout the 1930s.

The architects of Rabkrin's organizational and financial politics in the late 1920s had a very specific vision of the kind of state they wished to create. Functionaries such as Gol'tsman, Rozengol'ts, and Piatakov were bent on using their reforms primarily as a means to create a new industrial state dictatorship. For Stalin's state-builders, the Revolution was not a class revolution but a state revolution. Theirs was a vision of a *Machtstaat*, a power-state that operated free of economic and social constraints. Rabkrin's immediate goal was to overcome the centrifugal forces that threatened the state's control over resources. Many of the agency's policies were aimed specifically at undermining the powerful regional blocs and commercial interests that wielded influence in the economy. But, as syndicate and Vesenkha finance officials so perceptively realized, the arbitrary command over resources that Rabkrin's reforms were designed to achieve was antithetical to rational economic planning and administration. As syndicate officials pointed out on numerous occasions, Rabkrin's various reform plans—to restrict credit and centralize money control, and to centralize administrative mechanisms for allocating resources—would actually hinder rather than facilitate the growth of capital in the industrial economy.

Rabkrin's officials understood very well what they were doing. Their plans were consciously conceived. The centralizing reforms that so strangled the Soviet economy in the five-year plan era did not grow ad hoc out of the unanticipated problems of rapid industrialization. The goal was capital extraction, not capital formation. Rabkrin's leaders were not particularly concerned about the disruptive effects their financial and economic reforms would have on rational economic planning and capital growth. Their aim was to create mechanisms that would allow the state to mobilize the maximum amount of resources from the population and the economy for industrial modernization. *Zagotovka sredstv naseleniia* (procuring the means of the population), the term Stalinist officials used to describe their mobilization campaigns, reflected the extractive character of the state's policies.

And yet, despite the economic irrationality of Stalinist industrial policies, those policies embodied a technological and engineering rationality that was essentially modern and utopian. Rabkrin's industrializers truly believed in the transforming power of modernization. In the long run, they believed, the productive capacity of modern industry would resolve all problems of economic scarcity and remake social relations in the rational image of modern technology and organization theory. Revolutionary modernization could free Russia, and first of all the Russian state, from the constraints that had bound it in backwardness and subservience to the Western industrial powers.

Faith in the liberating power of technology wedded to the state was not peculiar to Soviet Russia; it was strong throughout post–World War I Europe.[10] As is well known, Rabkrin's officials derived many of their ideas from models of advanced cartel and state capitalism and the mobilized European economies of World War I. But it was during the first years of the Bolshevik regime that key individuals in the agency gained experience as economic and administrative "commanders." They based their policies not on the war economy of Germany or England but on their own revolutionary war experience.

Numerous historians have pointed to the similarities between the mobilization of Soviet society for industrialization during the first five-year plan years and the Bolsheviks' mobilization of the economy between 1918 and 1921. The similarities are not coincidental, and the earlier period served as more than just inspiration. To transform the Soviet state of the late 1920s, Rabkrin's high officials drew consciously and specifically on the financial and organizational techniques they helped pioneer during the revolutionary war. They hoped to recreate, on a larger scale, the militarized economic system of that era. Their conception of statism combined the rationalized power of modern German and American industry with the economic administration characteristic of a country under martial law. For Stalin's state-builders, state involvement in economic construction was a sign not of backwardness but of modernity.[11]

It is difficult to reconcile this vision of statism with the regime's avowed goal of building socialism. Certainly what Stalin's state-builders created was a noncapitalist state, in the sense that private property and trade were severely restricted. Yet statism, as Stalin's state-builders conceived it, was not the same as socialization of property. The kind of statism embodied in Gol'tsman's reforms shifted the criterion of the state's legitimacy away from social and economic justice—social welfare—to mastery of new technologies and projection of industrial might on a world scale.[12]

[10]For a summary of these trends in Western Europe, see Charles Maier, "Between Taylorism and Technocracy: European Ideologies and the Vision of Industrial Productivity in the 1920s," *Journal of Contemporary History* 2, no. 5 (1970): 27–61, and *Recasting Bourgeois Europe*. For Germany see Detlev Peukert, *The Weimar Republic: The Crisis of Classical Modernity*, trans. Richard Deveson (New York, 1992), esp. sec. 3 and pp. 112–18, 275–77. Peukert emphasizes an *inherent* contradiction in German modernism similar to the one I posit for the modernism of Soviet Russia's industrializers. See also Mary Nolan, *Visions of Modernity: American Business and the Modernization of Germany* (New York, 1994), chap. 7. In *The Third Rome: National Bolshevism in the USSR* (Boulder, 1987), Mikhail Agursky emphasizes the peculiarly nationalist and reactionary origins of statist thinking among Soviet leaders. There were certainly strong nationalist elements in Soviet political discourse, but Agursky's argument that Soviet statism was anti-Western ignores the modernist, Western-oriented trends among Soviet industrializers.

[11]On state support of industrialization as an indication of backwardness, see Alexander Gerschenkron, *Economic Backwardness in Historical Perspective* (New York, 1962).

[12]For the argument that the Stalinist state was socialist because it was noncapitalist, see Kotkin, *Magnetic Mountain*, pp. 2, 6, 357. Davies also confuses statist confiscation of property with socialization; see *Soviet Economy in Turmoil*, Introduction, n. 12.

Many people accepted the argument that a strong state was needed to protect socialism from capitalist encirclement. V. N. Mantsev, the head of the syndicates, for example, finally conceded that for a time it would be necessary to strengthen the elements of state socialism. As we have seen, however, Mantsev's idea of state socialism differed fundamentally from the ideas of industrial dictatorship that motivated Gol'tsman, Piatakov, and Rozengol'ts. Mantsev, like other syndicate and economic officials, was not opposed to state governance of the economy but was wary of a statist dictatorship.

In the late 1920s numerous proposals were put forward for ordering the economy along noncapitalist lines, from the commercial socialism of the syndicates to the decentralized "communal" socialism proposed by Vesenkha's various republic chiefs. Indeed, the system of state industry that existed at the end of NEP was more complex than we have traditionally believed. It was not just one system but several. At least three economic cultures operated simultaneously and in conflict with one another. The commercial state being built by the syndicates in the late 1920s was far more influential than we have imagined, and it presented a dynamic challenge to the inefficient bureaucratic economy run by Vesenkha. The syndicates' vision of a commercial state represented the best hope for integrating economic planning with commercial mechanisms in a new kind of market socialist economy. But just as the syndicates were trying to consolidate their hold on the economy, Rabkrin's officials were beginning to push their own methods onto Vesenkha. The techniques of economic mobilization developed by Rabkrin proved a threat both to the commercial state envisioned by the syndicates and to Vesenkha's ponderous but stable bureaucratic empire. The military-campaign economy that Rabkrin imposed on the industrial system, with its culture of *nachal'stvo*, its constant shortages and built-in waste, and its crisis-management administration, proved the biggest threat to rational planning and systematic administration. Rabkrin's vicious attack on the Vesenkha system was certainly directed against the private market and trade aspects of NEP, but it was also an attack on rational planning and administration in a socialist commercial economy. The statization of the industrial economy that occurred during the 1930s should not be equated with the socialist transition from private to public ownership of property. What Rabkrin's state-builders wanted to construct was an industrial state dictatorship, not a state-managed industrial system committed to social and economic justice. Whatever else we may call the Soviet industrial state that emerged during the first five-year plan, it was neither planned nor socialist.

Such was the industrial system Ordzhonikidze helped to create. As other historians have noted, Ordzhonikidze's attitudes changed when he took command of the economy in 1930, and he came increasingly to identify with and defend the industrial bureaucracies of which he had charge.[13] This is not to say that Ordzhonikidze found no fault with his subordinates. He continued to criticize his industrial managers, at times rounding on them severely. Yet even as he criticized them, he reassured them of his protection. At a 1931 production conference, for example, he upbraided industry's leaders for the economy's poor performance and warned them that they could not escape responsibility by blaming everything on wrecking, for there were no more wreckers left in industry.[14] In March 1934 Ordzhonikidze criticized industrial heads as "lacking any discipline" and "not knowing the simplest thing." Even as he declared that "it would be easy to get rid of the lot of you," however, he told them that the "more difficult but necessary task" was to "train poor workers into good ones."[15]

As these comments indicate, by the early and mid-1930s Ordzhonikidze was seeking ways to stabilize the state's industrial dictatorship and to regularize its routines. He realized the need somehow to integrate the militarized campaign economy with the methods of systematic management. Thus the same Ordzhonikidze who in 1930 lauded Bolshevik tempos and revolutionary leadership in 1934 urged his managers to "work quietly, steadily, not at a frenetic pace." The same Ordzhonikidze who in the late 1920s called bureaucratism a scourge argued in 1934 against the 17th Party Congress resolutions to eliminate all forms of systematic administration. In Narkomtiazhprom meetings in March of that year he cautioned against another "root reorganization." In approaching the question of administrative reform, industrial leaders needed to "go slow, with much study." Above all, he declared, the leaders of industry needed to ensure administrative stability so as not to derail progress in fulfilling the new five-year plan.[16]

There was irony in Ordzhonikidze's statements, and that irony surely was not lost on Stepan Birman, who attended the March 1934 meeting. In 1929 Birman, the maverick industrial leader, had made the same criticism of Ordzhonikidze's plans to overhaul Vesenkha as Ordzhonikidze was making of those who demanded radical change in 1934. Ordzhonikidze was not alone in his change of attitude. Many of his subordinates, especially his former Rabkrin comrades, expressed similarly cautious views after their move to Vesenkha and then to Narkomtiazhprom. The former *Rabkrinovtsy*, now the commanders of industry, complained about "those who did nothing but criticize from the outside." Yet criticizing from the outside was, of course, exactly what these industrial commanders had done when they unleashed Rabkrin's virulent campaign against the coun-

[13]See, e.g., Fitzpatrick, "Sergo Ordzhonikidze."
[14]*Pervaia vsesoiuznaia konferentsiia*, p. 31.
[15]RTsKhIDNI, f. 85, op. 29, d. 67, l. 91.
[16]RTsKhIDNI, f. 85, op. 29, d. 67, ll. 91, 87, 99, 88.

try's industrial administration in the late 1920s. Now, in 1934, Mikhail Kaganovich, like Ordzhonikidze, cautioned against scrapping functional forms of management without "seriously considering how to replace them." Like Ordzhonikidze, Kaganovich warned against "rushing into destructive reorganization."[17]

Ordzhonikidze demonstrated his change in attitude most dramatically in clashes with the police as he tried to keep them out of industry's domain. As early as 1931, Ordzhonikidze declared it "absolutely unacceptable" that the police continue to have so much influence in factory affairs. When the Central Committee met with industrial leaders in June 1931, Ordzhonikidze demanded several times that officials of the state prosecutor's office be "categorically forbidden" to investigate factories or even to enter a factory. According to Ordzhonikidze, he persuaded the Politbiuro to accept this condition.[18]

His commitment to stability and to the unchallenged dictatorship of the industrial state brought Ordzhonikidze to his final conflict with Stalin. As other scholars have noted, it was the dictatorship of state and Party bureaucracies that Stalin feared most as a constraint on his personal, arbitrary power.[19] Yet Ordzhonikidze and other leaders of heavy industry were striving to create just such a dictatorship. Stalin may have suspected this of Piatakov, Rozengol'ts, Gol'tsman, and Mikhail Kaganovich. In a perverse way, he was correct when he called them all Trotskyites. These men had developed their ideas about statism, political economy, and society in their formative years with Trotsky during the revolutionary war. But Ordzhonikidze was another matter. He had been a loyal supporter of Stalin since well before the Revolution. Now Ordzhonikidze's loyalty to his commissariat and his commitment to the power and stability of the state must have looked to Stalin like a personal betrayal.[20] It is difficult to know when Ordzhonikidze became aware that Stalin's personal rule was detrimental to the dictatorship of the Party and the state. Intriguing hints abound about Ordzhonikidze's knowledge of or participation in discussions of ways to curtail Stalin's power during the early 1930s. Whatever Ordzhonikidze may have thought or done then, in 1936 he clashed openly with the general secretary over Stalin's decision to purge the state system, beginning with the industrial bureaucracies. Stalin's determination to rule alone and the threat posed to his personal rule by a strong state and Party dictatorship led to Ordzhonikidze's suicide in early 1937. Ordzhonikidze, like many others, fell victim to Stalin's despotism.

[17]Ibid., l. 68.
[18]Ibid., op. 28, d. 7/8, l. 136.
[19]For a fuller explication of this argument, see Getty, *Origins of the Great Purges*; Lewin, *Making of the Soviet System*, esp. chaps. 11 and 12; Rittersporn, *Stalinist Simplifications*.
[20]On Stalin's ability to create in his followers the slavish mentality demanded by a true despot, see Lewin, *Making of the Soviet System*, pp. 25–26, 276–79, 304–10.

Glossary

Donugol' Donetskii gosudarstvennyi kamennougol'nyi trest po proizvodstvu i pro-
dazhe kamennogo uglia i antratsita (Donets State Coal Trust)

Gipromez Gosudarstvennyi institut po proektirovaniiu metallicheskikh zavodov
(State Design Institute for Metal Factories)

Glavchermet Glavnoe upravlenie po chernoi metallurgii (Chief Administration for
the Iron and Steel Industry)

glavk, glavki glavnoe upravlenie, glavnye upravleniia (chief administration[s])

Glavmashinstroi Glavnoe upravlenie mashinostroeniia (Chief Administration for
Machine Building)

Glavmetall Glavnoe upravlenie metallicheskoi promyshlennosti (Chief Administration of the Metal Industry)

Gomzy Gosudarstvennye metallicheskye zavody (State Metal Factories)

Gosbank Gosudarstvennyi bank (State Bank)

Gosplan Gosudarstvennaia planovaia komissiia (State Planning Commission)

Iugostal' Gosudarstvennyi iuzhnyi metallurgicheskii trest (State Southern Metallurgical Trust)

Iuzhmashtrest (IuMT) Iuzhnyi mashinostroitel'nyi trest (Southern Machine Building Trust)

Izvestiia News; the government's daily newspaper

kharakteristika professional and political biography, kept on file for every state official

khozraschet khoziaistvennyi raschet (economic [profit and loss] accounting)

kombinat integrated organization; production units of various types combined under a single administration

Komsomol Kommunisticheskii soiuz molodezhi (Communist Youth League)

Komsomolskaia pravda Komsomol truth; newspaper of the Communist Youth League

Krasnyi profintern Red International Trade Union machine building factory,
Briansk

Krasnyi proletarii   Red Proletariat engineering factory, Moscow

Krasnyi putilovets   Red Putilov metal factory, Leningrad

Kuznetskstroi   Kusnetsksoe stroitel'stvo (Kuznetsk Metallurgical Factory Construction)

Lenmashtrest   Leningradskii mashinostroitel'nyi trest (Leningrad Machine Building Trust)

Magnitostroi   Magnitogorskoe stroitel'stvo (Magnitogorsk Metallurgical Factory Construction)

Mashinoob"edinenie (Moob)   Gosudarstvennoe ob"edinenie mashinostroitel'nykh zavodov (State Association of Machine Building Factories)

Metall   Metal; trade newspaper of the metal syndicates

Mosmashtrest (MMT)   Moskovskii mashinostroitel'nyi trest (Moscow Machine Building and Engineering Trust)

nachal'nik   an industrial "chief"; a shop administrator

nachal'stvo   command leadership

narkom   narodnyi komissar (people's commissar)

Narkomfin   Narodnyi komissariat finansov (People's Commissariat of Finance)

Narkomput' (NKPS)   Narodnyi komissariat putei soobshcheniia (People's Commissariat of Means of Communication [Transportation])

Narkomtiazhprom   Narodnyi komissariat tiazhelei promyshlennosti (People's Commissariat of Heavy Industry)

Narkomtorg   Narodnyi komissariat vneshnei i vnutrennei torgovli (People's Commissariat of Domestic and Foreign Trade)

Narkomtrud   Narodnyi komissariat truda (People's Commissariat of Labor)

neplanovost'   lack of planning; lack of established procedure

ob"edinenie   association

Orgametall   State Engineering Design Bureau (also a newspaper)

paishchiki   institutional shareholders of trade syndicates

piatiletka   five-year plan

planovost'   proper or regular administrative procedure

Politbiuro   Political Bureau; ruling organ of the Communist Party

Pravda   Truth; Communist Party daily newspaper

proizvodstvennoe ob"edinenie   production association

Puti industrializatsii   Path of industrialization; monthly journal

Rabkrin (RKI)   Narodnyi komissariat raboche-krest'ianskoi inspektsii (People's Commissariat of Workers' and Peasants' Inspection)

rabkrinovtsy   Rabkrin officials

rabochii selok   workers' village

samoderzhavie   autocracy

samokritika   self-criticism

Serp i Molot   Sickle and Hammer metallurgical factory, Moscow

Shakhty   Mines; name given to trial of mining engineers accused of sabotage in 1928

Soiuzneft'   Gosudarstvennoe vsesoiuznoe ob"edinenie neftianoi i gazovoi promyshlennosti (All-Union State Association of the Oil and Gas Industry)

Soiuzstankoinstrument (SSI)   Vsesoiuznoe stankostroitel'noe i instrumental'noe ob"edinenie (All-Union Engineering and Toolmaking Association)

sotsialisticheskoe sorevnovanie   socialist work competition

Sovnarkom Sovet narodnykh komissarov (Council of People's Commissars)

Sovtorg   Soviet state trading organization

spetseedstvo   specialist baiting

spetsy   specialists

Stal'   Vsesoiuznoe ob"edinenie metallurgicheskoi, zheleznorudnoi i margantsevoi promyshlennosti (All-Union Association of the Iron and Steel, Iron Ore, and Manganese Industry)

Stankotrest   Vsesoiuznyi stankostroitel'nyi trest (All-Union Machine Tool and Engineering Trust)

STO   Sovet truda i oborony (Council of Labor and Defense)

Tekhnika upravleniia   Techniques of management; Rabkrin newspaper

Torgovo-promyshlennaia gazeta (TPG)   Trade-industrial journal; Vesenkha newspaper

tsekh   factory shop

udarnichestvo   shock work labor movement

udarnik   shock worker

upolnomochnyi   an official with specially designated authority

Uralmet   Ural'skii metallicheskii trest (Urals Metal Trust)

vedomstvennaia militsiia (vedmilitsiia)   civil police units assigned to patrol factories

Vesenkha (VSNKh)   Vysshii sovet narodnogo khoziaistva (Supreme Council of the People's Economy)

vreditel'   wrecker or saboteur

vreditel'stvo   wrecking

Za ratsionalizatsii   For rationalization; Rabkrin newspaper

Zemplan   Agricultural planning department in Gosplan

Bibliography

PRIMARY SOURCES

Archives

Gosudarstvennyi arkhiv Rossiiskoi Federatsii (GARF)
f. 374   Narodnyi komissariat raboche-krest'ianskoi inspektsii
f. 1235 Vserossiiskii tsentral'nyi ispolnitel'nyi komitet
f. 5286 Protokoly i stenogrammy Obshchestva rabotnikov nauchnoi organizatsii truda pri Narodnom komissariate raboche-krest'ianskoi inspektsii i Vsesoiuznom sovete narodnogo khoziaistva SSSR
f. 5446 Sovet narodnykh komissarov
f. 5451 Vsesoiuznyi tsentral'nyi sovet professional'nykh soiuzov SSSR
f. 5469 Vsesoiuznyi sovet rabochikh metallistov: Protokoly i stenogrammy Tsentral'nogo komiteta
f. 5515 Narodnyi komissariat truda SSSR: Protokoly i stenogrammy Prezidiuma.
f. 7952 Materialy gosudarstvennogo arkhiva istorii fabrik i zavodov.

Rossiiskii gosudarstvennyi arkhiv ekonomiki (RGAE)
f. 3429 Vsesoiuznyi sovet narodnogo khoziaistva SSSR i Narodnyi komissariat tiazheloi promyshlennosti
f. 3915 Vsesoiuznyi sovet sindikatov
f. 4086 Glavnoe upravlenie metallicheskoi promyshlennost'iu i Glavnoe upravlenie mashinostroeniem
f. 5715 Vsesoiuznyi mashinotekhnicheskii sindikat
f. 5716 Gosudarstvennoe ob"edinenie mashinostroitel'nykh zavodov
f. 5735 Gosudarstvennoe ob"edinenie mashinostroitel'nykh zavodov
f. 7733 Narodnyi komissariat finansov
f. 7880 Protokoly i materialy zasedanii pravleniia Vsesoiuznogo tresta stankostroeniia i Vsesoiuznogo ob"edineniia stanko-instrumental'nogo stroeniia

Rossiiskii tsentr khraneniia i izucheniia dokumentov noveishei istorii (RTsKhIDNI)
f. 17   Tsentral'nyi komitet
f. 85   Lichnyi fond G. Ordzhonikidze

Articles

Aizenman, G. A. "Vnutrizavodskoi transport v mashinostroitel'noi promyshlennosti pre seriinom i massovom proizvodstve." *Za ratsionalizatsiiu*, 1928, no. 6, pp. 11–13.

Al'perovich, E. "Sovetskoe stankostroenie na novom etape." *Planovoe khoziaistvo*, 1933, nos. 7/8, pp. 45–53.

——. "Stankostroenie v Germanii i v SASSh." *Torgovo-promyshlennaia gazeta*, 31 December 1927, p. 3.

——. "Stanok i instrument: Osnovnoe sveno mashinostroeniia." *Izvestiia*, 9 September 1930, p. 2.

Avdienko, M. "Sdvigi v strukture proletariata v pervoi pitiletke." *Planovoe khoziaistvo*, 1932, nos. 6/7, pp. 145–53.

Birman, S. P. "Iugostal'." *Metall*, 1929, no. 2, pp. 111–26.

——. "Osnovnye momenty raboty Iugostali, 1928–1929." *Metall*, 1929, no. 10, pp. 102–14.

——. "Perevod zavodov na khoziaistvennyi raschet i struktura apparata pravleniia tresta: Iz prakhtiki Iugostali." *Metall*, 1927, nos. 1/4, pp. 83–112.

Bochko, N. D. "Semichasovoi rabochii den'." *Metall*, 1931, nos. 2/3, pp. 93–100.

Charnovskii, N. F. "Ekonomicheskie i tekhnicheskie predposylki 'Fordizatsii' proizvodstva." *Metall*, 1927, no. 6, pp. 61–64.

Dimanshtein, Ia. B. "O rekonstruktsii zavodov Iugostali." *Metall*, 1930, nos. 3/4, pp. 3–16.

Dobrovol'skii, B. N. "O finansovom polozhenii metallopromyshlennosti." *Metall*, 1927, nos. 1/4, pp. 22–35.

——. "Reorganizatsiia proektirovanogo dela." *Metall*, 1930, nos. 3/4, pp. 24–30.

G-ii. "Uroki Iugostali." *Za ratsionalizatsiiu*, 1929, no. 8, pp. 26–29.

G. S. "Osnovnye linii tekhnicheskoi rekonstruktsii promyshlennosti." *Metall*, 1929, no. 11, pp. 115–17.

Granovskii, E. "Organizatsiia truda i ispol'zovanie rezervov v tiazheloi promyshlennosti." *Planovoe khoziaistvo*, 1934, no. 10, pp. 105–14.

Grechnev-Chernov, A. S. "Ratsionalizatsiia v metalloobrabotivaiushchei promyshlennosti." *Metall*, 1929, no. 7, pp. 75–88.

Grubokov, N. A. "Mashinostroenie v 1929–1930." *Metall*, 1929, no. 9, pp. 7–27.

Gumilevskii, N. "Kharakteristika sostava rabochei sily, zaniatoi v metallopromyshlennosti." *Metall*, 1930, no. 2, pp. 19–32.

I. G. "E. O. Shatan, Problema rabochei sily v osnovnykh promyshlennykh raionakh." *Metall*, 1928, no. 1, pp. 115–23.

K. "Ratsionalizatorskaia rabota v trestakh i predpriiatiiakh metallopromyshlennosti." *Za ratsionalizatsiiu*, 1928, no. 8, pp. 17–24.

Kaganovich, M. "Direktivy o spetsializatsii zavodov nuzhno vypolnit'." *Za ratsionalizatsiiu*, 1929, no. 4, pp. 34–39.

——. "Mashinostroenie v vtoroi piatiletke." *Planovoe khoziaistvo*, 1934, no. 3, pp. 17–31.

——. "Opyt tekhnicheskogo planirovaniia v mashinostroenii." *Planovoe khoziaistvo*, 1935, no. 3, pp. 29–38.

——. "Sovremennoe polozhenie i ocherednye zadachi ratsionalizatsii raboty v promyshlennosti." *Za ratsionalizatsiiu*, 1928, no. 6, pp. 1–4.

——. "Uroki istekshego goda." *Za ratsionalizatsiiu*, 1929, no. 9, pp. 1–4.

"Kak u nas nanimaiut rabochikh." *Metallist*, 1929, no. 12 (28 March), pp. 4–5.

Kheifets, L. M. "K voprosu o sovremennom sostoianii mashinostroeniia." *Metall*, 1931, no. 1, pp. 86–97.

——. "Mashinostroitel'nye promyshlennosti Germanii i SASSh." *Metall*, 1929, no. 12, pp. 93–102.

——. "Problema zameshcheniia importa oborudovaniia." *Metall*, 1928, no. 12, pp. 55–63.

Khirnov, A. "O pervoi vsesoiuznoi konferentsii po ratsionalizatsii mashinostroitel'noi promyshlennosti." *Za ratsionalizatsiiu*, 1929, no. 5, pp. 4–5.

Khrennikov, S. A. "Rol' tekhnicheskikh sil v razvitii metallopromyshlennosti." *Metall*, 1925/26, nos. 1/2, pp. 75–81.

Klimov-Verkhovskii, B. P. "Mashinostroitel'naia konferentsiia Gosplana SSSR." *Metall*, 1929, no. 3, pp. 31–42.

Koniukov, N. D. "Vsesoiuznyi mashinotekhnicheskii sindikat v 1928/1929." *Metall*, 1929, no. 4, pp. 100–110.

Kopelovich, M. P. "Voprosy organizatsii upravleniia proizvodstvom v metallopromyshlennosti." *Metall*, 1927, no. 9, pp. 5–12.

Kovartsev, S. M. "Planirovanie proizvodstva." *Metall*, 1931, no. 1, pp. 3–9.

Kuperman, O. M. "Kon'iunktura mashinostroeniia." *Metall*, 1929, no. 9, pp. 105–12.

——. "Mashinostroitel'naia promyshlennost' na putiakh rekonstruktsii." *Puti industrializatsii*, 1930, nos. 11/12, pp. 77–84.

——. "Mashinostroitel'naia promyshlennosti 1928–1929." *Metall*, 1929, no. 11, pp. 95–100.

——. "Mashinostroitel'naia promyshlennost' v pervoi treti 1929/1930." *Metall*, 1930, no. 2, pp. 106–14.

——. "Sebestoimost' produktsii VOMT." *Metall*, 1931, nos. 5/6, pp. 34–41.

Kuz'minov, Iu. "V bor'be za osvoenie novymi zavodami." *Planovoe khoziaistvo*, 1934, no. 2, pp. 57–76.

Kvasha, Ia. "Mashinostroenie i vosproizvodstvo oborudovaniia v narodnom khoziaistve." *Planovoe khoziaistvo*, 1933, nos. 5/6, pp. 37–69.

Lipovetskii, L. "Kakie mashinotresty nam nuzhny?" *Za ratsionalizatsiiu*, 1929, no. 6, pp. 18–19.

Maksimov, P. "Sesonnye kolebaniia v sovetskom sel'skokhoziaistvennom mashinostroenii." *Planovoe khoziaistvo*, 1935, no. 4, pp. 18–36.

Mezhlauk, V. I. "Metallopromyshlennosti pered litzom Partii i Sovetskoi vlasti." *Metall*, 1925/26, nos. 1/2, pp. 3–11.

Miliukov, A. A. "Zadachi finansirovaniia metallopromyshlennosti v novom operatsionnom godu." *Metall*, 1925/26, nos. 1/2, pp. 36–47.

Oborin, V. F. "Stankostroitel'naia promyshlennost' v Anglii, Germanii, i SSSR." *Vestnik metallopromyshlennosti*, 1932, no. 10, pp. 56–64; no. 11, pp. 53–56; no. 12, pp. 47–49.

"Obzor piatiletnogo plana razvitii mashinostroenii." *Metall*, 1929, nos. 5/6, pp. 3–86.

"O chem molchat stanki." *Metallist*, 1929, no. 11 (21 March), pp. 6–7.

Orentlikher, M. F. "O meropriiatiiakh k razvitiiu nashego stankostroeniia." *Metall*, 1925/26, nos. 10/12, pp. 154–58.

——. "Problema stankostroeniia v SSSR." *Metall*, 1928, nos. 3/4, pp. 123–28.

——. "Sostoianie i perspektivy stankostroeniia SSSR." *Metall*, 1927, no. 6, pp. 74–81.

——. "Tekhnicheskie sdvigi v stankostroenii kapitalisticheskikh stran i nashi zadachi." *Planovoe khoziaistvo*, 1934, nos. 8/9, pp. 21–32.

Ossovskii, Ia. Ia. "K voprosu ob organizatsii rabochei sily kak faktora proizvodstva." *Metall*, 1930, nos. 10/12, pp. 15–28.

Ostrovskii, M. G. "Provedenie 7-chasovogo dnia v metallopromyshlennosti." *Metall*, 1928, nos. 5/6, pp. 144–161.

——. "Vrediteli v metallopromyshlennosti." *Metall*, 1930, nos. 10/12, pp. 3–7.

Pepper, Dzh. "Itogi pervoi piatiletki v oblasti spetsializatsii, kooperirovaniia i kombinirovaniia mashinostroeniia." *Planovoe khoziaistvo*, 1932, no. 3, pp. 101–22.

Perel'man, E. S. "Opyt VMTS po postroike novykh mashin." *Metall*, 1930, no. 1, pp. 27–36.

——. "O sinditsirovanii mashinostroeniia." *Metall*, 1925/26, nos. 4/5, pp. 101–11.

——. "Puti mashinostroeniia." *Metall*, 1927, no. 6, pp. 65–73.

——. "Voprosy sebestoimosti i tsen v mashinostroenii." *Metall*, 1928, nos. 8/9, pp. 83–100.

"Perevybory fabzavkomov metallistov." *Izvestiia*, 12 June 1930, p. 4.

"Piatiletnyi plan rekonstruktsii metallicheskoi promyshlennosti." *Metall*, 1929, nos. 5/6, pp. 3–86.

Piterskii, A. "Sobstvennaia prodovol'stvennaia baza tiazheloi promyshlennosti." *Planovoe khoziaistvo*, 1935, no. 4, pp. 66–75.

"Problema intensifikatsii truda." *Za ratsionalizatsiiu*, 1929, no. 8, pp. 1–4.

"The Problem of Labour Output in Soviet Russia." *International Labor Review* 13 (May 1926): 684–716.

Rabkrinovets. "Problema segodniashchego Urala." *Metall*, 1930, nos. 3/4, pp. 52–61.

Radchenko, Ia. "K voprosu o vnedrenii khozrascheta." *Puti industrializatsii*, 1930, no. 14, pp. 37–41.

Rakovskii. "Sotssorevnovanie i tekuchest' rabochei sily." *Puti industrializatsii*, 1930, nos. 15/16, pp. 32–41.

"Rationalizierungsbestrebungen im Ruhrbergbau." *Bergarbeiterzeitung*, June 1924.

"Resoliutsiia soveshchaniia predstavitelei ratsionalizatorskikh grupp pri organakh RKI." *Za ratsionalizatsiiu*, 1929, no. 9, pp. 14–16.

Rostovtsev, P. P. "Ratsionalizatorskie meropriiatie po zavodam Mosmashtresta." *Za ratsionalizatsiiu*, 1929, no. 4, pp. 50–52.

Rubinshtein, B. G. "Orgametall." *Metall*, 1928, no. 10, pp. 119–26.

Sandomirskii, S. B. "O reorganizatsii upravleniia mashinostroeniem i metalloobrabotkoi." *Metall*, 1930, no. 1, pp. 5–14.

"Sebestoimost' na Krasnom Sormove ne snizhena." *Metallist*, 1929, no. 14 (15 April), pp. 8–9.

Shakhnazarov, M. M. "Proizvoditel'nost' truda i zarabotnaia plata v metallopromyshlennosti." *Metall*, 1925/26, nos. 1/2, pp. 71–74.

Shkundin, Z. "Voprosy upravleniia promyshlennost'iu na sovremennom etape." *Planovoe khosiaistvo*, 1934, no. 3, pp. 78–100.

Sipachev, A. "Dva goda piatiletki Mosmashtresta." *Metall*, 1930, no. 1, pp. 106–27.

Spektor, G. A. "Balans oborudovaniia na 1931 g. i zadachi mashinostroeniia." *Metall*, 1931, nos. 2/3, pp. 3–19.

Stetsenko, A. S. "Poteri v promyshlennosti i mery bor'by s nimi." *Metall*, 1931, nos. 2/3, pp. 82–92.

Stremlianova, N. "K voprosu ob organizatsii rabochei sily na predpriiatii." *Metall*, 1931, nos. 2/3.

Sukharevskii, B. "Sovershenie tekhnicheskoi rekonstruktsii i voprosy mekhanizatsii promyshlennosti." *Planovoe khoziaistvo*, 1934, no. 1, pp. 65–96.

Tirzbanurt, T. "K voprosu o sotsialisticheskikh formakh organizatsii truda." *Udarnik*, 1932, no. 2 (January), pp. 20–29.

Trakhmer, B. S. "K voprosu o reorganizatsii material'nykh chastei zavodov Iugostali." *Metall*, 1925/26, nos. 8/9, pp. 23–30.

Veitsman, S. E. "Puti razvitiia mashino-tekhnicheskogo sindikata." *Metall*, 1928, no. 1, pp. 56–68.

Vovsi, M. "K voprosu o tekuchesti rabochei sily v promyshlennosti." *Puti industrializatsii*, 1930, no. 14, pp. 25–36.

"Zadachi inzhenerno-tekhnicheskoi sektsii." *Metallist*, 1929, no. 11 (March), pp. 3–4.

Zelikson, G. "Postroenie promfinplana na predpriiatii." *Metall*, 1931, nos. 2/3, pp. 58–69.

Zolotarev, A. "Sovetskoe mashinostroenie—vedushchee sveno tekhnicheskoi rekonstruktsii." *Planovoe khoziaistvo*, 1933, nos. 7/8, pp. 19–44.

Zubzhinskii, N. A. "Deviatii mesiatsev GOMZy." *Metall*, 1929, no. 10, pp. 115–28.

——. "Rabota GOMZy 1926/1927." *Metall*, 1928, no. 2, pp. 100–111.

Books

Barun, M. A. *Osnovnoi kapital promyshlennosti SSSR.* Moscow, 1930.

Belen'kii, Z. M. *Rezultaty obsledovaniia NKRKI kapital'nogo stroitel'stva VSNKh SSSR.* Moscow, 1929.

Biulleten' po uchetu truda: Itogi 1931 goda. Moscow, 1932.

Biulleten' TsIK Soiuza SSSR: Stenograficheskii otchet. Moscow, 1929.

Bulyzhnik, S. *Udarnye brigady na rabote.* Moscow, 1929.

Charnovskii, N. F. *Tekhno-ekonomicheskie printsipy v metallopromyshlennosti.* Moscow, 1927.

Chistka sovetskogo apparata. Moscow, 1930.

Desiat' let Orgametalla, 1924–1934. Moscow, 1935.

Differentsiatsiia zarabotnoi platy v fabrichno-zavodskoi promyshlennosti za 1927 i 1928 gg. Moscow, 1929.

Dinamika rossiiskoi i sovetskoi promyshlennosti. Moscow, 1928.

Direktivy po ratsionalizatsii proizvodstva. Moscow, 1929.

Dzerzhinskii, F. *Problemy proizvoditel'nosti truda.* Moscow, 1925.

Dzerzhinskii, F., et al. *Problemy proizvoditel'nosti truda.* 4 vols. Moscow, 1925–26.

——. *Voprosy truda v promyshlennosti: Sbornik statei.* Moscow, 1926.

Ermanskii, O. *Neotlozhennie zadachi ratsionalizatsii.* Moscow, 1925.

——. *Pis'ma o ratsionalizatsii: 3-oe izdanie.* Moscow, 1934.

——. *Teoriia i prakhtika ratsionalizatsii.* Moscow, 1924.

Frishman, S. B. *Vrednaia ustanovka organov ratsionalizatsii na predpriiatiiakh: Kritika inzhenera Popova.* Moscow, 1933.

Gastev, A. K. *Kak nado rabotat'.* Moscow, 1924/1972.

Gerchuk, Ia. P. *Sezonnye kolebaniia v promyshlennosti.* Moscow, 1930.

Gol'tsman, A. Z. *Upravlenie promyshlennost'iu v Germanii i v SSSR.* Moscow, 1930.

——. *Voprosy planirovaniia narodnogo khoziaistva.* Moscow, 1927.

Granovskii, E. L., and B. Markus. *Ekonomika sotsialisticheskoi promyshlennosti.* Moscow, 1940.

Grossman, V. Ia. *Sotsialisticheskaia ratsionalizatsiia promyshlennosti: Itogi i blizhaishie zadachi.* Moscow, 1932.

Ingulov, I. *Protiv demogogii i khvostizma: O vzgliadakh oppozitsii na ratsionalizatsiiu proizvodstva.* Moscow, 1927.

Inzhenerno-tekhnicheskie kadry promyshlennosti: Materialy sektora truda, ratsionalizatsii i sebestoimosti PTEU, VSNKh SSSR. Moscow, 1930.

Itogi i materialy pervoi Moskovskoi oblastnoi konferentsii VKP(b). Moscow, 1929.

Izderzhki proizvodstva i proizvoditel'nosti truda v promyshlennosti. Moscow, 1935.

Kachestvennye pokazateli raboty promyshlennosti VSNKh za 1931 god: Sebestoimost' i tekhniko-ekonomicheskie pokazateli. Moscow, 1932.

Kantorovich, V. Ia. *Sindikatskaia sistema.* Moscow, 1929.

Kapital'noe stroitel'stvo promyshlennosti. Moscow, 1928.

Kaplun, S. I. *Statistika professional'nogo travmatizma za 1928.* No. 24, *Mashinostroenie i obrabotka metallov.* Moscow, 1933.

Khavin, A. *Ot udarnykh brigad k udarnym tsekham i zavodam.* Moscow, 1929.

Khrashchevskii, L. *Itogi raboty Ural'skoi promyshlennosti za 1929/1930 gg.* Sverdlovsk, 1931.

Kombinirovanie v usloviiakh kapitalizma i v SSSR: Stenogramma dokladov v Institute promyshlenno-ekonomicheskogo issledovaniia, VSNKh. Moscow, 1931.

Kontsentratsiia fabrichno-zavodskoi i trestirovannoi tsenzovoi promyshlennosti (po materialam godichnogo obsledovaniia 1925/26 g. i posledyiushchikh let). Moscow, 1929.

Kuibyshev, V. *Itogi i perspektivy khoziaistvennogo stroitel'stva SSSR: Doklad na 2-i sessii TsIK SSSR 17/X/27 g.* Moscow, 1927.

——. *Ratsionalizatsiia promyshlennosti.* Moscow, 1928.

——. *Sistema promyshlennogo upravleniia.* Moscow, 1927.

Leder, V. L., ed. *Sovremennoe sostoianie rabot po ratsionalizatsii v promyshlennosti SSSR.* Moscow, 1926.

Lepse, I. *Zadachi soiuza metallistov: Doklada k 8-omu s"ezdu VSRM.* Moscow, 1929.

Logiiko, F. *Opyt ratsionalizatsii metalloobrabatyvaiushchego zavoda.* Khar'kov, 1930.

Materialy o gubkonferentsii masterov-metallistov, 11–12 iiunia 1926. Moscow, 1926.

Materialy po kachestvennym pokazateliam raboty promyshlennosti v 1931. Moscow, 1932.

Metallopromyshlennost' za 10 let. Moscow, 1927.

Mezhlauk, V. I. *Metallopromyshlennost' v 1924/1925.* Moscow, 1925.

Mints, L. E. *Komandnyi sostav promyshlennosti, transporta, i sel'skogo khoziaistva v SSSR.* Moscow, 1926.

Mordukhovich (Mokhov), Z. *Ispol'zovanie trudovykh resursov i podgotovka kadrov.* Moscow, 1932.

——. *Na bor'bu s tekuchest'iu rabochei sily.* Moscow, 1931.

Mutsenek, Ia. *Ratsionalizatsiia i zarabotnaia plata.* Kiev, 1930.

Na Novom Etape sotsialisticheskogo stroitel'stva. Moscow, 1930.

O kulture vzaimosameniaemogo proizvodstva, o sovremennykh rezhushchikh instrumentakh, i o kulture prisposoblenii. Moscow, 1928.

Ol'khov, V. *Za zhivoe rukovodstvo sots-sorevnovaniem.* Moscow, 1930.

Ordzhonikidze, G. K. *Stat'i i rechi.* Vol. 2, 1926–1937. Moscow, 1957.

Osnovnye linii tekhnicheskoi rekonstruktsii promyshlennosti SSSR: K piatiletnomu planu promyshlennosti SSSR. Vol. 2. Moscow, 1929.

Osnovnie momenty rekonstruktsii promyshlennosti SSSR. Moscow, 1930.

Otchet brianskogo okruzhnogo komiteta VKP(b). Bezhitsa, 1930.

Otchet o rabote Brianskogo raionnogo komiteta VSRM, ianvar' 1928–aprel', 1929. Bezhitsa, 1929.

Otchet o rabote inzhenerno-tekhnicheskii sektsii Moskovskogo raionogo komiteta VSRM, 11.2.1927 po 1.9.1928. Moscow, 1928.

Otchet zavodskogo komiteta VSRM gosudarstvennogo mekhanicheskogo zavoda K. Libknikhtu za period s 22 dek., 1929 g. po aprelia 1930. Bezhitsa, 1930.

Patschau, Herbert. *Die Maschinenindustrie im deutschen Reich.* Berlin, 1937.

Perel'man, E. S. *Mashinostroenie v SSSR.* Moscow, 1931.

Perepis' oborudovanii promyshlennosti, 1932–1933: Metaloobrabatyvaiushchee oborudovanie SSSR. Moscow, 1933.

Perepis' oborudovanii promyshlennosti, 1932–1934: Oborudovanie metalloobrabatyvaiushchei promyshlennosti. Moscow, 1935.

Pervaia vsesoiuznaia konferentsia rabotnikov sotsialisticheskoi promyshlennosti: Stenograficheskii otchet. Moscow, 1931.

Pervyi god sotsialisticheskogo sorevnovaniia Moskovskykh metallistov. Moscow, 1930.

Piatnadtsatyi let bor'by za sovetskoe mashinostroenie. Moscow, 1932.

Pis'mennyi, Ia. K., ed. *Mashinostroitel'naia promyshlennost' SSSR: Spravochnik zavodov, stroitel'stv, trestov, i glavk upravlenii soiuznoi, respublikanskoi, i mestnoi mashinostroitel'noi i metalloobrabativaiushchei promyshlennost'iu.* 4 vols. Moscow, 1933–1935.

Professional'nyi sostav personala zavodskoi promyshlennosti na 1-oi noiabre 1927. Moscow, 1928.

Rabinovich, A. *Problema proizoditel'nosti truda.* Moscow, 1925.

Rabochyi den' v fabrichno-zavodskoi promyshlennosti v 1928. Moscow, 1928.

Rashin, A. *Sostav fabrichno-zavodskogo proletariata SSSR.* Moscow, 1930.

Ratsionalizatsiia promyshlennosti SSSR: Rabota komissii prezidiuma VSNKh, SSSR. Moscow, 1928.

Rezoliutsii pervoi vsesoiuznoi konferentsii po planirovaniiu proizvodstva metalloobrabatyvaiushchei i elektropromyshlennosti. Moscow, 1931.

Romanov, M. M. *Trud v SSSR i v kapitalisticheskikh stranakh.* Moscow, 1931.

Rozenfel'd, I. A. *Promyshlennaia politika SSSR, 1917–1925.* Moscow, 1926.

Rozengol'ts, A. P. *Za sotsializm protiv biurokratizma: Doklad o rabote TsKK-NKRKI na XVI s"ezde KP(b)U.* Moscow, 1930.

——, ed. *Promyshlennost': Sbornik statei po materialam TsKK VKP(b)-NK RKI.* Moscow, 1930.

Rubinshtein, Modest. *Kapitalisticheskaia ratsionalizatsiia.* Moscow, 1929.

Sebestoimost' i proizvoditel'nost' truda po otrasliam narodnogo khoziaistva v 1931. Moscow, 1932.

Shatan, E. O. *Problema rabochei sily v osnovnykh promyshlennykh raionakh.* Moscow, 1928.

XVI konferentsiia VKP(b), aprel' 1929: Stenograficheskii otchet. Moscow, 1962.

XVI s"ezd vsesoiuznoi kommunisticheskoi partii (b), 26 iiunia-13 iiulia 1930: Stenograficheskii otchet. Moscow, 1935.

Shukgalter, L. Ia., ed. *Rabota nepreryvnym potokom: Sbornik statei.* Moscow, 1930.

Shuvalov, K. *Shturm tekhniki.* Leningrad, 1931.

Sindikatskaia sistema. Moscow, 1929.

Soiuznaia promyshlennost' v tsifrakh: Tempy rosta i faktora razvitiia. Moscow, 1929.

Soiuz rabochikh metallistov. *Materialy k 3-oi konferentsii masterov metallistov, 4.10.1928: Kapital'noe stroitel'stvo i rabota soiuza sredi masterov.* Moscow, 1928.

Sokolov, A. *Sovetskoe stankostroenie.* Moscow, 1932.

Sostav rukovodiashchikh rabotnikov i spetsialistov soiuza SSR. Moscow, 1936.

Sostoianie raboty Moskovskikh profsoiuzov i blizhaishie zadachi soiuza metallistov: Materialy k 7-oi gubkonferentsii 31.10.1928. Moscow, 1928.

Sotsialisticheskaia ratsionalizatsiia i bor'ba s poteramy. Moscow, 1929.

Sotsialisticheskoe sorevnovanie v promyshlennosti. Moscow, 1930.

Sotsialisticheskoe stroitel'stvo SSSR. Moscow, 1935.

Statistika professional'nogo travmatizma za 1925 god. Moscow, 1930.

Stenograficheskii otchet pervoi proizvodstvennoi konferentsii Uralmeta, 13–16 ianvaria, 1929. Sverdlovsk, 1929.

Stremlianova, N. G. *Organizatsiia truda na mashinostroitel'nom zavode: Opyt Klimovskogo zavoda.* Moscow, 1931.

——. *Tekuchest' i ispol'zovanie rabochei sily.* Moscow, 1932.

Strumilin, S. G. *Problemy ekonomiki truda: Ocherki i etiudy.* Moscow, 1925.

Tekhnicheskaia rekonstruktsiia narodnogo khoziaistva SSSR v pervoi piatiletke. Moscow, 1934.
Tekhno-ekonomicheskie pokazateli po novom i rekonstruktirovannym zavodam mashino-stroeniia i metalloobrabotki. Moscow, 1930.
Tezisy k Moskovskomu oblastnomu s"ezdu metallistov. Moscow, 1929.
Trud v SSSR: Statisticheskii spravochnik. Moscow, 1936.
Trud v SSSR: Statistiko-ekonomicheskii obzor, oktiabr' 1922–mart 1924. Moscow, 1924.
Trudy konferentsii tekhniko-normirovochnykh biuro metallo-elektropromyshlennosti. Moscow, 1925.
Trudy pervogo vsesoiuznogo soveshchaniia po ratsionalizatsii proizvodstva, 4–9 noiabr' 1925. Moscow, 1926.
Tsaguriia, M. *Osvoenie novymi predpriiatiiami i novoi tekhnikoi v tiazheloi promyshlennosti.* Moscow, 1934.
TsIT i ego metody NOT. Moscow, 1970.
Tsyperovich, G. V. *Glavkizm.* Moscow, 1924.
Udarnye brigady. Moscow, 1929.
Varzar, V. E. Bazarov. *Svod statisticheskikh dannykh po fabrichno-zavodskoi promyshlennosti s 1887 po 1926.* Moscow, 1929.
V bor'be s proryvom: Itogi rabot obshchzavodskoi proizvodstvenno-tekhnicheskoi konferentsii udarnikov kolomenskogo mashinostroitel'nogo zavoda. Moscow, 1933.
Vseukrainskaia proizvodstvennaia konferentsiia rabochikh metallistov zavodov Iugostali, 28 iuniia–5 iuliia, 1928 goda: Stenograficheskii otchet. Khar'kov, 1928.
Wegleben, F. *Die Rationalizierung im deutschen Werkzeugmaschinenbau.* Berlin, 1924.
Zagorsky, S. *Wages and Regulation of Conditions of Labour in the USSR.* Geneva, 1930.
Zarabotnaia plata rabochikh krupnoi promyshlennosti v oktiabre 1934 g. Moscow, 1935.

SECONDARY SOURCES

Acherkan, N. S. *Razvitie stankostroitel'noi i instrumental'noi promyshlennosti v SSSR.* Moscow, 1958.
Andrle, Vladimir. *Workers in Stalin's Russia: Industrialization and Social Change in a Planned Economy.* Brighton, 1988.
Agursky, Mikhail. *The Third Rome: National Bolshevism in the USSR.* Boulder, 1987.
Avdakov, Iu. K. *Gosudarstvennaia promyshlennost' SSSR v perekhodnom periode.* Moscow, 1977.
——. *Proizvodstvennye ob"edineniia i ikh rol' v organizatsii upravleniia sovetskoi promyshlennost'iu, 1917–1932.* Moscow, 1973.
Azrael, Jeremy. *Managerial Power and Soviet Politics.* Cambridge, Mass., 1966.
Bailes, Kendall. "The American Connection: Ideology and the Transfer of American Technology to the Soviet Union, 1917–1941." *Comparative Studies in Society and History,* 23 (July 1981): 421–48.
——. "The Politics of Technology: Stalin and Technocratic Thinking among Soviet Engineers." *American Historical Review* 79 (April 1974): 445–69.
——. "Technology and Legitimacy: Soviet Aviation and Stalinism in the 1930s." *Technology and Culture* 17 (January 1976): 55–81.
——. *Technology and Society under Lenin and Stalin: Origins of the Soviet Technical Intelligentsia.* Princeton, 1978.
Ball, Alan. *And Now My Heart Is Hardened: Abandoned Children in Soviet Russia, 1918–1930* (Berkeley, 1994).
——. *Russia's Last Capitalists: The Nepmen, 1921–1929.* Berkeley, 1987.
Barmine, Alexander. *Memoirs of a Soviet Diplomat: Twenty Years in the Service of the U.S.S.R.* Westport, Conn., 1973.

Beissinger, Mark. *Scientific Management, Socialist Discipline, and Soviet Power.* Cambridge, Mass., 1988.

Billon, S. A. "Soviet Management Structure: Stability and Change." In *Evolution of International Management Structures,* ed. Harold F. Williamson. Newark, Del., 1979.

Boffa, Giuseppe. *The Stalin Phenomenon.* Trans. Nicholas Fersen. Ithaca, 1992.

Brady, Robert. *The Rationalization Movement in German Industry.* Berkeley, 1933.

Braverman, Harry. *Labor and Monopoly Capital: The Degradation of Work in the Twentieth Century.* New York, 1975.

Burns, Emile. *Russia's Productive System.* London, 1930.

Carr, E. H. *The Bolshevik Revolution.* New York, 1952.

——. *Socialism in One Country, 1924–1926.* 3 vols. London, 1959–64.

——. *The Twenty Years' Crisis, 1919–1939: An Introduction to the Study of International Relations.* New York, 1946.

Carr, E. H., and R. W. Davies. *Foundations of a Planned Economy, 1926–1929.* 2 vols. London, 1969.

Chapman, Herrick. *State Capitalism and Working-Class Radicalism in the French Aircraft Industry.* Berkeley, 1991.

Chase, William. *Workers, Society, and the Soviet State: Labor and Life in Moscow, 1918–1929.* Urbana, 1987.

Childers, Thomas. *The Nazi Voter: the Social Foundations of Fascism in Germany, 1919–1933.* Chapel Hill, 1983.

——. "The Social Language of Politics: The Sociology of Political Discourse in the Weimar Republic." *American Historical Review* 95, no. 2 (1990): 331–58.

Cooper, J. "The Development of the Soviet Machine Tool Industry, 1917–1941." Ph.D. thesis, University of Birmingham, 1975.

Coopersmith, Jonathan. *The Electrification of Russia, 1880–1926.* Ithaca, 1992.

Davies, R. W. *The Soviet Economy in Turmoil, 1929–1930.* Cambridge, Mass., 1989

Danilov, Viktor. *Rural Russia under the New Regime.* Trans. Orlando Figes. Bloomington, 1988.

Direktivy KPSS i Sovetskogo pravitel'stva po khoziaistvennym voprosam. Vol. 2, 1929–1945. Moscow, 1957.

Dobb, Maurice. *Soviet Economic Development since 1917.* New York, 1966.

Drobizhev, V. Z. *Glavnyi shtab sotsialisticheskoi promyshlennosti: Ocherki istorii VSNKha, 1917–1932.* Moscow, 1966.

——. "Rol' rabochego klassa SSSR v formirovanii komandnykh kadrov sotsialisticheskoi promyshlennosti, 1917–1936 gg." *Istoriia SSSR,* 1961, no. 4, pp. 55–75.

Erlich, Alexander. *The Soviet Industrialization Debate 3, 1924–1928.* Mass., 1960.

Filtzer, Donald. *Soviet Workers and Stalinist Industrialization: The Formation of Modern Soviet Industrial Relations, 1928–1941.* Armonk, N.Y., 1986.

Fitzpatrick, Sheila. "Ascribing Class: The Construction of Social Identity in Soviet Russia." *Journal of Modern History* 65 (December 1993): 745–70.

——. *Education and Social Mobility in the Soviet Union, 1921–1934.* Cambridge, 1979.

——. "'Middle-Class Values' and Soviet Life in the 1930s." In *Soviet Society and Culture: Essays in Honor of Vera S. Dunham,* ed. Terry Thompson and Richard Sheldon, pp. 20–38. Boulder, 1988.

——. "The Problem of Class Identity in NEP Society." In Fitzpatrick et al., *Russia in the Era of NEP,* pp. 12–33. Bloomington, 1991.

——. "Sergo Ordzhonikidze and the Takeover of VSNKh." *Soviet Studies* 36 (April 1985): 153–72.

——. "Stalin and the Making of a New Elite, 1928–1939." *Slavic Review* 38, no. 2 (1979): 377–402.

Gaposhkin, O. *Potochnyi metod v promyshlennosti SSSR*. Moscow, 1946.

Gerschenkron, Alexander. *Economic Backwardness in Historical Perspective*. New York, 1962.

Getty, J. Arch. *The Origins of the Great Purges: The Soviet Communist Party Reconsidered*. New York, 1985.

Graham, Loren. *The Ghost of the Executed Engineer: Technology and the Fall of the Soviet Union*. Cambridge, Mass., 1993.

Grannick, David. *Red Executive: A Study of the Organization Man in Russian Industry*. New York, 1960.

——. *Soviet Metal Fabricating and Economic Development*. Cambridge, Mass., 1967.

Graziosi, Andrea. "At the Roots of Soviet industrial relations and practices: Piatakov's Donbass in 1921." *Cahiers du monde russe* 36 (1995): 95–138.

——. "'Building the First System of State Industry in History': Piatakov's VSNKh and the Crisis of NEP, 1923–1926." *Cahiers du monde russe et soviétique* 32 (1991): 539–81.

——. "'Visitors from Other Times': Foreign Workers in the Prewar *Piatiletki*." *Cahiers du monde russe et soviétique* 29 (April–June 1988): 161–80.

Hatch, John. "Bringing Economics Back In: Industrial Arbitration and Collective Bargaining during NEP." Paper presented at the conference "The Making of the Soviet Working Class," Michigan State University, 9–11 November 1990.

——. "The 'Lenin Levy' and the Social Origins of Stalinism: Workers and the Communist Party in Moscow, 1921–1928." *Slavic Review* 48, no. 4 (1989): 558–77.

Herf, Jeffrey. *Reactionary Modernism: Technology, Culture, and Politics in Weimar and the Third Reich*. Cambridge, 1984.

Hogan, Heather. "Financiers, Engineers, and the 'Imperatives' of Economic Modernization." Paper presented at the 22d National Convention of the American Association for the Advancement of Slavic Studies, Washington, D.C., 18–21 October 1990.

——. *Forging Revolution: Metalworkers, Managers, and the State in St. Petersburg, 1890–1914*. Bloomington, 1993.

Hounshell, David. *From the American System to Mass Production: The Development of Manufacturing Technology in the United States, 1800–1932*. Baltimore, 1984.

Ikonnikov, S. N. *Sozdanie i deiatel'nost' ob"edinennykh organov TsKK-RKI v 1923–1934 gg*. Moscow, 1971.

Industrializatsiia SSSR: Dokumenty i materialy, 1926–1928. Moscow, 1969.

Industrializatsiia SSSR: Dokumenty i materialy, 1929–1932. Moscow, 1970.

Industrializatsiia SSSR: Dokumenty i materialy, 1933–1937. Moscow, 1971.

Jasny, Naum. *Soviet Industrialization, 1928–1952*. Chicago, 1961.

Khlevniuk, O. V. *Stalin i Ordzhonikidze: Konflikty v Politbiuro v 30-gody*. Moscow, 1993. Published in English as *In Stalin's Shadow: The Career of Sergo Ordzhonikidze*, trans. David S. Nordlander. Armonk, N.Y., 1995.

——. *Udarniki pervoi piatiletki*. Moscow, 1989.

Khlevniuk, O., and R. W. Davies. "The Role of Gosplan in Economic Decision-Making in the 1930s." CREES Discussion Papers, SIPS no. 36, University of Birmingham, 1993.

Khlevniuk, O., Aleksandr Kvashonkin, L. P. Kosheleva, and L. A. Rogovaia. *Stalinskoe politbiuro v 30-e gody*. Moscow, 1995.

Kommunisticheskaia Partiia Sovetskogo Soiuza v rezoliutsiiakh s"ezdov, konferentsii i plenumov TsK. Vols. 2 and 3. Moscow, 1954, 1970.

Koritskii, E. B., et al. *Sovetskaia upravlencheskaia mysl' 20-kh godov*. Moscow, 1990.

Kosheleva, L. P., L. A. Rogovaia, and O. Khlevniuk. *Pis'ma I. V. Stalina V. M. Molotovu, 1925–1936 gg.: Sbornik dokumentov*. Moscow, 1995.

Kotkin, Stephen. *Magnetic Mountain: Stalinism as a Civilization.* Berkeley, 1995.

Kozlov, V. A., and O. V. Khlevniuk. *Nachinaetsia s cheloveka: Chelovecheskii faktor v sotsialisticheskom stroitel'stve.* Moscow, 1988.

KPSS v rezoliutsiakh. Vol. 2. Moscow, 1954.

Kuromiya, Hiroaki. "*Edinonachalie* and the Soviet Industrial Manager, 1928–1937." *Soviet Studies* 36, no. 2 (1984): 185–204.

——. "The Crisis of Proletarian Identity in the Soviet Factory, 1928–1929." *Slavic Review* 44, no. 2 (1985): 280–97.

——. *Stalin's Industrial Revolution: Politics and Workers, 1928–1931.* Cambridge, 1988.

Lampert, Nicholas. *The Technical Intelligentsia and the Soviet State.* New York, 1979.

Lewin, Moshe. "The Disappearance of Planning in the Plan." *Slavic Review* 32 (June 1973): 271–87.

——. *The Making of the Soviet System: Essays in the Social History of Interwar Russia.* New York, 1985.

——. *Political Undercurrents in Soviet Economic Debates.* Princeton, 1974.

——. *Russia/USSR/Russia: The Drive and Drift of a Super-State.* New York, 1995.

Maier, Charles. "Between Taylorism and Technocracy: European Ideologies and the Vision of Industrial Productivity in the 1920s." *Journal of Contemporary History* 2, no. 5 (1970): 27–61.

——. *Recasting Bourgeois Europe: Stabilization in France, Germany, and Italy in the Decade after World War I.* Princeton, 1988.

Makeenko, M. M. *Ocherki razvitiia mashinostroeniia SSSR, 1921–1928.* Moscow, 1962.

Merkle, Judith. *Management and Ideology: The Legacy of the International Scientific Management Movement.* Berkeley, 1980.

Meyer, Gert. *Sozialstruktur sowjetischer Industriearbeiter am Ende der zwanziger Jahre: Ergebnisse der Gewerkschaftsumfrage unter Metall-, Textil-, und Bergarbeitern, 1929.* Marburg, 1981

Nolan, Mary. *Visions of Modernity: American Business and the Modernization of Germany.* New York, 1994.

Nove, Alec. *An Economic History of the Soviet Union.* London, 1969.

Osokina, E. A. *Ierarkhiia potrebleniia: O zhizni liudei v usloviiakh stalinskogo snabzheniia, 1928–1935.* Moscow, 1993.

Petrochenko, P. *Organizatsiia i normirovanie truda v promyshlennosti SSSR: Istoriko-ekonomicheskii ocherk.* Moscow, 1971.

Peukert, Detlev. *The Weimar Republic: The Crisis of Classical Modernity.* Trans. Richard Deveson. New York, 1991.

Rees, E. A. *State Control in Soviet Russia: The Rise and Fall of the Workers' and Peasants' Inspectorate, 1920–1934.* New York, 1987.

Reiman, Michal. *The Birth of Stalinism: The USSR on the Eve of the Second Revolution.* Bloomington, 1987.

Resheniia Partii i pravitel'stva po khoziaistvennym voprosam. Moscow, 1967.

Rieber, Alfred. "The Sedimentary Society." In Edith W. Clowes et al., *Between Tsar and People: Educated Society and the Quest for Public Identity in Late Imperial Russia.* Princeton, 1991.

Rittersporn, G. T. *Stalinist Simplifications and Soviet Complications: Social Tensions and Political Conflicts in the USSR, 1933–1953.* New York, 1991.

Rogger, Hans. "Amerikanizm and the Economic Development of Russia." *Comparative Studies in Society and History* 23 (July 1981): 382–420.

Rosenberg, William G., and Lewis H. Siegelbaum, eds. *Social Dimensions of Soviet Industrialization.* Bloomington, 1993.

Rozenfel'd, Ia. S., and N. N. Klimovskii. *Istoriia mashinostroeniia SSSR*. Moscow, 1961.
Scott, John. *Behind the Urals: An American Worker in Russia's City of Steel*. Bloomington, 1989.
Seiranian, F. G., ed. *O Sergo Ordzhonikidze: Vospominaniia sovremennikov*. Moscow, 1981.
Shakhovoi, V. A. "Organizatsionnye formy upravleniia metallopromyshlennost'iu, 1917–1932." Candidate diss., Moscow State University, 1971.
Shanin, Teodor. *The Awkward Class: Political Sociology of the Peasantry in a Developing Society*. London, 1972
Shearer, David R. "The Language and Politics of Socialist Rationalization: Productivity, Industrial Relations, and the Social Origins of Stalinism at the End of NEP." *Cahiers du monde russe et soviétique* 32 (October/December 1991): 581–608.
Siegelbaum, Lewis H. "Production Collectives and Communes and the 'Imperatives' of Soviet Industrialization, 1929–1931." *Slavic Review* 44 (Spring 1986): 65–84.
——. "Soviet Norm Determination in Theory and Practice, 1917–1941." *Soviet Studies* 36 (January 1984): 45–68.
——. *Stakhanovism and the Politics of Productivity in the USSR, 1935–1941*. New York, 1988.
Siegelbaum, Lewis H., and Ronald Grigor Suny. "Making the Command Economy: Western Historians on Soviet Industrialization." *International Labor and Working-Class History*, 43 (Spring 1993): 65–76.
Siegelbaum, Lewis H., and Ronald Grigor Suny, eds. *Making Workers Soviet: Power, Class, and Identity*. Ithaca, 1994.
Sobranie postanovlenii pravitel'stva SSSR, 1924–1949. Moscow, 1957.
Souvarine, Boris. *Stalin: A Critical Study of Bolshevism*. New York, 1939.
Tekhniko-ekonomicheskoe planirovanie. Moscow, 1949.
Tucker, Robert C., ed. *Stalinism: Essays in Historical Interpretation*. New York, 1977.
Valentinov (Vol'skii), N. *Novaia ekonomicheskaia politika i krizis partii posle smerti Lenina. Gody raboty v VSNKh vo vremia NEP*. Stanford, 1971.
Viola, Lynn. *Best Sons of the Fatherland*. New York, 1987.
Ward, Chris. "Languages of Trade or Languages of Class? Work Culture in Russian Cotton Mills in the 1920s." In *Making Workers Soviet: Power, Class, and Identity*, ed. Lewis H. Siegelbaum and Ronald Grigor Suny, pp. 194–219. Ithaca, 1994.
——. *Russia's Cotton Workers and the New Economic Policy: Shop Floor Culture and State Policy, 1921–1929*. Cambridge, 1990.
Webb, Steven B. "Tariffs, Cartels, Technology, and Growth in the German Steel Industry, 1879–1914." *Journal of Economic History* 40 (June 1980): 309–30.
Weber, Max. *The Theory of Social and Economic Organization*. Trans. A. M. Henderson and Talcott Parsons. New York, 1947.
Winkler, Hans August. *Organisierter Kapitalismus: Voraussetzungen und Anfänger*. Göttingen, 1974.
Zaleski, Eugene. *Planning for Economic Growth in the Soviet Union, 1918–1932*. Chapel Hill, 1971.
Zelenko, G. I. "Podgotovka kvalifitsirovannoi rabochei sily." In *Voprosy truda v SSSR*. Moscow, 1958.

Index

Accounting (*khozraschet*), 40–42, 72, 121,
  160, 205–6, 208
  and factory reconstruction, 220–21, 224–
  25
Al'perovich, E., 87, 158, 161
  as head of Soiuzstankoinstrument, 209–11
  and industrial modernization, 142–46
Astashev, A., 173, 176

Backwardness, 18, 141, 143, 147, 152, 230,
  235, 238. *See also* Modernization
Bailes, K., 135–36
Bardin, I., 219, 222–24
Birman, S.:
  as head of Iugostal', 41, 48–50, 67, 93–
  94, 101–4, 113, 123
  in Vesenkha, 170, 241
Budget, 40–42, 89–90
Bureaucratic left, 81–82, 129
Butenko, B., 222

Capitalism, 36
  and European reconstruction, 1, 3–4
  and left opposition, 82–83
  Manchesterian and organized, 116
  and NEP, 5–6, 81–83
Carr, E. H., 1, 9–10, 12
Charnovskii, N., 138–41, 143, 152, 201
Chernov, A., 173–74
Chubar', V., 124–25
Corporatism, 225–29

Davies, R., 10, 12,
Davydov, G., 175, 190–96

Deitz engineering firm, 150, 155
Dobrovol'skii, B., 138, 174–76
Donugol', 35–37
Dotsenko, I., 175–76

Factories:
  and corporatism, 225–29
  and localism, 226–29
  occupational cultures in, 229–31, 233–35
  reconstruction and accounting in, 224–
  25
  reconstruction and labor in, 16, 216–20,
  223–24
  reconstruction and production relations
  in, 220–26
  reconstruction and wages in, 216–18,
  222–24
  and revival of shop contracting in, 224–
  25
  technological reconstruction of, 211–
  17
Falkner-Smit, M., 115–16
Fascism, 1
Feigin, V., 84–85
Fitzpatrick, S., 17–18
Ford, Henry/Fordism, 32, 138–42, 235
France, 4
Functionalism, 32–34, 159–60
  collapse of, 220–28
  and workers, 157–58
Fushman, A., 70–75, 81, 86

Gastev, A., 117
Gendin, Ia., 171, 177, 181–82

Germany, 1, 3–4, 89–90, 116, 130, 139–40,
144, 147, 150, 153, 155
and credits to Soviet industry, 48–50
as industrial model, 33, 117–21, 126,
142–43, 235, 239
Ginzburg, A., 98, 122
Gipromez, 47, 86, 88, 96, 138
purge of, 190
Glavchermet, 32, 101
Glavelektro, 32,
Glavki:
competition among, 34–37
organization of, 29, 32
and regionalism, 44–46
reorganization of, 111–14, 168, 171–73,
184–89
and syndicates, 55–56
and trusts, 29–30, 42–43
and Vesenkha, 43–44
See also entries for individual glavki
Glavkism, 114, 120
Glavmashinstroi:
and engineering syndicate, 56–57, 60, 61,
66
and mobilization campaigns, 93, 100–101
organization of, 32
purge of, 190, 196–203
and regionalism, 46
and reorganization, 128, 141, 145, 171–87
and Spektor case, 192–96
staff shortages and daily work in, 42–43,
171–87
Glavmetall, 29, 31–32, 42, 45–46, 192
purge of, 190–91, 196–203
Goffman, A., 159
Gokhman, I., 197–202
Gol'tsman, A., 79–81, 83, 87, 90–91, 95, 96
and reorganization, 115–22, 125–33, 167
Gomzy, 31, 35, 38, 40, 45–46
purge of, 190
Gorbunkov, A., 144, 146–55, 158, 161
Gosbank, 49, 61, 81, 86, 98
and credit reform, 70–75, 116–17, 119,
121, 132
Gosplan, 77, 84, 112, 121, 171
Great Leap Forward, 2, 8–9, 134–35
Grossman, V., 79, 221
Gurevich, A., 79–82, 95, 102, 104

Iakovlev, Ia., 78–79, 84, 122
Ianovskii, M., 173, 175–76
Industrial Party trial, 138, 173
Industrialization:
as class war, 16, 160
contradictions of, 160
and corporatism, 225–27
and localism, 226–29

and planning, 11
and socialist construction, 2, 160–61
and state building, 9–13, 16–17, 82–83,
115–17, 132, 238–39
See also Great Leap Forward
Italy, 1, 4
Iugostal', 36, 40, 41, 45, 67, 80, 90, 93, 101,
113
and German credits, 48–50
purge of, 190
and Rabkrin, 47–50, 102–04
and reorganization, 170, 188

Kaganovich, L., 79, 102–3
and 1930 crisis, 185
and purges, 189–90
Kaganovich, M., 79, 81, 87, 95, 104, 137,
144–46, 242
Kheifets, M., 138–41
Khodorov, I., 114
Khrennikov, S., 173, 190
Klimovsk textile machine-building factory,
155–58
Klimov-Verkhovskii, B., 42, 44
Kolomensk factory, 31
Kombinaty, 35–36, 56–57, 63, 168
Komsomol, 87, 146, 152–54
Koniukov, N., 58–66, 122, 171, 181
Kosior, I.:
defends trusts, 54–55, 66–69, 99, 102
and industrial reorganization, 113, 171
and Iugostal', 45–46
vs. regionalism, 129–30
vs. syndicates, 66–70
Krasnyi Profintern, 35, 38, 45–46, 201, 210
Krasnyi Proletarii:
and industrial reorganization, 170
in Mosmashtrest, 31, 35, 128, 144, 146–55
occupational stratification and conflicts
in, 147–55, 221–22
rationalization and reconstruction of,
207–8, 212
in Soiuzstankoinstrument, 207–8
Krasnyi Putilov, 32, 34, 43, 210
Krupp, 33,
Kuibyshev, V., 25–26, 49–50, 94, 98, 101–3,
105, 114, 122, 129, 131, 159, 176
and 1930 crisis, 185
Kuznetskstroi, 219, 221–26, 230

Labor:
aristocracy of, 80
and factory reconstruction, 136, 140,
143–44, 156
militarization of, 83, 117, 129, 233
and revolution, 5
and socialist competition, 160–61, 233

Labor (*cont.*)
  and wages, 216–20, 223–24
  See also Workers
Lampert, N., 135
Left opposition, 82–83
Lenin, V., 4–5, 115–16
Lenmashtrest, 32, 45–46, 63–64, 101–2
  and reorganization, 177
Lewin, M., 10, 17–18
Lipovetskii, L., 137
List, N., 147, 154
Lobov, S., 102–4, 123–24, 129

MAN, 33
Mantsev, 68–70, 125–33, 194
Mashinoob''edinenie, 35–36, 46, 145
  origins and operation of, 168–87
  purge of, 196–203
Mass production, 136–42, 146, 149, 160
  at Klimovsk factory, 155–56
  myth of, 235
Matrozov, I., 40, 111–12, 141
Mezhlauk, V., 45, 69, 171, 193–96
Mikhailov, M., 46–47, 63–64, 101–2
Mikoyan, A., 185, 149–50, 155
Modernity, 16–17
  and socialism, 158–59
  and Stalinism, 2–3, 238–39
Modernization, 16, 21, 83, 138, 161
  contradictions of, 230, 232–39
  effects of on labor, 136, 142–43, 156,
    216–20
  and industrial strategy, 136–47, 160
  at Klimovsk factory, 155–56, 158
  and occupational conflicts, 16–17, 136
  of production, 211–20
  and Stalinism, 2–3, 21, 238–39
Molotov, V., 84, 149–50, 155
Mosmashtrest, 31–32, 35, 64, 97, 128, 147,
    151, 154
  and industrial reorganization, 170

Nachal'stvo, 221–25, 237, 241, 240
Narkomfin, 7, 86, 97, 137
Narkomtiazhprom, 81, 159, 204–5, 236,
    241–42
Narkomtorg, 60, 88, 119, 121, 125
National socialism, 1
NEP, 4–8, 27–28, 38, 51, 54, 60, 69, 75, 79,
    96, 117, 134
  and bureaucratic left, 81–83, 129
  and capitalism, 6–7
  end of, 240
  and industrialization, 9–13
  and left opposition, 82–83
  reconceptualization of, 12–13
Neplanovost', 175–78, 185, 236

NKTPS, 88, 101
NOT, 117, 159

Oborin, F., 100–101, 175, 199
OGPU, 48, 87, 102, 105–6, 134, 154
  and purges, 189–90, 196
  and Spektor case, 193–96
Ordzhonikidze, S., 74, 83–84, 90, 100, 104,
    115, 137, 160
  and bureaucratic dictatorship, 240–42
  on bureaucratism, 206, 236
  and conflict with Stalin, 242
  as head of Narkomtiazhprom, 81, 159,
    204–5, 241–42
  as head of Rabkrin, 73, 77–80, 85, 91, 95,
    159, 196
  as head of Vesenkha, 79–81, 134, 144, 159
  on *nachal'stvo*, 223, 237, 241
  on *neplanovost'*, 236
  and 1930 crisis, 185
  and 16th Party Congress, 104–6
Orentlikher, N., 58, 61, 138, 141–43
Orgametall, 47, 58, 86–87, 142–46
Organizatsiia rabotnikov NOTa, 159

Peters, Ia., 85, 196
PEU, 29, 42, 47, 58, 97, 176
  and Spektor case, 193–96
Piatakov, G., 70–75, 78, 80, 86, 100, 116–17,
    124, 129, 132
  and bureaucratic left, 81–83
Politbiuro, 20, 77–78
Portenko, K., 45–47, 201–2
Preobrazhenskii, E., 82–83
Production associations:
  administrative and market forces in,
    206–11
  origins and organization of, 167–72
  rationalization of, 209
Purges, 189–91, 202–3
  *See also entries for individual persons and
    institutions*

Rabkrin, 26–27
  and industrial modernization, 136–42,
    144–46, 160–61
  and industrial reorganization, 114–15
  and Iugostal', 47–45, 102–4
  and mobilization campaigns, 95–102, 132
  and NEP, 26, 79
  and NOT, 159
  and planning, 92–95
  and purges, 196–202
  and specialists, 142–63
  and syndicate reforms, 70–75
  vs. Vesenkha, 26–27, 85–86, 88–92, 102–
    6, 136–37, 144–46, 154–55

Rabkrin (*cont.*)
  and war communism, 96
  work methods of, 85–88, 90–92
Rationalization, 35–37, 79, 104, 125, 132,
    138, 147, 160, 232
  in production associations, 209
  and shock work, 15
  as specialization, 38, 139–41, 145–46,
    149, 168, 209, 212–13
Regionalism, 38–39, 44–46, 48–50, 55, 104,
    112, 147
  and industrial reorganization, 122–24,
    126–33, 137, 167–68, 181–83, 238
Rozengol'ts, A., 78–79, 81–83, 93, 95–96,
    99, 104, 131, 137
  and 1930 crisis, 185
  on bureaucratism, 188–89
Rozmirovich, E., 159
Rukhimovich, M., 100, 114, 129–30

Samokritika, 151–52
Sandomirskii, S., 172–73, 175–76, 189
Satel', E., 151–52, 154
Scientific (systematic) management, 32–34,
    80, 117, 159
  collapse of, 220–31
  See also Functionalism
Serp i Molot, 122
Shock work, 15, 154, 160, 233–34
  and technological modernization, 219
Shostakovskii, B., 191–92
Shtern, A., 97–100
Shukhgalter, L., 138, 140–41
Shvetsov, D., 190–92
Siemens, 33
Socialism, 18
  and modernity, 158–59
  and Stalinism, 2, 10, 21, 239–40
  and syndicates, 55–56, 240
Soiuzstankoinstrument (SSI), 145, 170, 206–
    11
Sovnarkom, 36, 44, 66, 73, 77–78, 89, 91,
    97–98, 122, 173, 177
Sovtorg, 60
Specialists, 106
  and antispecialist campaign, 14–16, 134–
    36, 161
  and mobilization campaigns, 100–101
  and purges, 189–92, 202–3
  and Rabkrin, 142–63
  and Stalinist industrialization, 15–16,
    134–136, 138–42, 158, 160–62
  See also entries for individual specialists
Spektor, G., 192–96
Stal', 104, 168, 170, 180
Stalin, J., 1–3, 8, 18, 76, 78–79, 83–84, 98,
    100, 105, 162, 242

Stalinism:
  contradictions of, 20–21, 160–61, 236–
    38
  as despotism, 2–3, 18–19, 242
  as economic system, 2, 10–11
  and Great Leap Forward, 2, 8, 134–35
  and modernity, 2–3, 158–59, 238–39
  and revolutionary war, 5, 17–19
  and socialism, 2, 10, 18, 21, 239–40
  and social support, 13–14, 17–18, 21,
    159–62
  and specialists, 14–17, 134–36, 158–59,
    161–62
  and statism, 3, 10, 17, 240
  and syndicates, 54–55, 75
  and technocracy, 159
  as totalitarianism, 2–3
Stankotrest, 145, 154, 206, 209
STO, 43, 66
Stremlianova, N., 155–58, 161
Syndicates:
  and credit, 70–75
  and glavki, 55–56
  and Gosbank-Rabkrin reforms, 70–75
  and industrial modernization, 138–44
  as institutional entrepreneurs, 54–55, 68–
    69
  and local trade networks, 59–60
  as monopolies, 55
  and NEP, 54–55, 69
  and regionalism, 55
  and reorganization, 111–14, 117–19, 132,
    168, 180–86
  and socialism, 55–56, 240
  and Stalinism, 54–55, 75
  and trusts, 53–56, 66–70
  See also entries for individual syndicates

Taylor, Frederick, 32–33, 117, 159
Technical leadership, 112, 121
Technocracy, 16, 135, 158–59
Technology, 136, 138, 142–43, 152
  and factory reconstruction, 211–17
  and modernization, 158, 230, 238
  movement for mastery of, 153–54, 162
  and reconstruction at Klimovsk factory,
    155–56
  and social progress, 158–59
  and state power, 117, 239
Tolokontsev, A., 45–46, 61, 66, 100, 102–3,
    141
  and 1930 crisis, 185
  and reorganization, 171
Trotsky, L., 78–84, 100
  and bureaucratic left, 82–83
  and left opposition, 81–83
  and NOT, 117, 129

Trusts:
  commercial activities of, 37–40
  competition among, 34–37, 48–50
  and glavki, 29, 32, 42–43
  and industrial reorganization, 111–14,
    120, 132, 167–71, 179–80, 184–89
  organization of, 29–32
  reconstruction of, 47–50
  and regionalism, 35–36, 38–39, 44–46,
    48–50
  and syndicates, 53–56, 66–70
  See also entries for individual trusts
TsKK, 78–79
TsSU, 115

Ukraine, 5, 33–34, 36, 46, 49–50, 78–79, 84,
    88, 96, 103, 113, 122–23, 130
United States, 116–17
  as industrial model, 137, 139–40, 144,
    147, 235, 239
Uralmet, 31, 46, 179
Urals, 46, 48–49, 57, 64, 101, 123, 130, 168,
    170, 182

Valentinov, N., 82, 98
Veitsman, S., 64, 138
Vesenkha:
  and industrial reorganization, 111–14,
    125–33, 167–68, 179–80, 184–86
  and mobilization campaigns, 100–101,
    185–86
  organization of, 28–37
  vs. Rabkrin, 26–27, 85–86, 88–92, 136–37
  and regionalism, 44–46, 48–50

Vsesoiuznaia assosiatsiia inzhenerov (VAI),
    147–48
Vsesoiuznyi mashinotekhnicheskii sindikat
    (VMTS), 138, 142–43
  commercial activities of, 58–59, 60–62
  and credit, 60–62
  and local trade organizations, 59–60
  in Mashinoob''edinenie, 171, 180–84
  origins and operation of, 56–58
  reorganization of, 66–69, 145, 186
  and trusts, 59, 62–66
Vsesoiuznyi sovet sindikatov (VSS), 68, 70,
    72, 113–14, 125

War communism, 5, 128–29
  as administrative model, 81, 83, 96–97,
    100, 239
Workers:
  aristocracy of, 80
  and factory culture, 228–30, 233–34
  and factory modernization, 136, 140,
    143–44, 156, 228–30
  and functional management, 117,
    157–58
  and labor conscription, 83, 117, 233
  modernization and wages, 216–20, 223–
    24
  and opposition politics, 149
  and revolution, 5–6
  and socialist competition, 160–61,
    233
  and support for Stalin, 14
  See also Labor
World War I, 1–4, 239